Translational Systems Sciences

Volume 22

In 1956, Kenneth Boulding explained the concept of General Systems Theory as a skeleton of science. He describes that it hopes to develop something like a "spectrum" of theories—a system of systems which may perform the function of a "gestalt" in theoretical construction. Such "gestalts" in special fields have been of great value in directing research towards the gaps which they reveal.

There were, at that time, other important conceptual frameworks and theories, such as cybernetics. Additional theories and applications developed later, including synergetics, cognitive science, complex adaptive systems, and many others. Some focused on principles within specific domains of knowledge and others crossed areas of knowledge and practice, along the spectrum described by Boulding.

Also in 1956, the Society for General Systems Research (now the International Society for the Systems Sciences) was founded. One of the concerns of the founders, even then, was the state of the human condition, and what science could do about it.

The present Translational Systems Sciences book series aims at cultivating a new frontier of systems sciences for contributing to the need for practical applications that benefit people.

The concept of translational research originally comes from medical science for enhancing human health and well-being. Translational medical research is often labeled as "Bench to Bedside." It places emphasis on translating the findings in basic research (at bench) more quickly and efficiently into medical practice (at bedside). At the same time, needs and demands from practice drive the development of new and innovative ideas and concepts. In this tightly coupled process it is essential to remove barriers to multi-disciplinary collaboration.

The present series attempts to bridge and integrate basic research founded in systems concepts, logic, theories and models with systems practices and methodologies, into a process of systems research. Since both bench and bedside involve diverse stakeholder groups, including researchers, practitioners and users, translational systems science works to create common platforms for language to activate the "bench to bedside" cycle.

In order to create a resilient and sustainable society in the twenty-first century, we unquestionably need open social innovation through which we create new social values, and realize them in society by connecting diverse ideas and developing new solutions. We assume three types of social values, namely: (1) values relevant to social infrastructure such as safety, security, and amenity; (2) values created by innovation in business, economics, and management practices; and, (3) values necessary for community sustainability brought about by conflict resolution and consensus building.

The series will first approach these social values from a systems science perspective by drawing on a range of disciplines in trans-disciplinary and cross-cultural ways. They may include social systems theory, sociology, business administration, management information science, organization science, computational mathematical organization theory, economics, evolutionary economics, international political science, jurisprudence, policy science, socio-information studies, cognitive science, artificial intelligence, complex adaptive systems theory, philosophy of science, and other related disciplines. In addition, this series will promote translational systems science as a means of scientific research that facilitates the translation of findings from basic science to practical applications, and vice versa.

We believe that this book series should advance a new frontier in systems sciences by presenting theoretical and conceptual frameworks, as well as theories for design and application, for twenty-first-century socioeconomic systems in a translational and trans-disciplinary context.

More information about this series at http://www.springer.com/series/11213

Hanna Lehtimäki • Petri Uusikylä •
Anssi Smedlund
Editors

Society as an Interaction Space

A Systemic Approach

Springer

Editors
Hanna Lehtimäki
University of Eastern Finland
Kuopio, Finland

Petri Uusikylä
Frisky & Anjoy
Helsinki, Finland

Anssi Smedlund
Research and Development
Finnish Institute of Occupational Health
Helsinki, Finland

ISSN 2197-8832 ISSN 2197-8840 (electronic)
Translational Systems Sciences
ISBN 978-981-15-0068-8 ISBN 978-981-15-0069-5 (eBook)
https://doi.org/10.1007/978-981-15-0069-5

This Springer imprint is published by the registered company Springer Nature Singapore Pte Ltd.
The registered company address is: 152 Beach Road, #21-01/04 Gateway East, Singapore 189721, Singapore

Preface

This book brings together perspectives from systems theory, complexity theory, practice theory, actor network theory, and social network theory to provide a many-sided discussion on value co-creating processes in society. The cross-disciplinary examination of value co-creation is necessary as the digitalization and social media continue to blur the boundaries between the traditional societal, political, and economic institutions. With perspectives from political science, public administration, sociology, business administration, and knowledge management, the book highlights the role of institutions in value co-creation, giving new perspectives on relational dynamics between government, companies, and citizens. These insights fill the gaps between service science and political science by integrating institutional logics into the concepts of value co-creation.

The topics in this book examine society as an interaction space. This book discusses the new logics and transformation mechanisms of economic activity, citizen participation, governance and policy-making in the face of technological innovations, market-based reforms, and the threat of disconnect between citizens and policy-making. The focus is on value co-creation in complex adaptive systems where institutions, individuals, and businesses negotiate value and interests in networked relations.

The chapters in this book present empirical cases and insight on innovative governance and policy-making, digital society, active participatory citizenship, and individual-level interaction in value co-creation. The cases are written in the context of Nordic countries, which are recognized as world leading democracies. With systems approach, the book articulates a social reality that comprises interacting and interconnected parts that cannot be captured with only micro or macro levels of analysis. The book addresses society as a configuration of institutions, people, and technologies that are embedded in institutionalized rules, cultural meanings, and practices and, thus, provide valuable insight on the service-centered view of markets and society. The book is recommended to students and scholars interested in understanding and envisioning the future democratic landscape. This book provides valuable insight to readers who seek forward-looking discussion and empirical examples on value co-creation in complex adaptive systems.

The book is organized into four parts: Part I, "Governance as an Interaction Space"; Part II, "Policy and Evaluation as an Interaction Space"; Part III, "Innovation as an Interaction Space"; and Part IV, "Civic Society as an Interaction Space."

There are three chapters in Part I. These chapters question the prevalent assumptions in governance and outline new perspectives on addressing complexity in the interconnected society. Discussions on co-creation in public services, hybrid governance, and ways of reintegrating civil society and other non-state sectors into public policy analysis provide fruitful insight for future governance and public decision-making.

In Chap. 1, "The Hidden Side of Co-Creation in a Complex Multi-Stakeholder Environment: When Self-Organization Fails and Emergence Overtakes," Harri Jalonen, Alisa Puustinen, and Harri Raisio explore the unforeseen and undesirable consequences of co-creation. Using the concepts of self-organization and emergence, they draw attention to the challenges in co-creation that is typically seen as affirmative interaction between multiple parties. They introduce a framework which shows how ideal co-creation might turn into participative diversion, pop-up participation, or even unintended co-destruction.

In Chap. 2, "Perspectives on Hybridity," Jan-Erik Johanson and Jarmo Vakkuri enrich understanding about economic and social interaction as hybrid arrangements in micro-, meso-, and macro-levels of activity. The empirical examples they present show that hybrids consist of pairwise interactions and network constellations between business firms and public agencies.

In Chap. 3, "Bringing Society Back In: Actors, Networks, and Systems in Policy-Making," Volker Schneider draws attention to the embeddedness of policy in the web of political, economic, scientific, and media subsystems of society in understanding how different societies cope with important challenges, such as climate change. By a comparison of major policy theories, he makes a plea for reintegrating a macroscopic perspective in public policy analysis.

Part II has three articles that examine the practice of public policy and evaluation in the future. Addressing societal complexity as a driver for change, the chapters in this part provide novel views and suggestions on new approaches in policy-making and evaluation.

In Chap. 4, "Mission-Oriented Public Policy and the New Evaluation Culture," Kaisa Lähteenmäki-Smith and Petri Virtanen introduce a framework to improve public policy-related evaluation practice for a more adaptive and anticipatory evaluation approach that is better in tune with complex interactions and interdependencies that emerge in policy agenda today. They argue that the mission-driven policy-making calls for a systems-based perspective and consideration of the diversity of policy interventions ranging from traditional budgetary or legislative instruments to experimentation and piloting. The focus of evaluation, in turn, ranges from the accountability to evaluation criteria, time scale, motivation, as well as type of intervention used.

In Chap. 5, "Systemic Evaluation Approach to Meet the Challenges of Complexity," Mika Nieminen, Kirsi Hyytinen, Vesa Salminen, and Sampsa Ruutu suggest a new integrative evaluation approach which combines foresight, multi-criteria evaluation, and system dynamic modelling into the evaluation process. They argue that the traditional linear evaluation approaches are not able to address the dynamic interrelationships and feedback mechanisms involved in the increasingly complex social environment.

In Chap. 6, "Participative Policy-Making in Complex Welfare System: A Delphi Study," Hanna-Kaisa Pernaa presents a Delphi study of the possibilities and obstacles of participative policy-making (PPM) in municipal welfare services. The outcomes of the study indicate that regardless of technological preparedness and the structural opportunities offered by a reform, cultural inertia and unawareness generate attitudes inhibitory on PPM practices.

Part III, "Innovation as an Interaction Space," has four chapters that draw from complexity theory, systems thinking, actor-network theory, and social network theory. The chapters point to directions on ways of theorizing relational phenomenon in complex settings. Examining creativity, risk-taking, emerging innovative market, and industry transformation with relational theory lenses allow for capturing the dynamics of interconnectedness between actors and institutions.

In Chap. 7, "How Overlapping Connections Between Groups Interact with Value Differences in Explaining Creativity," Antti Gronow, Anssi Smedlund, and Aasa Karimo draw on network theory and sociology of valuation and examine creativity in groups. Their study shows that overlapping connections that groups have with each other and differences in within-group values explain coming up with new ideas and practices.

In Chap. 8, "Disaster Management as a Complex Adaptive System: Building Resilience with New Systemic Tools of Analysis," Petri Uusikylä, Paula Tommila, and Ida Uusikylä apply systems thinking and complexity theory to introduce an alternative perspective to study disaster preparedness and risk reduction (DP/DRR) systems. Their study shows that an understanding of the interconnectedness of risk elements and the joint impact on the risks, along with an understanding of the relations and connections between the disaster risk agencies and stakeholders, is beneficial in creating a more versatile understanding of the risk preparedness and, thus, a higher resilience of preparedness actions.

In Chap. 9, "Translations in Biobanking: Socio-Material Networks in Health Data Business," Ilpo Helén and Hanna Lehtimäki draw attention to the interaction between material and human actors in an emerging innovation-based market of personalized medicine. Their study examines innovation as a manifold and transformative texture of socio-material relations in which a prospect of innovation is conjoined with and put to the test by multiple human and nonhuman actors. The chapter highlights the dynamic and malleable nature of socio-material relations as the groundwork of innovation by showing how innovation and business become entangled through translations.

In Chap. 10, "Digital Platforms and Industry Change," Mikko Hänninen and Lauri Paavola explore how digital platforms shape industry dynamics and transformation. Based on a broad literature review, they introduce a theoretical model for understanding the phases through which digital transformation in industry takes place.

There are five chapters in Part IV, "Civic Society as an Interaction Space." These chapters look at interaction between individuals and draw attention to the bottom-up processes in complex societies. The chapters explore online and off-line interaction and provide insight on how social ties are formed and maintained, how emotions play a role in interaction, and how sensory technologies can be used in measuring emotions. Furthermore, the last two chapters present experiences from using novel methods for participative processes in governance and engagement of citizens in deliberative democracy and co-production of social innovations.

In Chap. 11, "Facilitating Organizational Fluidity with Computational Social Matching," Jukka Huhtamäki, Thomas Olsson, and Salla-Maaria Laaksonen examine organizations as fluid communicative compositions of collaborative ties. Their chapter provides perspectives on how computational social matching can enhance interaction both on the societal and organizational levels. The authors describe three strategies for professional social matching: social exploration, network theory-based recommendations, and machine learning-based recommendations.

In Chap. 12, "Emotions in Customer Experience," Tiina-Kaisa Kuuru, Lauri Litovuo, Leena Aarikka-Stenroos, and Nina Helander suggest a framework to identify how different types of emotions build customer experience. They present a literature review and provide conceptual clarity on emotions in customer experience.

In Chap. 13, "Sensory Technologies for Improving Employee Experience and Strengthening Customer Relationships," Jari Jussila, Virpi Sillanpää, Mika Boedeker, and Nina Helander examine emotions in value co-creating interaction between employees and customers. Their study uses modern sensory technologies to measure emotional states and to better understand how positive and negative emotions impact job satisfaction, employee experience, and customer satisfaction.

In Chap. 14, "Individual Conditions for Co-production of a Social Innovation in a Living Lab: Case Sunshine PopUp Park," Kaisa Henttonen, Minna Takala, Kirsmarja Blomqvist, Anne Horila, and Anna-Maija Nisula present a case study on participative processes and the empowerment of citizens in local co-production of social innovation. Their study shows how collaboration between the private, public, and third sectors support citizen involvement, encourage people to contribute to improving societal well-being, and enhance partnerships between citizens, regions, and the profit and nonprofit sectors.

In Chap. 15, "Security Cafés: A Deliberative Democratic Method to Engage Citizens in Meaningful Two-Way Conversations with Security Authorities and to Gather Data," Alisa Puustinen, Harri Raisio, and Vesa Valtonen present a deliberation and data collection method developed for security authorities and researchers to access the opinion of the general public on issues of importance to their safety and security.

The editors believe that this book, with its insightful theorizing and empirical examples on interconnectedness and complexity in the modern society, will add a valuable contribution to "cultivating a new frontier of systems sciences for contributing to the need for practical applications that benefit people," as declared in the description of the Translational Systems Sciences book series.

Kuopio, Finland — Hanna Lehtimäki
Helsinki, Finland — Petri Uusikylä
Helsinki, Finland — Anssi Smedlund
9 July 2019

Contents

Part I
Governance as an Interaction Space

Chapter 1
The Hidden Side of Co-Creation in a Complex Multi-Stakeholder Environment: When Self-Organization Fails and Emergence Overtakes

Harri Jalonen, Alisa Puustinen, and Harri Raisio

Abstract Co-creation is typically defined as a mode of collaborative action, which is based on the complex combination of both top-down designing and bottom-up organizing from service beneficiaries. As a practice, co-creation is seen in an affirmative light. It is seen to provide a solution for many service planning, delivery and implementation problems faced by governments and public service organizations. However, in addition to improvement of means of providing public services, co-creation also introduces many challenges. Using the concepts of self-organization and emergence this conceptual chapter explores the hidden side of co-creation, i.e. situations which may produce unforeseen and undesirable consequences. The chapter contributes to both public service research and complexity sciences by introducing a framework which describes how ideal co-creation might turn into participative diversion, pop-up participation or even unintended co-destruction.

1.1 Introduction

Co-creation has become a kind of a "silver bullet": something to provide a solution for the fiscal and service delivery problems faced by governments and public service organizations worldwide. Co-creation has been justified on several grounds, of which the most alluring are perhaps that co-creation conceives service users as

H. Jalonen (✉)
Turku University of Applied Sciences, Turku, Finland
e-mail: harri.jalonen@turkuamk.fi

A. Puustinen
Emergency Services Academy Finland, Kuopio, Finland
e-mail: alisa.puustinen@pelastusopisto.fi

H. Raisio
University of Vaasa, Vaasa, Finland
e-mail: harri.raisio@uwasa.fi

H. Lehtimäki et al. (eds.), *Society as an Interaction Space*, Translational Systems Sciences 22, https://doi.org/10.1007/978-981-15-0069-5_1

active partners rather than passive service users, co-creation promotes collaborative relationships between service providers and users and co-creation puts the focus on the effectiveness of services (Brandsen et al. 2018). Seemingly, co-creation is based on the ideal of active citizenship and on the logic of effective production, combining the complementary and substitutive capabilities possessed by different stakeholders, particularly citizens who use services. Hence, co-creation can be conceptualized as a mode of cooperative action, which is based on the complex combination of both top-down steering (from government and service providers to service users) and bottom-up organizing (from service users and service providers to government).

As a practice, co-creation is seen in an affirmative light. It is identified with the progress and improvement of the state of affairs without much questioning. Apart from potential benefits of co-creation, this chapter explores situations in which co-creation comes something unintended and unexpected that should be examined closely. It is expected that co-creation produces not only new thoughts, ideas and solutions, but also new kinds of political, ethical, economic, cultural and managerial dilemmas. As an example, the skewness in distribution of the participants in co-creation processes means that the most active ones and the ones in higher social status tend to dominate in participation and the voice of the rest remains unknown. Instead of value co-creation, the result can be something that Williams et al. (2015) describe as public value failure and co-contamination.

Using the complexity lens, this exploratory and conceptual chapter focuses on dilemmas introduced by "bottom-up organizing" of co-creation—particularly on self-organization processes, which produce emergent patterns that no-one chose or wanted. At the heart of the argument is that higher-level (good) behaviour emerges from the self-organizing interactions within the system. Consequently, managers and organizations have been advised to build up cooperation-friendly conditions that allow the positive emergence to happen. Without questioning the appealing ideas concerning the power of self-organization and emergence, however, this chapter focuses on the dark side of self-organization and emergence. Exploring several examples where the process of self-organization has caused unproductive, unwanted and unintended emergence, this chapter claims that co-creation has the faces of Janus; on the one hand, co-creation may improve the effectiveness of services, while on the other hand, it introduces new dilemmas and unexpected outcomes.

The objective of the chapter is to theoretically explore the meaning of self-organization and emergence in complex co-creation settings and to seek potential new theoretical frames to address the phenomenon. The chapter contributes to the whole by introducing a theoretically sound framework, which sheds light on the promises and pitfalls of co-creation. Particularly, the chapter increases understanding of the dark side of co-creation, which has focused mainly on the deliberate rejection of responsibility, failing accountability, rising transaction costs, loss of democracy, reinforced inequalities, implicit demands and co-destruction of public value (Steen et al. 2018). In a way, we aim to tackle the challenge which Voorberg et al. (2015: 1346) describe "we cannot definitely conclude whether co-creation can be considered as beneficial". This chapter contributes both to the complexity sciences and to the public service research. The chapter supplements complexity theory as it sheds light on the negative implications of emergence and self-organization. In this sense, the chapter rectifies the positive bias in complexity literature—particularly in management-oriented literature—which mostly conceives emergence, and its cousin self-organization, as useful for organizations. The chapter also contributes to the public service research by providing theoretically founded explanations for unintended and unexpected consequences of co-creation. In doing so, the chapter provides an interpretation, which is potentially useful for understanding the difficulties in finding the evidence of the benefits of co-creation (cf. Voorberg et al. 2015; Brandsen et al. 2018).

This chapter is structured as follows: after the introduction, Sect. 1.2 presents our definitional understanding of the complexity of co-creation and discusses the concepts of self-organization and emergence. Section 1.3 presents the promises of co-creation by explaining two opposite service logics, "linear value delivery logic" and "interactive value creation logic". In addition, the section discusses preliminary findings from the co-creative pilots conducted in ten European countries. Sections 1.4 and 1.5 focus on examples of different forms of co-creation such as the exploitation or "participatory diversion" and exploration in the form of fourth sector type "pop up participation", i.e. self-organized civic activity (see Mäenpää and Faehnle 2017; Raisio et al. 2019). In Sect. 1.6, we study how systemic distortion, or even co-destruction, may emerge out of co-creation. We will provide a variety of real-life examples adopted from several past and ongoing research projects in which the authors are involved. Finally, in Sect. 1.7, we close our argument by proposing a framework highlighting the different sides of co-creation and its many features.

1.2 Co-creation Through "Complexity Lenses"

It sounds reasonable to claim that co-creation processes are complex by nature. Complexity does not only refer to situations that are difficult to understand or complicated to handle, but to a basic property of a co-creative system. Seeing through complexity thinking, it is not necessary to consider complexity as neither "bad" nor "good"; it is just that it helps us to understand the nature of the world—and the systems—we live in (Mitleton-Kelly 2003: 46–47). The strength of complexity thinking is that it may explain why the whole is more (or less) than the sum of its parts and how all its components come together to produce overarching patterns as the system evolves and adapts (Mitleton-Kelly 2003; Stacey 2010). It may even provide a new way to combine the science and art of management (Richardson 2008).

In recent years, complexity thinking has been used widely as a theoretical framework in public policy and administration studies. As some examples, Christensen and Lægreid (2011) used complexity thinking in searching for hybrid public administration, Morçöl (2012) attempted to develop a coherent and exhaustive complexity-informed framework for public policy, Cairney (2012) explored the challenges to be overcome before complexity theory can become valuable in politics and policy making, Geyer (2012) provided a "complexity cascade" to be applied in policy making in education and health sector, Klijn and Koppenjan (2012) tried to build a bridge between complexity thinking and governance network theory, Ansell and Geyer (2017) introduced "pragmatic complexity" as a new foundation for moving "evidence-based policy making" and Murphy et al. (2017) used the complexity leadership approach to manage entanglement in public sector systems. Despite of growing interest in complexity thinking, it seems that a lack of a common understanding of complexity still exists in the field of public policy and administration (Gerrits and Marks 2015), and also a lack of empirical studies that test the theory in different contexts.

Following the logic of Cilliers (2005) and Richardson (2008), however, we believe that complexity thinking could help to reveal limits to what is known about organizations, and therefore it also enables us to understand more about what we can and cannot achieve with management based on linear logic and causal reasoning. For our purpose, we use complexity thinking as conceptual frames to understand and explain why initiatives of co-creation in complex multi-stakeholder environments sometimes fail.

Complexity in co-creation derives from two interlinked sources. First, the process itself is complex due to the interdependence of a variety of stakeholders. Interdependency points out that actions by any stakeholder may affect—constrain or enable—related stakeholders and the whole system. Interdependencies between stakeholders allow information and other intangible resources to travel within and outside the co-creative system, and they can be used either for creating something new and potentially valuable for strengthening the status quo. Second, stakeholders have different and contradictory expectations and demands for co-creation. The valuation of benefits and costs of co-creation is based on incommensurate measures. While some put emphasis on effective service delivery, others appreciate that provided services meet users' needs.

We agree with Bourgon (2009), who claims that governments must accept that "no single actor, not even the State, controls all the levers that are required to achieve the results people really care about". In addition, we believe that the key to the problem—and its solution—are complex systems that merge the activities of multiple stakeholders. Seeing co-creation as a complex system forces to focus on system-level results. The system-level approach stresses the reality that public, private and third sector organizations must work in synergy with citizens to achieve the desired outcomes and create public value (Bouckaert and Halligan 2008).

Drawing on the complexity of problems and diversity of perspectives, we think that it would be worthwhile to search for the secret of co-creation from the self-organizing and emerging nature of the relationships within the system and between the system and its environment. Adapting Mitleton-Kelly (2003) and Stacey (2007) and many other complexity scholars, we refer with *self-organization* to a more or less spontaneous process without outside applied coercion or control. The process of self-organization, in turn, is necessary to produce *emergence*—a new level of order. A clichéd saying "the whole is more than the sum of its parts" implicates that self-organization can produce emergence, which cannot be predicted or decided in advance. Emergence cannot be fully understood on the basis of what is known about the components of the system. Self-organizing activity, which may lead to the emergent order of the "whole", is fundamentally based on the number and the strength of the connections between the participants and the differences between the participants. This argument can be based on the principle of "requisite variety" (Ashby 1956). Requisite variety refers to a state where systems' internal variety is sufficient to match the environmental variety. The greater the diversity of the system, the more adaptability and fitness it has (Uhl-Bien and Arena 2017). The diversity of the system's parts spreads into the rest of the system as a result of connections. Instead of being "a magical sundering of causality", we see emergence and self-organization as "an outcome of variegated and constructed dynamics generated out of interactions" between the lower level actors that constitute the system (Hazy et al. 2007). This means that while the complex system is aggregated from its parts, the interplay of these parts produces emergent patterns, which cannot be analytically reducible to the constituent parts (Stacey 2010). While emergent phenomena are seen occurring on the macro level (Goldstein 1999), however, the emergent whole has causal power in affecting micro-level components and processes. Blitz (1992), for example, has portrayed the duplex nature of emergence as "downward causation".

In practice this could mean, for example, that emergence results from the self-organizing process where each participant—public organizations, private companies and non-profit organizations—continually decide with which other organizations to engage, and what information and other resources to exchange with them (cf. Jalonen and Juntunen 2011). Citizens also have important roles in co-creation processes of many public services, such as social and health care services. They participate and influence the production and outputs, for example, by providing information about their health and by exercising rehabilitation actions. Co-creative practices simultaneously emerge from the decisions and actions taken at the micro level, and they also affect on those micro-level decisions and actions.

Although both self-organization and emergence have been widely accepted as central phenomena within the complexity literature, there are, however, some differences in their interpretations. On the one hand, there is an approach that sees the emergent whole as bubbling up from the micro-level interaction. The emergent whole represents "global" whereas self-organization coincides with "local". From this point of view, self-organization and emergence can be used to explain why things "just happen" without a visible reason (e.g. Stacey 2007). Self-organization and emergence are something very opposite from participants' intentions. A strong argument for this is given by Mintzberg (1979), who has described emergent strategies as "strategies without clear intentions, actions simply converging into patterns". Taking this view seriously means also that self-organization and emergence are always unique processes in the sense that the search for generalized and average characteristics of those processes should be abandoned (cf. Aasen 2009).

On the other side of the spectrum are researchers who call into question the "spontaneity" of self-organization and emergence. Hazy et al. (2007), for example, suspects the existence of pure spontaneous self-organizing processes of creating order out of chaos. Particularly, he is concerned of the moral message "spontaneity" implies when it is applied literally. Hazy et al. (2007) challenges the notion that "simply put together the right conditions and the hoped-for result will 'bubble up' or 'emerge' on their own, spontaneously and fully-formed as new processes and strategies that dramatically increase the competitive advantage of the organization". He ironically continues, "as many managers and scholars soon learned, it doesn't happen that way. Emergence in real organizations requires constant attention, support and resources, and the 'success' of emergence [...] depends in large measure on the quality of resources and attention that individuals and managers bring to the process." However, it is important to notice that Hazy et al. (2007) and those like-minded do not argue against the existence of emergence or self-organization—all they suggest is that emergence and self-organization are processes that can and also should be guided.

Whether seeing emergence and self-organization as "spontaneous" or as "guided" processes, what is of importance is that both views accept that the twenty-first century challenges cannot be solved without collaboration between different participants. It is reasonable to assume that co-creators are facing wicked problems (cf. Rittel and Webber 1973). Wicked problems are problems which have no definitive formulation; solutions are not true or false; there is no test for a solution; every solution has a consequence; they do not have simple causes; and they have numerous possible explanations which in turn frame different policy responses (Raisio et al. 2018; Daviter 2017). Therefore, we suggest that it would be useful to study the challenges of co-creation with "the lens of self-organization and emergence". Not least because self-organization and emergence have built-in potential to pull co-production in two directions—*success* and *failure*—at the same time. The rest of this chapter discusses how the process of self-organization may create emergent co-creation patterns that are not in accordance with the interests of the participants involved in the practices.

1.3 Promises of Co-creation

In many studies from the 1980s and onwards, *co-production* has been identified as the new emerging paradigm for delivering public services (e.g. Bovaird 2007). Benefits of co-production are cited as including better service quality, customer-oriented services and less costly public services. The rising interest in co-production was mainly due to the economic pressures that state agencies and public organization were facing in delivering public services. It can be claimed that this is still the case in the late 2010s, but co-production has also received some extra attention for being able to enhance the citizen orientation in public services, to promote the role of the underprivileged and to encourage the actions of a civil society (e.g. Brandsen and Pestoff 2006). It has been employed in a predominantly positive manner as one of the remedies from keeping public services from collapsing all together. A bit simplified, co-production is based on linear and goods-dominant logic of value creation (cf. Vargo and Lusch 2004) and resonates with the New Public Management movement (Hood 1991). Public services are seen as "vehicles" in which value is embedded and through which value is delivered to users.

Despite of many benefits related to co-production, it has also been questioned on the basis that the reality of public services is an increasingly complex, fragmented and interdependent world (Osborne 2018). Arguably the linear value delivery logic does not work in the complex reality where value is realized in use and in a particular context. *Co-creation* has been proposed as a strategic direction for taking seriously the critique of co-production. Co-creation builds on the idea that people who use services work with professionals to design, create and deliver services. It has been suggested that the involvement of end-users in the planning process as well as in service delivery is what distinguishes co-creation from co-production (Osborne and Strokosch 2013; Voorberg et al. 2015). Co-creation assumes "an interactive and dynamic relationship where value is created at the nexus of interaction" (Osborne 2018: 225). This conceptualization of co-creation suggests a clean break with New Public Management thinking, because value for the service user and the public service organization are not created by a linear process of production but rather through an interaction in which the service user's wider life experience is part of the context (ibid.). In other words, public services cannot deliver value to the users but they can make a "service offering" that has the potential to create value for users (ibid.).

Under the umbrella of co-creation, users' roles can vary from co-implementers to co-designers and even co-initiators (Voorberg et al. 2015). As co-implementers, users participate in delivering services; as co-designers, users decide how the service delivery is to be designed, and as co-initiators, users set the agenda to be followed by the public body (ibid.).

The Co-creation of Service Innovation in Europe project[1] was launched to increase service innovations based on co-creative design. The project aims to develop initiatives that advance the active shaping of service priorities by end users and their informal support networks, and contribute to social inclusion through co-creating public services by engaging diverse citizen groups and stakeholders in varied public services. In addition, the project focuses particularly on the potential of ICT to widen participation in co-creating public services. The project includes several real-life pilot projects developing innovative solutions to complex social challenges. The following brief analysis of the promises of co-creation is based on Rapid Evidence Assessment (REA) about the current state of co-creation in ten European countries (Sakellariou 2018). REA is a type of evidence review that aims to provide an informed conclusion on the volume and characteristics of an evidence base, a synthesis of what that evidence indicates and a critical appraisal of that evidence. The main purpose was to get a thorough evidence synthesis to inform policy and practice and to explore what is effective and what is not.

First, the odds of successful implementation of co-creation can be increased by ensuring the participation and commitment of groups closely working with the

---

[1]The CoSIE project will be executed in 2017–2020 and it is funded by the European Union's Horizon 2020 research and innovation programme under grant agreement No 770492. See more at https://cosie.turkuamk.fi/.

target groups and service users themselves in the co-creation process already during the planning phase of co-creation initiatives. Instead of strictly defined objectives and procedures that must be followed, the key is to encourage the stakeholders to search applicable solutions through interaction. Involvement and interaction enable that the development and outcomes are actually serving users targeted purpose.

Second, the greatest challenge and at the same time the significant basic element in co-creation is the persuasion of the service providers and service users to participate. While co-creation promotes the power of service users, however, we find that the role of public servants should not be underestimated when initiating and implementing co-creation projects. When they are well informed, trained and committed to co-creation methods and goals they become the key players in enhancing co-creation. The key is that public servants understand and accept that outcomes might be something very different than first anticipated, and that co-creation is possible only when it is conducted in close and respectful collaboration with all stakeholders.

Third, in promoting and ensuring the diversity of "co-creators", it is important to use a wide range of different ways by which they can participate. By combining physical (e.g. citizen panel) and virtual spaces (e.g. social media), it is possible to enable different voices to be heard and improve the fit between services offered and services needed.

Forth, although co-creation processes are primarily bottom-up processes, they can and should, however, be supported by a legal framework and governmental guidelines. It was found out that regulatory support can create fruitful conditions for co-creation to flourish and an open space for the implementation of co-creation.

Despite the potentiality and popularity of co-creation, it does not mean that co-creation is easily implemented and that it functions under all circumstances. Co-creation is not self-evidently valuable as means in itself. Failures are to be expected, and co-creation has the potential of becoming co-destruction. These different sides of co-creation are illustrated in Fig. 1.1. When successfully implemented, co-creation gives people a possibility to communicate, express their views and ideas and feel part of the design and implementation process, but it can also have unintended and unwanted consequences if implemented without proper design and with poor engagement of various stakeholders. Next, we will turn our attention to the various darker sides of co-creation and explore the different features found therein.

1.4 Participatory Diversion: An Illusion of Co-creation

Co-creation as described above is an ideal type of construction. As such, it is an objective to be pursued, but it must be accepted that it is rarely realized in its full capacity. Several factors challenge the realization of the ideal. These are, among others, the trivialization of public participation (e.g. Fung 2015), "rescripting" of community aspirations (e.g. Parker et al. 2015) and using co-creation as a mere legitimizing (e.g. Virta and Branders 2016) or placating (Lee Jenni et al. 2015) tool.

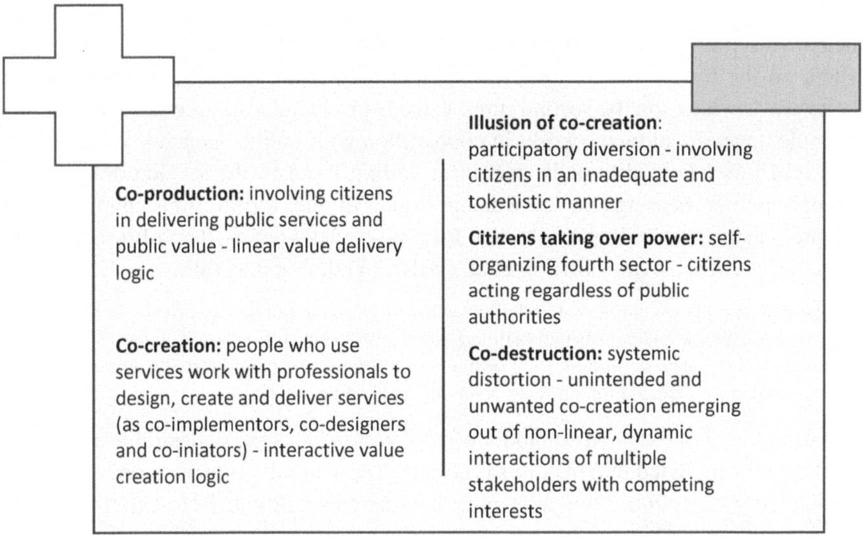

Fig. 1.1 The bright and dark side of co-creation

We consider these different barriers to genuine co-creation to form collectively a category we call *participatory diversion*. With participatory diversion, we refer to situations where public authorities, consciously or unconsciously, involve citizens in co-creation processes that are inadequate and at worst, a mere illusion of participation. In such situations, the ownership and control of co-creation processes remains exclusively with public sector actors, and citizens stay as mere bystanders.

As a phenomenon, participatory diversion is not a novel one. Already in 1969, Sherry Arnstein highlighted such negative participatory processes in her, now famous, *ladder of public participation*. This typology consists of eight levels of public participation. From the bottom up, the two first rungs are manipulation and therapy. For Arnstein (1969) these belong to a class of non-participation. On these levels, the aim is not in genuine participation, but in "educating" or "curing" the participating citizens. The next three rungs, informing, consultation and placation, form a class of tokenism. When participation is understood as tokenistic, the participating citizens may have a voice, to a degree. However, the decision-making power remains with the official decision-makers. The final rungs, partnership, delegated power and citizen control, belong to a class of citizen power. Power is then shared with or fully redistributed to citizen participants. Of the rungs, partnership seems to fit best the ideals of co-creation (see also Rock et al. 2018).

Arnstein's ladder of public participation was a product of its time, and has since been criticized as well as developed further (see e.g. Tritter and McCallum 2006; Hurlbert and Gupta 2015). For example, Torfing et al. (2016) point out the antiquatedness of citizen control—the self-government of the people—idealized by Arnstein. In response to an ever more complex operating environment, where collaboration, instead of any such single actor strategy, is called for, they present their own typology, *a ladder of co-creation*. This typology consists of five levels, where on the lowest rung citizens are empowered and encouraged to co-produce their own services. On the second rung, value is produced also for other citizens, for example through voluntary work, in cooperation with public agencies. On the third rung, citizens take additionally part in providing input to the service design (e.g. through public hearings or crowdsourcing). On the fourth rung, participation advances to mutual dialogue between different societal actors. The fifth rung is the most comprehensive one. Torfing et al. (2016: 11) define it as follows:

> The final rung is when relevant and affected actors from the public and private sector participate in institutional arenas that facilitate collaborative innovation based on joint agenda-setting and problem definition, joint design and testing of new and untried solutions, and coordinated implementation drawing on public and private solutions.

However, the above-described ladder of co-creation lacks the undesirable and detrimental rungs included in Arnstein's typology. These are the rungs we understand as participatory diversion. One such rung is what Fung (2015: 521) calls "the park bench problem". This refers to a situation where the choices and stakes of co-creation processes are trivial, akin to having a power to decide on the colour of park benches. Citizens then have a possibility to take part and influence, but not in a truly meaningful way. This triviality may eventually lead to widespread disappointment and even apathy. The issue of triviality occurs in certain branches of government more strongly than in others. For example, Virta and Branders (2016) highlight security governance as one such area, where participatory processes are often depoliticized and even circumvented by the public authorities. The possibility of citizens having an authentic voice on questions of safety and security may seem for public authorities as too unpredictable, uncontrollable and ambiguous (see also Torfing et al. 2016; Raisio et al. 2019).

On another rung, a situation may exist where citizens are initially promised a stronger voice in co-creation processes, but which eventually is rescripted. Citizen input is then rewritten to "planning language", downplayed and even written out of the final product. The promised partial ownership and control of the process becomes a mere illusion (Parker et al. 2015). This can be understood as a tokenistic practice where public authorities make perfunctory gestures of including citizens in the co-creation of public services (see Torfing et al. 2016).

As a third example of participatory diversion, we highlight the usage of co-creation as a legitimating device and a tool for placation (see e.g. Lee Jenni et al. 2015; Virta and Branders 2016). In such situations, participatory processes are used to legitimate plans and decisions that have already been made. The aim is to gain support through informing and placating citizens. Citizens' role is then akin to participating in "a kind of customer feedback event" (Virta and Branders 2016: 1151). All the examples above are such where initiating, planning and implementing public services becomes something that is fundamentally done *for*, not *with* the citizens.

1.5 Self-Organizing Fourth Sector: Citizens Taking Over Power

Participatory diversion, however, does not automatically lead to passivity or apathy. Citizens may also begin to rebel and radical social movements may emerge. Due to increasing dissatisfaction with the public authorities, citizens are then striving to find ways to have a stronger impact and even take over power. These actions often take forms such as demonstrations and marches, but may eventually extend beyond democratic forms of protest and even include civil disobedience and violence (Kotus and Sowada 2017). While we acknowledge the importance of such actions, in this section of the article, we highlight a more prosocial model of *fourth sector* type civic activity, which does *not act against* public authorities, but *acts regardless of* them. Mäenpää and Faehnle (2017): 78) define the activity in question as follows:

> By the fourth sector, we refer to the area of civil society that, with its quick, lightly organised, proactive and activity-centred nature, is structured outside of the third sector, or the field of non-governmental organisations.

The definition highlights a do-it-yourself (DIY) spirit and a yes-in-my-backyard (YIMBY) attitude. Mäenpää et al. (2017) consider digitalization as one of the key reasons for the rise of such fourth-sector type activity. Technology enables continuous, real-time and place-independent communication, which manifests, for example, in social media groups emerging around topical issues. This leads to citizens being more empowered than ever to act and take matters into their own hands (Faehnle et al. 2017).

As examples of fourth sector type civic activity, Mäenpää and Faehnle (2017) consider, among others, local movements, peer-to-peer trade and services, social peer support and hacktivism. Also, Böse et al. (2006), studying the cultural sphere in Vienna and Belgrade, have written of fourth sector. They consider fourth sector to be identified by its transitory, subversive and fluid nature and being exemplified by DIY cultural activity. Rask et al. (2018) have examined fourth sector in the context of responsible research and innovation. For them, the fourth sector "is an emerging field, composed of actors or actor groups whose foundational logic is not in the representation of established interests, but rather, in the idea of social cooperation through hybrid networking" (ibid. 46). Fourth sector has been studied also in the context crises and disasters (see Raisio et al. 2019). In this context, the fourth sector includes spontaneous volunteers and emergent citizen groups who, for example, take part in tasks such as search and rescue, providing food, drink, and shelter, and collecting and distributing relief supplies. As an example, in the refugee crises of 2015, public authorities all over Europe were overwhelmed by the informal self-organized responses of citizens in providing support, such as shelter and provisions, for refugees (see Lorenz et al. 2018). In this context, Raisio et al. (2019: 14–15) define the fourth sector as:

> [being] composed of self-organized actors or actor groups who are not affiliated with any formal organizations and who engage in emergent short-term activities. Fourth-sector

activities are neither good nor bad per se, but are determined by complex situational dynamics. The fourth sector can become active in all phases of a crisis or disaster by taking on diverse tasks and roles. Resilient and agile fourth-sector actors adapt to the actions of formal actors according to circumstances. Over time, the actors in the fourth sector often disappear, although it is possible that they merge, for example, with a third-sector organization.

Self-organization is one of the defining characteristics of the fourth sector (see Rantanen and Faehnle 2017; Raisio et al. 2019). In the context of urban development, Boonstra and Boelens (2011: 113) provide a definition of self-organization that is well suited to describe the fourth sector type civic activity: "initiatives that originate in civil society from autonomous community-based networks of citizens, who are part of the urban system but independent of government procedures". Such self-organizing civic activity has been considered to include various positive aspects. Among the foremost is the fourth sector's adaptability and agility. Self-organizing civic activity is based on improvisation and creativity, often making fourth-sector actors capable of acting more flexibly, unconventionally, and quicker than actors in other sectors, whose actions are limited by various rules and regulations (Mäenpää and Faehnle 2017; Polanska 2018; Raisio et al. forthcoming). In addition, owing to them having a certain elasticity, fourth-sector practices may be an attractive way of contributing for citizens who cannot, or do not want to, engage in activities for a prolonged period (see Polanska 2018). This reflects the changing nature of volunteering. Instead of traditional volunteering based on committing their time to third-sector organizations, individuals desire more autonomy, are prepared for an episodic style of volunteering, and develop more loyalty to causes important to them than to a specific organization. (See Grönlund 2016; McLennan et al. 2016.)

The growth of the fourth sector, at least in the context of participatory diversion, "turns the tables" between public authorities and citizens. To put it simply, it is then not so much citizens who adapt to the actions of the public authorities, but public authorities who adapt to the new operating environment, that is, the emergence of the self-governing fourth sector. Mäenpää and Faehnle (2018: 43) define the relationship between the fourth sector and public authorities as *hybrid governance* (see also Johanson and Vakkuri 2017). They consider this as more suitable than, for example, co-governance or partnership due to two factors. First, fourth sector actors are cautious of too tight a relationship, as it "might melt their identity and operating methods with those of others, fearing that they would thus diminish their own role as actors." Second, as fourth sector actors, due to their self-organizing, fluid and temporary nature, are not legal entities, public authorities "cannot share responsibility for decisions with these civic actors, and cannot make legally binding contracts where the other party is not a legal entity." Hybrid governance is then more about interaction processes between different societal actors than decision-making power or contracts (ibid.).

Mäenpää and Faehnle (2018) have tried to outline such interactions in their eight-step model of hybrid governance. The steps include ones where the fourth sector acts on its own (step 1), where fourth sector actors are in dialogue with public authorities (step 4), and where the dynamic fourth sector and the more rigid public sector form an integrated system (step 8). Public authorities can then choose, context-wise, different strategies to react and adapt to the self-organizing fourth sector. The choice is then not a simplistic binary decision, for example, between *control* or *enable* (see Raisio et al. 2019).

1.6 Systemic Distortion Leading to Co-destruction

Public authorities (mis)using co-creation in the form of participatory diversion or citizens acting regardless of public authorities in harmless self-organizing civic activity are not the ideal type of co-creation described in the third chapter of this article. However, they are not particularly dangerous or destructive either. They just disguise some other sort of action as co-creation. Organizations and organizing have always had a darker side, which has also been acknowledged and studied in several disciplines (Bella et al. 2003; Linstead et al. 2014). On the other hand, self-organization and emergence, as well as co-creation, have all too often been treated in a merely affirmative light (Bella 2006). We have an inherent tendency to believe that when bringing people together in an organized setting, good deeds and things will automatically arise.

In the case of co-creation, seen through the lenses of complexity, we would like to draw the attention to systemic effects, to the logic of systemic distortion. Systemic distortion may happen even when "good people" come together in "good faith" to do "good things", like in co-creation (King et al. 2002: 163). No-one intends to do any harm, but the evil emerges out of the interconnections of the parts and the non-linear, dynamic interactions (Bella 2006; Bella et al. 2003; see also Kotus and Sowada 2017). Systemic distortion is more likely when there are multiple stakeholders with competing interests and competing goals, and when power imbalances are present. Such situations have been studied for example in health care (Friedman et al. 2007), the tobacco industry (Bella 1997) and crisis and emergency situations (Johannessen 2018). That is also precisely the case with co-creation. Regardless of the actual substance and context of the co-creative actions, there are by definition multiple stakeholders—at least public authorities, NGOs, private sector actors and citizens, in many combinations. They might have an overall common goal, for example the production of better public services or more civic participation, but they always have (slightly) competing interests. The power imbalance is also notable. Public authorities are considered the legitimate power holders in many cases of co-creation whereas the others compete for the power and resources left from there.

In order for the systemic distortion to emerge, there must also be systemic distortion of information in the given system (see e.g. Bella 2006; Bella et al. 2003; King et al. 2002). This refers to a situation where some information is ignored, distorted, left unsaid or misinterpreted. It creates a continuous reinforcing cycle of misinformation, misinterpretation and misconduct. The distortion of information is often not intentional—it comes naturally in social systems, where people promote their own interests, tend to blame "others" for mistakes, or do not want to blame anyone, covering up for mistakes in order not to disturb the system or put anyone into shame and so on (ibid.). This in turn may lead to systemic organizational defensive routines, where our espoused theories and theories-in-use differ—we do not act the way we say or believe we do (see e.g. Argyris 1999). Systemic distortion worsens even further when we realize that most often we actually think in a linear manner—A leads to B, or B is a consequence of A—not in systemic terms, cyclically or in circles (King et al. 2002). In other words, we ignore feedback loops, systemic effects and non-linearity that characterize complex systems.

Systemic distortion in co-creation may lead into what we would like to call *co-destruction*. It is the opposite of ideal co-creation, an unintended and unwanted co-creation. It is the dark side that emerges when self-organization fails. Kotus and Sowada (2017) point out one form of co-destruction in their article where they describe different types of participation in urban management. They call it disorder: not only is there actually no participation (no co-anything), but the entities or actors involved do not even perform their basic functions. Everyone considers themselves being treated unfairly and having no say in the process. Everyone is having a growing desire to seize power and take more radical steps (Ibid: 81). This is a case where the self-organizing fourth sector (see Chap. 5) is striving to take over power, but at the same time feeling dis-empowered. Public authorities are not only performing a participative diversion, but they are directing their efforts to provoke confrontation and authoritarian rule. Interests and goals are hidden, action is not open, power imbalance and battle is notable, as is the systemic distortion of any information possibly available in the system.

A somewhat different example of systemic distortion was uncovered in the social and health care sector in Finland at the time of writing the article. A large private company providing housing and care for the elderly was charged for widespread neglect of customers all over the country. Opening up the case brought forth a classic case of systemic distortion of information inside the organization. The situation can be analysed as an example of co-destruction. Public authorities and the private sector were co-creating, or at least co-producing the services, and also the customers or their advocates were actively involved. The goal and intention was undoubtedly good—high-quality services for the elderly. Not one of the actors involved was intentionally malicious. But there were, and are, multiple stakeholders with varying interests and power imbalances. The public authorities mainly responsible for financing the services obviously wanted the services inexpensively. The customers also wanted the services inexpensively, but also with good quality. The company wanted to make profit. Customers had the least power in the process, being often disadvantaged due to physical and mental conditions. Since there is lack of services for elderly in the society, it is more or less a seller's market, hence often leaving the public authorities without much choice. Adding to this was the shortage of care personnel. The lack of personnel led to situations where there was neglect of customers, or even open misconduct. This had to be covered. And the cover-up had to be covered. Soon no-one knew what the real situation was or had been. The "others" were blamed. Public authorities blamed the company, when customers of their advocates complained. The personnel said they were not listened to by the management. The management said they did not know about the situation etc. The vicious cycle of co-destruction was operating in the "context of normal behaviours acted out by a number of well-intended people" (King et al. 2002: 163).

1.7 Discussion and Conclusions

While co-creation is a lucrative concept within public services, it has also been criticized for being too vague. Gebauer et al. (2010), for example, have pointed out that co-creation has been used inter-changeably with co-production, and for many (e.g. Voorberg et al. 2017: 366) co-creation has been limited solely to "the involvement of citizens in the initiation or design of public services". Emphasizing *value* co-creation in the public service context has also been seen as problematic. Osborne (2018), for example, has identified four reasons why value creation in public services differs from private service firms. First, for public services the retention of customers and repeat business is likely to be a sign of service failure, whereas for firms they are key objectives. Second, many service users in public services (e.g. prisoners) are coerced to use services. Third, the concept of customer is blurred in public services because of multiple end-users and stakeholders with conflicting ideas about what is valuable. Fourth, public service users have a dual role as both a service user, but also a citizen who may have a broader societal interest in the outcome of a service (ibid.). The problem of value co-creation is well presented in the co-destructive case of elderly care described in the previous Chap. 6.

Ideal co-creation works in an environment of dynamic balance between exploitation and exploration (see Fig. 1.2). Exploitation is characterized as refining,

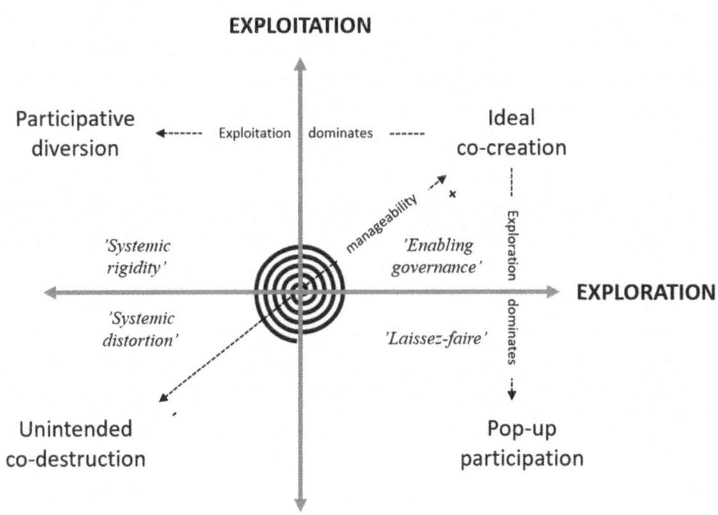

Fig. 1.2 The matrix of co-creation

selecting, implementing and executing operations, whereas exploration is an organizational activity based on searching, risk-taking, playing, experimenting, discovering and innovating (March 1991). While exploitation rests on established routines and modes of routines, exploration emphasizes the identification of new opportunities and alternatives (ibid.). The ideal co-creation is also controllable in a sense that there are shared goals, intentions and values. There is a feasible convergence of all parties involved, and at best ideal co-creation is characterized by enabling governance. Where there is exploration, but the exploitation in the situation decreases, we enter the era of pop-up participation or a self-organizing fourth sector. From the part of public authorities, it is a sort of "laissez-faire" governance. Let the civil society deal with it, if they are willing to. When exploration activities decrease and exploitation remains at high levels, we face the participative diversion. It is a form of pseudo-co-creation, an illusion of participation and collaboration. It is characterized by systemic rigidity, again mostly from the part of the public authorities wishing to stay in control. Too much exploitation will not foster co-creation. Finally, where there is no exploitation and no exploration, at worst, we enter co-destruction powered by systemic distortion.

The simultaneous appearance of exploitation and exploration is called organizational ambidexterity (e.g. Uhl-Bien and Arena 2018). In the general sense of the word, ambidextrous refers to being able to use both arms. In relation to this, Fig. 1.2 presents *a matrix of co-creation*, where, in the upper right corner of the matrix, actors taking part in co-creation processes are—metaphorically speaking—able to use both of their arms, to innovate and to produce, to be ambidextrous. In the upper left corner, actors work one-armed, only using their left arm, and not being able to take advantage of the full potential of the co-creation processes. The same applies to the bottom right corner, where actors are only using their right arm. In the former case the strong, but inflexible and tense left arm goes with public authorities. In the latter case the frail, but flexible and loose right arm belongs to civil society. In the bottom right corner of the matrix, all actors are collectively altogether armless, and at the mercy of (destructive) self-organization and emergence.

Participative diversion, pop-up participation and unintended co-destruction are all outcomes of co-creation that Bovaird (2007: 857) describes as socially undesirable. They are also compatible with the findings of De Vries (2010 in Steen et al. 2018: 288) who argue that even in the case of no explicit misuse by anyone, the tension between private and public value means that service professionals cannot use individual citizens' opinion as an indication of what is preferred by all citizens nor good for the community/society. Following the logics of Brandsen and Pestoff (2006), Bovaird (2007) and Voorberg et al. (2015), Fox et al. (2019) suggest that co-creation implies re-thinking of democratic processes. Whether value is created depends on how citizens interact with the government and public service providers. Thus, we also conclude that the democracy dimension of co-creation should not be undervalued. We argue, in accordance with Verschuere et al. (2018: 246), in favour of three criteria that need to be met: first, there is a need for "a sufficient and truthful *professional support*", from public or non-profit organizations; second, there is a need for "a minimal level of *competency*" of co-creating citizens; third, there is need for "the *salience* of the service provided", i.e. the importance of the content of co-creation. Seen through "complexity lenses", self-organization cannot produce beneficial emergent patterns if the actors involved in the process lack the knowledge or motivation to join co-creative activities. This leads us to ask how the democratic aspect of co-creation is unintentionally eroded. One possible avenue for further research is to analyse the dilemmas the digital technologies entail. While this work has already started (see e.g. Lember et al. 2019; Jamieson et al. 2019), we think that by using complexity concepts it is possible to get new insights in a way that can also be used in developing digitally enabled co-creative practices.

Acknowledgements This paper was created in conjunction with the Co-creation of Service Innovation in Europe (CoSIE) project. The project has received funding from the European Union's Horizon 2020 research and innovation programme H2020-SC6-COCREATION-2017 under grant agreement No 770492. www.cosie-project.eu

References

Aasen, T. M. B. (2009). *Innovation as social processes. A participative study of the Statoil R & D program Subsea Increased Oil Recovery (SIOR)*. Oslo: Norwegian University of Science and Technology.

Ansell, C., & Geyer, R. (2017). 'Pragmatic complexity' a new foundation for moving beyond 'evidence-based policy making'? *Policy Studies, 38*(2), 149–167.

Argyris, C. (1999). *On organizational learning* (2nd ed.). Oxford: Blackwell Business.

Arnstein, S. R. (1969). A ladder of citizen participation. *Journal of the American Institute of Planners, 35*(4), 216–224.

Ashby, W. R. (1956). *An introduction to cybernetics*. London: Chapman & Hall.

Bella, D. A. (1997). Organized complexity in human affairs: The tobacco industry. *Journal of Business Ethics, 16*, 977–999.

Bella, D. A. (2006). Emergence and evil. *Emergence: Complexity and Organization, 8*(2), 102–115.

Bella, D. A., King, J. B., & Kailin, D. (2003). The dark side of organizations and a method to reveal it. *Emergence: Complexity and Organization, 5*(3), 66–82.

Blitz, D. (1992). *Emergent evolution: Qualitative novelty and the levels of reality*. Dordrecht: Kluwer Academic Publishers.

Boonstra, B., & Boelens, L. (2011). Self-organization in urban development: Towards a new perspective on spatial planning. *Urban Research & Practice, 4*(2), 99–122.

Böse, M., Busch, B., & Sesic, M. D. (2006). Despite and beyond cultural policy: Third and fourth sector practices and strategies. In U. H. Meinhof & A. Triandafyllidou (Eds.), *Transcultural Europe: Cultural policy in a changing Europe* (pp. 131–156). New York: Palgrave Macmillan.

Bouckaert, G., & Halligan, J. (2008). *Managing performance: International comparisons*. New York: Routledge, Taylor and Francis.

Bourgon, J. (2009). New directions in public administration: Serving beyond the predictable. *Public Policy and Administration, 24*(3), 309–330.

Bovaird, T. (2007). Beyond engagement and participation: User and community coproduction of public services. *Public Administration Review, 67*(5), 846–860.

Brandsen, T., & Pestoff, V. (2006). Co-production, the third sector and the delivery of public services. *Public Management Review, 8*(4), 493–501.

Brandsen, T., Steen, T., & Verschuere, B. (Eds.). (2018). *Co-production and co-creation. Engaging citizens in public services*. London: Routledge.

Cairney, P. (2012). Complexity theory in political science and public policy. *Political Studies Review, 10*, 346–358.
Christensen, T., & Lægreid, P. (2011). Complexity and hybrid public administration—Theoretical and empirical challenges. *Public Organization Review, 11*, 407–423.
Cilliers, P. (2005). Knowledge, limits and boundaries. *Futures, 37*, 605–613.
Daviter, F. (2017). Coping, taming or solving: Alternative approaches to the governance of wicked problems. *Policy Studies, 38*(6), 571–588.
De Vries, P. (2010). *Handboek Ouders in de School*. Amersfoort: CPS.
Faehnle, M., Mäenpää, P., Blomberg, J., & Schulman, H. (2017). Civic engagement 3.0—Reconsidering the roles of citizens in city-making. *Yhteiskuntasuunnittelu, 55*, 3.
Fox, C., Jalonen, H., Baines, S., Bassi, A., Marsh, C., Moretti, V., & Willoughby, M. (2019). *Co-creation of public service innovation—Something old, something new, something borrowed, something tech* (Reports from Turku University of Applied Sciences 259). Turku: Turku University of Applied Sciences.
Friedman, L. H., King, J. B., & Bella, D. A. (2007, July–August). Ending the blame game. Seeing systems in health care organizations. *The Physician Executive, 2007*, 20–29.
Fung, A. (2015). Putting the public back into governance: The challenges of citizen participation and its future. *Public Administration Review, 75*(4), 513–522.
Gebauer, H., Johnson, M., & Enquist, B. (2010). Value co-creation as a determinant for success in public transport services: A study of the Swiss federal railway operator (SBB). *Managing Service Quality, 20*(6), 511–530.
Gerrits, L., & Marks, P. (2015). How the complexity sciences can inform public administration: An assessment. *Public Administration, 93*(2), 539–546.
Geyer, R. (2012). Can complexity move UK policy beyond 'evidence-based policy making' and the 'audit culture'? Applying a 'complexity cascade' to education and health policy. *Political Studies, 60*, 20–43.
Goldstein, J. (1999). Emergence as a construct: History and issues. *Emergence: Complexity and Organization, 1*(1), 49–72.
Grönlund, H. (2016). Vapaaehtoistoiminta vuonna 2025 [Volunteering in 2025]. In E. Innola (Ed.), *Kohti kattavampaa varautumista [Towards more comprehensive preparedness]* (pp. 57–61). Helsinki: The Security Committee.
Hazy, J. K., Goldstein, J. A., & Lichtenstein, B. B. (2007). *Complex systems leadership theory new perspectives from complexity science on social and organizational effectiveness*. Mansfield: ISCE Publishing.
Hood, C. C. (1991). A public management for all seasons? *Public Administration, 69*(3), 3–19.
Hurlbert, M., & Gupta, J. (2015, June). The split ladder of participation: A diagnostic, strategic, and evaluation tool to assess when participation is necessary. *Environmental Science & Policy, 50*, 100–113.
Jalonen, H., & Juntunen, P. (2011). Enabling innovation in complex welfare service systems. *Journal of Service Science and Management, 4*(4), 401–418.
Jamieson, D., Wilson, R., & Martin, M. (2019). The (im)possibilities of open data. *Public Money and Management, 39*(5), 364–368.
Johannessen, S. O. (2018). *Strategies, leadership and complexity in crisis and emergency operations*. New York: Routledge.
Johanson, J.-E., & Vakkuri, J. (2017). *Governing hybrid organisations. Exploring diversity of institutional life*. London: Routledge.
King, J., Down, J. T., & Bella, D. A. (2002). Learning to think on circles. *Journal of Management Inquiry, 11*(2), 161–170.
Klijn, E.-H., & Koppenjan, J. (2012). Governance network theory: Past, present and future. *Policy & Politics, 40*(4), 587–606.
Kotus, J., & Sowada, T. (2017). Behavioural model of collaborative urban management: Extending the concept of Arnstein's ladder. *Cities, 65*, 78–86.

Lee Jenni, G. D. L., Peterson, M. N., & Katz, J. (2015). Military perspectives on public relations related to environmental issues. *Journal of Public Relations, 27*(4), 353–369.

Lember, V., Brandsen, T., & Tõnurist, P. (2019). The potential impacts of digital technologies on co-production and co-creation. *Public Management Review*. https://doi.org/10.1080/14719037.2019.1619807.

Linstead, S., Maréchal, G., & Griffin, R. W. (2014). Theorizing and researching the dark side of organization. *Organization Studies, 35*(2), 165–188.

Lorenz, D. F., Schulze, K., & Voss, M. (2018). Emerging citizen responses to disasters in Germany. Disaster myths as an impediment for a collaboration of unaffiliated responders and professional rescue forces. *Journal of Contingencies and Crisis Management, 26*(3), 358–367.

Mäenpää, P., & Faehnle, M. (2017). Civic activism as a resource for cities. *Helsinki Quarterly, 1*, 68–81.

Mäenpää, P., & Faehnle, M. (2018). Urban civic activism: Solutions for the governance of a self-organising urban community. *Helsinki Quarterly, 2*, 38–45.

Mäenpää, P., Faehnle, M., & Schulman, H. (2017). Kaupunkiaktivismi, jakamistalous ja neljäs sektori [Civic activism, sharing economy and the fourth sector]. In P. Bäcklund, J. Häkli, & H. Schulman (Eds.), *Kansalaiset kaupunkia kehittämässä [Citizens developing the city]* (pp. 239–259). Tampere: Tampere University Press.

March, J. G. (1991). Exploration and exploitation in organizational learning. *Organization Science, 2*(1), 71–87.

McLennan, B., Whittaker, J., & Handmer, J. (2016). The changing landscape of disaster volunteering: Opportunities, responses and gaps in Australia. *Natural Hazards, 84*(3), 2031–2048.

Mintzberg, H. (1979). *The structuring of organizations*. Englewood Cliffs: Prentice-Hall.

Mitleton-Kelly, E. (2003). Ten principles of complexity and enabling infrastructures. In E. Mitleton-Kelly (Ed.), *Complex systems and evolutionary perspectives on organizations: The application of complexity theory to organizations* (pp. 23–50). New York: Pergamon.

Morçöl, G. (2012). *A complexity theory for public policy*. London: Routledge.

Murphy, J., Rhodes, M. L., Meek, J. W., & Denyer, D. (2017). Managing the entanglement: Complexity leadership in public sector systems. *Public Administration Review, 77*(5), 692–704.

Osborne, S. (2018). From public service-dominant logic to public service logic: Are public service organizations capable of co-production and value co-creation. *Public Administration Review, 20*(2), 225–231.

Osborne, S., & Strokosch, K. (2013). It takes two to tango? Understanding the co-production of public services by integrating the services management and public administration perspectives. *British Journal of Management, 24*, 531–547.

Parker, G., Lynn, T., & Wargent, M. (2015). Sticking to the script? The co-production of neighbourhood planning in England. *Town Planning Review, 86*(5), 519–536.

Polanska, D. V. (2018). Going against institutionalization: New forms of urban activism in Poland. *Journal of Urban Affairs*. Published online. https://doi.org/10.1080/07352166.2017.1422982

Raisio, H., Puustinen, A., & Vartiainen, P. (2018). The concept of wicked problems: Improving the understanding of managing problem wickedness in health and social care. In W. Thomas, A. Hujala, S. Laulainen, & R. McMurray (Eds.), *The management of wicked problems in health and social care* (pp. 3–20). London: Routledge.

Raisio, H., Puustinen, A., Norri-Sederholm, T., & Jalava, J. (2019). "Those who agree to play on our terms will be taken in": A qualitative study of the perceptions of public authorities and NGO representatives regarding self-organizing fourth-sector activity. *Public Administration Quarterly, 43*(3), 4–44.

Rantanen, A., & Faehnle, M. (2017). Self-organisation challenging institutional planning: Towards a new urban research and planning paradigm—A Finnish review. *The Finnish Journal of Urban Studies, 55*, 3.

Rask, M., Mačiukaitė-Žvinienė, S., Tauginienė, L., Dikčius, V., Matschoss, K., Aarrevaara, T., & d'Andrea, L. (2018). *Public participation, science and society: Tools for dynamic and responsible governance of research and innovation*. New York: Routledge.

Richardson, K. A. (2008). Managing complex organizations: Complexity thinking and the science and art of management. *Emergence, Complexity and Organization, 10*(2), 13–26.
Rittel, H., & Webber, M. (1973). Dilemmas in a general theory of planning. *Policy Sciences, 4*(2), 155–169.
Rock, J., McGuire, M., & Rogers, A. (2018). Multidisciplinary perspectives on co-creation. *Science Communication, 40*(4), 541–552.
Sakellariou, A. (2018). *Rapid evidence appraisal of the current state of co-creation in ten European countries* (Reports from Turku University of Applied Sciences 251). Turku.
Stacey, R. D. (2007). *Strategic management and organisational dynamics: The challenge of complexity to ways of thinking about organisations*. London: Prentice Hall.
Stacey, R. (2010). *Complexity and organizational realities: Uncertainty and the need to rethink management after the collapse of investment capitalism*. London: Routledge.
Steen, T., Brandsen, T., & Verschuere, B. (2018). The dark side of co-creation and co-production of co-production and co-creation. In T. Brandsen, T. Steen, & B. Verschuere (Eds.), *Co-production and co-creation. Engaging citizens in public services* (pp. 284–293). London: Routledge.
Torfing, J., Sørensen, E., & Røiseland, A. (2016). Transforming the public sector into an Arena for co-creation: Barriers, drivers, benefits, and ways forward. *Administration & Society*. https://doi.org/10.1177/0095399716680057.
Tritter, J. Q., & McCallum, A. (2006). The snakes and ladders of user involvement: Moving beyond Arnstein. *Health Policy, 76*(2), 156–168.
Uhl-Bien, M., & Arena, M. (2017). Complexity leadership: Enabling people and organization for adaptability. *Organizational Dynamics, 46*, 9–20.
Uhl-Bien, M., & Arena, M. (2018). Leadership for organizational adaptability: A theoretical synthesis and integrative framework. *The Leadership Quarterly, 29*(1), 89–104.
Vargo, S., & Lusch, R. (2004). Evolving to a new dominant logic for marketing. *Journal of Marketing, 68*(1), 1–17.
Verschuere, B., Vanleene, D., Steen, T., & Brandsen, T. (2018). Democratic co-production: Concepts and determinants. In T. Brandsen, T. Steen, & B. Verschuere (Eds.), *Co-production and co-creation. Engaging citizens in public services* (pp. 243–251). London: Routledge.
Virta, S., & Branders, M. (2016). Legitimate security? Understanding the contingencies of security and deliberation. *The British Journal of Criminology, 56*(6), 1146–1164.
Voorberg, W. H., Bekkers, V., & Tummers, L. G. (2015). A systematic review of co-creation and co-production: Embarking on the social innovation journey. *Public Management Review, 17*(9), 1333–1357.
Voorberg, W. H., Bekkers, V., Fleming, A., Timeus, K., Tonurist, P., & Tummers, L. J. (2017). Does co-creation impact public service delivery? *Public Money & Management, 37*(5), 365–373.
Williams, B. N., Kang, S.-C., & Johnson, J. (2015). (Co)-contamination as the dark side of co-production: Public value failures in co-production processes. *Public Management Review, 18*(5), 692–717.

Chapter 2
Perspectives on Hybridity

Jan-Erik Johanson and Jarmo Vakkuri

Abstract It is too simplistic to see hybridity only as a type of organisation. Hybrids appear in micro, meso, and macro levels of activity consisting of pairwise interactions and network constellations between business firms and public agencies. Cleantech industry, health policy national innovation systems, and global air travel are showcases of hybrid activities in higher than organisational level of analysis. The current classifications of organisations do not acknowledge the existence of hybrids. The denial of existence of hybrids are embedded in the classification principles which have not followed the evolution of economic and social activities. It is also the case that seeing the reality as more simple than it really is provides heuristic tools to understand complex hybrid arrangements.

2.1 Introduction

Looking at hybrids from the perspective of public administration research, we refer to institutional settings in which corporations with both public and private owners may operate according to public interest or activity, or in which private (for-profit or nonprofit) firms increasingly take care of public service provisions. In practice, hybrid forms of governance may thus assume many forms: government-owned corporations, public–private partnerships, social enterprises, commissions, public procurement, purchaser–provider models, and contracting out. More specifically, the notion of hybridity, can be considered to cover the following:

1. Mixed ownership. Consider the current forms of organising important societal functions, such as energy delivery and supply and the infrastructure in different countries of the world. These societal functions are often organised as state-owned enterprises (SOEs) that aim to combine the politically driven goals of modern nation states while exploiting business logics and operating on global financial markets (Thynne 2011).

J.-E. Johanson (✉) · J. Vakkuri
Tampere University, Tampere, Finland
e-mail: jan-erik.johanson@tuni.fi; Jarmo.vakkuri@tuni.fi

H. Lehtimäki et al. (eds.), *Society as an Interaction Space*, Translational Systems Sciences 22, https://doi.org/10.1007/978-981-15-0069-5_2

2. Goal incongruence and competing institutional logics. Think about institutions that aim to balance the logic of profit seeking vis-à-vis the logic of societal effectiveness. While these organisations—in terms of ownership—may quite often be purely private firms, their activities are shaped by different forms of ambiguity and ambivalence. They should be able to employ different but parallel institutional logics. They should be able to provide financial value for their shareholders but also social impacts on society and citizens. Consider social enterprises, the objective of which is to 'do well by doing good', where 'good' refers to legitimate social aims, and 'well' is understood as being profitable (Reay and Hinings 2009; Kreps and Monin 2011; Pache and Santos 2013; Ebrahim et al. 2014).
3. Multiplicity of funding arrangements. Think about modern megaprojects such as the International Space Station, the Beijing–Shanghai High-Speed Railway, the Airbus A380 aircraft, or the Channel Tunnel connecting the UK and continental Europe. These projects not only take time and massive amounts of financial and intellectual resources but also institutional collaboration between public and private actors (Greve and Hodge 2007).
4. Public and private forms of financial and social control. There can be different types of control systems applied to systems of service delivery. In general, forms of control may include, for instance, the regulatory control of markets, professional self- (or clan-) control, and customer-driven market control within a single system of service delivery (Kickert 2001; Jordana and Levi-Faur 2004). Modern control systems are defined by the simultaneity of different dimensions of control. It is probably more important to understand whether control is exercised by an external or internal party. In hybrid settings, forms of control are usually mixed and influenced by multiple pressures of control from both inside and outside forces.

2.2 Hybridity and Its Variants

The aim of this chapter is to broaden the view of hybridity in social activities, contexts, and organisations. It is our contention that the dichotomous perspective of public and private action has constrained our understanding regarding what hybrids and hybridity actually involve. This is not to state that we cannot comprehend the cognitive rationales of the distinctions between public and private. However, the clear-cut public and private sector delineation that prevents us from seeing institutional life in all its richness. Hybridity, we contend, is one aspect in exploring such richness. For us, it is erroneous to see such an exploration process as creating monstrous hybrids, institutional weirdos, or an increase in theoretical complexity for its own sake.

Our process of enhancing understanding of the public, the private, and the hybrid is divided into several elements. We discuss hybridity at different levels of social and economic action. Furthermore, we combine levels of hybridity with some traditional discussions in social theory associated with social structures. Finally, this chapter concludes by discussing hybrid structures and activities as institutional, political, and cognitive practices in the context of uncertainty avoidance. We study ideals of administrative pragmatism and decision-making heuristics as reasoning for why it may make sense to rely on a clear distinction of the public and private (Tilly 2006). In this chapter, we provide a variety of case illustrations from different contexts of hybrid activities.

There are number of analytic perspectives available for the study of hybrid governance. One can distinguish levels of hybridity according to the number of participants in social intercourse, which results in singular, dyadic, and triadic levels of analysis. Another way of separating hybrid activities is to see them as abstractions beginning from the low level of analysis (micro) and progressing into more general and larger levels (meso and macro). Yet another option is to see hybrids as entities. Most typically, hybrids are seen as organisational entities with a distinctive border separating them from their environments, but it is equally possible to see collective entities of hybrids as comprising industries or organisational fields (see Fig. 2.1). The following discussion elaborates on these perspectives in more detail.

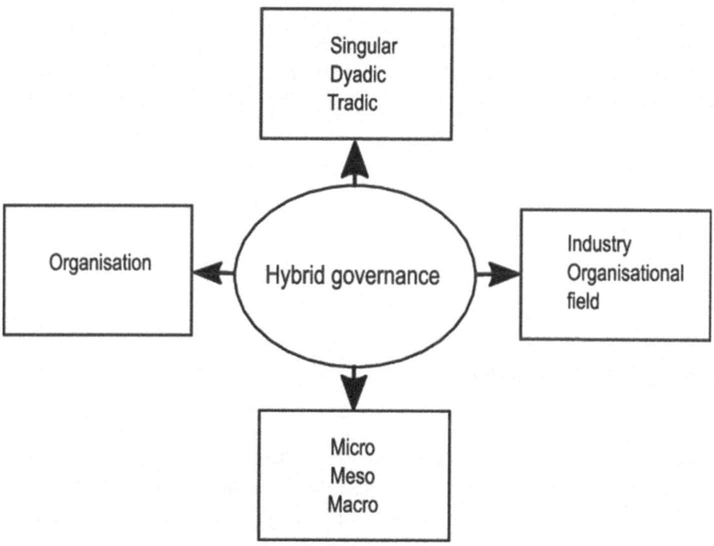

Fig. 2.1 Analytic perspectives on hybrid governance

There is more than meets the eye? Hybridity as levels of societal activities.

Hybrids and hybridity are often associated with the notion of hybrid organisations. In this association, we tend to assume that if an organisation incorporates features from both public and private forms of institutional action, it is regarded as a hybrid organisation. Such features, as previously discussed, may include ownership, objective setting, finance, and control (Bozeman and Moulton 2011). This type of reasoning has resulted in several studies and research programmes exploring how to delineate the public from the private and how to define hybridity in the context of modern organisations.

The argument that hybridity only resembles one form of organisational action in society is probably more an elucidation of us living amidst a world of organisations than a true representation of hybridity in social life (Simon 1991). To some extent, we have learnt to use organisations as an important frame for our thinking to inform ourselves of how social action takes place. Educational activities are conducted by educational 'organisations' or 'schools', and people are cured in health care 'organisations' or 'hospitals'. Organisational logics can easily be applied. Almost anything can be labelled as an 'organisation'.

However, thinking about entities assumes that an organisation can be easily distinguished from its environment. It is not easy to do this in the context of organisational settings, let alone in the context of hybrid organisations. Furthermore, one of the most interesting things is, in fact, environment, the framework that sets the scene for organisations, policies, actions, and actors. For instance, Scott (1991) refers to an industry system as a single, concrete, and stable network of the identifiable and interacting components of the societal sector, which perform similar functions together with other members of their set that influence their operations in some manner. Whitley (2000: 7) talks about intellectual fields as a concept that describes 'a broader and more general social unit of knowledge production'. When we attempt to understand hybrid activities, organisational thinking may constrain us.

2.3 Levels of Hybridity

In social life, hybridity may be observed in distinct settings of institutional, political, and economic action. Therefore, we can think of three different levels of hybridity: hybrid systems, hybrid industries, and hybrid organisations. As the previous research discussion has primarily concentrated on hybrid organisations, our aim is to discuss further other levels of societal action influenced by hybridity; that is, levels of public–private interaction. Case illustrations of health policy (Case 2.1) and cleantech industry (Case 2.2) enable us to see hybridity as macro- and industry-level development.

Case 2.1 Hybrid Governance for Solving Tricky Problems of Health Policy
Maintaining and developing health among people is a complicated task in society. At the level of health policy, societies struggle to balance different criteria of rationality: cost containment, access to health services, and service quality (Kissick

1994), each of which provides important, albeit to some extent mutually exclusive, criteria for the governance of health care service provision. For instance, while it may be legitimate to ease the access to health care services, it may be difficult to do this in the context of finite financial resources and providing marginal quality improvements for existing health service users. Therefore, health care systems struggle to cope with the wicked tension between the unlimited needs of health service and the limited financial and intellectual resources for providing services (Kork and Vakkuri 2016).

In governing such an effort, countries of the world have adopted different strategies and institutional practices with which they have attempted to solve simultaneous problems of access, service quality, and financial balance. Health care service provision reveals important examples of hybrid systems. Financing comes from both public and private resource bases; organising and provision includes business firms, public organisations, and nonprofit organisations; and forms of control entail both government oversight and private and professionally organised practices.

Health care systems show different levels of hybridity (OECD 2015). For instance, the US's health care system is by definition a hybrid, as fundamental choices of health care activities are organised, financed, insured, and managed by both public and private interests and organisations (Sekhri et al. 2011). For instance, one half of the funding comes from private sources, and the other half comes from the government. However, even in publicly funded health services, the form of delivery is primarily private. The health policy is under intense scrutiny and policy debate in the USA because, in addition to well-documented problems of access to services, health care expenditures per GDP are significantly higher in the USA than in other countries (in the USA it is 16.4%, and the average of all OECD countries is 8.9%) (OECD 2015). Is this somehow associated with the hybrid nature of the US health care system, in which public services and goods are provided but also in which different sets of business profit-seeking motives are included and enacted? For instance, cost containment may be of different importance to different actors in the health care system. While it is too straightforward to make an argument about clear and unambiguous causal relationships between system properties and health impacts, there are several discussions and ideas emphasising the need for the systematic governance of health care systems as hybrid systems. These ideas have been labelled as, for instance, 'integrated governance' (Sekhri et al. 2011) or 'multisector partnerships' (Harris 2016).

***

It is complicated to talk about health as a purely private or purely public good. Health impacts may be wide-ranging and comprehensive, and they may spill over, but health can also be commodified and commercialised. Accordingly, the fundamental question in the governance of health systems is about selecting the best features of both public and private forms of health-maintaining activities and processes. But how to create solutions that would be able to utilise the best features of both systems? 'Integrated' modes of governance might be able to solve some of the problems that other forms of governance fail to address. What transaction cost analysis teaches us is to evaluate whether there is some concrete option to deal with governance problems other than the option that has already been adopted (Williamson 1985). Moreover, if a governance structure exists in the first place, it is viable, as it has already survived the institutional struggle of survival.

There are multiple uncertainties and contingencies in different governance forms. In order to solve fundamental health problems, hybrid forms of governance require new types of system-level coordination, rethinking roles for government and private business firms, and disclosures of transparent and comparable information on service provision, as well as an understanding of the explicit and implicit forms of hybrid contracting (Williamson 1999). It may be these contingencies which determine the actual possibilities of using hybrid forms of governance in health policy. However, an even more fundamental question is our approach to hybridity and our perceptions of how to define the success and failure of governance solutions. Do we think of these as a result of conscious and deliberate design, or as intended or unintended outcomes of institutional change (Scott 2000)?

Moving to another subject matter, we are interested in hybrid industries, a cluster of public and private actors pursuing public goals but within a more specific institutional field of action (Padgett and Powell 2012). As a case context for this, we can think of the 'cleantech' industry, in which several actors—including public policy makers, business firms, and multiple associations—aim to contribute to the common good of ensuring clean air by producing environmentally friendly technologies and solutions for the global marketplace. Third, we can discuss hybrid organisations pursuing public goals by employing parallel institutional logics. The selection of different industries in our study represents the differentiated orderings of worth by default (Stark 2009). As a field of activity, the area of health has been related to the civic order of worth in Europe, which is evaluated by the principle of collective welfare and its ability to distribute these services in an equal manner, whereas the USA has valued the world of markets in emphasising competition and buying and selling while providing health services.

The cleantech industry signifies the green order of worth by supplying environmentally friendly products, emphasising sustainability, and working for ecosystems. Within R&D, there is an inbuilt for technical efficiency, and for a long-term plan of the future combined with the world of markets. As a specific area of R&D, the cleantech industry is in its institutional infancy, as it combines features of the green, market, and industrial worlds. These ambiguities exemplify the difficulty of defining qualified objects within the cleantech industry. Is a low-emission diesel engine part of the green world on the basis of its modification, a part of the market world due to its ability to save on costs, or even a part of the industrial world due to its technical efficiency, to name a few possibilities?

Case 2.2 Hybridisation of Industries: Going Green Through Cleantech

The institutional emergence of industries is an interesting phenomenon and an extremely useful case for exploring hybrid forms of governance (Padgett and Powell 2012). Although many actors seek institutional clarity and wish to avoid uncertainty, this may not always apply to industrial fields. The current structure of industries is a social convention, which may be incongruous with what is happening in the real world of economic activities.

One such example is the cleantech industry, a nascent industrial field combining and transcending several categories of existing areas of industrial business firms and activities as well as distinct fields of public policies. According to O'Rourke (2009), in order to understand the emergence of the cleantech industry, two parallel trajectories of institutional changes should be considered. First, economic growth, particularly in North America and the USA, has largely been stimulated by entrepreneurial actors operating with new technologies and innovations. Quite often, this goes hand in hand with venture capitalists (VC) willing to invest in such new innovative technologies. O'Rourke recognises such a development in the background of the cleantech concept's emergence, dating this back to the early 2000s. The second parallel development was the degradation of our physical environment. Long-standing discussions on climate change started to be grounded on explicit indicators of that degradation. People began to attach new meanings to environmental problems, such as environmental disasters and changes in the ozone layers of the stratosphere. People also started to seek more sophisticated and eloquent evidence of climate change. They wanted to know more about what was going in their environments, and also how they would be able to contribute to solutions.

Interestingly enough, there had to be an intellectual shift to understand environmental problems in a new manner. The traditional idea of treating business and the environment as mutually exclusive elements of the market economy had to be changed. Environmental 'problems' had to be transformed into 'opportunities' for investments and VCs. This necessitated uses of new institutional logics, or frames, as O'Rourke (2009) names them, which indicate that new technologies are the most efficient means for solving environmental problems. In other words, as societal ends include environmental, ecologically sustainable, or social benefits to society, the most optimal means could be found in an effective system of business and entrepreneurial activities. Doing well by doing good began to be accepted as a proper form of business behaviour.

The case of the cleantech industry reflects the basic idea of an industry transcending the boundaries between traditional business industrial activities and societal aims such as reducing carbon dioxide emissions and facilitating a clean-energy supply chain. However, it is also apparent that the introduction and emergence of the cleantech industry disturbs the institutional status quo of existing industries. For instance, consider manufacturing industrial technologies aimed at developing hardware and software to increase manufacturing productivity and efficiency (Cooke 2008). In terms of cleantech development, this makes perfect sense. For instance, in order to contribute to the reduction of carbon dioxide emissions, a system of production economics needs to drastically improve the eco-efficiency of production processes. However, not all manufacturing industrial technologies are related to environmental problems or cleanliness. Optimality is the fundamental aim and starting point of any production process (Koopmans 1957). Therefore, industries are not easily distinguished from each other, or, to put it another way, technologies of optimality may serve almost any context of institutional and industrial action (Porter 1995).

***

This illustration may be used as a way to discuss the mechanisms of the emergence of hybrid industries. The cleantech industry could be seen as an institutional change mechanism that Padgett and Powell (2012) label incorporation and detachment. The cleantech industry has come to solve 'new' social aims using both old and novel technologies. Old technologies implying that, for example, economising production manufacturing processes are indeed an 'old' concept are now utilised in a new context for solving social and ecological problems. In addition, we are also dealing with several new technologies in terms of inventions for reducing carbon dioxide emissions. In doing this, many of the elements of the cleantech industry have been detached from their old contexts in industrial activities. By connecting old and new networks of industrial activities, revised social aims, and new forms of technology, economising production processes have—step by step—become incorporated into the context of cleantech.

2.4 Links Between Levels of Analysis

There is a fertile debate in many fields of research about levels of institutional action in society. One common approach is to discuss micro, meso, and macro levels. In (neoclassical) economics, there is a long tradition of analysing two distinct levels of economic activities; that is, micro and macro. Micro concerns the choice of individual economic agents, and macro refers to the aggregated consequences of such individual choices. According to Dopfer et al. (2004: 264), 'The sum of micro is macro, and the decomposition of macro is micro'. Naturally, these levels have intrinsic value of their own in the economics discipline, as microeconomics aims to understand the behaviour of rational economic agents—such as consumers, firms, and public agencies—while macroeconomics aims to understand the overall economic system and the determinants of macroeconomic planning in society. An important area of methodological discussion concerns the extent to which the interlinkages between these two levels and systems of economic action can be assumed, observed, or intervened through policy design (Dopfer et al. 2004).

Analysing evolutionary economics as a system of rules, Dopfer et al. (2004: 268) treat the meso level not as a transitionary or intermediary level between the macro and micro levels but as 'a thing . . . that is made of complex other things (micro) and is an element in higher order things (macro)'. The meso level constitutes the basis for evolutionary process and change. Such a meso trajectory is represented in the three-stage process of emergence, diffusion, and retention, in which rule systems shape and reshape the underpinnings of economic change. For Dopfer et al., the meso level is necessary to understand the forces and mechanisms of economic change. The micro vs. macro distinction is not always sufficient for that purpose.

According to this view, there is no direct link between the micro and macro levels of analysis. Rather, micro and macro are two perspectives that reveal structural aspects of the changes in meso populations. It is the meso level that constitutes the basic element of economic structure. The macro perspective offers a top-down view on the economic processes of the meso level, and the micro perspective signifies a bottom-up system perspective. The meso level of analysis includes industrial districts, regional knowledge clusters, learning regions, interfirm industrial organisations, national innovation systems, networks with weak and strong ties, and technical support communities. The dynamism of the meso level originates from the interplay between human experimentation and curiosity and the degeneration of rule structures, which guarantees that rule structures are prone to change (Dopfer 2013). To put it otherwise, the new rule generating action takes place at the meso level, which can be observed in micro level (organisations) and aggregated into the macro level (national economies).

Case 2.3 National Innovation Systems as a Meso-Level Hybrid Organisational Field

The discussions and developments of national innovation systems clearly point out some of the main features and challenges of a meso-level analysis of hybridity. National innovation systems represent an important area of public–private interactions within societies. Discussion of national innovation systems began in the late 1980s with the aim to provide an overall framework for a more systematic development of new technologies. In the background, there was a hope that the development of innovations would give mature industrialised countries a competitive edge over newly industrialised countries in Asia and elsewhere. There was also disillusionment about the linear innovation process, which begins with basic science and ends with a commercialised product through applied research, following the chain reaction from basic physics to large-scale development in big labs and leading to commercial applications and innovations. In its reliance on big science and the importance of national research laboratories, the linear model promotes the importance of the supply side in developing new technologies (Freeman 1995).

There were important links between different levels. National innovation systems appear in micro-level interactions. A triple helix grows out of the government-industry dyad into the government-university-industry triad. In this setting the third mission of universities (involvement in the socioeconomic development of society) enables entrepreneurial universities to establish innovation-generating interactions with business enterprises aiming to commercialise R&D innovations aided by government funding. As a result, universities can adopt a position of advancing regional economic development (Ranga and Etzkowitz 2013).

Definitions of national innovation systems underline the interaction between national institutions in developing new technologies (Freeman 1987). This development orients the focus on systemic failures to mismatches between basic research in the public sector and applied research in industry, as well as between the malfunctioning of technology-transfer institutions and the lack of absorptive capacity (the ability to recognise, assimilate, and apply new information to commercial ends) of firms (OECD 1997). One of the challenges in mapping national innovation systems is the lack of proper statistics to account for the various aspects of interactions within countries not present in systems of national accounting (Godin 2009).

Empirical findings of a 15-country comparative study of national innovation systems in small and large high-income countries and some developing countries suggest that the countries did not have coherent industrial policies. Where strong government industrial policies were executed, they led to failure as often as they led to success (Nelson 1992).

***

This examination of national innovation systems (Case 2.3) illustrates the benefits and problems of developing new meso-level constructs to understand hybrid systems. A construct such as national innovation systems highlights knowledge-creation activities as an area of interest in their own right. Innovation systems invite us to examine information-processing activities within universities, public research facilities, and corporate R&D in private enterprises. However, this perspective of national innovation systems has turned into normative demands for more coherent innovation and technology policies. The examination of a new meso-level construct did not come about without problems. First, the lack of proper data regarding the most important features (e.g. interaction of industries and organisations in the process of innovation), systems, and problems of compiling data for new purposes not acknowledged by existing statistics eludes the exact measurement of meso-level phenomena (Godin 2009).

2.5 Public Policy Considerations

In public policy literature, it has been common to discuss the micro, meso, and macro levels. In this literature, the micro level is often associated with 'organisations', the meso level with 'policy fields or areas', and the macro level with the overall 'politico-administrative system' (Van Dooren et al. 2015). In this context, the levels may have slightly different roles than in economics reasoning. In order to achieve society-level goals, there needs to be a reasonable consensus on the macro level. However, achieving society-level goals necessitates the decomposition of abstract political goals into more governable, implementable, and manageable objectives. Often, this takes place at the meso level, in different policy fields where general ideological stances turn into more specific policy agendas. This is why the overall political objective of, for instance, a more secure society is transformed into a more transparent and operationalised objective of, for example, reducing crime and violence in cities. Politics and policies need to be implemented, and they need to be accompanied with the necessary economic and human resources because this allocation decision is an important political choice in society (Wildavsky 1986).

If we accept the assumption that there are three levels of societal action, how would or should we modify these levels in the context of our discussion on hybrid governance and organisations? Can we presume that the same characteristics of institutional action that seem to work in economics, public policy, and organisational studies (i.e. there is a reasonably functioning division of labour for micro, meso, and macro concepts) will apply to our reasoning on hybridity?

Two important considerations need to be made. First, one needs to be candid enough to loosen the absolute primacy of organisational reasoning. Instead, we need to understand the collaborative action that takes place sometimes between organisations but also between individuals, groups, and other types of institutional actors. These other actors may fulfil the criteria of hierarchical organising, but they are not necessarily organisations in the exact sense of the word (Powell 1990; Williamson 1999).

Second, we may comprehend hybrid forms of action by discussing what is missing if we commit ourselves to organisational thinking only. Let us consider hybridity as a mix of public and private ownership, public and private sources of funding, public and private forms of control, and different and contrasting institutional logics and goal setting. Ownership is a pretty straightforward question in the context of hybridity. We may create typologies of public, private, and hybrid organisations in which hybrid organisations are usually referred to as ownership structures with both taxpayers' funding and private forms of capital (Thynne 2011). Funding is readily another issue, as we are moving to an area where the interest lies not in organisations as such but in projects and programmes. We may be dealing with PPP arrangements (Greve and Hodge 2007).

2.6 Hybrids as Singular, Dyadic, and Multilateral Structures

The number of participants is one of the building blocks of social and economic life (Simmel and Wolff 1964). The isolated individual (a singular being), the dyad (a group of two), and the triad (a group of three) are distinctive configurations which cover basic positions in social life (see Fig. 2.2). First, a singular being is not isolated from a social environment, as the singular being cannot exist without the idea

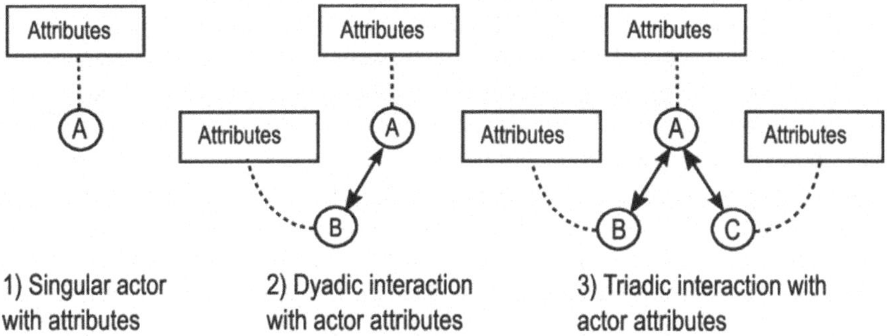

Fig. 2.2 Hybridity as singular, dyadic, and triadic structure

of separation from the others. In this way, an analysis of hybridity often denotes two separate aspects: (1) The very idea of hybridity refers to the idea of other forms that serve as a point of departure for hybrids to exist in the first place, and (2) a singular hybrid possesses attributes that give it its own idiosyncratic characteristics. In a theoretical sense, too much emphasis on the former delegates the role of the hybrid to a residual category of other beings, and emphasis on the latter gives it entitlement for its own existence.

The evolution of organisational forms, the variety of legally defined organisation structures, and organisation typologies are helpful in detecting hybridity in organisational life. It becomes relevant to ask questions such as the following: What are the origins and basic forms of organisation structures, and how do we distinguish organisations in different populations?

Case 2.4 Singular, Dyadic, and Triadic Hybridity in Global Air Travel
The international airline industry showcases public–private interaction on the grandest scale. Developments after World War II represented sharp increases in air travel on a global scale, even though the regulatory regime was founded on intergovernmental agreements and detailed restrictions on establishing new routes. Here, business models in the USA and other countries differed from one another. In the USA, transborder (legacy) carriers and domestic carriers were regulated but competitive private enterprises, whereas in many other countries airlines were national monopolies under government ownership (flag carriers). After the World War II era, international air travel was developed according to bilateral agreements of governments for the operation of routes between two countries after the World War II era. Chicago convention on international air transportation in 1944 established rules by which international air traffic would proceed. Most importantly, the convention gave sovereignty to governments to rule their airspace, which meant that foreign aircraft needed domestic government approval to enter its airspace, and commercial airlines could not negotiate agreements involving two or more airspaces. Consequently, the commercial rights of airlines in international routes were governed by bilateral agreements between each country pair. The developments of the regulatory environment, however, signified two different regimes during the post-war period. The first was highly regulated, the second less so (Hanlon 2007).

The old bilateral agreements included agreements on traffic rights, capacity, designation, and other issues. Traffic rights defined the routes airlines could fly, including destinations that could be served within, between, and beyond bilateral partners. The details of these rights were defined through principles known as 'freedoms of the sky'. Capacity defines the number of flights that can be operated or passengers that can be carried between bilateral partners. Designation refers to the number of airlines bilateral partners can nominate to operate services. Some agreements required airlines to submit ticket prices to aeronautical authorities for approval, and the agreements may have contained ownership criteria that airlines had to meet to be designated under the bilateral agreement. In the old regime, capacity restrictions were open to renegotiation, designation was limited to one or a few airlines, and the pricing of fares was based on the principle that, if the host country was unsatisfied with the fare of the foreign carrier, it could unilaterally adjust it. In the old regime, the details of coordination extended to setting rules for other aspects of aviation services, such as in-flight entertainment. The bilateral agreements and national monopolies produced a mixture of public and private institutions in a de facto cartel of international aviation services (Richards 2001).

In the new regime, the contractual arrangement of the Chicago convention still exists, but the restrictiveness of such contracts has eased greatly. The US policy of open skies agreements after 1977 gave the initial impetus for more liberalised markets of international air travel. In these agreements, no host country can unilaterally limit the volume of traffic and frequency of service provided by the partner's carrier. Agreements allow the partner to name multiple air carriers for designated routes, and, in pricing, partners can unilaterally change the fare without the other partner's approval. According to these agreements, any carrier from a partner country can fly into any domestic airport with as much capacity and frequency as it wishes. The deregulation has increased airline competition and decreased ticket prices (Hanlon 2007: 16).

Probably the biggest change eroding the basis of the post–World War II regulation regime was change in the European Union, which affected the bilateral nature of the air traffic agreements. Measures for the liberalisation of air transport in the European Union came into force in 1993, largely replacing the bilateral air transport agreements signed in the past between EU member countries and making it possible for EU nationals to establish air transport activity anywhere in the European Union (OECD 2015).

To circumvent restrictions on bilateral agreements when operating in foreign countries, many airlines began to build alliances with other airline carriers. By forging an alliance with another carrier, an airline can expand its network and provide customers with many more itinerary combinations than it could on its own. Most notably, there are three global airline alliances in the world: Star Alliance, SkyTeam, and Oneworld. More than a decade after their formation, half of the seating capacity in the world and around 80% of intercontinental traffic between Asia, Europe, and America were served by airlines enrolled in these alliances (Tugores-García 2013).

***

This airline case illustration (Case 2.4) relates to the different kinds of hybrid groupings in the following ways. Within the airline industry, hybridity appears in many forms. On the organisational level, private stock-hold companies, government-owned flagship carriers, and hybrid ownership formed by both public and private shareholders continue to operate in airspaces. The main change in the institutional logics has been the abandoning of the airlines as public utilities and the introduction of competition to replace government regulation. Despite deregulation efforts, governments hold considerable influence in the final say of allowing or denying the operation of foreign airlines in national airspace. The aircraft-manufacturing business is concentrated to only a few manufacturing firms, which are connected to national governments through direct government stakes, contracting deals, and/or military aircraft development.

Singular. The most obvious demarcation line between airlines as singular entities is the ownership structure, which might involve purely private shareholders (private), both public and private shareholders (mixed or hybrid forms), and predominantly government-owned entities (public). The privatisation and hybridisation of airlines have seemingly reduced governments' financial control of airlines. The combined influence of deregulation and increased competition also signifies that operating an airline is a burden for public finances, as witnessed in the bankruptcies of some flag carriers, such as Sabena in Belgium in 2001, Swissair in Switzerland in 2001, and Air Canada in 2003 (European Commission 2014).

In terms of ownership, out of the top 100 airlines, the top 60 have private ownership, 15 have mixed ownership, and the remaining 25 have state ownership (Hanlon 2007). The trend has been that formerly government-owned national flag carriers have been privatised. There is, however, significant regional variation in the ownership structures of the airlines. The USA, Europe, and Latin America are dominated by private airlines, whereas emerging airline markets in the Middle East are dominated by government-owned operators, and airlines in Africa and Asia Pacific are divided roughly into equal shares of public and private operators (IATA 2011).

Dyadic. The dyadic nature of air travel originates from the bilateral air service agreements between national governments that made decisions about how transborder traffic between two countries operated (Prokop 2014). The hybrid twist originates from the fact that such agreements aim at establishing operating rights for commercial airlines. In a formal sense, every agreement introduces a link between national governments and approved foreign airlines (public/private/hybrid).

Triadic. The global constellation of the airline industry has resulted in a tripartite alliance structure of three major alliances, which together account for the majority of global travel. All three alliances include an internal triadic constellation of the USA, European, and Asian carriers. The formation of three global air alliances is a typical hybrid constellation according to transaction cost logic. They are not organisations arranged under unified command or a hierarchical, vertical division of labour, nor do they represent unsecured transactions of atomistic markets. Instead, the alliances are tied together through cooperative agreements in code sharing, scheduling, and shared loyalty programmes.

2.7 The Beauty of Simplification in Distinguishing Public from Private

This chapter has dealt with the multifaceted nature of hybridity in social life and institutional organising. The focus of examination has been on the area between the public and private sectors, between government agencies and private enterprises. The simple starting point of the examination was to find out what the space is in between private enterprise and government action, which is signified by the notion of hybrids, hybridity, hybrid action, and hybrid governance. These notions cannot easily be reduced to the existing categorisations of the public and private sectors. Case extracts of health system, cleantech industry, national innovation systems, and airline travel illustrate the multifaceted nature or hybrid arrangements. The outcome of such examination is that we begin to see distinctions between public and private, government, and business enterprises as impoverished deviations from the richness of hybrids rather than as pure types of existence.

How should we approach the distinction between public and private activities in society? Does that distinction reflect the 'true' state of affairs in organising, or is it more a reflection of the ways in which we as human beings perceive that distinction? To what extent is it real, and to what extent is it socially constructed, a product of human sense-making procedures, or an outcome of administrative pragmatism (Berger and Luckman 1967; Sokal 1996)? One obvious conclusion may be that we cannot possess any understanding of public and private distinctions without the social and linguistic constructions we have created to conduct such a process of comprehension.

It would be unfair to maintain that the dichotomy of the public and private does not incorporate rationalities, albeit hidden rationalities, for decision-makers. Rather, there may be several hidden rationalities, interpretive schemes, and locked-in histories that make sense. It is important to discuss the beauty of black-and-white constructions of organisational and institutional life. We can do this by asking what attracts actors and decision-makers to abstain from adding levels of complexity and ambiguity in policy making. We need to address the beauty of simplification, which is not a normative, prescriptive approach but a descriptive perspective of decision-making.

We can use Daniel Kahneman's work (Kahneman 2012) on human cognition and human perception as one pioneering perspective in order to understand the mechanisms of distinctions, simplifications, and heuristics in human decision-making. The deliberate choice to focus on distinctions between the public and private can be seen as a decision that is shaped by different societal, political, and individual rationalities and guided by several decision-making rules and interpretive schemes of human decision-making (Vakkuri 2010). Those rationalities are limited, bounded, and, as such, associated with a large research tradition on bounded rationality in human choice. Bounded rationality is a theory of decision-making that attempts to take into account the two aspects: the cognitive limitations of decision-makers and the structures of their working environments (Simon 1955). Cognitive limitations include, for example, memory, limited comprehension of causal relationships, and shortage of time. The structure of environments—the context to which public managers have to adapt—is a source of ecological rationality indicating external limitations (Gigerenzer 2000). Understanding decision-making as it happens in practice necessitates an analysis of both aspects.

Decision-makers' assessments are biased and often neglect baseline effects. In other words, initial starting points are sometimes too significant for ultimate choices (Tversky and Kahneman 1974). Therefore, there may be important gains, or 'scale economies', when relying on the clear-cut distinction between public and private. Even small events may reshape the trajectories of reforms. Reforms emphasise the timing and sequencing of policy events to enable increasing returns to reform processes. The lesson for a policy reformer would preferably be to influence the course of reform actions earlier, not later. Accordingly, the costs of shifting reform paths from distinctions between public and private to more ambiguous and hybrid forms of governance tend to become higher in the long run. Institutional locked-in structures and ergodic institutional processes are known to persist in time, particularly in complicated areas of societal change and public policy. We may discover different forms of inherent administrative pragmatism within distinctions of public and private (Pierson 2000).

Decision-making heuristics are one type of rule system. There can be search rules of two types: searching for alternatives for action (defining the choice set) and searching for cues for judging the alternatives (Hey 1982). Search can be random, ordered, or based on imitation and emulation. When should a specific decision-making rule or heuristic be employed? Would this help us understand why and how the strong commitment to public and private distinctions develops? An answer may be found in the individual history of a decision-maker. For example, if a manager of a hybrid organisation learns to use a rule when there is little time to make a decision, the use of such a rule will more likely be used later in choice situations with time pressures. It is obvious that the preceding situation makes it possible to influence judgments and choices by designing situations in which tasks incorporate or simulate initial learning conditions. Another explanation is outcome feedback. Since outcome feedback is the main source of information for evaluating the quality of judgement rules, knowledge of how task variables both affect outcomes and influence the way outcomes are coded and stored in memory becomes critical in explaining heuristics. This makes it important to understand the perceived causalities of public managers in their decision-making (Weiner 1986). In other words, decision-makers using the clear-cut distinction between public and private need to be convinced of the assumed cause-effect relationships between decisions made and outcomes produced. Decision-makers ask themselves how they can determine the relationship between the distinction and the outcome achieved. Where can they see the benefit in the distinction? How do they value those benefits?

References

Berger, P., & Luckman, T. (1967). *The social construction of reality*. London: Penguin Books.

Bozeman, B., & Moulton, S. (2011). Integrative publicness: A framework for public management strategy and performance. *Journal of Public Administration Research and Theory, 21*(Suppl. 3), i363–i380.

Cooke, P. (2008). Cleantech and an analysis of the platform nature of life sciences: Further reflections upon platform policies. *European Planning Studies, 16*(3), 375–393.

Dopfer, K. (2013). *Evolutionary economics* (Vol. 1308). Jena: Max-Planck-Institut für Ökonomik.

Dopfer, K., Foster, J., & Potts, J. (2004). Micro-meso-macro. *Journal of Evolutionary Economics, 14*(3), 263–279.

Ebrahim, A., Battilana, J., & Mair, J. (2014). The governance of social enterprises: Mission drift and accountability challenges in hybrid organizations. *Research in Organizational Behavior, 34*, 81–100.
European Commission. (2014). State aid for airline restructuring: Does it give you wings? Issue 10. Competition Directorate—General of the European Commission.
Freeman, C. (1987). *Technology, policy, and economic performance: Lessons from Japan*. London; New York: Pinter Publishers.
Freeman, C. (1995). The national system of innovation in historical perspective. *Cambridge Journal of Economics, 19*(1), 5–24.
Gigerenzer, G. (2000). *Adaptive thinking: Rationality in the real world*. New York; Oxford: Oxford University Press.
Godin, B. (2009). National innovation system. *Science, Technology & Human Values, 34*(4), 476–501.
Greve, C., & Hodge, G. (2007). *The challenge of public-private partnerships: Learning from international experience*. Cheltenham: Edward Elgar.
Hanlon, J. (2007). *Global airlines: Competition in a transnational industry*. Oxford: Elsevier.
Harris, G. (2016). Transforming health through multisector partnerships. *North Carolina Medical Journal, 77*(4), 286–289.
Hey, J. (1982). Search for rules for search. *Journal of Economic Behavior and Organization, 3*(1), 65–81.
IATA. (2011). *Vision 2050*. Singapore: IATA.
Jordana, J., & Levi-Faur, D. (2004). *The politics of regulation: Institutions and regulatory reforms for the age of governance*. Cheltenham; Northampton: E. Elgar.
Kahneman, D. (2012). *Thinking, fast and slow*. London: Penguin Books.
Kickert, W. (2001). *Public management and administrative reform in Western Europe*. Cheltenham: Elgar.
Kissick, W. L. (1994). *Medicine's dilemmas: Infinite needs versus finite resources*. New Haven: Yale University Press.
Koopmans, T. (1957). *Three essays on the state of economic science*. New York: McGraw-Hill.
Kork, A., & Vakkuri, J. (2016). Improving access and managing healthcare demand with walk-in clinic: Convenient, but at what cost? *International Journal of Public Sector Management, 29*(2), 148–163.
Kreps, T., & Monin, B. (2011). "Doing well by doing good"? Ambivalent moral framing in organizations. *Research in Organizational Behavior, 31*(2), 99–123.
Nelson, R. (1992). National innovation systems: A retrospective on a study. *Industrial and Corporate Change, 1*(2), 347–374.
O'Rourke, A. (2009). *The emergence of cleantech*. New Haven: Yale University.
OECD. (1997). *National innovation systems*. Paris: OECD Publishing.
OECD. (2015). *Health at a glance 2015: OECD indicators*. Paris: OECD Publishing.
Pache, A., & Santos, F. (2013). Inside the hybrid organization: Selective coupling as a response to competing institutional logics. *Academy of Management Journal, 56*(4), 972–1001.
Padgett, J., & Powell, W. (2012). *Emergence of organizations and markets*. Princeton: Princeton University Press.
Pierson, P. (2000). Increasing returns, path dependence, and the study of politics. *American Political Science Review, 94*, 251–268.
Porter, T. (1995). *Trust in numbers: The pursuit of objectivity in science and public life*. Princeton: Princeton University Press.
Powell, W. (1990). Neither market nor hierarchy. In B. Staw & L. Cummings (Eds.), *Research in organizational behavior* (Vol. 12, pp. 295–336). Greenwich: JAI Press.
Prokop, D. (2014). Government regulation of international air transportation. In J. Peoples (Ed.), *The economics of international airline transport* (pp. 45–60). Bingley: Emerald.
Ranga, M., & Etzkowitz, H. (2013). Triple helix systems: An analytical framework for innovation policy and practice in the knowledge society. *Industry and Higher Education, 27*(4), 237–262.

Reay, T., & Hinings, C. (2009). Managing the rivalry of competing institutional logics. *Organization Studies, 30*(6), 629–652.
Richards, J. (2001). Institutions for flying: How states built a market in international aviation services. *International Organization, 55*(4), 993–1017.
Scott, R. (1991). Unpacking institutional arguments. In W. Powell & P. Dimaggio (Eds.), *The new institutionalism and organizational analysis* (pp. 164–182). Chicago: The University of Chicago Press.
Scott, W. (2000). *Institutional change and healthcare organizations: From professional dominance to managed care*. Chicago: University of Chicago Press.
Sekhri, N., Feachem, R., & Ni, A. (2011). Public-private integrated partnerships demonstrate the potential to improve health care access, quality, and efficiency. *Health Affairs, 30*(8), 1498–1507.
Simmel, G., & Wolff, K. (1964). *The sociology of Georg Simmel*. New York: The Free Press.
Simon, H. (1955). A behavioral model of rational choice. *The Quarterly Journal of Economics, 69*(1), 99–118.
Simon, H. (1991). *Models of my life*. New York: Basic Books.
Sokal, A. (1996). Transgressing the boundaries: An afterword. *Dissent, 43*(4), 93–99.
Stark, D. (2009). *The sense of dissonance: Accounts of worth in economic life*. Princeton: Princeton University Press.
Thynne, I. (2011). Ownership as an instrument of policy and understanding in the public sphere: Trends and research agenda. *Policy Studies, 32*(3), 183–197.
Tilly, C. (2006). *Regimes and repertoires*. Chicago: University of Chicago Press.
Tugores-García, A. (2013). *Analysis of global airline alliances as a strategy for international network development*. Cambridge: Massachusetts Institute of Technology.
Tversky, A., & Kahneman, D. (1974). Judgment under uncertainty: Heuristics and biases. *Science, 185*(4157), 1124–1131.
Vakkuri, J. (2010). Struggling with ambiguity: Public managers as users of NPM-oriented management instruments. *Public Administration, 88*(4), 999–1024.
Van Dooren, W., Bouckaert, G., & Halligan, J. (2015). *Performance management in the public sector*. Milton Park: Routledge.
Weiner, B. (1986). *An attributional theory of motivation and emotion*. New York: Springer.
Whitley, R. (2000). *Divergent capitalisms: The social structuring and change of business systems*. Oxford; New York: Oxford University Press.
Wildavsky, A. B. (1986). *Budgeting: A comparative theory of the budgeting process*. Oxford: Transaction Publishers.
Williamson, O. E. (1985). *The economic institutions of capitalism: Firms, markets, relational contracting*. New York: Free Press.
Williamson, O. E. (1999). *The mechanisms of governance*. New York: Oxford University Press.

Chapter 3
Bringing Society Back in: Actors, Networks, and Systems in Public Policy

Volker Schneider

Abstract A key thesis of this contribution is that the analysis of policy processes in the last decades has focused too much on governmental and conventional political actors, on the one hand, and too much on actor-centered bottom-up perspectives. As the microfoundation of social explanations has moved to the fore, actor constellations became the core of policy explanations and contextual factors and systemic perspectives moved into the background. The chapter proposes a renewed perspective on public policy with the aim to bring social factors back into play, particularly at macrostructural level. This means not only that non-governmental, civil society organizations and social relations should be given greater consideration, but even more important are various forms of structural differentiation at the macro level of societies which should be reintegrated into policy explanations.

3.1 Introduction

The manner in which we think about society, politics, and policy-making, how we try to understand and explain the causes and effects of state intervention and "societal problem processing" (Mayntz 1982), has been less a continuous process of knowledge enhancement than a discontinuous advancement that repeatedly was influenced by fashion waves—coming, going, and returning. However, this does not mean that no progress has happened. Scientific progress, at least in the social sciences, is no gradual ascending process in which the shelves in the warehouse of knowledge are increasingly replenished. New perspectives trigger shifts in the focus of analysis, improve precision and explanation in some areas, but deteriorate analysis in others. Important explanatory factors sometime step into the background until they get rediscovered after the fashion wave has faded.

The main thesis of this contribution is that the analysis of policy processes in recent decades has focused too much on governmental and conventional political actors, on the one hand, and too much on actor-centered bottom-up perspectives. As

V. Schneider (✉)
University of Konstanz, Konstanz, Germany
e-mail: volker.schneider@uni-konstanz.de

H. Lehtimäki et al. (eds.), *Society as an Interaction Space*, Translational Systems Sciences 22, https://doi.org/10.1007/978-981-15-0069-5_3

the microfoundation of social explanations has moved to the fore in the past decades, actor constellations became the core of policy explanations. City Hall policy then was treated in a similar way as national policy-making or even negotiations in global politics. This pushed contextual factors and systemic perspectives into the background.

The following proposal for a renewed perspective on public policy aims to bring social factors back into play, particularly at macrostructural level. This means not only that non-governmental and civil society organizations should be given greater consideration, but even more important are various forms of structural differentiation at the macro level of societies which should be reintegrated into policy explanations.

Such macroscopic perspectives seem to be particularly fruitful in cross-national analysis. In this respect, for example, it is important to identify not only differences in the policy subsystems, but more generally in their embeddedness in the web of political, economic, scientific, and media subsystems of society in order to understand how different societies cope with important challenges. An example of the fruitfulness of such a macroscopic perspective is climate policy, where the social origins of this creeping policy problem also suggest a societal perspective for coping with this challenge. In this policy domain, we can clearly see how varying national political systems and their interaction with science, economy, and media have differential influence on the perception and communication of this policy problem as well as the translation of this awareness into concrete policy formulation and implementation processes (Schneider et al. 2013; Satoh et al. 2018). From a more comprehensive view, this problem of adaptation in the process of social evolution is a central topic of complexity-oriented approaches (Schneider and Bauer 2007).

The plea for a macroscopic perspective in comparative policy analysis will be bolstered in this chapter by a comparison of major policy theories which show the range of how policy explanations can incorporate societal factors into their *explanans*. It will be shown that many theories, frameworks, and approaches shift major societal determinants into the background.

This paper proceeds in five sections. After this introduction, a conceptual part first aims to specify the variants of meaning of the central concepts—public policy and society—in this essay. The third part compares two dozen policy theories in terms of their analytical dimensions and the role that societal aspects play in description and explanation. In the fourth section, a proposal is presented on how macrostructures of "society at large," different forms of societal differentiation, and particularly civil society and other non-state sectors should be reintegrated into public policy analysis. The paper concludes with a short summary.

3.2 Public Policy and Society

Before we enter into the comparison of theories, we have to clarify what we mean by the central concepts exposed in the title of this essay. These are not self-explanatory and often ambiguous. As so often in the social science, there is conceptual confusion, and this is very often due to the fact that the meaning of these concepts is based on their multiple positions in the different "theory nets" (Stegmüller 2013) in which they are embedded.

3.2.1 Society as Part and Whole

Recent overviews in social sciences and philosophy show that there are multiple versions of the society concept (Schwinn 2011). For instance, within *Grand Theories* à la Parsons and Luhmann, the term is theoretically much more presuppositional (Parsons 1966; Luhmann 1977). A sociological systems theory conceives society as a supra-individual entity with emergent characteristics. It includes specialized social spheres or "subsystems" such as economy, culture, and politics at the national and global level. The German language offers the terminus *Gesamtgesellschaft* (society at large) for such a comprehensive view.

Marxists use the term "social formation" for this inclusive view, which encompasses the totality of all social relations and conditions. Both the Marxist and the system perspectives are examples of a holistic view in which society "hovers" above its members.

With regard to Luhmann's inclusive concept of society, it must be noted that it covers all subsystems of the social, from economy, law, politics, media, education, etc. and of course includes social entities such as the state although Luhmann has often stressed that the system perspective makes the concept of the state obsolete. A further specificity of his society concept is that it includes solely communication relations and subsystem-specific codes of communicative interchange and completely ignores that also other relations such as energy exchange exist in all types of societies.

In contrast to this "society at large" concept, we can distinguish *society* as a subsystem of this supra-system. We find this use in German "Staatswissenschaft" (science of the state) of the eighteenth and nineteenth century. Society herein was distinguished from other social spheres such as the economy, the law, and the state. The most prominent perspective of this kind of differentiation had been provided by Hegel, treating society as a specialized sphere which is separated from family on the one hand and the state on the other (Hegel 1820). In Hegel's dialectical conception, bourgeois society was the antithesis to the family, a contradiction in the social world that was resolved by intermediate powers such corporations and the police, and finally the state as superior force of integration. However, Hegel also used the concept of the *political state*, which comes closer to the conventional concept of government to be distinguished from the state as such.

Hegel was influenced by Enlightenment philosophy. Influential were Montesquieu, who distinguished between "l'état politique" and "l'état civile," and British social philosophers like Locke, Smith, Hume, and Ferguson which supported the idea of an autonomously self-regulated sphere to be separated from the state. Ferguson coined the notion of "civil society." Cohen and Arato argue very convincingly that the conceptual separation of state and society was a result of Enlightenment philosophy in which society in a way was mobilized against the absolutist state (Cohen and Arato 1994).

For Marx, for his part influenced by Hegel and the British philosophers, the state lost the superior macro position and became a part of society, i.e., a power instrument of the rulers in a class society to defend their social supremacy. Marx used the concept of society at the highest, inclusive level, but stressed that in capitalist societies economic conditions would dominate all others relationships.

A narrower society concept is used in the sociology of Simmel and Weber. For Simmel, society is not a supra-individual but only an inter-individual entity, the sum of relationships that socialize people. Important in this perspective is his idea of intersecting social circles.

Weber is a special case. He never explicitly defined the concept of society in his main work entitled "Economy and Society" where it remains unclear whether economy is juxtaposed with society or whether economy represents a certain order of society. However, he also speaks of *Vergesellschaftung* (socialization), which he distinguishes from *Vergemeinschaftung* (communitarization) in the sense of Tönnies, who uses the narrowest concept of society.

In Tönnies' writings, society is not just a network of relations but a specific type of relational configuration that is based on contractual agreements. For social relations such as kinship, friendship, and neighborhood that create social proximity, he reserved the concept of community. This connotation of society thus is close to the original meaning of the Latin word societas, which designates contractual agreements for the joint pursuit of common interests.

On the basis of this conceptual analysis, at least six versions of this term can be distinguished. Society can be:

- A super system, including everything social (people and their relations) in a country or the whole planet (world society) (S_1)
- A system with emergent, supra-individual properties that encounters individuals as superior power (S_2)
- A non-governmental subsystem that is separated from the state (S_3)
- A subsystem that is non-governmental but also separated from economy or business (S_4)
- An inter-individual entity, i.e., a network of social relations (S_5)
- A network of contractual relations (S_6)

The main differences are thus that S_1 and S_2 conceive society as the all-inclusive macro level, from whose perspective state and politics represent only subsystems. S_3 and S_4 treat society as a subsystem of "society at large," and S_5 and S_6 understand society only as network of relations. More recent approaches to social theory, which speak of "sectors close to the state" or "societal capacity to act" (Mayntz and Scharpf 1995), for example, or which conceptualize the "penetration of society by state power" as the infrastructural power of the state (Mann 1984), tend to use the terms S_3 and S_4. There are few philosophers and theoreticians who combine S_2 with the concept of the state (Etzioni 1968; Willke 1995; Bunge 1998).

3.2.2 Public Policy and Governance

The term "public policy" has also been around since centuries, but a more theory-inspired sophisticated use only emerged since the 1950s, when policy sciences and policy analysis emerged. Implicitly, this term was understood to designate exclusively government action, although the word policy is more abstract and can be applied to all principled strategies of action at all social levels (individual, organization, state, society). Lasswell, a central initiator of policy analysis, used the term "policy" in this general way (Lasswell and Kaplan 1952). Only later the term was narrowed down to public policy or state policy-making. Thomas Dye defined policy analysis as "finding out, what the governments do, why they do it, and what difference it makes" (Dye 1972). This conceptual restriction to government action was clearly an effect of the Bringing-the-State-Back-In movement, in the course of which the political system was "besieged by the state" (Easton 1981) and finally defeated in such a way that even pure sociologists spoke only of "the organizational state" (Laumann and Knoke 1987). The German political scientist Manfred Schmidt translated this branch of research as "state activity research" (Schmidt 1993).

This state-centric perspective was only broken up by governance research, in which the formulation and implementation of collective decisions was conceived as the production of public and common goods, in which also a broad spectrum of private actors and non-governmental coordinating mechanisms could be involved (Mayntz 2003). Private actors in this function were referred to as "private interest governments" (Streeck and Schmitter 1985).

Particularly Ostrom demonstrated in her "Governance of Commons" that non-state actors can provide important contributions to societal problem-solving (Ostrom 1990). Governance became an extended view of policy processes in which a wide range of actors, organizational forms, and coordinative regimes were included into the analysis and reconstruction of societal problem-solving mechanisms (Mayntz 2003; Schneider 2004; Grande 2012).

But here, too, we must exercise conceptual caution since governance is a pretty ambiguous concept. A narrow version equals governance with public policy, reducing this activity domain to the state sector. A broader concept of public policy conceives state policy-making only as a subset of governance, which includes governmental and non-governmental actors, as well as hierarchies and networks as coordinating mechanism. The most extended concept of governance is provided by industrial economics and includes in addition markets as coordinative mechanisms (Williamson 1979).

The concept of society and the public policy perspective are very different centers of theoretical gravity around which different scientific discourses revolve. However, we can combine both conceptual perspectives. Society can be mapped as a landscape with different areas and levels that influence policy-making and governance processes. From this perspective, society impacts on public policy from three different directions:

- Influences from "society at large," i.e., the macro level of society where specific patterns of functional differentiation and the particular interconnectedness of societal subsystems are shaping policy processes
- Influence by the relational level by which the whole spectrum of networks shows effectiveness
- Influences from the actor level, i.e., non-governmental actors from civil society and private business participate in policy formulation and implementation

Society thus influences policy processes through various pathways. In the next part of this chapter, a meta-theoretical inquiry will examine in which policy theories such influences were taken into account.

3.3 Policy Theories and the Impact of Society on Policy-Making

The theories (in the broadest sense) which have been developed to explain or understand public policy-making can be thought of as a landscape that has been increasingly populated over the last 100 years. As the architectural settlement shows geographical differences, there are also different cognitive constructions in theory formation, ranging from metaphors to paradigms, approaches, and frameworks, to formal theories of policies as research objects.

In this theory landscape, a large number of villages and agglomerations emerged that makes it difficult to maintain a clear overview. The following is an attempt to map this landscape. Many theories and frameworks are listed in reviews and textbooks. Because a systematic account is not yet available, our classification presented here will include only two dozen theories. The theories to be compared are listed in Fig. 3.1, including classical social science theories of the early twentieth century up to most recent perspectives in policy analysis. They are grouped into different types of theory, ranging from grand theories, which have a general and overarching claim to explanation, to middle-range theories, which explain sub-areas of the social, to mini theories, which deal with only a few variables or aspects. Approaches and frameworks tend to represent networks of theories and methods specified to the explanandum "policy process" or "outcome."

From a comparative perspective, we will examine these with respect to a dozen properties, such as levels of analysis, facets of reality, relationships, and societal subsystems. For each feature, we check whether it is taken into account in a particular theory.

Levels. Theories can have a purely individualistic orientation and try to trace policies back to the micro level (mostly based on methodological individualism), and most popular here is rational choice. The counterpart is holism. Holistic theories explain policies by macrostructures, and most prominent here is Marxism in which all societal spheres (politics, law, culture, etc.) are derived from the operating logic of capitalist economy.

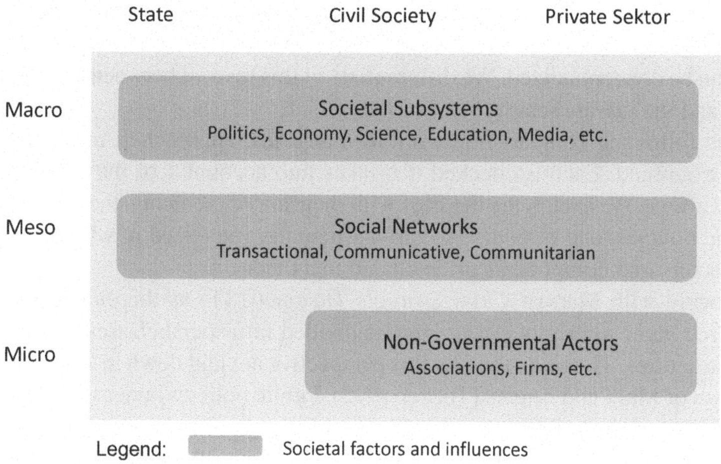

Fig. 3.1 Societal influences on public policy

Between micro and macro, there are further layers that may be distinguished. Looking bottom-up, the next societal layer is the level or organizations. Individuals join such collective constructions as members or employees by creating corporate actors with emergent properties (Coleman 1974; Mayntz 1986). Above this level are social groups or classes, and the highest level of a macro-societal perspective is the level of societal subsystems based on functional (politics, economy, science, etc.) or institutional (State, Civil Society, Private Sector) differentiation.

Facets. The second group of dimensions differentiates between three facets of social reality—the material, institutional, and ideational. The material facet refers to concrete, physical, biological, etc. interests, resources, and interactions. Typical material interests refer to human basic needs. The institutional facet refers to rules and norms that structure problem perception, interests, and actions. This institutional sphere is sometimes difficult to separate from the ideational. For instance, sociological institutionalism is merging both facets.

The ideational facet refers to cognitive representations of reality. It is the sphere of ideas, beliefs, and images. Recent policy theories put emphasis on this facet by analyzing discourses, frames, and narratives in the policy process.

Relations. Links or ties between policy actors are an important aspect of actor constellations in the policy process. Although the spectrum of possible relationships is huge (Borgatti et al. 2009), a rough distinction is made between three main types of relationships that are relevant for policy processes. Firstly, these are transactional relationships involving a utilitarian orientation in the exchange of resources (Williamson 1975). Secondly, relations may relate to communication and exchange of information (Leifeld and Schneider 2012). Thirdly, communitarian relationships can be involved, such as friendship or face-to-face meetings that generate social proximity and trust (Odella 2011).

Spheres. In contrast to the vertical differentiation of society into levels, a horizontal differentiation into domains with different rights of action and institutional status can be conceptualized. We differentiate in this respect between the state, civil, society and the private sector.

In the following comparison, two dozen theories, approaches, and frameworks will be examined. Each is checked if it takes into account 1 of the 12 dimensions outlined above. We sketch the theories with their major elements, their explanations of public policies, and of course we are particularly interested in whether and how social factors and components are included in a theory.

We begin with Marxist *Class Struggle Theory* (CST) as the oldest framework considered here, where society at large is divided into social classes based on economic structures. The basic traits of this perspective are laid down in *The Communist Manifesto* of Marx and Engels (Tucker 1972). Public policies here express the material interests of the ruling class or alliance of classes. In this perspective society comes in at the macro level as well as the actor level, where large societal aggregates (classes) but also individual capitalists shape politics and policy-making. Civil society came into the play only by neo-Marxists such as Gramsci.

Pluralist group theory (PGT) broadened this understanding of policy-making as power struggle to a group conflict that is not only restricted to material interest but also includes ideational groups (Bentley 1967). This pluralist perspective conceives policies as a resulting vector in a parallelogram of forces, and society enters the picture at the macro level by background factors generating these group structures.

It was only with *System Theories* (ST) that concepts became popular in which societies had to deal with challenges and problems of adaptation to preserve societal orders (Parsons 1966; Luhmann 1969). Policy sciences emerged at that time, when systemic thinking flourished. Its basic idea was that societal problems could be better solved if scientific expertise would be pooled across disciplines. Some of these approaches applied cybernetic models to politics and conceived governing as a process of self-regulation in which the political system detects undesirable states and initiates corrective action by the formulation of public policies (Almond 1956; Easton 1957).

Such theories have a holistic and functionalist orientation. In the 1980s, the derivation of policies as functionally necessary problem-solving was increasingly criticized (Elster 1982). The critics from the individualistic camp in contrast emphasized the micro level as the appropriate level of analysis, and collective action in policy processes was explained by the rational choice of actors in the pursuit of their material and power interests.

Individualist exchange theories first developed in sociology and subsequently diffused into political science, particularly by James Coleman's model of political exchange (Coleman 1990). This way *Exchange Theory* (ET) entered the realm of policy studies, often using the sophisticated mathematical modelling of exchange and bargaining relations. In these models, social embedding fades completely into the background (Knoke et al. 1996).

The new grand theory, which largely superseded systems theory, was *Rational Choice Theory* (RCT) in which policy preferences and outcomes are explained by rational interaction of individuals or organizations (Shepsle and Bonchek 1997). While the analysis usually includes the micro level and only in rare instance the meso level, rational choice theory ignores aspects of social embedding.

Neo-corporatism (NC) is as a combination of group theory and exchange theory at the macro level of a political system. Policies in this perspective are bargained compromises between the government and large societal groups, particularly capital and labor (Schmitter and Lehmbruch 1979). Since the concrete structure of organized interests and also the tendency of governments to negotiate often have historical causes, societal influences of policy processes play an important role in this theoretical perspective. The distinction between corporatist and pluralist societies has therefore established itself not only in policy research but also in comparative politics (Lijphart 1999).

Some mini-theories explore only the influence of one or only a few variables on public policy. Each of these theories focuses on a singular type of actor. *Power Resources Theory* (PRT) explains public policies, e.g., the expansion of the welfare state, largely by the organizational power of trade unions (Korpi 1985). Governing Party Theory (PGT) explains public policy mainly by party politics and the impact of governing parties or party coalitions. It hypothesizes, for example, that it makes a difference in government spending or privatization whether left-wing or right-wing parties rule (Schmidt 1996). From a societal perspective, party government theory is state-centric and narrows the spectrum of actors to conventional politics, while power resource theory, like neo-corporatism theory, at least includes the trade unions as "societal superpowers" in their explanations.

The *Networked Governance Approach* (NGA) sees networks as a distinct form of governance (Powell 1987). It emphasizes on the one hand the involvement of a pluralistic spectrum of actors in the formulation and implementation of policies and combines this with theoretical concepts of exchange and negotiation in order to describe a polycentric and a network-shaped constellation of actors in the production of public policies (Kenis and Schneider 1991; Mayntz 1993). Societal aspects come into play in this perspective by the wide-ranging actor structure (e.g., also private and civil society are included) but also by the analysis of network structures.

Historical-Institutionalist (HI) approaches strongly emphasize the impact of evolutionary, historically grown formal and informal institutional arrangements on policy-making (Thelen 1999). Examples are the structuring of policy subsystems by long-term social processes. For instance, to use a recent example, the German energy system transformation cannot be explained without reference to the traditional strength of the German environmental movement (Rinscheid et al. 2019). This approach is open to the influence of societal factors on public policy, whether through actors, institutions, or ideas.

A specialized rational choice perspective close to the party government and power resources approaches is Tsebelis' *Veto Player Theory* (VPT), which also relies on the institutionalist perspective (Tsebelis 2002). Policy influence here is derived from veto positions that policy actors acquire via institutional structures and party system configurations. This may be, for instance, the power of a second parliamentary chamber to veto a law or the power to stop action by each of the coalition partners in a party government. Political systems differ by their number of veto players, and mathematical analysis in rational decision-making then claims that the greater the number of veto players is, the more difficult it is to generate policy change. A serious shortcoming of this theory in our perspective is that societal factors only play a marginal role.

There are further neo-institutionalist approaches that combine actor-centered with institutional analysis and assume that actors are constrained but also enabled by institutional systems specifying sets of rules that are relevant in policy processes.

The *Institutional Analysis and Development* (IAD) framework of Ostrom (Ostrom 2011) emphasizes that policy-making systems not only contain rules that specify actor's attributes and interaction outcomes, but also position in policy arenas ("access rules") and relations structuring information exchange ("Information rules") (Ostrom 1986).

The *Actor-Centered Institutionalism* (ACI) (Mayntz and Scharpf 1995; Scharpf 1997) conceptualizes policy systems by multiple actors with different interests, specific action orientations, and typical conflict constellations. Diverse institutional arrangements mediate conflicts and facilitate or hamper certain policy outcomes (e.g., structural reforms of redistribution). Since institutions facilitate coordination, various forms of coordination imply different transaction costs. Scharpf (1997) distinguishes between positive and negative coordinations. In the first mode, all actors bargain with all other actors on each policy option, while in the second, all policy options are excluded to which at least one actor objects. This reduces coordination and transaction costs. Society comes in here only by actor constellations and institutions that include societal actors.

A new conceptual development in a similar direction is the *Ecology of Games* (EoG) approach (Lubell 2013). Its central idea underscores nestedness and overlap of policy games. Actors are involved in multiple and cross-cutting conflictual relations, and policies are explained by decisions that maximize the different player's combined outcomes. An instructive example of such a game network is Scharpf's analysis of economic policy of the 1970–1980s where games between party governments and trade unions had been linked with voting games (Scharpf 1997). Another example is the concatenation of an innovation game with a regulatory game, by which coordination problems and technological frictions in technology policies can be explained (Dutton et al. 2012).

Recently, this perspective has been linked to the *Collaborative Governance* (CG) approach (Emerson et al. 2012). Specific arrangements and relations are emphasized which facilitate and support cooperation, information sharing, and joint problem-solving. The CG thus adds a clear relational facet to the IAD and ACI perspectives by combining the analysis of conflict constellations with institutional affiliations and collaborative contacts. Here too, it depends on how inclusive actor constellations are conceptualized in order to include societal aspects into the policy process.

A special perspective is taken by *Ecological System Theories* (EST) which seems to be a new Grand Theory that integrates different versions of evolutionary approaches and complexity theory. This stream of thought was prominent in multiple variants during the last decades (human ecology, population ecology, and organizational ecology). Eco-approaches apply biological concepts of the eco-sphere to social areas, and some of these concepts are also applied to policy-making. This perspective examines habitats, resources, and multiplex relations between species (symbiosis, mutualism, but also predatory relations, etc.) to determine equilibria and adaptation capabilities of these systems. Particularly in the field of innovation policy, this perspective is quite popular, and a number studies cover "innovation ecosystems" (Ferasso et al. 2018). In such systems, different "organizational species" interact in complex ways: universities, research organizations, business firms, finance capitalists, trade associations, and governmental policy-makers. This perspective is not only open to all areas of society but is also sensitive to a variety of organizational forms ("species") and the multiplexity of relations that are involved in policy-making (Shaw and Allen 2018).

The relational dimension plays an essential role in *Social Capital Theory* (SCT) (Putnam 1995). Recently, this perspective has acquired the status of a new Grand Theory in the social sciences. In policy analysis too, this theory gained currency, particularly in network studies. It emphasizes interpersonal relations under the assumption that a particular class of relationships generates long-term trust and reciprocity. A strong influence on this perspective had the assertion that multiple membership relations in associations are of great importance for the emergence of social trust. This idea is close to Simmel's idea of intersecting social circles, and it brings Tocqueville's idea back to memory that membership in associations is an effective remedy against individualism, which ultimately would destroy social cohesion.

Another group of policy approaches highlights the role of ideas in policy processes. One of these is the *Policy Paradigm Framework* (PPF) operating at the macro level of politics. In applying a Kuhnian perspective to the world of policy-making, policy conflicts are largely understood as struggles among "policy paradigms," such as between Keynesianism and Monetarism in economic policy-making (Hall 1993). Policy preferences and outputs are explained by the dominance of a given policy paradigm or by paradigm change. Society comes in at the macro level at which such world views are shaped.

An approach applying a similar principle at the level of belief systems is the *Advocacy Coalition Framework* (ACF) (Sabatier 1988). Its central premise is that policy actors form advocacy coalitions based on competing beliefs. Beliefs are embedded in systems with hierarchical structures. There is a deep core of basic convictions about normative and ontological aspects of the world, and at the periphery are secondary beliefs on instrumental and informational aspects that adapt to changing circumstances most easily. ACF assumes that policy brokers mediate the conflicts between coalitions and belief change occurs by means of external shocks, communication, and learning. Since communication plays an important role in maintaining coalitions, there is a range of relations to be studied in this perspective.

Societal factors only play a role if actor coalitions include also societal actors and extensive networks.

The *Multiple Streams Framework* (MSF), too, has an ideational orientation and is mainly interested in the first phases of the policy cycle (Zahariadis 2007). It views policy-making not as a rational decision process but as a contingent confluence of three autonomous processes: (1) a process in which problems are defined; (2) a process in which ideas for problem solutions emerge and diffuse; and (3) processes at the macro level of politics (elections, legislative turnover, etc.) that support or suppress policy issues. The coupling of these streams opens policy windows in which political entrepreneurs can push their issues on the policy agenda. Societal factors flow in here via the level of macro-politics and private interest groups.

A closely related perspective is *Punctuated Equilibrium Theory* (PET) which combines group interaction and macro dynamics in political systems (Baumgartner and Jones 1993). Its key idea is that policies usually evolve incrementally and only occasionally depart from a steady path by big aberrations. Such policy punctuations depend on the capacities of groups for agenda setting. PET distinguishes between subsystem politics and macro-politics, and issues may shift from a rather technical matter to a macro-political issue when there is a switch in policy images. Society comes in by the same trajectories as in the MSF.

In the last few years, various currents of ideational policy research have emerged, which not only analyzes discourse formations but also emphasizes power structures. Discourse involves power in the sense that policy problems are defined in a way that certain social groups benefit by a given definition. One approach of this view is the *Narrative Policy Framework* (NPF) which emphasizes the role of narratives in the definition of situations (Shanahan et al. 2011). Social factors play a role here insofar as the general predominance of certain narratives in society has an influence on the perception of policy problems.

Another group of theories emphasizes the economic sphere of society at large. These are the *Varieties of Capitalism* (VoC) theory (Hall and Soskice 2001) and *Post-Democracy Theory* (PDT) (Crouch 2004). In contrast to the ideational approaches just discussed, these two perspectives focus strongly on the material sphere of politics, and both bring into play a modernized version of Marxism in which macroanalysis and economic structures are placed at the center of the analysis.

VoC has a clear macro-orientation in explaining policies but includes society only partially. Just as Marxism holistically understands current society as a social formation shaped by the capitalist economy, this approach emphasizes the dominance of economic interests and constraints in political processes. Its innovative point is that different versions of capitalisms exist. Capitalist economies (based on specific institutional settings) vary in their economic and social policy performance due to different forms of coordination (market versus state plus associations, to put it simply). In order to explain policies, this approach emphasizes the role of large companies and associational structures in the business sector.

PDT is currently quite popular and can also be applied to policy analysis (Schneider 2015). The prefix "post" pretends a trend reversal of democracy since the 1980s when globalization transformed large corporations into the main business actors and marginalized business associations and trade unions. Governments would get dependent on the expertise from large corporations, and policy formulation would move to small circles including central government and the business elite. Elections and parliamentary debates would decline to pure theatrical spectacles, boosted by media conglomerates with little effect on policy formulation. PDT is clearly macro oriented by emphasizing large material structures but also aspects of ideational domination. Society as subsystem comes in particularly through private business and institutional structures of the economic system, but also by links to science and education systems.

A comparison of the different theoretical profiles in Table 3.1 shows that, with a single exception, all the theories have different property characteristics with respect to the 12 dimensions. This becomes evident when we translate the property profiles into binary vectors to perform multidimensional scaling and cluster analysis (Chatfield and Collins 1980).

Table 3.1 Theories and approaches in public policy analysis

		Levels			Facets			Relations			Spheres		
THEORIES & APPROACHES	Abbreviations	Macro	Meso	Micro	Material	Ideational	Institutional	Transactional	Communicative	Communitary	State	Civil Society	Private Sector
Grand Theories													
Class Theory	CST	■	□	□	■	□	□	□	□	□	■	■	■
Eco-Systems Theory	EST	■	■	□	■	□	■	■	■	■	■	■	■
Rational Choice Theory	RCT	□	■	■	■	□	■	□	□	□	■	■	■
Social Capital Theory	SCT	□	■	■	□	□	■	■	□	■	■	■	□
Systems Theory	ST	■	□	□	■	■	■	■	■	□	■	■	■
Middle Range Theories													
Exchange Theory	ET	□	■	■	■	□	□	■	□	□	■	■	■
Party Government Theory	GPT	□	■	□	■	□	■	□	□	□	■	□	□
Historical Institutionalism	HI	■	■	□	■	■	■	□	□	□	■	■	□
Neocorporatism Theory	NC	□	■	□	■	□	■	■	□	□	■	■	□
Networked Governance Theory	NGT	□	■	□	■	□	■	■	■	■	■	■	■
Post-democracy Theory	PDT	■	■	□	■	■	□	□	□	□	■	□	■
Punctuated Equilibrium Theory	PET	□	■	□	□	■	■	□	□	□	■	□	□
Pluralist Group Theory	PGT	■	□	□	■	■	■	□	□	□	■	■	□
Power Ressources Theory	PRT	□	■	□	■	□	■	□	□	□	■	■	□
Varieties of Capitalism Theory	VoC	■	■	□	■	□	■	■	□	□	■	□	■
Veto Player Theory	VPT	□	■	□	■	□	■	□	□	□	■	□	□
Frameworks and approaches													
Advocacy Coalition Framework	ACF	□	■	■	□	■	□	■	■	□	■	■	□
Actor-Centered Institutionalism	ACI	□	■	□	■	■	■	□	□	□	■	■	□
Collaborative Governance	CG	□	■	□	■	□	■	■	■	■	■	■	□
Ecologies of Games Theory	EoG	□	■	□	■	□	□	■	□	□	■	■	■
Institutional Analysis and Development	IAD	□	■	■	■	□	■	□	□	□	□	■	□
Multiple Streams Approach	MSA	□	■	■	■	■	□	□	□	□	■	■	■
Narrative Policy Framework	NPF	□	■	■	□	■	□	■	■	□	■	■	■
Policy-Paradigm Framework	PPT	■	■	□	□	■	□	□	□	□	■	□	□

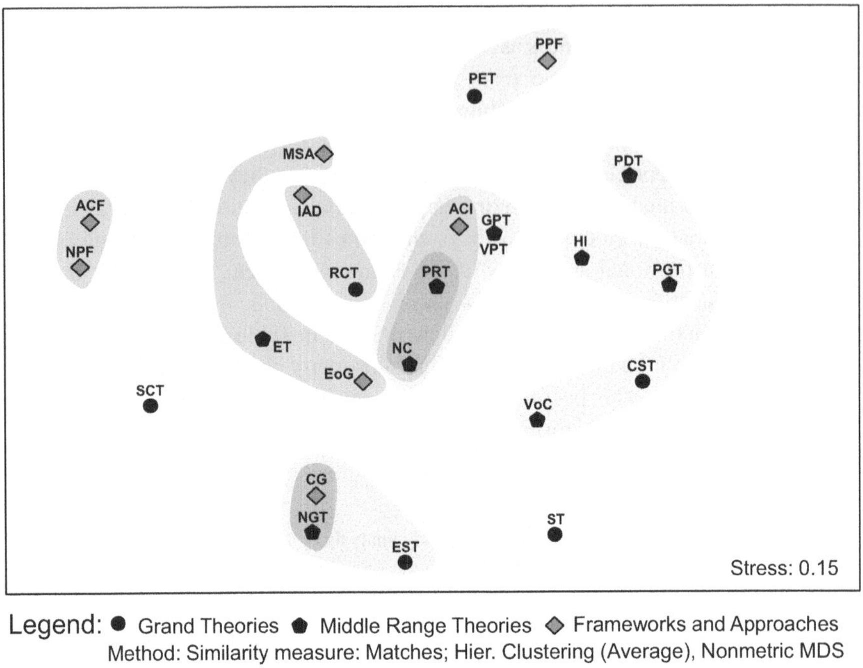

Fig. 3.2 Clusters of theories and approaches

The integrated results of this analysis are shown in Fig. 3.2 where the 24 theories are grouped into 4 clusters:

- The largest cluster is located at the top of the diagram and consists of actor-centered and institutionalist theories.
- The second largest cluster in the lower half includes three ideational theories, two relational theories, and one macroscopic theory.
- The cluster to the left comprises includes ecological, systemic, and relational theories.
- The cluster at the right border includes two theories that are actor-centered but also include some macroelements in the analysis.

In spatial terms, the EoG approach and the class structure theory are close to the theories involving varieties of a systemic perspective.

3.4 Actors, Networks, and Systems in Public Policy

Conceptual analysis and theory mapping have shown that policy-making is not just a matter of state activities and politics, but also societal factors and relationships come in at several levels and venues. Firstly, from the broader spectrum of actors, in which not only governmental actors but also non-governmental actors from civil society and private business are involved in policy-making. Secondly, societal influences occur via social relationships that facilitate exchange of resources, discourses on policy topics, and social bonds that generate social capital. Thirdly, individual actors not only join in organizations and social movements, but also assume specific social positions in the increasingly complex societal division of labor. Policy actors thus have structural positions in the policy process that are dependent on patterns of functional, institutional, relational, and organizational differentiation. In order to make use and integrate these different conceptual perspectives, we draw on five different literatures: Social Network Analysis, Governance Theory, Systems Theories (of societal differentiation), Eco-System Theories, and Organizational Ecologies.

3.4.1 Institutional Differentiation Between Societal Sectors

Most institutionalist theories and approaches agree with the assertion that institutions are social rules that enable certain actions and restrict others. They structure action situations and stabilize mutual expectations. This leads to distinct categories of actors that are equipped with varying opportunities and constraints. We conceptualize these social processes as mechanisms of *institutional differentiation* that ultimately distribute action resources and control positions among the actors. In our context they regulate access to policy arenas and allocate decision-making power. Some of the theories outlined above put large emphasis on this role of institutions. In particular Ostrom has tried to systematize the various rules by distinguishing between access rules, position rules, area rules, authority rules, etc. (Ostrom 1986).

On an abstract level, each rule configuration—as governance structure—represents a complex distribution of control. In this respect, a broad spectrum of institutional mechanisms and societal status is conceivable. Firstly, between hierarchy, networks, and the atomistic market as an extreme point of decentralized control and, secondly, between the public and the private sector.

The most important dimension of differentiation is the distinction between "the private" and "the public." Since these status positions are in most cases determined by sets of rules, an institutional status is always based on a "bundle of rights" which allows many combinations. This leads to the observation that a private or a public status is not a binary institutional state such as black and white, but there are many shades between the two poles. If one looks just at public administration, one can find a spectrum of diverse organizational forms ranging from pure state-controlled organizations via independent agencies to public corporations that are only indirectly under public control (Gill 2002).

The spectrum of differentiation between the public and the private sector organizations also includes an intermediate area, which some designate as the "third sector," others as civil society or a non-governmental sphere. These terms are not very sharp, and sometimes they denote very different things and are even inconsistent.

For instance, the term "non-governmental organizations" usually does not contain all organizations with a non-governmental status and excludes, for instance, business firms. The term "civil society" no longer refers to the entire non-governmental part of society, as British moral philosophy used it, but excludes business with its companies and associations.

The business world, too, is no longer involved in policy processes only by business associations, but there is a variety of organizational forms (Streeck et al. 2006; Grote et al. 2008). The public-private axis of institutional differentiation thus covers multiple organizational forms, a situation that has similarities with biodiversity in ecosystems. In this respect, it makes sense to make use of organizational ecology approaches to describe these differentiation processes at organizational level. This aspect will be discussed in more detail below.

3.4.2 Relational Differentiation in Multiplex Networks

Another venue for social influences in political processes is personnel and organizational networks. As described in the previous part, from a functional point of view, we can differentiate between three network forms:

- *Transactional networks* in which the focus is on the utilitarian exchange of resources on a quid pro quo basis. These may include not only material items such as money and personnel, but also technical information and specialized expertise.
- *Communicative networks* in which symbolic interaction, discourse, argumentation, and persuasion with regard to policy goals and instruments are at stake.
- *Communitarian networks* in which social bonds based on friendship, neighborhood, and "intersecting social circles" become effective in the creation of mutual trust and social cohesion.

Networks based on these types of relations involve all the categories of actors in the institutionally differentiated spectrum described above. Among the theories discussed, the networked governance approach particularly emphasizes this relational level in the production of public policies. However, networks should not only be reduced to this governance perspective (Pappi 1993). For some time now, ideational and institutional frameworks such as the ACF and the HI also include communicative networks in their analysis and examine whether, for example, belief changes are induced by information exchange and collective learning (Weible 2005; Rinscheid et al. 2019).

From a macro perspective, it is interesting to see which network roles the various actors play in a total network (Ferligoj et al. 2011). The respective roles are of course dependent on the network type. For instance, in a communication network roles can be sender and receiver, leader, follower, exchanger, gatekeeper, multiplier, etc. (Friemel 2010). Roles in the resource networks can be producer, user, exchanger, distributer, etc. By social network analysis, relational structures can be examined both at the individual and group level as well as at the macro level of total networks. In this way, specific macrostructural positions can be conceived as roles in a total network.

3.4.3 Functional Differentiation and Societal Subsystems

A further path of societal influence in public policy-making is functional differentiation at the macro level of societies and the effects of these structures on policy actor constellations. Functional differentiation impacts on the partition of actor constellations into various subsystems. Laumann and Pappi applied such concepts in the late 1970s and therefore represent a rare combination of systemic and relational analysis (Laumann and Pappi 1976).

The affiliation of actors to societal subsystems implies specific action orientations. Each subsystem is focused on specific criteria of relevance that are important within specialized social spheres. In politics, the name of the game is "how to gain and retain power," in business "how to make money," in science "how to find truth," in the media sector all is about "attention," and so on. Luhmann's merit was to systematize this basic idea of communicative differentiation. However, the baseline of this logic of differentiation we can find in many theories. In some respects, we can trace this idea back to the ancient Greeks: In *Politeia* and in *Politikos*, Plato has emphasized the different action orientations of statesmen, helmsmen, doctors, and shepherds.

The affiliation of policy actors to specific societal subsystems thus implies that macrostructures influence their basic orientations, e.g., scientists have different objectives than politicians or businessmen. Systems theories à la Parsons and Luhmann but also actor-centered perspectives to functional differentiation share this idea of subsystemic specific modes of orientation (Luhmann 1977; Mayntz et al. 1988; Schimank 2015).

In the light of diversity and complexity of modern societies, Luhmann's macro perspective appears more attractive than that of Parsons because it expands the rather parsimonious fourfold AGIL scheme to an almost unlimited array of societal subsystems. Not only politics, economy, and culture differentiate into partially autonomous spheres, but also science, education, the media sector, and many more societal domains emerge in the great division of societal labor. A serious shortcoming of Luhmann's perspective, however, is its mono-relational focus. Society is exclusively based on communication and domain-specific codes. Communication may be an important facet of society, but there are additional levels and building parts of the complex social fabric that makes up our modern world. In addition to communication, there are multiple relations involved which connect individuals and organizations on many levels. Of particular importance is the exchange of resources, a kind of counterpart to energy exchange in ecosystems.

More recent system-theoretical approaches try to overcome the holistic and mono-relational deficits of the old theories à la Parsons and Luhmann. They address both the multi-layeredness and the multiplexity of social structures in their analysis. For some time now, these have been discussed as the third wave of systems theory (Schneider and Bauer 2007; Schneider 2012; Waldherr 2017).

The reduction of societal relations to communication leads to a kind of "pigeon hole thinking" with respect to systemic differentiation, in which each subsystem is completely sealed off and self-referential like Leibniz's windowless monads. However, inter-systemic links and overlaps between social subsystems, for example, between science and politics, or between the science and education are so obvious and omnipresent that it is surprising that Luhmann did not capture these outstanding features. Societal subsystems are intertwined, nested, and embedded in complex ways.

The key features of modern societies are critical infrastructures and "large technical systems" like energy systems, transport and telecommunication systems (Mayntz and Hughes 1988). These systems are transversal to functional subsystems and often interpenetrate these subsystems. A major feature of modern societies is precisely that different societal components are functionally so densely coupled that a failure in one part has fatal effects on many other parts. The idea of self-referential closure may be plausible for symbolic systems, but for society at large it is unrealistic. More convincing is Bunge's systemic perspective of societal subsystems that are interconnected and embedded in other systems via "exo-structures" (Bunge 1996).

3.4.4 Organizational Differentiation and Policy Ecologies

A more refined form of institutional differentiation is treated here as organizational variation. This refers to specific organizational forms and makes use of ecological approaches to understand how "organizational species" adapt to specific habitats. Among the theories discussed above, it is the EOG and the Ecological Systems Theories in particular that are closest to such a perspective.

The higher granularity of this differentiation can be demonstrated using the example of the economic and the scientific subsystems. The organizational ecology of the business world related to politics has become much more complex, and the spectrum of organizational forms is nowadays much more diversified. It ranges from direct lobbying by individual companies to manager round tables, think tanks, forums, and even business movements.

A number of these organizations have the so-called boundary spanning functions by working at the intersections of systems, e.g., by mediating between politics and business or science and politics. Such cross-system organizations include various forms of organized business interests that mediate between business and politics. There are also specialized organizations at the interface between business, science, and politics, such as think tanks financed by private industry who also perform important lobbying functions. Even political parties can be seen as particular organizational species that perform complex mediation functions between civil society and the state (Mair 1994).

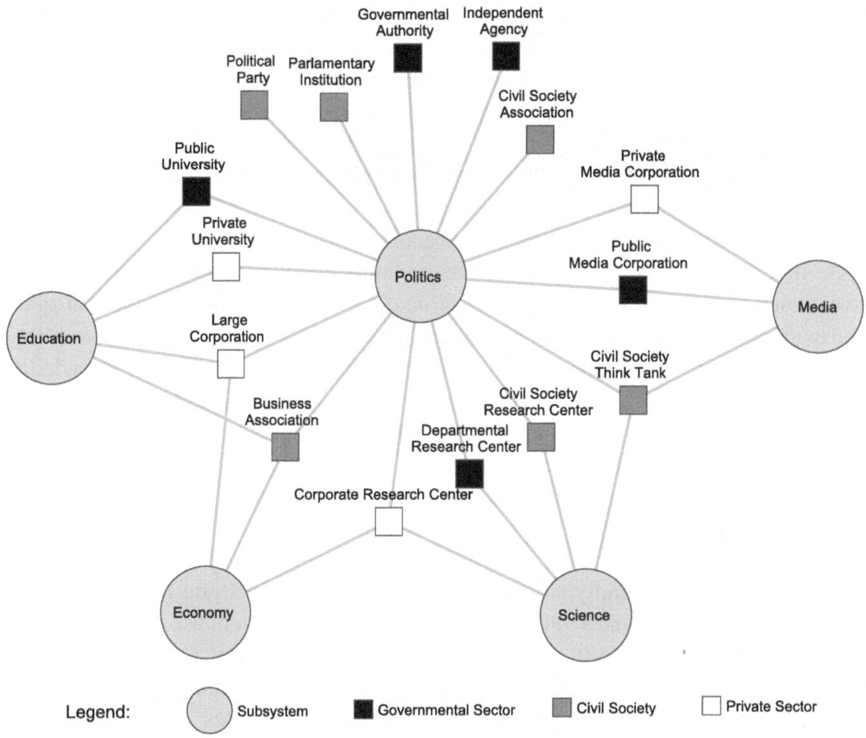

Fig. 3.3 Societal subsystems and organizational forms

At the systems level, institutional and ecological perspectives should be integrated in a fruitful way. In this perspective, not only specialization patterns between social systems are important for the analysis, but also the differentiation into specialized organizational species. If one tries to model adjacent subsystems in a geometric way, then one quickly reaches an upper limit with more than three subsystems. Figure 3.3 therefore attempts to represent organizational forms associated with multiple subsystems by means of affiliation relations. The organizational forms indicate their institutional status by different scales of gray.

Organizations that belong to two or more subsystems have boundary spanning functions and must mediate the different systemic orientations with each other. A public think tank in the field of civil society, for example, has to mediate between the different logics of politics, science, and not least the media system, which is becoming increasingly important also in policy processes (Waldherr 2017).

Macro perspectives stressing structural differentiation between the economy, politics, and science should be combined with the aforementioned ecological approaches. In each subsystem, specific organizations develop that are particularly adapted for specific tasks. Within the economic system, the corporate organization of large firms, the specific role of business associations, and the variety of finance institutions are important aspects of the social organization of this subsystem. In this respect, the institutional differentiation perspective within the VoC approach can be combined with an ecosystem perspective. Different organizational fields occupy different habitats with specific resources, conditions of survival, and interest positions. For instance, in the current research on climate policy, it is important to distinguish between the traditional and the green economy. Both have different material interests and not simply different preferences due to different belief systems.

Another instructive example is the science system, which differs strongly among countries: by the variety of specialized organizations and by the networks in which these organizations are embedded. If we are not only interested in beliefs or narratives that are dominating given organizational contexts, but also assume that good and evidence-based knowledge can significantly improve collective problem-solving, it is of great importance how the production process of policy-relevant knowledge is working in a country, and how this knowledge is distributed and is funneled into relevant policy venues. For instance, if we take independent public organizations in the German science system such as Max Planck and Fraunhofer Institutes or public universities, we assume a more reliable production of facts-based knowledge on climate change than knowledge produced by a think tank that is financed by the oil industry.

In this respect, the analyses made at the Max Planck Institute for the Study of Societies in the 1980s and 1990s of the German science system are very instructive (Hohn and Schimank 1990). In Germany, besides research at almost exclusively public universities, there is a very important field of non-university public research, which is carried out by Max Planck and Fraunhofer Institutes. In addition, as in other countries, much of the research takes place in the private sector (Grande and Häusler 1994). A further special organizational form in the science system is departmental research (Barlösius 2010). Overall, the organizations of the German science system form a specific organizational ecology that has specific effects in various science-related policy fields.

From a systemic and complexity-theoretical perspective, it is important to identify both the internal structural differentiation (endo-structures) of a system and its interconnectedness with the other subsystems such as politics and the economy (exo-structures). Especially in international comparative policy research, such structural comparisons promise to be particularly fruitful. As part of a larger international research network (Broadbent 2016), we are currently investigating how political, economic and scientific subsystems interact in Germany and Japan (Satoh et al. 2018). Our analysis shows that climate policy-making is embedded quite differently into the national systems of policy knowledge production and distribution. The reliance on evidence-based knowledge in German policy-making seems to be more intense and also more pluralistic than in Japan. Germany differs from Japan particularly by the fact that its organizational ecology is more diversified and civil society organizations are more strongly involved in the production and exchange of policy-relevant knowledge. We assume that this difference explains to a large part the differential performance of the two countries in this policy domain.

3.5 Conclusion

This chapter began with the observation that in recent decades the analysis of public policies has focused too much on the micro and meso levels and too narrow on governmental and conventional actor constellations. This narrowing of the analytical perspective gets particularly clear, when we compare the current situation with that of 50 years ago. At that time, a systemic view based on an inclusive concept of society included not only non-governmental actors, but also other societal subsystems were also regarded as important context factors for the processing of societal by means of public policy.

Since the 1980s, policy analysis has become increasingly state-centered in its main orientation, especially in light of the "bringing-the-state-back-in" movement. Only governance broadened the analytical perspective again by including non-state actors and non-hierarchical coordination mechanisms in the analysis of policy processes.

However, this enhancement is not enough. This chapter argues for a systematic and comprehensive inclusion of societal factors in the analysis of public policies whereby particularly the influences from the macro level play an important role. From a conceptual point of view, therefore, it was first clarified which ideas about society and governance can be combined in a public policy perspective. In a comparison of two dozen theories, an immense opportunity space of theories and approaches was outlined, as to how societal aspects can influence policy-making. Based on the conceptual and metatheoretical analysis, a new perspective was presented to combine several approaches. In this respect, it is particularly important to embed the analysis of actor constellations into structures of societal differentiation on the macro level. In addition, also actor positions with regard to specific network roles should be taken into account. Institutional differentiation structures between the state and the private sector should be linked on the one hand with structures of functional differentiation and on the other hand with structures of relational differentiation in order to be able to analytically grasp the complex social embedding and entanglement of social subsystems in modern policy processes. Ultimately, it is argued that approaches and analytical elements of complexity theory should be made fruitful for the analysis of public policies.

References

Almond, G. A. (1956). Comparative political systems. *Journal of Politics, 18*, 391–409. https://doi.org/10.2307/2127255.

Barlösius, E. (2010). Ressortforschung. In D. Simon, A. Knie, & S. Hornbostel (Eds.), *Handbuch Wissenschaftspolitik* (pp. 377–389). Wiesbaden: VS Verlag für Sozialwissenschaften.

Baumgartner, F. R., & Jones, B. D. (1993). *Agendas and instability in American politics*. Chicago: University of Chicago Press.

Bentley, A. F. (1967). *The process of government: A study of social pressure*. Cambridge: Harvard University Press.
Borgatti, S. P., Mehra, A., Brass, D. J., & Labianca, G. (2009). Network analysis in the social sciences. *Science, 323*, 892–895.
Broadbent, J. (2016). Comparative climate change policy networks. In J. N. Victor, A. H. Montgomery, & M. Lubell (Eds.), *The Oxford handbook of political networks*. Oxford: Oxford University Press.
Bunge, M. (1996). *Finding philosophy in social science*. New Haven: Yale University Press.
Bunge, M. (1998). *Social science under debate: A philosophical perspective*. Toronto: University of Toronto Press.
Chatfield, C., & Collins, A. J. (1980). *Introduction to multivariate analysis*. London: Springer—Science + Business Media.
Cohen, J. L., & Arato, A. (1994). *Civil society and political theory*. Cambridge: MIT Press.
Coleman, J. S. (1974). *Power and structure of society*. New York: Norton.
Coleman, J. S. (1990). *Foundations of social theory*. Cambridge: Harvard University Press.
Crouch, C. (2004). *Post-democracy*. Cambridge: Polity.
Dutton, W. H., Schneider, V., & Vedel, T. (2012). Ecologies of games shaping large technical systems: Cases from telecommunications to the Internet. In J. M. Bauer, A. Lang, & V. Schneider (Eds.), *Innovation policy and governance in high-tech industries* (pp. 49–75). Berlin: Springer.
Dye, T. R. (1972). *Understanding public policy*. Englewood Cliffs: Prentice-Hall.
Easton, D. (1957). An approach to the analysis of political systems. *World Politics, 9*, 383–400. https://doi.org/10.2307/2008920.
Easton, D. (1981). The political system besieged by the state. *Political Theory, 9*, 303–325. https://doi.org/10.1177/009059178100900303.
Elster, J. (1982). Marxism, functionalism, and game theory. The case for methodological individualism. *Theory and Society, 11*, 453–482.
Emerson, K., Nabatchi, T., & Balogh, S. (2012). An integrative framework for collaborative governance. *Journal of Public Administration Research and Theory, 22*, 1–29. https://doi.org/10.1093/jopart/mur011.
Etzioni, A. (1968). *The active society: A theory of societal and political processes*. New York: Free Press.
Ferasso, M., Wunsch Takahashi, A. R., & Prado Gimenez, F. A. (2018). Innovation ecosystems: A meta-synthesis. *International Journal of Innovation Science, 10*, 495–518. https://doi.org/10.1108/IJIS-07-2017-0059.
Ferligoj, A., Doreian, P., & Batagelj, V. (2011). Positions and roles. In *The SAGE handbook of social network analysis* (pp. 434–446). London: Sage.
Friemel, T. N. (2010). Netzwerkanalytische Methoden zur Identifizierung von Kommunikationsrollen. In C. Stegbauer (Ed.), *Netzwerkanalyse und Netzwerktheorie* (pp. 179–190). Wiesbaden: VS Verlag für Sozialwissenschaften.
Gill, D. (2002). Signposting the zoo. *OECD Journal on Budgeting, 2*, 27–79. https://doi.org/10.1787/budget-v2-art3-en.
Grande, E. (2012). Governance-Forschung in der Governance-Falle?–Eine kritische Bestandsaufnahme. *Politische Vierteljahresschrift, 53*, 565–592.
Grande, E., & Häusler, J. (1994). *Industrieforschung und Forschungspolitik: staatliche Steuerungspotentiale in der Informationstechnik*. Frankfurt/Main: Campus.
Grote, J. R., Lang, A., & Schneider, V. (2008). *Organized business interests in changing environments: The complexity of adaptation*. New York: Palgrave Macmillan.
Hall, P. A. (1993). Policy paradigms, social learning, and the state: The case of economic policymaking in Britain. *Comparative Politics, 25*, 275–296.
Hall, P. A., & Soskice, D. (2001). *Varieties of capitalism: The institutional foundations of comparative advantage*. Oxford: OUP.
Hegel, G. W. F. (1820/2004). *Grundlinien der Philosophie des Rechts*. Frankfurt/Main: Suhrkamp.

Hohn, H.-W., & Schimank, U. (1990). *Konflikte und Gleichgewichte im Forschungssystem: Akteurkonstellationen und Entwicklungspfade in der staatlich finanzierten ausseruniversitären Forschung*. Frankfurt/Main: Campus.

Kenis, P., & Schneider, V. (1991). Policy networks and policy analysis: Scrutinizing a new analytical toolbox. In B. Marin & R. Mayntz (Eds.), *Policy networks. Empirical evidence and theoretical considerations* (pp. 25–59). Campus: Frankfurt/Main.

Knoke, D., Pappi, F. U., Broadbent, J., & Tsujinala, Y. (1996). *Comparing policy networks: Labour politics in the U.S., Germany, and Japan*. Cambridge: Cambridge University Press.

Korpi, W. (1985). Power resources approach vs. action and conflict: On causal and intentional explanations in the study of power. *Sociological Theory, 3*, 31–45.

Lasswell, H. D., & Kaplan, A. (1952). *Power and society: A framework for political inquiry*. London: Routledge and Kegan Paul.

Laumann, E. O., & Knoke, D. (1987). *The organizational state: Social choice in national policy domains*. Madison: University of Wisconsin Press.

Laumann, E. O., & Pappi, F. U. (1976). *Networks of collective action: A perspective on community influence systems*. New York: Academic.

Leifeld, P., & Schneider, V. (2012). Information exchange in policy networks. *American Journal of Political Science, 56*, 731–744.

Lijphart, A. (1999). *Patterns of democracy: Government forms and performance in thirty-six countries*. New Haven: Yale University Press.

Lubell, M. (2013). Governing institutional complexity: The ecology of games framework. *Policy Studies Journal, 41*, 537–559. https://doi.org/10.1111/psj.12028.

Luhmann, N. (1969). Moderne Systemtheorien als Form gesamtgesellschaftlicher Analyse. In T. W. Adorno (Ed.), *Spätkapitalismus oder Industriegesellschaft?* (pp. 253–266). Stuttgart: Ferdinand Enke.

Luhmann, N. (1977). Differentiation of society. *The Canadian Journal of Sociology, 2*, 29–53.

Mair, P. (1994). Party organizations: From civil society to the state. In R. S. Katz & P. Mair (Eds.), *How parties organize: Change and adaptation in party organizations in western democracies* (pp. 1–22). London: Sage.

Mann, M. (1984). The autonomous power of the state, its origins, mechanisms and results. *European Journal of Sociology, 25*, 185–213. https://doi.org/10.1017/S0003975600004239.

Mayntz, R. (1982). Problemverarbeitung durch das politisch-administrative system: Zum Stand der Forschung. In J. J. Hess (Ed.), *Politikwissenschaft und Verwaltungswissenschaft* (pp. 74–89). Wiesbaden: VS Verlag für Sozialwissenschaften.

Mayntz, R. (1986). Corporate actors in public policy: Changing perspectives in political analysis. *Norsk Statsvitenskapelig Tidsskrift, 2*, 7–25.

Mayntz, R. (1993). Modernization and the Logic of Interorganizational Networks. *Knowledge, Technology & Policy, 6*, 3–16.

Mayntz, R. (2003). New challenges to governance theory. In H. P. Bang (Ed.), *Governance as social and political communication* (pp. 27–40). Manchester: Manchester University Press.

Mayntz, R., & Hughes, T. P. (1988). *The development of large technical systems*. Frankfurt: Campus.

Mayntz, R., & Scharpf, F. W. (1995). *Gesellschaftliche Selbstregelung und politische Steuerung*. Frankfurt/Main: Campus.

Mayntz, R., Rosewitz, B., Schimank, U., & Stichweh, R. (1988). *Differenzierung und Verselbständigung: zur Entwicklung gesellschaftlicher Teilsysteme*. Frankfurt/Main: Campus.

Odella, F. (2011). Social networks and communities: From traditional society to the virtual sphere. In M. Safar & K. Mahdi (Eds.), *Social networking and community behavior modeling* (pp. 1–25). Hershey: Information Science Reference.

Ostrom, E. (1986). An agenda for the study of institutions. *Public Choice, 48*, 3–25.

Ostrom, E. (1990). *Governing the commons: The evolution of institutions for collective action*. Cambridge: Cambridge University Press.

Ostrom, E. (2011). Background on the institutional analysis and development framework. *Policy Studies Journal, 39*, 7–27.
Pappi, F. (1993). Policy-Netze: Erscheinungsform moderner Politiksteuerung oder methodischer Ansatz? In A. Héritier (Ed.), *Policy-analyse (Sonderheft der Politischen Vierteljahresschrift 24)* (pp. 84–94). Wiesbaden: Westdeutscher Verlag.
Parsons, T. (1966). *Societies: Evolutionary and comparative perspectives*. Englewood Cliffs, NJ: Prentice-Hall.
Powell, W. (1987). Hybrid organizational arrangements: New form or transitional development? *California Management Review, 30*, 67–87.
Putnam, R. D. (1995). Bowling alone: America's declining social capital. *Journal of Democracy, 6*, 65–78.
Rinscheid, A., Eberlein, B., Emmenegger, P., & Schneider, V. (2019). Why do junctures become critical? Political discourse, agency, and joint belief shifts in comparative perspective. *Regulation and Governance*. https://doi.org/10.1111/rego.12238.
Sabatier, P. A. (1988). An advocacy coalition framework of policy change and the role of policy-oriented learning therein. *Policy Sciences, 21*, 129–168.
Satoh, K., Nagel, M., & Schneider, V. (2018). *Faith in scientific expertise and the organizational distribution of knowledge: Climate change policy networks in Germany and Japan*. Paper presented at the ECPR-Conference in Hamburg.
Scharpf, F. W. (1997). *Games real actors play: Actor-centered institutionalism in policy research*. Boulder: Westview Press.
Schimank, U. (2015). *Differenzierung und Integration der modernen Gesellschaft: Beiträge zur akteurzentrierten Differenzierungstheorie 1*. Wiesbaden: Springer.
Schmidt, M. G. (1993). Theorien der international vergleichenden Staatstätigkeitsforschung. In A. Héritier (Ed.), *Policy analyse (Sonderheft der Politischen Vierteljahresschrift 24)* (pp. 371–393). Wiesbaden: Westdeutscher Verlag.
Schmidt, M. G. (1996). When parties matter: A review of the possibilities and limits of partisan influence on public policy. *European Journal of Political Research, 30*, 155–183. https://doi.org/10.1111/j.1475-6765.1996.tb00673.x.
Schmitter, P. C., & Lehmbruch, G. (1979). *Trends toward corporatist intermediation*. Beverly Hills: Sage.
Schneider, V. (2004). State theory, governance and the logic of regulation and administrative control. In A. Warntjen & A. Wonka (Eds.), *Governance in Europe* (pp. 25–41). Baden-Baden: Nomos.
Schneider, V. (2012). Governance and complexity. In D. Levi-Faur (Ed.), *The Oxford handbook of governance* (pp. 129–142). Oxford: Oxford University Press.
Schneider, V. (2015). Towards post-democracy or complex power sharing? Environmental policy networks in Germany. In V. Schneider & B. Eberlein (Eds.), *Complex democracy: Varieties, crises, and transformations* (pp. 263–279). Berlin: Springer.
Schneider, V., & Bauer, J. M. (2007). *Governance: Prospects of complexity theory in revisiting system theory* (pp. 1–37). In: Annual meeting of the Midwest Political Science. Retrieved from Https://pdfs.semanticscholar.org/0007/4f01be487919b7cd9dc0ce9a173436d82d6c.pdf
Schneider, V., Leifeld, P., & Malang, T. (2013). Coping with creeping catastrophes: National political systems and the challenge of slow-moving policy problems. In B. Siebenhüner, M. Arnold, K. Eisenack, & K. Jacob (Eds.), *Long-term governance for social-ecological change* (pp. 221–238). New York: Routledge.
Schwinn, T. (2011). Von starken und schwachen Gesellschaftsbegriffen. Verfallsstufen eines traditionsreichen Konzepts. In *Soziale Differenzierung* (pp. 27–44). Wiesbaden: VS Verlag für Sozialwissenschaften.
Shanahan, E. A., McBeth, M. K., & Hathaway, P. L. (2011). Narrative policy framework: The influence of media policy narratives on public opinion. *Politics and Policy, 39*, 373–400.

Shaw, D. R., & Allen, T. (2018). Studying innovation ecosystems using ecology theory. *Technological Forecasting and Social Change, 136*, 88–102. https://doi.org/10.1016/J.TECHFORE.2016.11.030.

Shepsle, K. A., & Bonchek, M. S. (1997). *Analyzing politics: Rationality, behavior, and institutions*. New York: W.W. Norton.

Stegmüller, W. (2013). *The structuralist view of theories: A possible analogue of the Bourbaki programme in physical science*. Berlin: Springer.

Streeck, W., & Schmitter, P. C. (1985). Community, market, state—And associations? The prospective contribution of interest governance to social order. In W. Streeck & P. C. Schmitter (Eds.), *Private interest government* (pp. 1–29). London: Sage.

Streeck, W., Grote, J. R., Schneider, V., & Visser, J. (2006). *Governing interests: Business associations facing internationalization*. London: Routledge.

Thelen, K. (1999). Historical institutionalism in comparative politics. *Annual Review of Political Science, 2*, 369–404. https://doi.org/10.1146/annurev.polisci.2.1.369.

Tsebelis, G. (2002). *Veto players: How political institutions work*. Princeton: Princeton University Press.

Tucker, R. C. (1972). *The Marx-Engels reader*. New York: Norton.

Waldherr, A. (2017). Öffentlichkeit als komplexes System. Theoretischer Entwurf und methodische Konsequenzen. *Medien & Kommunikationswissenschaft, 3*, 534–549. https://doi.org/10.5771/1615-634X-2017-3-534.

Weible, C. M. (2005). Beliefs and perceived influence in a natural resource conflict: An advocacy coalition approach to policy networks. *Political Research Quarterly, 58*, 461–475.

Williamson, O. E. (1975). *Markets and hierarchies: Analysis and antitrust implications: A study in the economics of internal organization*. New York: Free Press.

Williamson, O. E. (1979). Transaction-cost economics: The governance of contractual relations. *Journal of Law and Economics, 22*, 233–261. https://doi.org/10.1086/466942.

Willke, H. (1995). *Ironie des Staates. Grundlinien einer Staatstheorie polyzentrischer Gesellschaft*. Frankfurt/Main: Suhrkamp.

Zahariadis, N. (2007). The multiple streams framework: Structure, limitations, prospects. In P. A. Sabatier (Ed.), *Theories of the policy process* (pp. 97–115). Boulder: Westview.

Part II
Policy and Evaluation as an Interaction Space

Chapter 4
Mission-Oriented Public Policy and the New Evaluation Culture

Kaisa Lähteenmäki-Smith and Petri Virtanen

Abstract In this chapter, our aim is to develop a framework to improve public policy-related evaluation practice for a more adaptive and anticipatory evaluation approach, better in tune with complex interactions and interdependencies that have emerged on our policy agenda today. One of the features of this space for interactions that is public policy is its mission orientation. Such an orientation is accompanied by the evolution of public policy instruments, which in turn necessitate new evaluation approaches. We are convinced that this requires developing a conceptual framework, which can be taken forward to test and further operationalise in situations where similar systemic transformations for policy development are elaborated upon.

Based on our work on public-sector leadership, we are proposing a framework for evaluation in a more mission-driven and systems-based perspective. The framework seeks to take better into consideration the diversity of policy interventions at our disposal, ranging from traditional budgetary or legislative instruments to experimentation and piloting. Changes are identified in the very characteristics of the societal problems we are trying to solve, as well as in the nature of policy, both subsequently requiring a more multifaceted scope of evaluation, an emerging practice being towards a more mission-oriented one as well as a more nuanced approach depending on whether one is interested in the multi-organisational performance, policy service delivery or quality of outputs and impacts from policy initiatives and projects. The focus of evaluation in turn ranges from the accountability to evaluation criteria, timescale, motivation, as well as type of intervention used.

K. Lähteenmäki-Smith (✉)
MDI, Helsinki, Finland
e-mail: kaisa.lahteenmaki-smith@mdi.fi

P. Virtanen
ITLA and University of Vaasa, Vaasa, Finland
e-mail: petri.virtanen@itla.fi

H. Lehtimäki et al. (eds.), *Society as an Interaction Space*, Translational Systems Sciences 22, https://doi.org/10.1007/978-981-15-0069-5_4

4.1 Introduction

This chapter builds upon a new conceptual treatise about phenomenon-based and systemic evaluation practice. The authors argue that our society as an interaction space is full of complex societal phenomena, which are best approached in a more systems-based, holistic fashion, rather than through piecemeal, one-dimensional or sectoral solutions. The main idea of the chapter is to discuss the new approach and role of public policy evaluation practice and to link the theoretical, conceptual and practical reasoning concerning evaluation embedded to the practice of public policy in society. In this chapter, we maintain that evaluation is a part of a systemic public policy—when the more conventional policy instruments evolve to fit in better with experimental governance, so do evaluation practice as well. Public policy evaluation, in all its varieties, is an important nucleus in the value chain comprised of complex adaptive public policy systems where decision-makers, institutions, organisations, citizens and public service users make sense and try to pinpoint the value of public interventions, increasingly brought about by various public, semipublic or market-oriented service ecosystems.

Societal complexity is also an essential driver of change from the perspective of public management doctrines and public policy evaluation ideals. As for the public management doctrines, the New Public Management (NPM) came into the scene during the 1990s as radical and innovative insight, conquering the bureaucratic bastions of Weberian task-oriented public policy and administrative world. NPM's promise was to put emphasis on effectiveness of public interventions. Soon after the turn of the new millennia, the New Public Governance (NPG) started to replace NPM as the dominant public-sector management doctrine by providing new understanding about governance issues and societal power networks and putting emphasis on the effectiveness and financial efficiency of public interventions. The NPG has served its purpose as a conceptual and theoretical model of public policy-making and public policy evaluation, yet from the current perspective, it offers much less potential to practical challenges public-sector policy-makers face in their everyday work, serving their citizens and administrations. It seems that societal complexity and related interconnectedness turned out to be too much for the NPG discourse and practice.

Phenomenon-based public policy offers an approach based on strategic agenda setting and implementation through holistic, cross-sector thinking, familiar from pedagogy all through the 2010s, only recently having made a serious transition to policy-making, with themes such as social inclusion, circular economy or inclusive and sustainable growth becoming central themes on the government agenda (e.g. Cairney and Geyer 2017). These holistic and horizontal phenomena are also particularly well-suited for more mission-oriented policy design, as the interactions and interdependencies which emerge when policies are defined through mission-driven processes restructure the agenda setting itself (e.g. Mazzucato 2018a, b).

The potential and promise of a more phenomenon-based policy, better in line with mission-driven approaches to our societal agenda, lies in three main characteristics of approaching policy: (1) capacity for better policy consistency and coherence, which can in turn be more effective in achieving policy impacts; (2) systems approach, making the causalities, root causes and interconnections more visible and by so doing raising more attention to the knowledge and evidence base of policies; and (3) more open and inclusive dialogue, across the sectors and policy spheres, which can be seen as having intrinsic value of its own and may lead to more inclusive policies and more deliberative-style public policy-making.

In this chapter, we ask *how evolving phenomenon-based public policy-making and mission-oriented public policy governance consequently reshape the traditional landscape of public policy instrument and especially the existing public policy practices.* We intend to explore the idea *how evaluation fits in with phenomenon-based experimental governance.*

In the following, our approach builds upon multiple theoretical and conceptual research discussions, which cut across the domains of public institutions, public policy, public-sector leadership, public services, public policy evaluation and accountability. Among these discussions, which are of direct relevance for evaluation practice and culture, are fundamental themes such as (1) **the decreased predictability and accelerating speed of change in public-sector leadership and the evolution of public policy instruments** (e.g. Van Wart 2003, 2013, 2017; Van der Wal 2017; Doz et al. 2018; Bourgon 2017; Bähr 2010); (2) **the interconnectedness of decision-making and the need for cross-sectoral collaboration, in line with the society as an interaction space**; (3) **the mission-oriented public policy** brought about by the complexity of the societal challenges and evolving ecosystems, touching upon the very public value notions themselves (from segregation to climate change and digitalisation to platform economy including new funding and investment methods such as alliances, impact investments and social impact bonds) (e.g. Mazzucato 2018a, b; Mazzucato and Semieniuk 2017); (4) **the innovative leadership methods and practices** (including experimentation, social innovation and co-creation) (e.g. Stephan et al. 2016; Bason 2017, 2018; Moussa et al. 2018; Mulgan 2013, 2018); (5) the **digital, more customer-oriented services, citizen participation and deliberation in service development** (e.g. Greve 2015; Osborne 2018; Crosby et al. 2017; Virtanen and Stenvall 2018); and finally (6) **the transformation and crisis of representative democracy** (e.g. Haskell 2000; Micklethwait and Wooldridge 2015). Whilst we see these as part and parcel of the cultural shift from a centralised and sector-based approach to policy, our main focus will be on the changes brought about by complexity or interactions and how they are connected to a more phenomenon-based and mission-driven thinking.

This chapter is organised as follows. *Firstly*, we will discuss the complexities of society from the point of view of public policy evaluation, focusing on the systemic nature of societal problems today's societies currently face throughout the globe. *Secondly*, we 'bring in' new approach to public policy which draws heavily on the current discussions about the role of state, public institutions and public policy in targeting societal problems and implementing public interventions to alleviate the negative effects of these problems and especially so-called wicked problems. *Thirdly*, we propose a framework for public policy evaluation for a more phenomenon-based (e.g. climate change, social exclusion, loneliness) governance system. The proposed framework seeks to take better into consideration the diversity of policy interventions ranging from traditional budgetary or legislative instruments to experimentation and piloting. Policy target identification subsequently requires a more multifaceted scope of evaluation, an emerging practice being towards a more mission-oriented one as well as a more nuanced approach depending on whether one is interested in the multi-organisational performance, policy service delivery or quality of outputs and impacts from policy initiatives and projects. The focus of public policy evaluation in turn ranges from the accountability to evaluation criteria, timescale, motivation as well as type of intervention used. *Fourthly*, our analysis concludes with ideas for further research agenda around the subject.

4.2 Does Societal Complexity Fit in with Our Administrative Structures?

A more mission-driven approach to policy is necessitated by the inability of our sector-based policies to respond to our societal challenges. Diverse societal phenomena that we meet in the society today are complex (and in some cases wicked) by their nature. Their causes and influences, as well as the mechanisms they reflect, are so multifaceted that they require more comprehensive and cross-border approaches if they are to be understood, analysed and let alone solved. They no longer cater for sector-based administrative solutions in policy practice. Their characteristics complicate any attempts to find suitable solutions for their evaluation, be in terms of impact or effectiveness, success and performance or, perhaps more acutely still, in terms of legitimacy (e.g. Termeer and Dewulf 2018; Laakso et al. 2017). Examples of such phenomena include the effect of climate change on human behaviour and consumer choices, social exclusion of certain groups in our society, the new economic potential and activity brought about by circular economy or platform economy.

Conceptually *a phenomenon* can be a simple object of observation, something that is perceived, but the reasons or explanations for which are unclear and the fundamental causalities or determining factors cannot be directly perceived. Such phenomena thus need to be observed and understood more comprehensively, from various points of view, systematically and beyond administrative or disciplinary boundaries. The term 'phenomenon-based learning' has perhaps been the most often used one as educational approaches and curricula have increasingly been approached in this way. Phenomenon-based learning as a concept refers to the holistic teaching of real-world phenomena, which crosses educational boundaries and takes the characteristics of the question, of the phenomenon in question as the starting point for the search of answers in the learning process.

From the perspective of learning and public policy implementation, complexity itself is not the main problem. Harnessing complexity is a truism and impossible as a thought. Complexity becomes problematic only when we try to solve the drivers and consequences of complexity with old mindsets. As already referred to above, in order to respond to the needs of complex adaptive systems, we need to be increasingly curious about the new solutions for identifying policy tools and instruments able to respond to the system transformation needs, as well as capable of identifying the potential directions for action within confines of the possible (policy change/societal transformation), adaptive and reflexive policy-making and evaluation approaches to fit the needs of such a system (e.g. Shine 2015; Innes and Booher 1999; Thomas 2012). Phenomena can be seen as clusters of complex issues or conundrums, which need to be seen, understood and developed into policy interventions through a systems approach. At their most basic, a phenomenon is a policy challenge or development, which needs to be perceived as part of a wider system and subject matter, instead of separate individual parts.

At present, governance and decision-making deals with issues and phenomena such as the exclusion of young people, climate change or changing nature of work and economic dynamics of a society in a wide range of administrative sectors and through separate budget resources, making the coming to grips with the phenomenon more difficult, with policy measures losing effectiveness, efficiency and coherence and becoming even mutually counter-productive. The lack of a shared understanding of any issue at hand itself thus makes making decisions on such phenomena particularly difficult. When it comes to allocating public funds towards a phenomenon-based agenda, it is clear that without a more phenomenon-based budgeting, i.e. budget or at least part of the budget being designed in a phenomenon-targeted fashion, the organisational momentum or administrative sectors and their sectoral interests quickly win ground, with financial resources allocated to key strategic goals, which do not necessarily share a common understanding of the cross-sector issues to be tackled.

4.3 Mission-Oriented Public Policies as a Means of Creating Joint Societal Value

Mission orientation in policy can be useful for making societal value easier to grasp. We often hear that government does not create value in itself, but rather it facilitates or enables its creation and redistributes value through taxation and by various redistribution mechanisms such as welfare benefits and social and healthcare services. From the perspective of mainstream economic thinking—and austerity policies within the umbrella of public policies (the assumption that public debt is an extreme enemy for economic growth and individual well-being, which should be handled by cutting government spending)—the narrative that government should limit itself to addressing market failure or restraining actions that may disrupt the market has been extremely powerful since the 1980s and especially after the 1990s (e.g. Mazzucato 2018b). Most strikingly, perhaps, this discussion has related to the banking sector and its role in solving the financial crises over the last few decades.

Mertens (2019), for instance, has argued that the European Investment Bank has become a centre of gravity in long-standing political attempts to increase the investment firepower of the European Union since the 1990s through gradual process of institutional innovation, network formation, market creation and depth management.

This narrative of the 1980s and 1990s has been interesting in many ways—also from a historical perspective. Reinert (1999) has analysed the role played by the government sector in promoting economic growth in Western societies since the Renaissance, and his conclusion is that the antagonism between state and market, which has characterised the end of the twentieth century, is a relatively new phenomenon: since the Renaissance one very important task of the state has been to create well-functioning markets by providing a legal framework, standards and credit and creating an infrastructure for markets to function.

Summarising, the role of government, public policy and public institutions has been debated over the centuries. According to Mazzucato (2018a, b: 229–230), these public entities have been considered as necessary but unproductive actors (as spenders and over-reaching regulators) throughout the history of economic thought—rather than value creators. Recent economic crises have underlined the fact that 'government failure' is not the 'whole picture'. Mulgan (2013: 45–46) refers to the 2008/2009 financial crises and argues that governments step in when markets fail: when economy is in turmoil, people turn more to their families and communities.

The concept of public value is at the heart of mission-oriented public policies when we consider public sector's role and capabilities in pursuing societal value and value creation as a process. From today's perspective, it is important to note that public good, public value and value creation are not synonyms, even though they may get easily conflated in media and in the everyday discussions. Whereas public good refers to outputs governments deliver (based on the public policy instruments), public value is then a much broader term, referring also to co-creation processes (by various societal actors and partners), intermediate effects and networks providing and expressing them. Value creation, then, refers to ways in which different service-dominant ways of human, physical and intangible capabilities and capacities are established, mobilised and orchestrated in economic and social markets together to produce new goods, goods-related services, aiming at individual well-being and ultimately societal betterment through the process of co-shaping and co-creation.

The new treatise about creating public value brings about new 'big questions' about government and the public sector. It is not the size, budget or regulatory power, which make the difference, but how public institutions involve themselves in the betterment of society. From today's perspective, mainstream economic thinking of the 1980s and 1990s, especially public choice theory, appears somewhat too narrow for the challenges the world and governments are facing. This view holds the idea that—from the perspective of economic and social value creation—all societal sectors (government, business, the third sector) maintain the idea that all of these institutions reinforce, nourish and help each other in the pursuit of common goal. This requires the presence of finance from public sources across the entire innovation chain; the deployment of mission-oriented policies which create new technology, innovation and industrial landscapes and ecosystems; and the entrepreneurial and lead investor role of public actors within the domain of public policies.

Summing up, more intelligent public policy is policy that is appropriate to the task at hand, feasible, timely and proportional to the objectives set. It has also an internal dynamic that allows for a future-oriented, more anticipatory way of working. Anticipatory governance or policy here does not only refer to the ability of governments to design policies to meet the needs of the future by better anticipating problems before they occur, often with the help of Big Data and monitoring, or to the process by which governments ensure acceptance of their measures (or industry for their technological standards) through the inclusion of the public in their introduction to the public sphere. It also relates to the ability, capacity and willingness of governments to engage and commit themselves to considering broader policy changes or individual policy measures with the help of a futures perspective, be it through foresight, scenarios or public panels, where the shared understanding of policies and the options available to governments in designing them are opened to public scrutiny and deliberation, with the help of systematic future methodologies and technologies (about this discussion from the perspective of governance in the framework of the fourth industrial revolution, see Schwab 2017).

Social impact and mission orientation are means of not only achieving a more phenomenon-based thinking, i.e. of starting from the societal challenge and task at hand and working one's way from there, but also seeking to find the solutions through variable and flexible pathways than of basing the activity to a planning-based structure of steps and milestones. Here the phenomenon-driven agenda can also benefit from experimental culture and the policy tools and instruments at its disposal.

Mission focus in public policy has a close link to phenomenon because it is a way to build agenda, commitment and ownership to an identified policy challenge. Although the phenomenon-based societal challenges are not technologically solved, their solution can benefit from lessons learned from ambitious technologic missions such as the US Space Administration's Apollo programme or Internet invention or various breakthroughs in bio- or nanotechnology. Similar thinking is now needed in implementing a new agenda for innovation and growth policy (e.g. OECD or EU visions to enable 'smart', 'inclusive' and 'sustainable' growth). Examples of such societal missions include 100 non-carbon cities in the climate change area by 2030, clean marine environment by 2025 and, in the human welfare area, reducing the human burden of memory sickness by 2030.

Societal missions in Mazzucato's (2018a, b) approach combine the following features, which may be taken as essential also for phenomenon-based thinking, when it is perceived as a serious commitment to mission-oriented and societally relevant cross-sectoral leadership practice:

- Courage: significant societal relevance and potential impact and ability to achieve change, allowing for the mobilisation of significant resources, actors and commitment across the society.
- Clear direction and measurability: despite its large-scale and long time span, societal missions should be formulated into clearly measurable measures, which

can be broken into steps and stages, milestone to be achieved through collaboration.
- Ambitious and realistic measures from the point of view of the private sector: policy measures should be formulated in a manner that allows for the private sector to partake in the public-sector interventions. This type of collaborative effort would bring the added value of the public sector into the private sector sphere (and vice versa).
- Cross-border dimension: crossing the boundaries of disciplines, sectors and society is characteristic to phenomenon-based policy as a whole and also for significant missions across the sectors.
- Partnerships: solutions bring together actors across disciplines and fields of expertise, also requiring new kinds of joint initiatives for development and ownership of them (partnership orientation). In this respect, mission-driven innovation can also lead to systemic changes through ecosystem formation.
- Diversity of possible solutions and bottom-up orientation: missions should not be achievable by a single development path, or by a single technology, but rather they should be open to being addressed by different types of solutions. A mission-based approach is typically very clear on the expected outcome, but the trajectory through which it is achieved is to be based on a bottom-up approach of multiple solutions, which can also be open to experimentation and adjusted along the way.

The variety of alternative paths and means by which the objectives (phenomenon-based or otherwise) can be achieved requires a broad perspective on the evaluative options available. Policy diversity is paralleled by evaluation diversity, ranging from methods to data and rationale of evaluation.

4.4 Mission-Driven Policy Accompanied by Changing Landscape of Public Policy Instruments

As the logic of policy changes, so do the relevant instruments. It becomes increasingly important to understand which instruments are suited for which situation, context and purpose. The urgency to develop sustainable and relevant evaluating methods and frameworks for policy is exacerbated by the need that it is increasingly difficult to identify and differentiate the tools that are best suited for dealing with any policy issue (e.g. whether a policy challenge in fact is complex, wicked or tame; Newman and Head 2017). The agenda for a more phenomenon-based governance model, which better responds to the trends referred to above, necessitates a fundamental re-thinking of evaluation methods, practices and cultures.

The 'new public-sector landscape' should be seen in the context of the public sector's role as a provider of stability, rule of law and democracy, seeking to ensure that the renewal and government reforms are firmly embedded in the pursuit of transparency and openness. Such radical re-thinking of the government requires a parallel redesign of the whole framework for evaluation, as it can no longer be sufficient to provide an evaluation set-up that simplifies the interventions to a temporally limited (ex ante/ex post) scale or sometimes artificial underestimation of the importance of networks and their impacts (external-internal distinction).

Taken together, these perspectives can be summed up as promoting the role of central government as an enabler of phenomenon-based good governance in the future. The transformation of governance culture requires commitment and process ownership of the society as a whole, not only ideas and proposals from expert organisations. If there is to be an evaluation culture, it should be one owned by the public, at the heart of accountability and public policy ethos.

The evaluation framework is necessitated by the shift from a simple to a complex system in policy challenges such as the inclusion of the young and fighting segregation. The need for policy innovation and more phenomenon-based policy is at the same time appreciative of relevant scale and small wins (e.g. Termeer and Dewulf 2018; Thomas 2012), rather than seeking to promote solutions for complex policy challenges and missions that defy easy solutions or one-dimensional frameworks and framing attempts.

Complex adaptive systems cannot be served by linear public policy intervention models, which only target one area of policy development, one agent or actor or individual policy sector. This type of policy design for complex systems in our view brings about a need for evaluation framework, which is at the same time experimental in nature at best randomised controlled trial (RCT)-based or research driven, e.g. basic income experiment in Finland), strategically timely (both ex ante and ongoing, e.g. sustainability experiments), multidimensional/perspective (e.g. municipal employment experiments) and learning-oriented (e.g. small-scale circular economy experiments) (e.g. Annala and Berg 2016).

In addition to the legislative route, there are numerous other ways of designing policy and public-sector intervention, as is indicative in the example provided by the UK Policy Lab (see below). The diversity of available options for any government, policy-maker or policy designer is such that when faced with a phenomenon-based need for change or transformation, we often overlook the multiplicity of the options, at the expense of easy or familiar options. Throughout the OECD countries, the predominance of traditional roles such as funder, regulator or legislator has been very strong. However, in many cases the softer options of collaborator or stewards may be more effective in terms of promoting change.

Conceptually speaking, the UK Policy Lab model comes close to various models of government intervention which have adopted dialogic approaches to traditional decision-making processes. The UK Policy Lab model draws to a great extent from the idea of collective intelligence, which has been developed within the framework of Nesta in the UK (e.g. Mulgan 2013, 2018) and consists of broad themes related to better understanding of facts and experiences, more inclusive decision-making and gaining better and more comprehensive oversight of what is done and accomplished by government, private and third-sector organisations (Table 4.1).

This type of more sophisticated way of identifying public-sector intervention can also make visible the tension inherent in the political and policy timescale: whilst the political sphere seeks to proceed rapidly and view solutions in an electoral cycle

Table 4.1 Framework for government interventions (the UK Policy Lab 2018)

Styles of government intervention	Early-stage intervention	Framing, piloting and market forming	Scaling, mainstreaming and market building	Moving in mature markets and policy ecosystems
Government as **collaborator** working with others to build evidence and develop ideas	*Champion*, i.e. build case for change and retain alliances for action	*Convening power*, i.e. draw together expertise from across system	*Connecting networks*, i.e. encourage government experts and citizens to co-create change	*Co-producing*, i.e. co-deliver by steering different actors from across the system to deliver outcomes
Government as **steward** steering a sector through influence and information	*Agenda setting*, i.e. build awareness and confidence in new opportunities by providing thought leadership	*Strategy and skills planning*, i.e. prepare for changing workforce demands and consequences of change	*Educating and informing*, i.e. ensure regulation is sufficiently understood and citizens know what's available for them	*Giving a voice*, i.e. creating platforms for citizens and stakeholders to protect vested rights and interests
Government as **customer** buying goods and commission services	*Catalyst*, i.e. review, identify and invest in key opportunities with strategic value	*Standard setting*, i.e. develop standards for data collection and presentation	*User-centred commissioner*, i.e. understanding citizens' needs and contracting services that deliver best impact	*Levering buying power*, i.e. utilise public procurement to encourage investment and protect consumer rights
Government as **provider** designing, providing and modifying public services	*Innovator*, i.e. create test beds, sandboxes and trials in real-world settings	*Service redesign*, i.e. establish legitimacy for more human-centred services, harnessing political will for change	*Service provider*, i.e. provide services directly or indirectly through funding and target setting	*Choice architect*, i.e. nudging behaviour so that the default is both attractive and easy
Government as **funder** stimulating or leading investment	*Early adopter*, i.e. invest in the early exploration of new opportunities with strategic value	*Fiscal incentives*, i.e. direct finance to stimulate new thinking that can drive future opportunities	*Grants and subsidies*, i.e. incentivise behaviour change through grants or other incentives	*Platform provision*, i.e. scale up proven ideas through existing infrastructure and public services
Government as **regulator** regulating a sector and coordinating enforcement	*Encourage voluntary codes*, i.e. self-regulation, without legislation, allowing for greater flexibility	*Governance*, i.e. ensure regulation supports the conditions for change and delivers the policy intent	*Building a regulatory environment*, i.e. ensure regulation enables the intended policy outcomes	*Compliance*, i.e. support enforcement and harmonise regulatory compliance environment
Government as **legislator** making laws and amending legislation	*Green papers*, i.e. publish proposals for discussion with stakeholders and the public	*White papers and draft bills*, i.e. publish proposals for consultation and pre-legislative scrutiny	*Primary and secondary legislation*, i.e. support a bill through parliament and enact legislation	*Amend rules*, i.e. statutory instruments (rules, orders) created by delegated authorities (e.g. secretary of state)

Source: Policy Lab 2018, available at: https://www.slideshare.net/Openpolicymaking/styles-of-intervention-for-government-policymaking

perspective and therefore prone to (at least seemingly) 'technical', 'orderly' or even 'simple' solutions, for policy-making the picture is necessarily more nuanced. Here moving from an operational to a more strategically formulated policy rationalisation is necessary, and even further, the vision of any government can only achieve change in relatively short term, but by seeking to formulate vision in a longer strategic perspective, also the cross-generational perspectives come to focus. Here the shift entails moving from a problem- or solution-based rationale to mission-based approach.

4.5 The Plethora of Available Policy Instruments Necessitate New Evaluation Frameworks

Evaluation frameworks also need to adapt, because they need to respond to policy change, which comes with more experimental governance. If traditional policy instruments proliferate by nature, then how do evaluation approaches evolve? This is the question we turn next. At the outset, governments are already increasingly developing and benchmarking instruments and new methods, which can provide them with new solutions. Policy experimentation represents one of the key facets of this new systemic approach to governance innovation. The type of policy trials and strategic experiments explored is diverse, thereby necessitating a multi-method evaluation approach. The main types include open-ended, through result- or even mission-driven *experimentation* (most in line with the aspirations of traditional thinking for evidence-informed policy), *piloting for early implementation* (e.g. inspiring and facilitating cultural change), *piloting for demonstration* (more testing for validation purposes than open-ended learning) and *operationalising policy through experimentation* (e.g. 'trailblazing').

As such, the framework proposed (see Annex 1) seeks to address the evaluation paradox discussed by Termeer and Dewulf (2018), where evaluations seek to judge policies as solutions for problems that per definition defy solutions and in relation to which 'one can always do better', i.e. additional efforts might increase the chances of finding a better solution. The framework thus seeks to address the usual responses to the paradox, namely paralysis (of doing nothing in face of finding the evaluation too daunting) and overestimation (the false assumption that a wicked problem can indeed be solved and addressing it through focusing on one single aspect or standpoint).

In terms of evaluation that is of relevance for pressing current phenomena, we are quickly faced with the conundrum of intervention and policy relevance. Can policy intervention make a difference in terms of policy change, systems change or impact? Here we are referring to the new role of the public sector and its role in enabling investment thinking in long-term systems change, as well as facilitating the problem-solving and mobilisation of resources, where complex problem-solving is based on a very ambitious goal setting and resource orientation. The mission is a social phenomenon-driven challenge, such as climate change, social segregation or platform economy.

As we put forward earlier, public policies are increasingly interconnected, many issues having become interdependent and having an influence or impact on each other. Typical example is social exclusion of young people and the phenomena around the so-called NEET group (young people who are outside education, employment or training). Whilst there may be perfectly valid reasons for being in this position (e.g. taking a leap year), there are many among the young who end up in this position for reasons that are indicative of social exclusion. The first indications of social exclusion may become manifest in lack of early-year education, behavioural problems as small children, etc., though on the level of evaluative knowledge, it only becomes visible (through indicators) once the problem has already led to dropping out of education. In such cases the early symptoms and understanding the root causes could be decisive in better addressing the root causes, identifying solutions and implementing them through less costly and potentially more effective soft measures. As the indications of the core phenomenon involved are necessarily diverse and multifaceted, identifying effective means of policy intervention can be particularly difficult, but also potentially powerful, if successful.

In what follows, we make a distinction in between four evaluation scopes (i.e. where to focus evaluations). They are (1) mission-oriented public policy, (2) multi-organisational performance review in public administration, (3) public service delivery and (4) development initiatives, experiments and projects. Our suggestion thus is to make a distinction between different vertical levels in the planning and implementation of public policies and to build certain common elements in practical evaluation agendas at each level based on societal phenomena and vertical/horizontal accountability function and to take into account the new role of public organisations and service ecosystems.

In the proposed model, we address basically all conventional evaluation timescales—ranging from ex ante to ongoing and ex post (e.g. Scriven 1991)—but address special emphasis on ongoing or process evaluation, where learning is prioritised over accountability. At the core of the proposed model is the utilisation aspect of evaluative inquiry drawing heavily on Patton's *Magnum Opus* published at the late 1990s (Patton 1997). This is partly because utilisation-focused evaluation is still widely recognised as the most influential approach in current evaluation practice, but ultimately because the proposed model is a broader one through its disciplinary foundations, stemming from sociology of knowledge, diffusion of innovation, sociological perspectives on power and conflict, organisational sociology and multiple use of different research methods.

One of the advantages for evaluation practice of such an approach is its ability to accept ambiguity and ill-structured societal challenges, which escape easy answers and are very much dependent on the context, therefore inherently contingent (see, e.g. Schwandt 2013). For us, this is where the beauty and promise of the phenomenon-based approach to policy and evaluation lies: practitioners' problems and questions (by their definition practical in nature) can be assessed and (to at least some extent) solved parallel with general societal dilemmas or complex (or even wicked) problems which by their definition we may not be able to solve, but in seeking the solution can shed light on multiple perspectives into both the practical and contextual conditions in which the societal problem is faced. By so doing even the most practical evaluation questions may lead to significant findings for deepening the contextual understanding of the complex systemic nature of the broader phenomenon itself.

4.6 Mission-Driven Policy and Its Implications for Evaluation

The evaluation framework that is proposed in this chapter is based on the assumption that a shift from a simple to a complex system and its understanding both in terms of theory and practice is necessary, in order to better come to terms with the current megatrends and societal conundrums (e.g. climate change, urbanisation, social fragmentation). The policy challenges societies are faced with are less linear and increasingly require more cross-sectoral focus, more innovative contextual framing and more phenomenon-based policy. Yet the solutions proposed seek to find systemic solutions through small wins rather than grand universal solutions (e.g. Termeer and Dewulf 2018; Thomas 2012). They essentially defy easy solutions or one-dimensional frameworks and framing attempts and by so doing provide interesting learning opportunities across sectors, disciplines and areas of professional evaluation activity.

Both experimentation and exploration are required in complex adaptive systems, which cannot be served by linear public policy intervention models, targeting only one area of policy development, one agent or actor or individual policy sector. Therefore, we have found it illustrative and useful to approach such societal challenges through a 'phenomenon-based' systems approach.

Our analysis in this chapter calls for further conceptual focusing and clarification on the nature and role of government interventions and evaluation of public policies. It is easy to express the idea that 'the change of public policy' is immanent, but far more complex to answer the question why and with what kind of consequences experimentalist governance is evolving. We are convinced that further scrutiny should be situational and system-based and focused on change ('transformation of public sector, public institutions and public policies'). One possibility opens up by structural contingency theory which would help in explaining the structure and role of public policies and public organisations by analysing their adjustment to external factors, particularly changing circumstances that introduce uncertainty in decision-making. Contingency thinking might be useful because in it the assumptions concerning research subject—evolving role of government and public policy in this chapter's case—must be made about starting premises, agency boundaries and system specifics. This enables conceptual scientific inquiry to reach known truisms about the role of government, for instance—in this kind of analysis, it is evident that congruent arguments (e.g. 'the greater the task uncertainty, the more complex the structure') and contingent arguments (e.g. 'task uncertainty interacts with the structure of public policy adopted') are from the same kind of theoretical treatise but offer instantly different perspectives to the research foci.

Considering the multiplicity of intervention styles and possibilities for policy learning in any one decision-making event, the possibilities of using evaluative knowledge and information through feedback loops are almost endless. The challenges lie in making the porous nature of policy-making also better understood by both the evaluation knowledge providers and the knowledge users. Here the sharing opportunities for framing public policy issues should also be better used and more professionally facilitated. This allows for evaluation into policy-making to make a leap towards evaluation into transformation. This in our view is a leap every evaluator, as well as every public-sector decision-maker, should be willing to explore.

Our analysis in this chapter sets out the following research agenda:

- The detailed cultivation of the role of evaluation culture in the making of mission-oriented public policy.
- The new understanding of policy and institutional evaluation as an integral part of policy cycle. This challenge includes the idea of analysing public organisations and public service as value creators at local, regional, national and supranational levels of governance.
- Further theoretical treatise of the new public policy evaluation culture closely linked with the chains of value creating. This view also includes the new role of evaluation from the perspective of societal decision-making.
- Further conceptual reassessment of public-sector accountability. We maintain the view that accountability not only transfers to horizontal accountability, but it also paves way to new understanding of 'classical' bottom-up performance review and reporting.

4.7 Synthesis: Where Does the Mission-Driven Policy Lead Us in Our Search for New Evaluation Practice?

Our chapter has entertained the need for a more mission-driven approach, which could be better suited for the multiple interfaces and connections, which society as a multifaceted interaction space accommodates. Certain critical discussion topics arise from our analysis, and they all relate to the evaluation practice as well as to evaluation culture.

First, we would like to emphasise that the shift from issue- or problem-driven public policy to a phenomenon-based experimental governance entails an equally important shift in evaluation practice. If the aforementioned conclusion is valid, we need to pose a further question as to its implications for evaluation. What does the shift from sector-driven policy to strategy-driven policy or the shift from regulation-driven intervention to enabling-driven role for the government imply for evaluation?

An important part of the shift was already referred to above, namely diversity, which is necessarily part of the phenomenon-based policy development. Parallel to diversity, interaction and methods of selection form what is called adaptive capacity (Innes and Booher 1999), which is also important in designing a new systemic approach to evaluation. As learning and tolerance of failure are an important part of adaptive capacity, phenomenon-based evaluation also prioritises possibilities for learning. As this is the case, learning—and not naming and shaping—constitutes an essential ingredient as the motive to evaluate publicly funded interventions.

In order to design individual evaluations and transform evaluation practice, better suitable of capturing the phenomenon-based transboundary or cross-sector policies, one has to be sensitive to the variable geometry of most of the evaluation elements, from diversity of timescales and perspectives to more variable portfolio of alternative methods and data, as well as the intended use and perceived usefulness of evaluation. Together these factors fit into a perspective of neo-institutionalist theory, where the traditional rationality assumptions are put under scrutiny, the role of actors (also collective ones) is emphasised, the relationships in between organisational actors are made visible and interaction among organisations and organisational actors is increasingly prioritised (e.g. Saks 2016).

Second, new understanding of timescales is of particular relevance for the new evaluation culture. At the mission-oriented policy level, for instance, with the unit of analysis and the intended user of evaluation often being the national government, the tension between the required long-term perspective (of changing phenomena and their root causes) and the realities of a short-term policy cycle (of individual governments) is most pronounced. The outdated model of policy cycle with a linear process of feeding knowledge into decision-making has already some time ago been replaced by a more fuzzy and complex picture of public policy, marked by fluidity and concentric circles and feedback loops. How to accommodate the political will to be seen to act swiftly and effectively with the necessary long-term perspective of many of the processes that transformation actually entail? How to ensure cross-generational focus when the need to act quickly and achieve results during one government term is hanging overhead of politicians and policy-makers?

One reason could be found in framing evaluations around phenomenon-based themes that are more long term and systemic in nature (e.g. Agenda 2030 and the SDGs). Could they be included as a backdrop when farming individual, single-policy initiatives and measures? Could the relevance or coherence of any set of policy interventions be assessed against the number (or degree) of adherence (or coherence) with the set targets in the Agenda 2030? This has so far not been systematically explored, but there are attempts to this direction, such as those undertaken by the Finnish government in its budget preparations for 2018 and 2019. A more phenomenon-based budget could be in line with such a future-proofed focus of evaluative action.

A third issue to be considered is the perspective of knowledge deployment. The intended use and expected rationale for usefulness thus also needs reconsideration. Here we can refer to the variable intervention styles, as they clearly also necessitate a more varied toolkit of evaluation knowledge and data to be considered in decision-making.

Many of the situations where choices between alternative options for action and policy are made are marked by imperfect information, asymmetrical knowledge base and time pressure. In such situations it is essential also for the evaluators and producers of evaluation knowledge to acknowledge that without a counterbalance the risk of Big Data could be that organisations and individuals start making decisions and optimising performance for metrics, derived from algorithms, whilst in many cases Big Data only makes sense and can be framed in an understandable way when it is put into perspective and sense is made of the optimisation process, people, stories and actual experiences.

We hope that the model (see Annex 1) we proposed in this chapter for evaluation of phenomenon-based policy makes room for adaptive capacity, more porous and multifaceted evaluation designs and more attention to the narrative and framing of evaluative information. Our shared sense-making of what we have learnt through evaluation is as important as the numbers revealed by evaluative efforts.

4.8 Final Note: Implications for Practice, Theory and Research

In our view, the systems thinking that the multiplicity of potential intervention styles and methods allows calls for attention on professional practice or evaluators and policy-makers alike. Change that a more mission-driven and phenomenon-based policy entails is at the same time a cultural and functional one, and it has implications for policy practice and evaluation activity. The more diverse architecture of policy intervention that was presented allows for policy-makers to rely on a range of tools, methods and approaches and by so doing thereby also allows and in fact calls for more variety across the evaluation approaches applied. This changes their practice, theory and professional understanding. This also has implications for all aspects of policy formation, from agenda setting to implementation and evaluation, as well as to the professional skills required of policy-makers, practitioners and evaluators alike. One of the fundamental potentials for transformative change that we see in this complex terrain of intervention, evaluation and learning lies in fact in its nature as a sphere of interaction and collaborations, as the understanding of single interventions or their dynamics becomes secondary to understanding of the interactions, causalities and interfaces between the various spheres.

In this shift towards a more systems- and phenomenon-based approach, evaluation does not lose its relevance or its pertinence; rather the shift enriches the role of the evaluator and his or her professional practice. Experimentation is an inherent part of the more multifaceted intervention architecture, and here evaluation is more needed than ever, as the whole notion of experimentation calls for constant and rigorous reflection on the criteria of success and failure and the standards of effectiveness. In such an environment, professional practice or evaluation, just as professional practice of policy planning and interventions, becomes one where the interfaces, interactions, feedback loops and corrective actions are particularly important. This may also require more openness to the outside world and more interaction across the evaluation field as a whole, as no single perspective, method or professional practice alone can determine the value or success of a systemically positioned and farmed intervention.

Annex 1: Four Layers of Future Evaluation in the Domain of Public Policy and Public Organisations—A Holistic Perspective

Evaluation scope	Evaluation focus	Accountability focus	Key evaluation criteria	Evaluation timescale key focus	Evaluation motive	Public-sector intervention mode
1. Mission-oriented public policy	– Public policy – Policy coordination – Policy coherence – Policy deployment – Implementation	*Horizontal and vertical:* towards political decision-makers and the public	– Policy-goal attainment – Policy-goal refocus – Deadweight effects – Misplacement effects – Counterfactual effects	– Ex ante – 'Normal' ex post (after the intervention) – 'Extended' ex post (+3–4 years after the intervention)	– Policy choice successfulness – Societal betterment – Public sector as value creator in society	Transformation roles (driving new markets, opening new opportunities, changing roles in the longer term)
2. Multi-organisational performance review in public administration	– Public administration institutions – Public service multi-organisational ecosystems – Interaction	*Horizontal and vertical:* towards decision-makers, stakeholders, service users and the public	– Multi-organisational 'joint' efficiency – Resource deployment among various organisations – Multi-organisational effectiveness – Systemic change of public institutions	– Ex ante – Ongoing (performance reviews) – Ex post	Performance management of multi-organisational setting	Ecosystem roles (e.g. co-producer, choice architect, providing platforms and funding change processes)
3. Public service delivery	– Service-user engagement – Service (re-)design – Service co-creation	*Mainly horizontal*: towards service users	– Service experience – Service need satisfaction – Participation to co-creation – Empowerment	Ongoing, i.e. learning by co-creation	– Mutual learning – Societal engagement – Enhancing democracy	Service provider, service innovator, service redesign
4. Development initiatives, experiments and projects	Experimentation Nudging	*Horizontal and vertical*: towards political decision-makers and the public, organisational peers	– Lessons learned from experiments – Scaling possibilities of delivered experiments	– Ongoing – Ex post	Testing new ideas and initiatives	Steward, giving voice and support to change makers, choice architect, rule-maker

References

Annala, M., & Berg, A. (2016). Näkökulmia kokeilurahoitukseen—Ehdotus kokeilurahoitusalustan perustamisesta. Valtioneuvoston selvitys-ja tutkimustoiminnan julkaisusarja 14/2016. (Perspectives into Funding Experiments, study commissioned by the Finnish Prime Minister's Office in 2016).

Bähr, H. (2010). *Policy instruments in the European Union*. New York and London: Routledge.

Bason, C. (2017). *Leading public design. Discovering human-centred governance*. Bristol: Policy Press.

Bason, C. (2018). *Leading public sector innovation. Co-creating for a better society*. Bristol: The Policy Press.

Bourgon, J. (2017). *The new synthesis of public administration. Fieldbook*. Copenhagen: Dansk Psykologisk Forlag A/S.

Cairney, P., & Geyer, R. (2017). A critical discussion of complexity theory: How does 'Complexity Thinking' improve our understanding of politics and policymaking? *Complexity, Governance & Networks, 3*(2), 1–11.

Crosby, B. C., 't Hart, P., & Torfing, J. (2017). Public value creation through collaborative innovation. *Public Management Review, 19*(5), 655–669.

Doz, Y., Kosonen, M., & Virtanen, P. (2018). Strategically agile government. In A. Farazmand (Ed.), *Global encyclopedia of public administration, public policy and governance*. https://doi.org/10.1007/978-3-319-31816-5_3554-1.

Greve, C. (2015). Ideas in public management reform for the 2010s: Digitalization, value creation and involvement. *Public Organization Review, 15*(1), 49–65.

Haskell, J. (2000). *Direct democracy or representative government? Dispelling the populist myth*. New York: Routledge.

Innes, J. E., & Booher, D. E. (1999). Consensus building and complex adaptive systems. *Journal of the American Planning Association, 4*(65), 412–423.

Laakso, S., Berg, A., & Annala, M. (2017). Dynamics of experimental governance: A meta-study of functions and uses of climate governance experiments. *Journal of Cleaner Production, 169*, 8–16.

Mazzucato, M. (2018a). *Mission-oriented research and innovation in the European Union*. Brussels: European Commission.

Mazzucato, M. (2018b). *The value of everything. Making and taking in the global economy*. London: Allen Lane.

Mazzucato, M., & Semieniuk, G. (2017). Public financing of innovation: New questions. *Oxford Review of Economic Policy, 33*(1), 24–48.

Mertens, D. (2019). Building a hidden investment state? The European Investment Bank, national development banks and European economic governance. *Journal of European Public Policy, 1*(26), 23–43.

Micklethwait, J., & Wooldridge, A. (2015). *The fourth revolution. The global race to reinvent the state*. New York: Penguin Books.

Moussa, M., McMurray, A., & Muenjohn, N. (2018). Innovation and leadership in public sector organizations. *Journal of Management Research, 10*(3). Retrieved July 25, 2018, from http://www.macrothink.org/journal/index.php/jmr/article/view/13101/10416

Mulgan, G. (2013). *The locust and the bee. Predators and creators in capitalism's future*. Princeton and Oxford: Princeton University Press.

Mulgan, G. (2018). *Big mind. How collective mind can change our world*. Princeton: Princeton University Press.

Newman, J., & Head, B. W. (2017). Wicked tendencies in policy problems: Rethinking the distinction between social and technical problems. *Policy and Society, 36*(3), 414–429.

Osborne, S. P. (2018). From public service-dominant logic to public service logic: Are public service organizations capable of co-production and value co-creation? *Public Management Review, 20*(2), 225–231.

Patton, M. Q. (1997). *Utilization-focused evaluation*. Thousand Oaks: Sage.
Reinert, E. S. (1999). The role of the state in economic growth. *Journal of Economic Studies, 4/5*(26), 268–326.
Saks, M. (2016). A review of theories of professions, organizations and society: The case for neo-Weberianism, neo-institutionalism and eclecticism. *Journal of Professions and Organization, 2*(3), 170–187.
Schwab, K. (2017). *The fourth industrial revolution*. London: Penguin Book.
Schwandt, T. A. (2013). On the mutually informing relationship between practice and theory in evaluation. *American Journal of Evaluation, 35*(2), 231–236.
Scriven, M. (1991). *Evaluation thesaurus*. Thousand Oaks: Sage.
Shine, K. T. (2015). Policy-making as complex cartography? Mapping and achieving probable futures using complex concepts and tools. In R. Geyer & P. Cairney (Eds.), *Handbook on complexity and public policy* (pp. 171–189). Cheltenham: Edward Elgar.
Stephan, U., Patterson, M., Kelly, C., & Mair, J. (2016). Organizations driving positive social change: A review and integrative framework of change processes. *Journal of Management, 42*(5), 1250–1281.
Termeer, C. J. A. M., & Dewulf, A. (2018). A small wins framework to overcome the evaluation paradox of governing wicked problems. *Policy and Society*. https://doi.org/10.1080/14494035.2018.1497933. Retrieved January 3, 2019.
The UK Policy Lab. (2018). *The styles of intervention for government policymaking*. Retrieved January 3, 2019, from https://www.slideshare.net/Openpolicymaking/styles-of-intervention-for-government-policymaking
Thomas, M. (2012). The complexity conundrum: Why hasn't the gender gap in subjective political competence closed? *Canadian Journal of Political Science, 2*(45), 337–358.
Van Der Wal, Z. (2017). *The 21st century public manager*. London: Palgrave.
Van Wart, M. (2003). Public sector leadership theory: An assessment. *Public Administration Review, 63*(2), 214–228.
Van Wart, M. (2013). Administrative leadership theory: A reassessment after 10 years. *Public Administration, 91*(3), 521–543.
Van Wart, M. (2017). *Leadership in public organizations*. New York: Routledge.
Virtanen, P., & Stenvall, J. (2018). *Intelligent health policy. Theory, concept, practice*. Cham: Springer.

Chapter 5
Systemic Evaluation Approach to Meet the Challenges of Complexity

Mika Nieminen, Kirsi Hyytinen, Vesa Salminen, and Sampsa Ruutu

Abstract Traditional linear evaluation approaches are not able to address the dynamic interrelationships and feedback mechanisms involved in the increasingly complex social environment. To meet the challenges of complexity, new evaluation approaches are required. This chapter contributes to this discussion by suggesting a new integrative evaluation approach which combines foresight, multi-criteria evaluation and system dynamic modelling into the evaluation process. The developed methodology is applied in the evaluation of the Finnish Innovation Fund, Sitra.

5.1 Introduction

During the last few decades, our societies have become increasingly complex and systemic. This is due to various nested processes and developments related to technological, environmental and economic developments that have made the world and living increasingly networked and connected, phases of change more rapid and the results of change more unanticipated (e.g. Lawrence 2013). Techno-economic globalization has intensified interconnections between organizations and national economies (e.g. Castells 1996), and technological, social and economic development have become irreversibly amalgamated (e.g. Freeman and Louca 2002). Similar to economic development, socio-technical changes and related innovations

---

M. Nieminen (✉)
VTT Technical Research Centre of Finland, Tampere, Finland
e-mail: Mika.Nieminen@vtt.fi

K. Hyytinen
VTT Technical Research Centre of Finland, Espoo, Finland
e-mail: Kirsi.Hyytinen@vtt.fi

V. Salminen
4Front Ltd, Helsinki, Finland
e-mail: Vesa.Salminen@4front.fi

S. Ruutu
Gofore Ltd, Helsinki, Finland
e-mail: Sampsa.Ruutu@gofore.com

H. Lehtimäki et al. (eds.), *Society as an Interaction Space*, Translational Systems Sciences 22, https://doi.org/10.1007/978-981-15-0069-5_5

are taking place in complex systems that are generated and disseminated through collaboration between various interdependent actors (e.g. Edquist 2005; Geels and Schot 2007; Autio and Thomas 2013). In these systems, the relationships among the actors and socio-physical elements form complex direct and indirect causal linkages that increase the unpredictability in the system (Holland 1995). Problems encountered in these kinds of systems become "wicked" in the sense, in short, that there are no definite answers to them, only spatially and temporally one-off solutions (Rittel and Webber Melvin 1973).

Societal complexity calls for more advanced approaches with respect to governance mechanisms (see Lähteenmäki-Smith and Virtanen in this book) and information generation methods that contribute to governance. Linear and top-down approaches are unable to address the dynamic interrelationships and feedback mechanisms involved in the increasingly complex social environment. Therefore, there has been growing interest among evaluation scholars towards systemic evaluation approaches (e.g. Cabrera et al. 2008; Patton 2011; Forss et al. 2011; Hargreaves and Podems 2012; Williams and Hummelbrunner 2011; Mowles 2014; Nieminen and Hyytinen 2015; Hyytinen 2017) and attempts to develop novel evaluation approaches to meet the challenge of complexity. The specific character of systemic evaluation approaches has been their interest in the dynamic interrelationships between actors, actions and their contexts. The chief aim has been to understand the mechanisms of the complex interactions involved in producing end results and impacts (Cabrera et al. 2008).

While the recent literature includes system elements, the approaches and perspectives are dispersed across various research fields. Therefore, development of multi-method approaches and integration of the perspectives of social sciences and systems thinking are needed to provide more comprehensive approaches to evaluation (Hargreaves and Podems 2012; Patton 2011).

In this chapter, we contribute to this discussion by suggesting a new integrative evaluation approach which combines foresight, multi-criteria evaluation and system dynamic modelling into the evaluation process (Nieminen and Hyytinen 2015; Hyytinen 2017). It draws from the idea that the evaluation of dynamic and complex systems needs to include anticipatory elements, integrate a variety of actors and their views and take into account the complex direct and indirect interlinkages between different factors and actors affecting the system (Hyytinen 2017). The approach supports systemic change and its governance.

The developed methodology is applied in the evaluation of the Finnish Innovation Fund, Sitra, which operates as a high-mandate future-oriented change agency in Finland. Sitra is a unique organization focusing on societal reforms and which has been authorized by Parliament. Our aim is to provide understanding of how the new systemic evaluation approach can support strategic management and other development activities of an agency operating in a highly systemic environment. We do not report the evaluation and its results as such, but rather focus on methodological aspects and use the case to illustrate the application of our methodology. For those interested in the evaluation results, the evaluation report is publicly available with an executive summary in English.[1]

The chapter is structured as follows. In the following section, we introduce the multilevel perspective as a generic analytical framework for understanding systemic changes. In Sect. 5.3, we present a brief review of the earlier literature on systemic evaluation and examine the reasons why novel evaluation approaches are required. In Sect. 5.4, we introduce our evaluation approach, which integrates foresight, multi-criteria evaluation and system dynamic modelling into the evaluation process and describe how we have applied the approach in a concrete organization evaluation. In the final section, we discuss the pros and cons of the approach and suggest some future development ideas and potential application areas of the approach.

5.2 The Multilevel Perspective for Understanding Complex Systems

A useful and applicable theoretical framework for describing and analysing complex systemic change processes is the multilevel perspective (MLP) (Geels 2002, 2004; Geels and Schot 2007). Originally the framework was developed to describe changes in technological systems, but later it has been applied to understand wider socio-technical changes in various contexts. The theory emphasizes the dynamic and complex interaction between different levels of the system: socio-technical landscape at the top level, socio-technical regime at the middle level and niche innovations at the bottom level. Figure 5.1 illustrates the analytical levels of the socio-technical system.

According to the framework, the pressure to change in the system comes from the *socio-technical landscape*, which refers to an exogenous environment encompassing large-scale and long-term societal trends (e.g. striving for sustainability), cultural and normative values, policy beliefs and worldviews, as well as economic developments (e.g. depression, resource scarcity). Changes in the landscape consist of relatively slow-changing factors in society (Geels 2002, 2004; Kemp and Rotmans 2004).

In the middle of the model is the *regime* level, which refers to institutionalized practices, structures and self-evident action patterns of a system. The regime consists of five dimensions: available and used technologies, scientific institutions and paradigms, politics and administration, sociocultural values and symbols as well as users and markets, whose interaction maintains and changes the system. A regime can be, for instance, a certain industrial or societal sector. The regime level is the conservative element in the model. Typically, institutionalized practices and structures may create "lock-ins" to the system. Status quo is maintained so long as there is "compatibility" between the landscape level and the regime. If the structures and

[1] https://media.sitra.fi/2017/11/29120141/Selvityksia127.pdf

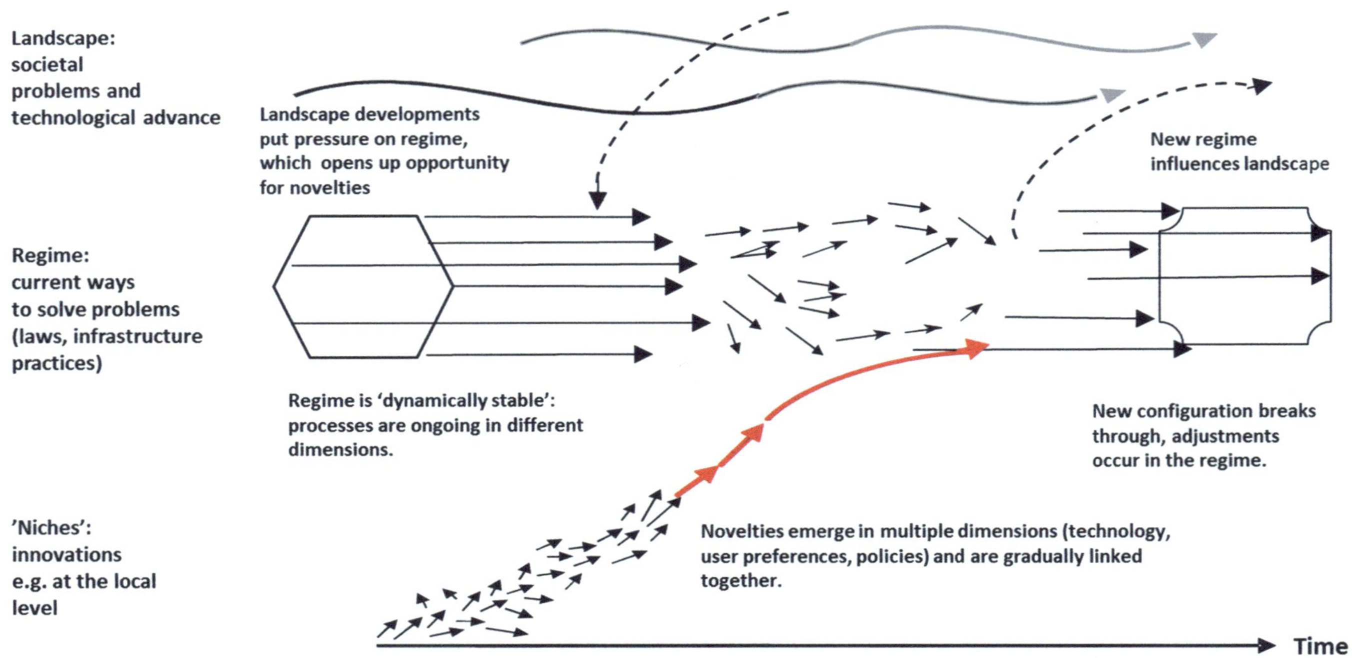

Fig. 5.1 Multilevel perspective of socio-technical change

action models in the regime are not compatible with the landscape, the regime is confronted with pressure from the landscape to change. This, in turn, may open up a window of opportunity for attempts to reform the regime (Berkhout et al. 2004; Geels 2002, 2004; Geels and Kemp 2007; Geels and Schot 2007; Kemp et al. 1998).

The third level in the framework, *niches*, refers to niche innovations and experiments that take place outside the regime. These renewals have the potential to reform or even transform the existing regime. A niche consists of a small niche market or protected and publicly supported segment where new innovation can be developed without fierce market competition that might kill it (ibid.).

The framework helps to analyse the long-term and dynamic process of system-level change by making visible the multiple actors, technologies, practices, resources and regulations that influence the development process. In addition, the framework shows that no single actor or factor in the system can promote systemic change alone. Instead, a system-level change requires the interaction of many actors and interconnections between parallel efforts to push through the change (Elzen et al. 2004; Geels 2002, 2004; Kemp et al. 2001; Kivisaari et al. 2004; Rip and Kemp 1998).

The analysis of dynamic complex systems from the multilevel perspective provides a fruitful starting point for the development of governance practices. In addition to multiple perspectives, the approach highlights that comprehensive understanding of a system and its development requires the integration of different methods (cf. Dyehouse et al. 2009; Williams and Imam 2007; Nieminen and Hyytinen 2015).

5.3 Towards Systemic Approaches in Evaluation

Traditionally, evaluations are based on linear approaches, crystallized in the idea of "logic models" (Kellogg Foundation 2004). These models consist of a linear continuum where inputs, activities, outputs, outcomes and impacts are connected by logical and causal pathways (Chen 2005; Dyehouse et al. 2009). While logic models can be acknowledged to be first attempts to understand a system, they do not explain the complex relationships and dynamics between system components and do not take into account that impacts emerge in a cyclic, complex and long-term process (Cozzens and Melkers 1997; Hansson 2006; Rip 2003; Tait and Williams 1999; van der Knaap 2006; Dyehouse et al. 2009; Kellogg Foundation 2004). While there are various variants of the linear approach, such as contribution analysis in which the core idea is that impacts are attributable to various contextual factors alongside the evaluated action (Mayne 2012), the basic idea of the approach remains the same.

Developmental evaluation is a promising evaluation approach (Patton 2011) that has been designed to conduct evaluation in complex societal environments. The main aim of the approach is to make sense of what emerges under the conditions of a complex system and to provide real-time responses to adapt to new conditions in the face of changes. At the core of the evaluation approach is a participatory process that supports multivoiced evaluation and continuous learning (Patton 2011). By means of anticipation, adjustment, reflection, multiple perspectives and continuous implementation, the approach increases understanding of the various factors and actors affecting the change and the various outcomes of it. The information gained by such an evaluation is especially valuable in complex and dynamic situations for supporting strategy building and development.

Other researchers have further developed and concretized Patton's ideas (e.g. Hargreaves and Podems 2012), among them systems researchers who have entered the field of evaluation and highlight the need for integrating systems thinking and specific methods with evaluation (Cabrera et al. 2008). Systems thinking and system dynamic modelling offer an alternative to the traditional evaluation approach, which relies on logic models and backward-looking input-output analyses. They make visible the "transformation processes that turn interventions into outcomes" (Chen 2005: 231). In this way, they tackle the challenge of "black-box evaluations: things go in and things come out, but what happens in between is a mystery" (Dyehouse et al. 2009: 187). By paying attention to the interaction between various actors and to long-term dynamic behaviour, system dynamic modelling helps to explain how complex interactions reduce, change or even hinder the emergence of impacts (Merril et al. 2013).

Despite a growing interest in systems thinking in evaluation during recent years (Cabrera et al. 2008; Dyehouse et al. 2009; Mayne 2012; Funnel and Rogers 2011; Patton 2011; Williams and Hummelbrunner 2011), systems approaches do not form the mainstream in the field; moreover, they are still unfamiliar to many evaluators. The plurality of systems approaches and methods and traditional barriers between research traditions are important background reasons for this situation and have hindered the utilization and integration of different systems approaches, especially among evaluators qualified in the social sciences (Hargreaves and Podems 2012).

5.4 An Integrative Approach: Foresight, Multi-criteria Evaluation and System Dynamic Modelling

In this chapter, we contribute to this discussion by suggesting a new integrative evaluation approach which combines foresight, multi-criteria evaluation and system dynamic modelling into the evaluation process (Nieminen and Hyytinen 2015; Hyytinen 2017). It draws from the idea that the evaluation of dynamic and complex systems needs to include anticipatory elements, integrate a variety of actors and their views and take into account the complex direct and indirect interlinkages between different factors and actors affecting the system (Hyytinen 2017).

Our evaluation approach is targeted at providing a comprehensive perspective on complex dynamic systems. To do so it integrates three perspectives, the *futures view, systems view* and *multi-actor view*, which are concretized with related methodologies (Hyytinen 2017). In the approach, *the futures view* orients towards long-term societal challenges, system-level drivers and forces that shape future directions. It emphasizes the possibility of many alternative futures (Martin and Irvine 1989; Martin 2010; Miles 2013) and an active stance in relation to their development (Miles 2013). The futures view can be concretized with various anticipatory methodologies, which contribute to the understanding of broad phenomena and directions for future development in society, e.g. demographic change, new social movements, shifts in political ideology, economic restructuring, emerging scientific paradigms and cultural developments (Geels 2005). Anticipatory approaches help to formulate scenarios for the development of a system and to set targets for reaching the most favourable vision. In this way, they support strategy and policy formulation and related decision-making. A central characteristic of such foresight-based approaches is an active stance: a shared view on how to "make the future together" (Martin and Irvine 1989).

The systems view understands the world in terms of wholes and relationships, rather than breaking the world into component parts (Hargreaves and Podems 2012; Sterman 2001). By emphasizing the structure and dynamics of the "whole", it increases understanding of the complexity of problems and of the variety of opportunities to solve them (Meadows 2008). From the methodological viewpoint, the systems view can be concretized with the integration of multi-criteria evaluation and system dynamic modelling (Hyytinen et al. 2014). Multi-criteria evaluation (Djellal and Gallouj 2013) provides information on the current stage of the system and the potential and realized impacts of selected actions from the perspectives of multiple values. It generates understanding of the past and current state of the prevailing system, including its structure and operations. Evaluation generates ex post evidence on how the actions taken have affected the development of the system. It helps to redirect policy instruments, i.e. to set ex ante operational targets for better performance and for better responses to the needs of the changing environment. System dynamic modelling (Forrester 2007; Sterman 2001) instead provides a formal and detailed analysis of the system's structure, including the interdependencies between system elements. It enables understanding of the complex interactions and feedback loops that affect the system dynamics. Improved understanding of the factors that enhance or hinder the emergence of opportunities for change helps to design robust strategies and policies and to find solutions to particular system-level problems. As an illustrative methodology, system dynamic modelling also fosters the emergence of "systems thinking" among the actors included. Constructing formal models and simulating policy options in the model help to understand impacts that are not usually that evident or visible.

The *multi-actor view* aims to promote flexibility, interconnectivity and cooperation. It drives the emergence of networked structures and highlights that the solutions to systemic problems require collaboration between multiple actors representing different sectors of society (Geels 2002, 2004; Windrum and García-Goñi 2008). In concrete terms, the multi-actor view concerns the participation of various relevant stakeholders in the evaluation process. Participatory approaches offer a multi-actor perspective on evaluation and support dialogue among various actors on setting the conditions for societal development. As the multi-actor view emphasizes the engagement of multiple actors, co-creation and networked decision-making (Rotmans and Loorbach 2009), it is beneficial for the implementation and diffusion of renewals.

5.5 A Systemic Evaluation in the Making

5.5.1 The Case Organization

The organization in which we piloted our approach was Sitra, the Finnish Innovation Fund.[2] Sitra is an independent public organization which reports directly to the Finnish Parliament, and its operations are funded by the return from endowment capital. It is an internationally unique think-and-do tank aimed at reforming Finnish society. Its mission is defined in legislation as "to promote stable and balanced development in Finland, qualitative and quantitative economic growth and international competitiveness and cooperation". For this purpose it establishes "projects that increase the efficiency of the economy, improve the level of education or research, or study future development scenarios".[3] Sitra defines itself currently as a "future house", whose mission "involves creating preconditions for reform, spurring everyone towards making a change and providing opportunities for co-operation. What it means in practice is that Sitra investigates, explores and develops operating models in close co-operation with other responsible operators (…)".[4]

Sitra's goals are large, systemic changes that involve multiple actors and impacts that are thus predominantly indirect and dependent on the actions of other actors. Sitra also facilitates changes by using various impact-generating mechanisms and measures. Theoretically, the interaction between Sitra and its operational environment can be described using the framework of a complex system where development is coevolutionary, based on the interaction of a number of elements and actors, and where impacts are usually indirect (e.g. Mitleton-Kelly 2007; Holling 2001; Holland 1995).

Wide social impacts may manifest themselves, for instance, in changes in behavioural patterns that are difficult to attribute to the operations of any one specific actor. The operations of the other actors create the changes in the system, and Sitra attempts to support the changes by collaborating with those actors. For instance, if the target is to renew the national economy, the actual actors are companies, various clusters of companies or the public administration, which regulates and steers the development of the national economy. Due to these indirect impact paths, there may also be considerable time gaps between actions and their observed impacts. On the

[2] See more of Sitra at https://www.sitra.fi/en/.

[3] Sitra law (only in Finnish) Laki Suomen itsenäisyyden juhlarahastosta. 24.8.1990/717 http://www.finlex.fi/fi/laki/ajantasa/1990/19900717

[4] https://www.sitra.fi/en/topics/facts-about-sitra/

other hand, change can take place rapidly if the interaction of the elements maintaining the system changes radically.

Due to this systemic nature of Sitra's goals and activities, it was evident that evaluation by traditional impact metrics would have been challenging and possibly misleading. Therefore, our approach was based from the outset on a systemic approach that we had previously started to develop (Nieminen and Hyytinen 2015; Hyytinen 2017) and now had an opportunity to develop further.

Sitra's organizational approach to supporting societal renewal is currently based on wide-ranging societal programmes in broad thematic areas, such as "capacity for renewal", "carbon-neutral circular economy" and "new working life and sustainable economy". Our case evaluation focused on Sitra's strategic area "Towards renewing and inclusive economy", which covers a broad range of actions and projects. At the time of the evaluation, we identified a total of 23 actions and projects in this area run at different periods during the years 2010–2017.[5]

5.5.2 *Data and Methods*

To create a holistic and multi-perspective understanding of Sitra's operations and complex impact paths in this area, we followed the idea of using a combination of various methods and data in a systemic evaluation (Dyehouse et al. 2009; Williams and Imam 2007; Patton 2011). In a system-based approach, triangulation (e.g. Denzin 2006) is of high importance as there are various system dimensions and actors involved, their significance in the processes is difficult to establish and the understanding of the whole necessitates learning about various perspectives, interests and connections in the system. Thus, we used various data sources and methods, from qualitative data and thematic interpretation to quantitative measurement and modelling, to develop a comprehensive understanding of the organization and its operations. In addition, we applied investigator triangulation, which helped to extend the scope of interpretations and validate them through joint discussion of the findings. We gathered the following three different sets of data:

- Documents, statistical material and organizational evaluation data, including Sitra's programme and project reports and other materials; stakeholders' strategy papers, reports, studies and web pages; and Sitra's internal evaluation and monitoring data. This data was used to create a general understanding of Sitra's operations, of the way Sitra had itself understood and created impact paths, and to tentatively assess the progress towards the impact goals and Sitra's role in them.
- Interviews of Sitra's programme and project managers and related stakeholders (totalling 14 persons from Sitra and 45 stakeholder representatives from 41

[5] The more detailed results are published in the evaluation report (executive summary is available in English; the whole report is available only in Finnish) and publicly available at https://media.sitra.fi/2017/11/29120141/Selvityksia127.pdf.

different organizations). This data served to generate a multi-perspective view of Sitra's operations and impacts. Especially important was to give a voice to the stakeholders, which assessed Sitra from their various societal and interest positions. A given action or impact might have different meanings depending on the value context and perspective of the observer. In a complex and indefinite systemic environment, there is rarely any definite answer to the emerging challenges or any clear-cut definition of a successful impact (e.g. Eoyang and Holladay 2013).

- Finally, we organized three stakeholder workshops to (a) strengthen the developmental dialogue and process with the stakeholders (cf. Patton 2011), (b) create a system dynamic model of Sitra's operations and systemic impact paths and (c) connect more explicitly the future perspective with the impact assessment with the help of system dynamic model. We used the model to understand and make visible the systemic complexity of Sitra's operations and operational environment as well as to create an anticipatory instrument for the future development of Sitra. Briefly, a system dynamic model is either a mathematical or descriptive model of the causal linkages and feedback loops among various actors and elements in a complex situation or environment (for a more detailed description of the method, see, e.g. Sterman 2001). We used the system dynamic model qualitatively to describe the systemic interconnectedness and interactions in the Sitra's operational environment. In practice, we discussed with the stakeholders the impact paths and causal linkages between various elements and actors and co-created with them a detailed descriptive model of Sitra's systemic operations (see the model in the following section).

5.5.3 Application of the Approach

As discussed previously (see Sect. 5.2), we used the multilevel perspective (MLP) (e.g. Geels and Schot 2007) as a general theoretical framework to position and interpret Sitra's activities in the Finnish politico-economic system. With this framework we were able to reflect on and conceptualize Sitra's societal role as an actor that facilitates renewal of the politico-economic system (regime in the MLP) and cultivates new solutions in protected programme spaces (niches in the MLP).

We used the framework to help enhance the multi-actor view of impact attribution. In order to identify the relevant actor and system dimensions with which Sitra is most likely to collaborate in order to support system-level changes, we used the MLP regime dimensions: in order to support societal renewal in the chosen strategic areas, Sitra should be able to identify and engage with these dimensions and actors and their interactions. This formed our initial "theory of change" (e.g. Funnel and Rogers 2011) with which we worked throughout the evaluation.

As it soon turned out that the original MLP dimensions (see Sect. 5.2) did not describe the actors with which Sitra was operating accurately enough, we adjusted the theoretical dimensions (although still in concordance with the original MLP approach) to better follow Sitra's operational environment. As the system dimensions in the MLP are rather general, they are likely to need adaptation and tailoring if a more detailed view is needed. The system dimensions and related actor categories we identified were (a) politics and government including politicians, policy-makers and civil servants; (b) the private sector, enterprises and entrepreneurs; (c) science, research and technology including universities and research institutes; (d) the third sector, i.e. NGOs; (e) private citizens; and (f) media and culture including journalists, media houses and cultural influencers.

This created the general "system framework" against which we evaluated the success of Sitra's processes as a system actor or "orchestrator" (Ritala et al. 2009) of various systemic renewal processes. As the assessment of the social impacts is highly challenging and attributable to various actors and system elements, it is important to understand how the impacts are generated, what kinds of impact paths there are and how effectively the various paths are addressed.

Table 5.1 presents a summary of our analysis across various programmes of the strategic area "towards renewing and inclusive economy" and provides a general view of our approach and an example of one way of implementing the approach. The table summarizes and simplifies our findings and interpretations based on the various data sources, from qualitative documents and interviews to quantitative sources. In the table, the symbol ++ indicates strong connection with and addressing of the system dimension, + indicates fair connection with and actions in the system dimension and – indicates no connection with or actions in the system dimension.

By using this system framework as the basis of the analysis, we were able to conclude that Sitra has the ability to address and engage different actors successfully through various channels. It has, for instance, contributed to public discussion, influenced policy-makers, facilitated network formation, negotiated and created shared goals and supported pilot projects. However, as indicated in the table, the focus of Sitra's activities is on politics, administration and the private sector. While this is understandable due to the nature of Sitra's mission as an actor supporting the renewal of society, it also makes visible a critical development need for broader impact pathways.

Another important dimension in our approach was qualitative case studies. We selected two projects from each key area to be studied more closely; these case studies served several important functions in the evaluation. The case studies:

(a) Helped to establish a more detailed view of impacts, impact paths and mechanisms
(b) Helped to form a multi-actor view of concrete actions and impacts
(c) Increased our understanding of systemic connections and dynamics and thus helped to create the first versions of the system dynamic model
(d) Provided evidence on societal impacts

One of the qualitative findings was that Sitra used various methods simultaneously to attain its goals and to reach a variety of stakeholders to support systemic changes. As a system orchestrator, it is important not only to address various systemic dimensions and corresponding actors but also to use various methods to

Table 5.1 An example of multidimensional analysis of impact paths: summary of Sitra's engagement with system dimensions and actors

Key domain (projects)	Politics	Admin.	Third sector	Citizens	Private sector	Science	Labour markets	Media	Technology
Leading public sector	++	++	-	-	-	-	-	-	-
Resource-wise citizen	-	-	-	++	++	-	-	-	++
Sustainabale welfare	+	+	++	++	+	+	+	++	-
Changeable working life	++	++	+	+	+	++	++	-	-
Circular economy	++	++	++	+	++	+	-	++	+
Isaacus	+	++	+	+	++	+	-	-	++
SUUNTA collaboration	++	++	-	-	+	-	-	-	-
Impact investing	++	++	++	+	++	-	+	-	-
Basic income trial	++	++	+	+	-	+	++	++	-
Carbon neutral industry	+	+	-		++	+	-	-	+
Active citizen	+	++	++	++	+	-	-	-	-
Sustainabale economic policy education	++	++	++	-	-	+	+	+	-
Resource wise region	+	++	+	+	+	+	-	+	+
Welfare from knowledge	++	++	+	+	++	+	-	+	++
Enabling information society	++	++	-	+	+	-	-	-	++
Industrial symbiosis	++	++	-	-	++	-	-	-	-
Green economy solutions	+	++	++	+	++	+	-	-	+
Welfare business from nature	-	-	-	+	++	+	-	+	+
Leadership	+	++	+		-	-	++	-	+
Energy programme	++	++	++	+	++	+	-	+	+

maximize the expected impact. This is important also from the governance perspective. The mechanisms used by Sitra included:

- "Sense making" about new concepts and ideas
- Setting agendas and facilitating conversations about societal challenges and new solutions
- Network building around recognized challenges or solutions
- Pilot projects and trials to test potential new solutions, establish new behaviours or practices and build political support
- Administrative renewals to support change by influencing policy-makers

One concrete example of how Sitra utilizes various mechanisms was the advancement of circular economy in Finland, an area in which Sitra had influenced governmental strategy documents, facilitated creating business ecosystems and pilots and influenced public discourse through the media.

The cases also underscored the importance of including various stakeholders and actors from different system dimensions in our evaluation. The various interpretations of impacts and impact paths fruitfully valorized Sitra's operations from different angles and provided evidence of different impact paths. Without relatively wide-ranging interviews, our view of the systemic mechanisms and significance of Sitra as a system orchestrator would have remained notably narrower. The interviews provided information on and assessments of Sitra's ways of acting and societal impacts. The cases corroborated our tentative view that the main benefit of Sitra is its ability to engage in systemic change in ways that are not possible for any other actor in the Finnish system. They also clearly indicated how complex and long term a process the materialization of a societal impact can be. The impact is dependent on various actors, their actions and right timing. The latter observation was revealed in several cases and seems to refer to the significance of the "window of opportunity" as defined in system transition theory (e.g. Geels and Schot 2007). From the network governance perspective, the cases also highlighted Sitra's need to deepen its already existing and wide interaction with stakeholders and increase transparency to enable the stakeholders to prepare and commit to the activities. This is critical for an actor whose impacts are dependent on other actors and indirect influencing.

The cases provided the basis for the system dynamic model of Sitra's societal activities and impact paths.[6] Tentative drafts of the model were created by the authors, but were further developed and discussed in collaborative and co-creative workshops to which we invited relevant stakeholder representatives and experts from Sitra. The workshops served to initiate and strengthen developmental dialogue between the stakeholders and Sitra and to create a shared understanding of the impact paths and feedback loops in Sitra's operational environment. The model presented in Fig. 5.2 summarizes the findings of the systemic evaluation in a condensed form and describes the complex dynamics, connections and mutual

[6] Before formulating the comprehensive system dynamic model, two narrower models were created to describe the dynamics of the two selected case areas. These models helped to create the comprehensive model.

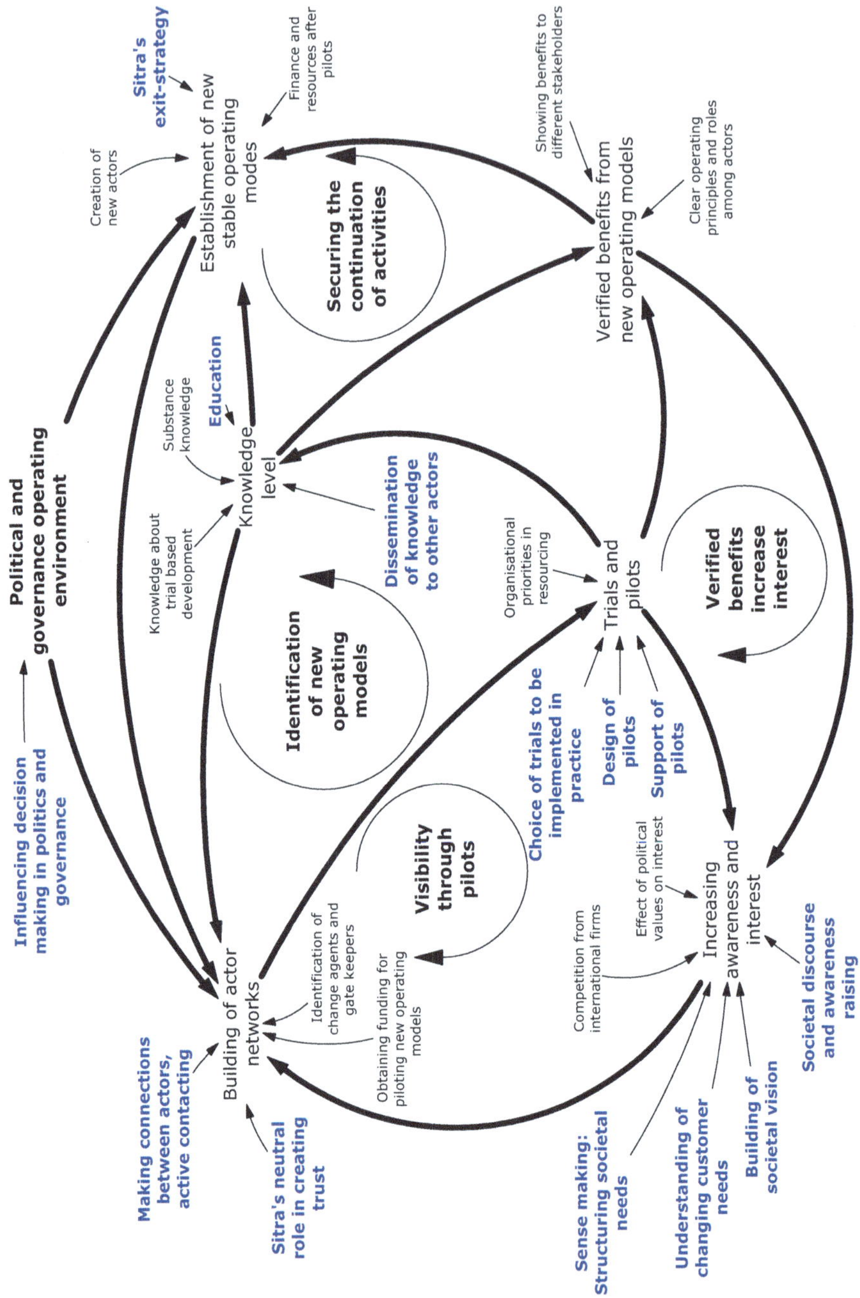

Fig. 5.2 System dynamic model of Sitra's actions and impact paths

dependencies of the various actions and impact paths. Besides being an instrument for understanding an organization's operational logic and impact creation, the model can also be used for anticipatory planning of future operations and for identifying network governance challenges.

In short, the model indicates how the advancement of new development themes requires awareness and interest in them to be raised. This is not, however, a simple process; various actions, from sense making to societal vision building, are needed. Furthermore, verified benefits increase interest, but benefits can only be verified by successful pilots and trials, which, in turn, are dependent on networks of actors who are interested in the development in question. At best, this may create a positive feedback loop, which increases awareness and the number of interested actors, which, in turn, makes new societal trials possible. However, some of these elements may remain too weak to initiate successful societal pilot activity and changes in practices, which also means that the societal impacts may remain modest.

The model also shows how Sitra's societal impact is highly dependent on other actors and on Sitra's ability to actively network these actors and "persuade" them to participate in solutions to societal challenges. This creates possibilities for new societal trials and pilots that raise knowledge and awareness of the issue and verify its benefits. These factors, in turn, affect, alongside political support, the stabilization of new operating models and practices in society.

Successful operation also requires a lot of learning, collection of information, codification of information and explaining or interpreting information ("sense making") to various actors. Knowledge and learning directly affect the establishment of new operating modes, the continuation of activities and network extension. Indirectly, they also increase awareness and interest, as well as new trials and pilots. From this perspective, knowledge and awareness raising can be seen as a central element of impact creation.

Although the model is a simplification of a complex reality, it indicates how complex and systemic the operational environment of a single organization can be. It suggests that evaluations based merely on linear models might lead to biased conclusions of the impacts and, especially, of the processes by which impacts are created. There are several concurrent and interconnected processes that directly or indirectly affect each other by either bolstering or diluting each other. In addition, alongside macro-level societal trends, such as economic development, a number of various actors are involved, and not all of the factors affecting their choices can be controlled.

5.6 Conclusions

In this chapter we have argued for a systemic evaluation approach, introduced an elaborated version of our earlier ideas (e.g. Nieminen and Hyytinen 2015; Hyytinen 2017) and illustrated an application of our approach in the case context of a Finnish organization operating as a future-oriented societal change agency.

Table 5.2 The three evaluation perspectives examined and their study approaches and research methods and contribution to systemic evaluation

Perspectives on evaluation	Study approaches and research methods	Contribution to evaluation
Futures view	MLP as an approach framing the analysis of documents and interviews	• Understanding of complex future developments • Directions for future developments • Managing transitions and supporting systemic change
Systems view	Multi-criteria evaluation as an approach to qualitative case studies	• Generating impact mechanisms • Connections to other system actors and dimensions • Making visible different values and interpretations of impacts
	System dynamic modelling to understand complex interrelations and feedbacks	• Generating impact paths • Understanding complex interrelations and feedback loops between impact mechanisms
Multi-actor view	Empowerment and developmental evaluation approach in participatory workshops	• Dialogic process of various stakeholders to generate impact paths • Reflectiveness and responsiveness to development needs • Dialogic process to support planning and transition management

As our social environment becomes increasingly complex and systemic, evaluation needs to tackle multidimensional, interconnected and indirectly developing systemic impacts. To provide a comprehensive view of this complex and systemic environment, evaluation should include anticipatory elements (futures view) and take into account the multitude of actors and their interests and views (multi-actor view) and the complex direct and indirect interlinkages between different factors and actors (systems view) (Hyytinen 2017). Table 5.2 summarizes the three perspectives to evaluation examined, how they were concretized as study approaches and research methods and their contribution to systemic evaluation.

We applied the multilevel perspective (MLP) as a general theoretical framework to formulate a systemic theory of change, to enhance the multi-actor view of impact attribution, to identify relevant actors and to analyse mechanisms to support systemic changes. The theoretical view was complemented empirically by using methodological triangulation (e.g. Denzin 2006), which supports the creation of comprehensive understanding of the various dimensions, perspectives, interests and connections in a system.

By utilizing various data sources, from documents to interviews, we first analysed to which extent our case organization was able to support systemic change and related processes by connecting itself to various system dimensions and actors and thus contributing to system change. This analysis was complemented by qualitative case studies, which provided a more detailed view of the impact mechanisms and impacts. In the final phase, a more detailed description of operations and impact paths was created in the form of system dynamic models, which were generated in the dialogic processes of various stakeholders. These models made visible the multiplicity of indirect causal linkages and feedback loops and provided a dynamic view of the future planning of operations.

We suggest that compared to various data-driven evaluation approaches, our systemic evaluation provides a more robust theoretical basis for understanding complex and indirect impact paths and, thus, also provides a more realistic view of change processes. The strength of the approach is that it identifies the multiplicity of actors and elements affecting the generation of impacts. Furthermore, the empirical analysis is based on a well-argued theoretical model. The rich and multifarious empirical data and stakeholder workshops supported the creation of a necessary multi-perspective view of the analysed processes. In a multi-actor system, there are various perspectives and value positions from which the impacts can be assessed. The approach also enhances our understanding of the complex feedback loops and intermediary linkages between various elements and actors in the system by using system dynamic modelling as a visualization tool. The modelling increases the precision of description of the attributing elements and actors. The approach also includes strong developmental evaluation-related characteristics, as the modelling is supported by collaborative and co-creative workshops, which further enhance dialogue between the organization and the stakeholders.

However, the approach also has its challenges. Firstly, the methodology is still in its early development phase, and more studies and pilots are needed to test the generalizability of the method. The approach should be tested and developed in various societal contexts and organizations to find its limits and to make it more concrete and easy to use. Secondly, testing the usability and relevance of various other analytical methods would be an important part of the integrative approach. Thirdly, system-level impacts are often difficult to define, and, due to their qualitative nature, they are difficult to measure with unambiguous indicators. Instead of concrete indicators, our approach has focused so far on the identification of impact mechanisms and paths. This sets a clear challenge for further methodological development: How should robust and dynamic indicators that are valid and reliable for describing systemic changes be developed? The development of systemic process and impact indicators would be highly desirable, especially for the governance, monitoring and steering of complex systems.

References

Autio, E., & Thomas, L. D. W. (2013). Innovation ecosystems. In M. Dodgson, D. Gann, & N. Phillips (Eds.), *Oxford handbook of innovation management* (pp. 204–288). Oxford: Oxford University Press.

Berkhout, F., Smith, A., & Stirling, A. (2004). Socio-technical regimes and transition contexts. In B. Elzen, F. W. Geels, & K. Green (Eds.), *System innovation and the transition to sustainability* (pp. 48–75). Cheltenham: Edward Elgar. https://doi.org/10.4337/9781845423421.00013.

Cabrera, D., Colosi, L., & Lobdell, C. (2008). Systems thinking. *Evaluation and Program Planning, 31*, 299–310.
Castells, M. (1996). *The rise of the network society, the information age: Economy, society and culture* (Vol. I). Cambridge and Oxford: Blackwell.
Chen, H. T. (2005). Theory driven evaluation. In S. Mathison (Ed.), *Encyclopedia of evaluation* (pp. 415–419). Thousand Oaks: Sage.
Cozzens, S., & Melkers, J. (1997). Use and usefulness of performance measurement in state science and technology programs. *Policy Studies Journal, 25*(3), 425–435.
Denzin, N. (2006). *Sociological methods: A sourcebook* (5th ed.). Piscataway: Aldine Transaction.
Djellal, F., & Gallouj, F. (2013). The productivity challenge in services: Measurement and strategic perspectives. *The Service Industries Journal, 33*(3–4), 282–299.
Dyehouse, M., Bennett, D., Harbor, J., Childress, A., & Dark, M. (2009). A comparison of linear and systems thinking approaches for program evaluation illustrated using Indiana Interdisciplinary GK-12. *Evaluation and Program Planning, 32*, 187–196.
Edquist, C. (2005). Reflections on the systems of innovation approach. *Science and Public Policy, 31*(6), 485–489.
Elzen, B., Geels, F. W., & Green, K. (2004). *System innovation and the transition to sustainability*. Cheltenham and Northampton: Edward Elgar.
Eoyang, G., & Holladay, R. (2013). *Adaptive action: Leveraging uncertainty in your organization*. Stanford: Stanford University Press.
Forrester, J. W. (2007). System dynamics—The next fifty years. *System Dynamics Review, 23*(2/3), 359–370.
Forss, K., Marra, M., & Schwartz, R. (2011). *Evaluating the complex: Attribution, contribution, and beyond*. London: Transaction Publishers.
Freeman, C., & Louca, F. (2002). *As time goes by: From the industrial revolutions to the information revolution*. Oxford: Oxford University Press.
Funnel, S. C., & Rogers, P. J. (2011). *Purposeful program theory: Effective use of theories of change and logic models*. San Francisco: Jossey-Bass.
Geels, F. W. (2002). Technological transitions as evolutionary reconfiguration processes: A multi-level perspective and a case-study. *Research Policy, 31*, 1257–1274.
Geels, F. W. (2004). From sectoral systems of innovation to socio-technical systems. Insights about dynamics and change from sociology and institutional theory. *Research Policy, 33*, 897–920.
Geels, F. W. (2005). *System innovation and the transition to sustainability. Theory, evidence and policy*. Cheltenham: Edward Elgar.
Geels, F. W., & Kemp, R. (2007). Dynamics in socio-technical systems: Typology of change processes and contrasting case studies. *Technology in Society, 29*(4), 441–455.
Geels, F. W., & Schot, J. (2007). Typology of sociotechnical transition pathways. *Research Policy, 36*, 399–417.
Hansson, F. (2006). Organisational use of evaluation. *Evaluation, 12*(2), 159–178.
Hargreaves, M. B., & Podems, D. (2012). Advancing systems thinking in evaluation: A review of four publications. *American Journal of Evaluation, 33*, 462–470.
Holland, J. H. (1995). *Hidden order: How adaptation builds complexity*. New York: Basic Books.
Holling, C. S. (2001). Understanding the complexity of economic, ecological, and social systems. *Ecosystems, 4*(5), 390–405. https://doi.org/10.1007/s10021-001-0101-5.
Hyytinen, K. (2017). *Supporting service innovation via evaluation: A future oriented, systemic and multi-actor approach*. Doctoral dissertation 14/2017, Aalto University publication series. VTT Science 146. Retrieved from http://www.vtt.fi/inf/pdf/science/2017/S146.pdf
Hyytinen, K., Ruutu, S., Nieminen, M., Gallouj, F., & Toivonen, M. (2014). A system dynamic and multi-criteria evaluation of innovations in environmental services. *Economics and Policy of Energy and the Environment, 3*, 29–52.
Kellogg Foundation. (2004). *Using logic models to bring together planning, evaluation & action logic model development guide*. Battle Creek: Kellogg Foundation. Retrieved from https://www.wkkf.org/resource-directory/resource/2010/w-k-kellogg-foundation-evaluation-handbook.

Kemp, R., Rip, A., & Schot, J. (2001). Constructing transition paths through the management of niche. In R. Garud & P. Karnoe (Eds.), *Path dependency and creation* (pp. 269–299). Mahwah: Lawrence Erlbaum.

Kemp, R., & Rotmans, J. (2004). Managing the transition to sustainable mobility. In B. Elzen, F. Geels, & K. Green (Eds.), *System innovation and the transition to sustainability: Theory, evidence and policy* (pp. 137–167). Cheltenham: Edgar Elgar.

Kemp, R., Schot, J., & Hoogma, R. (1998). Regime shifts to sustainability through processes of niche formation. The approach of strategic niche management. *Technology Analysis and Strategic Management, 10*(2), 175–195.

Kivisaari, S., Lovio, R., & Väyrynen, E. (2004). Managing experiments for transition: Examples of societal embedding in energy and health care sectors. In B. Elzen, F. W. Geels, & K. Green (Eds.), *System innovation and the transition to sustainability. Theory, evidence and policy* (pp. 223–250). Cheltenham: Edward Elgar.

Lawrence, K. (2013). *Developing leaders in VUCA environment*. Retrieved January 24, 2017, from http://www.growbold.com/2013/developing-leaders-in-a-vuca-environment_UNC.2013.pdf

Martin, B. R. (2010). The origins of the concept of 'foresight' in science and technology: An insider's perspective. *Technological Forecasting and Social Change, 77*, 1438–1447.

Martin, B. R., & Irvine, J. (1989). *Research foresight: Priority-setting in science*. London and New York: Pinter Publishers.

Mayne, J. (2012). Contribution analysis: Coming of age? *Evaluation, 18*, 270–280.

Meadows, D. H. (2008). Thinking in systems. A primer. Chelsea Green, White River Junction.

Merril, J. A., Deegan, M., Wilson, R., Kaushal, R., & Frederiks, K. (2013). A system dynamics evaluation model: Implementation of health information exchange for public health reporting. *Journal of the American Medical Informatics Association, 20*, 131–138.

Miles, I. (2013). Interactive impacts—Foresight as a product, service and coproduction process. In D. Dirk Meissner, L. Gokhberg, & A. Sokolov (Eds.), *Technology and innovation policy for the future: Potentials and limits of foresight studies* (pp. 63–82). Berlin: Springer.

Mitleton-Kelly, E. (Ed.). (2007). *Complex systems and evolutionary perspectives on organizations. The application of complexity theory to organizations*. Bingley, UK: Emerald.

Mowles, C. (2014). Complex, but not quite complex enough: The turn to the complexity sciences in evaluation scholarship. *Evaluation, 20*(2), 160–175. https://doi.org/10.1177/1356389014527885.

Nieminen, M., & Hyytinen, K. (2015). Future-oriented impact assessment: Supporting strategic decision-making in complex socio-technical environments. *Evaluation, 21*(4), 448–461.

Patton, M. Q. (2011). *Developmental evaluation: Applying complexity concepts to enhance innovation and use*. New York: Guilford.

Rip, A., & Kemp, R. (1998). Technological change. In S. Rayner & E. J. Malone (Eds.), *Human choice and climate change: Vol. 2. Resources and technology* (pp. 327–399). Battelle Press: Columbus.

Rip, A. (2003). Societal challenges for R&D evaluation. In P. Shapira & S. Kuhlmann (Eds.), *Learning from science and technology policy evaluation: Experiences from the United States and Europe* (pp. 35–59). Cheltenham: Edward Elgar.

Ritala, P., Armila, L., & Blomqvist, K.-M. (2009). Innovation orchestration capability—Defining the organizational and individual level determinants. *International Journal of Innovation Management, 13*(4), 569–591.

Rittel, H., & Webber Melvin, M. (1973). Dilemmas in a general theory of planning. *Policy Sciences, 4*, 155–169.

Rotmans, J., & Loorbach, D. (2009). Complexity and transition management. *Journal of Industrial Ecology, 13*(2), 184–196.

Sterman, J. D. (2001). System dynamics modeling: Tools for learning in a complex world. *California Management Review, 43*(4), 8–25.

Tait, J., & Williams, R. (1999). Policy approaches to research and development: foresight, framework and competitiveness. *Science and Public Policy, 26*(2), 101–112.

van der Knaap, P. (2006). Performance evaluation and performance management. Overcoming the downsides of policy objectives and performance indicators. *Evaluation, 12*(3), 278–293.

Williams, B., & Hummelbrunner, R. (2011). *Systems concepts in action. A practitioner's Toolkit*. Stanford: Stanford University Press.

Williams, B., & Imam, I. (Eds.). (2007). *Systems concepts in evaluation: An expert anthology*. Point Reyes: Edge Press of Inverness.

Windrum, P., & García-Goñi, M. (2008). A neo-Schumpeterian model of health services innovation. *Research Policy, 37*(4), 649–672.

Chapter 6
Participative Policymaking in Complex Welfare System: A Delphi Study

Hanna-Kaisa Pernaa

Abstract Shared, experience-driven and value-based perspectives in an ongoing interaction of agents constitute the basis of the coevolutionary dynamics of a complex system. The interpretation of good governance comprehends participation as increasingly fundamental in approaching policies in complex systems. This chapter presents a Delphi study of the possibilities and obstacles of participative policymaking (PPM) in municipal welfare services viewed by an expert panel consisting of 37 participants representing the executive managers of third-sector organizations, the chairmen of the municipal councils or welfare service boards and the leading office-holders of municipal welfare offices in Finland. The panel estimated and discussed the projections of participatory welfare policymaking in 2030. The outcomes of the study indicate that regardless of technological preparedness and the structural opportunities offered by a reform, cultural inertia and unawareness generate attitudes inhibitory on PPM practices. Albeit participative practices were considered influential to policymaking legitimacy as well as central to the nature of equal and flexible resource distribution, there were reservations about the inclusion of the participation. There were concerns over the validity and the liability of the decisions reached by participative means. Several undercurrents affecting the development of PPM were discernible in the conversations.

6.1 Introduction

Shared, experience-driven and value-based perspectives in an ongoing interaction of agents constitute the basis of the coevolutionary dynamics of a complex system. The ability to review and challenge the validity of a policy by various stakeholders requires a novel mindset of the policymaking process (McGlade and Garnsey 2006: 10–12; Boulton et al. 2015: 212–214, 219). Engaging the public in the ownership of policymaking processes has shaped the public administrative theories (e.g., Pyun and Gamassou 2018) and policymaking practices toward enabling coevolutionary

H.-K. Pernaa (✉)
University of Vaasa, Vaasa, Finland
e-mail: hanna-kaisa.pernaa@uva.fi

H. Lehtimäki et al. (eds.), *Society as an Interaction Space*, Translational Systems Sciences 22, https://doi.org/10.1007/978-981-15-0069-5_6

practices (Mitleton-Kelly 2011b). In the welfare service context, the small marginal group of large-scale service consumers (see Perttola and Pernaa 2016) should be of considerable relevance in the comprehension of the systemic policy influences. Yet although widely approved, the citizen participation in policymaking processes is developing at slow pace (Raisio 2010; Möttönen 2012; Monno and Khakee 2012).

This chapter presents a Delphi study of the future of participative policymaking development in Finnish public welfare services, viewed by an expert panel consisting of 37 participants representing the executive managers of third-sector organizations, the chairmen of the municipal councils or welfare service boards and the leading officeholders of municipal welfare offices. The panel estimated and discussed the projections of participatory welfare policymaking in 2030. The majority of research focused on the citizen engagement takes place in organizations and networks (Nabatchi 2012), usually with an objective to elucidate the variety of participative practices. This case study presents an untypical yet significant, policymaking experts' perspective to the unspoken inertia in the construction of civic engagement culture in policymaking practices. With respect to the fact of any model's inability to offer a comprehensive description of a complex system, this study provides examination and illumination of the prospects, incentives, impediments and undercurrents affecting the participatory development in Finnish welfare service policymaking. The main result of the study can be formulated as a contradiction between the complex systems' ability to create new order and the inability of polity to recast the social policies to be more responsive to the changing societal demands.

The chapter begins by describing the welfare service system complexity and the significance of the participative societal advocacy in the complex system coevolution and further, in the context of welfare policymaking. The introduction of the Delphi research method and the study description is followed by an outline of the study process and the discussion of the results.

6.2 Welfare Services as Complex Systems

Perceiving complexity sciences as a contributing field and complexity as a constituent part of policy processes is gaining ground in public administrative discourse (Eppel 2012, 2017). Any public administrative entity can be perceived as a complex social system with several levels, layers and clusters each composed of individuals with social interrelations. Even if the features of a single, interacting part contribute to the entity of a complex system, it cannot be scrutinized merely by its parts. A change in any part of the system does not indicate a linear and predictable outcome, but a variety of repercussions (Eppel 2017; Byrne 2001: 14). This "entanglement" of numerous elements and individuals enables creativity and dynamics and, furthermore, mutual dependence even between organizations and their environments (Haynes 2015: 19).

Understanding the parts of a system as components of the whole emphasizes the comprehension of their integration and mutual relationships (Capra and Luisi 2014:

63–64; 80–81). Welfare services[1] have an indirect relationship with political choices by bidirectional implications for national economy (e.g., Pierson 2000; Seaford 2014) and, more directly, the *salutogenic*[2] assets for individual health and well-being. Put in a complex entity of people with a varying scope of personal and subjective needs, welfare services can be understood and evaluated normatively on the basis set by independent welfare policies and their efficacy—or impotence—of prevailing societal conditions (Spicker 2008: 17–36).

The association of policymaking and knowledge utilization in public administration has transformed from the rational, information-based decisions to using the knowledge for the understanding and steering of complex realities (Parsons 2004) and to recognizing the interdependencies of economic, societal, and environmental policies (Adams and Wiseman 2003; Boulton et al. 2015: 212–213). As a result of this development, the public policymaking and governance requires progress from "apparent simplicity and rationality" of the bureaucratic and market rationalism toward "balance, accountability and engagement in complex policy environments" (ibid: 22).

The perception of a successful change in any human, complex system is one carried out by shifting of the approach from structures to processes (Capra and Luisi 2014: 81) and consequently appreciating and enabling the equal interplay between different dimensions and levels of interaction within the system (Goergen et al. 2010: 4–5). It is also intrinsic to its characteristics: the emergence of new phenomena arising from the connectivity and, at the same time, the ability to create new order. The multiple layers of the underlying and sometimes implicit causes of problem spaces take place contextually. The same also holds true for appropriate means of addressing issues distinctive to a particular system. Instead of seeking an all-embracing solution to several, sometimes overlapping issues, the primary administrative objective should be fostering an adaptable and enabling environment for coevolution (Goergen et al. 2010: 4–22).

6.3 Coevolution Claims Participation

Due to the anti-reductionist nature—the inability to analyze a complex system by examining its parts—evolution and holism, the two major components of complexity, are inseparable (Byrne 2001: 15). Societies seen from complexity perspective are in continuous evolution with emerging and changing dynamics, political and ideological movements and by—hopefully—learning from them. The process of choosing our societal objectives and our mutual interactions accordingly becomes

---

[1] In this study, "welfare" is understood in its widest sense, referring to the well-being of the citizens, and "welfare services" as a collective service provision to enhance it.

[2] The concept introduced by medical sociologist Aaron Antonovsky portrays the human *abilities and resources to develop positively*, underlining the societal arrangements to utilize those capabilities (Eriksson and Lindström 2014).

essential in the state of flux and proliferating uncertainty. Even if the increasing amount of data enhances the knowledge and awareness of interconnectedness in complex issues, it does not exclude ethical and moral discourse. The effect is emphasized in globally paramount issues, such as global warming. Scientific approach is essential but calls for extensive engagement in the process of creating ethical and justifiable policies (Mannermaa 1988; Dennard et al. 2008; Collins 2010).

It is characteristic of any complex, human system to have multiple and interrelated challenges with several dimensions and ways to address them. This becomes emphasized in decision-making and in fundamental systemic changes. The true respect of the complex, interactive dimensions affecting a problem space requires engaging the problem owners in its examination (Mitleton-Kelly 2011a). Accumulating the data and multifaceted elucidations of policy issues is a prerequisite for adapting them to local circumstances, to learn from them, as well as to create communal resilience (Boulton et al. 2015: 219). The general interest for lay participation in public policymaking has been increasing since the 1990s, simultaneously with the declining trust for political and societal institutions in the advanced western societies. The phenomenon coincides with the proliferating knowledge available for the public, rise in educational levels as well as the value shift from maximizing the economic wealth to the enhancing of subjective well-being (Inglehart 1999).

Even if the scopes of the complex issues can be comprehended to some extent, the means of addressing them can neither be definitive nor static. A creative and enabling environment for change promotion in a complex system has stated to be robust only along with coevolutionary qualities of its own (Goergen et al. 2010: 5; Mitleton-Kelly 2011a). Considering a variety of societal and even global issues, nongovernment organizations are found significant in initiating public engagement processes. In addition to the strong involvement of third-sector organized stakeholder groups, an even larger portion of actors of innovative public engagement comes from a fourth sector, "actors or actor groups whose foundational logic is not in the representation of established interest, but rather, in the idea of social cooperation through hybrid networking" (Rask et al. 2016: 3). While this phenomenon of proactive, self-organizing and emergent activism is mostly not acknowledged as a constituent element of societal activism, it is gaining ground on participative dynamics (Rask et al. 2018).

The demands for participative societal advocacy have shaped the public administrative bodies and practices by means of institutional innovations (Atkinson 2002; Warren 2009). Viewed in general, the phenomena of enhancing the civic engagement can be anticipated to expand further, beyond the domains of direct democracy and governance into more extensive discourse in scientific issues with societal and environmental impact (e.g., Köhler et al. 2015; Pernaa 2017; Blue 2018). An inevitable transformation of civil advocacy is acknowledged and included in the frameworks in various European programs in the ongoing process of "aligning research and innovation to the values, needs and expectations of European society" (RRI 2014; Euroscientist 2016).

6.4 The Welfare Policy Participation

Welfare policymaking requires acknowledging the system as an entity of interacting systems and further, as a coevolving and transforming ecosystem. The understanding of this interaction elucidates its consequences and changes the administrative *foci* to enabling the interaction and developing the discourse competency (Kernick 2008). The public administrative exploration of the welfare service systems traditionally emphasizes the internal structures and interrelation between the variety of service providers. The main theories of the public administration have all added their heterogenous characteristics in examining welfare systems, whether the subject has been a national or an organizational reform or any other objective to foster the public good. According to Pyun and Gamassou (2018), the trajectory of the theories from theoretical and practical predominance to public participation in decision-making indicates a societal desire to "getting back to the traditional values, that's to say, the general welfare and the social harmony" (p. 255). The trend is considered having gained strength in western societies by experiences of the Arab Spring and the development of electronic administrative applications.

Longitudinal studies in healthcare organizations have shown the distinctive characteristic of complex systems to strive for sustainability by creating new order through enabling coevolutionary processes (Mitleton-Kelly 2011b). Put in a national welfare service system context, the challenge of changing the policy inertia is demanding due to its "lock-in effect". In order for a reform to take place, the incentives have to overcome strong resistance by not only an institutional but also public path dependency. The more daring the intended change and its consequences to the systems arrangements are, the more likely it is preceded by a severe political and/or economic crisis (Hemerijck 2002). In retrospect, a "crisis" represents the lead-up to the turning point where the transformation of a complex system occurs. The previous state is unattainable due to the developments in causal and underlying, structural nexuses (Byrne 2001: 151). Complexity sciences aim to examine the instability, self-organizing capacities and emergent behavior below the apparent macro level or long-term stability, causing—if gaining a critical mass of significance—greater changes (Mitleton-Kelly 2003; Haynes 2015: 43; Cairney 2012).

Any policy addressing the future of a society is tinged with expectations, emotions and assumptions originating from its culture and history. The designated values-based objectives of a policy can therefore not be attained by solely evidence-based nor archived information. The core of the policy aspiration should consist of the public conceptions, even subjective, of the factors contributing to the present state (Appadurai 2013: 286–289). In the context of welfare policies, the accentuation of the subjective perceptions should be of the deviant, vulnerable and marginal groups (Raisio et al. 2014) that can also be considered as large-scale consumers of the welfare services (Perttola and Pernaa 2016). Welfare service organizations are balancing between their tolerant, customer-oriented values and a strain of efficacy and, simultaneously, not only smooth away deviant voices but "assume the right to define and diagnose normality and deviance" (Riikonen et al. 2004: 312).

The discrepancy between increasing demands of welfare services and diminishing fiscal resources calls for the policy principles implemented by the variety of domestic welfare services to be sensitive and adjustable with reference to the evidence of services beneficial to general well-being (Seaford 2014; Hemerijck 2002). Given the complexity and multiple dimensions of a welfare system with an extensive sphere of intergenerational influences, the necessary service rationalizations cannot be tackled by focusing on the structural dimension only (see Mitleton-Kelly 2011b). An inadequate recognition of healthcare complexity during a reform process can result in implementing linear and deficient solutions (Raisio 2009) and, thereby, unsuccessful outcomes (Vartiainen 2005).

6.5 Case Finland: The Description of the Study

The extensive efforts to rearrange welfare services in Finland highlight the desideratum of participative policymaking (PPM) discussion. By restructuring the municipal and regional duties—to enhance the well-being of the citizens and to reduce inequalities in health and well-being—the arrangement of and relations between welfare branches, different public entities, NGOs and private healthcare service providers create a multisectoral realignment where the perception of service users should not be ignored.

Finnish social and welfare services are slowly comprehending the importance of service users' expertise in developing the services to advance the well-being, and the ways of the citizens' consultancy are taking shape slowly (Raisio 2010; Möttönen 2012). Despite the efforts of Finnish ministries and public offices in developing citizens' engagement and municipal democracy (e.g., Ministry of Finance 2017, 2018), the experiments in participative policymaking have remained local and relatively small scale.

The purpose of the study was to discover and discuss the possibilities of addressing the challenges of welfare service complexity by participatory[3] instruments, involving the residents and service users in the municipal welfare policymaking. The study aimed at deepening the comprehension of the incentives and impediments affecting the participatory policymaking development in the welfare service ecosystem, by providing insight into the perceptions of experienced municipal policymakers[4] and the administrators of nongovernmental welfare organizations.

The research questions of the study were:

- Which factors are considered as fundamental to the participative welfare policymaking development in Finland?

[3] In this study, the concept of participation implies the desire to influence in welfare policies by a variety of participative practices.

[4] The municipal policymaking in Finland is presently built on the so-called dual model, local councilors making decisions based on proposals and details prepared by the office bearers.

- What are the undercurrents of the protracted development in participative welfare policymaking?

The study located temporally in a critical juncture of an extensive Finnish regional government, health and social service reform.[5] The reform originated from the 2004 PARAS reform to restructure municipalities and services, paved the way to the current, comprehensive social welfare and healthcare reform with an aim of the "equal provision of social welfare and health care services" (THL 2019). During the first week of the study in November 2015, the Ministry of Social Affairs and Health and the Ministry of Finance gave a significant outline for the service arranging responsibility to be transferred to the self-governing regions, wider than the present municipalities. Simultaneously, the current financing and the welfare service provision system would be rearranged. The timing served the study by offering a *tabula rasa* for the experts to consider the future of the Finnish welfare services without clear vision of the inchoate reform and, yet, with an awareness of inevitable and significant changes in the financing and administrative structure of the welfare services.

The study was implemented as a web-based Delphi study in October–December 2015 in three rounds, each active for 2 weeks. The analyses of the rounds were conducted within a week between them. The survey was built of future claims, which were anonymously assessed and commented by experts (henceforth referred to as panelists). The expert panel consisted of 37 participants, representing Finnish

- Representative chairpersons of the municipal councils/welfare service boards
- Leading municipal welfare department office bearers
- Executive managers of the third-sector welfare organizations

The panelists representing the municipal electives and officials were chosen with a random sampling from the statistics[6] provided by the Association of Finnish Local and Regional Authorities (Kuntaliitto n.d.). The panelists representing the third-sector welfare organizations were chosen with a random sampling from the statistics[7] provided by SOSTE, the Finnish federation for social affairs and health, an umbrella organization of 200 welfare NGOs. All of the selected panelists held a responsible position in their background institutions, with an assumption of considerable experience in welfare policymaking practices and/or welfare service user perspectives.

Fifty candidates were approached by e-mail, including a brief introduction to the study as well as the date and time for a more informative telephone discussion. During the second approach by telephone, further details of the study were discussed, and a total of 47 experts—consisting of 15 NGO representatives, 14 municipal chairs and 18 municipal officials—gave an approving response to participation.

[5] Due to the resignation of the government at the time, the preparations for the implementation of the reform were discontinued in March 2019.

[6] At the time of the study, Finland consisted of 317 municipalities.

[7] At the time of the study, a total of 200 NGOs was listed under the parent organization SOSTE.

From the original group, the amount of 37 experts were actively engaged in the study, with a varying degree of activity in its different parts, as well as in different claims.

The study was fully anonymous, enabling the participants to express their views as private individuals, free from organizational representativeness and group dynamics. To secure the anonymity, the panelists representing political decision-makers and office bearers were selected from different municipals with no announced, cooperative affiliations or consolidations.

6.6 The Delphi Method

The Delphi method has its origins in 1950s' war strategic research. The method was originally developed by the RAND Corporation for forecasting trends and complex problems by the experts of different fields to anticipate the changes in post-war Europe (Dalkey and Helmer 1963). Futurist Harold A. Linstone and physicist Murray Turoff have stated an extensive description of it (Linstone and Turoff 1975: 3): "[Delphi is] a method for structuring a group communication process so that the process is effective in allowing a group of individuals, as a whole, to deal with a complex problem". Delphi method and its modifications using the wisdom of crowds (Hiltunen 2011) have been widespread and accepted[8] not only among foresight practices but more widely as a technique in scientific research and decision-making support.

The special characters of the method can be identified as *anonymity, expertise knowledge* and *iteration*. In a Delphi process, the experts of various fields are brought together to deliberate a current, controversial question. The experts are asked to judge and argue the probability and desirability of future claims (Linturi and Rubin 2014) and conducted to an anonymous, written discourse on the subject, characterized by expertise instead of status or authority. The iteration is achieved by returning the analyzed results to the panelists, who are guided further to re-evaluate, argue or justify their assessments. Previous round forming a base for the next one results in a dialogue that aims to confront expert disputes without confrontation and to examine standpoints not necessarily supported by oneself (Linturi 2007; Kuusi 2002).

Linstone and Turoff (1975) have identified issues that can be effectively addressed by the method. Concerning public administration and well-being, the following attributes can be emphasized (Ziglio 1996):

- Issues not suitable for explicit analyzing techniques, but benefit from evaluations based on collective, subjective analysis
- Issues without "monitored" history or sufficient information of its present state nor future development

[8] For a description of the Delphi method stages of development, see Rieger (1986).

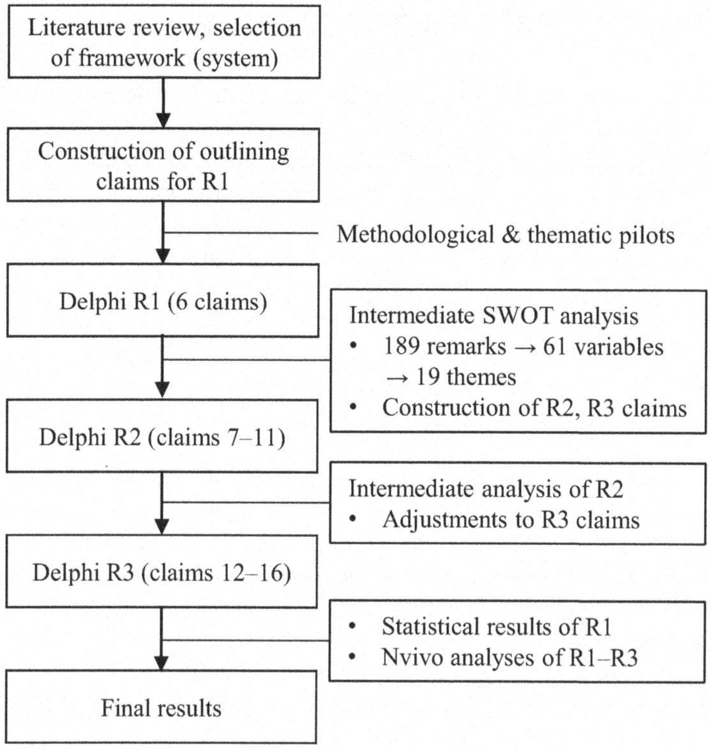

Fig. 6.1 Flow chart of the three-round, modified Delphi study process

– Issues that require multiple approaches in evaluating different policies

The study required an online platform for an anonymous discourse, with the ability to transform the data to be used in software applications for the analyses (in this study, SPSS and NVivo). The Delphi method and the open-source software eDelfoi[9] met the requirements of the study. The construction of the study began in May 2015, concurrently with method training and monthly workshops offered by the Finnish administrative and developing network of the software.

[9] Current version: *eDelphi* is a third version of a web-based software, introduced in the late 1990s by a corporation of Finnish futures scientists Linturi, Kuusi and Kaivo-oja. "eDelphi has been developed during 20 years together with Finnish future research institutions including University of Turku Futures Research Centre and Society for Futures Research" (http://www.edelphi.org).

6.7 The First Round of the Study: Construction

The flowchart (Fig. 6.1) describes the study process of the three-round, modified Delphi. The first round (R1) of a Delphi is commonly constructed by the panelists involved in the study, to generate a frame of reference to be used in the following rounds. In this study, to offer a comprehensive basis for an examination of an issue inevitably generating controversies, the early framing of the discussion consisted of predetermined, theory-based (described below) perspectives which were then assessed by the expert panel.

Before the actual study, R1 was tested twice: first, within an eDelfoi, workshop for comprehensibility and structural clarity, and second, regarding the contents by seven test panelists with long experiences in the fields of welfare service execution, research and policymaking. Adjustments and improvements were made after both tests.

R1 of the study consisted of six projections for 2030, considering the future of participative welfare policymaking system. The structure of R1 was built based on the theory of expansive learning, developed by an educationalist Yrjö Engeström (1987, 2015). First introduced in 1987, the theory based on the activity theory by psychologist Lev Vygotsky (Engeström 2001) provides a learning-based model for collective development.

The Engeström structure of a human activity system (Fig. 6.2) was selected as a structured framework to study welfare policymaking as a social system. The following reasons supported the use of the framework:

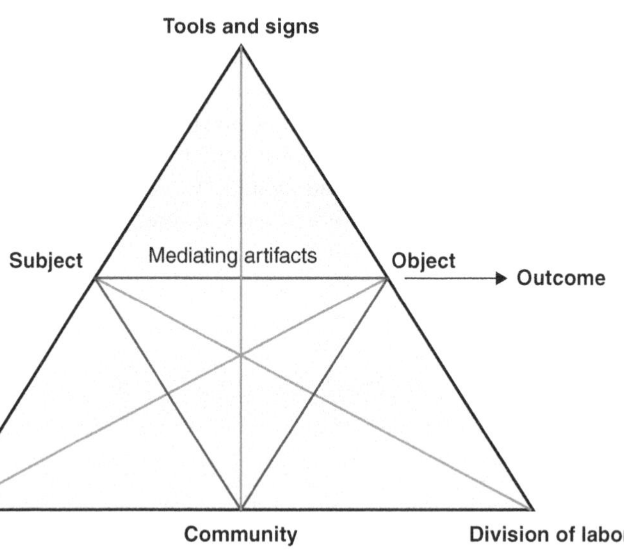

Fig. 6.2 The structure of the human activity system (Engeström 1987: 78)

- The "activity" in the human activity system are human interactions within a larger system with a variety of entities, objectives, rules and norms. The activities are studied in real-life practices rather than analyzed knowledge states, detached from the entity (Jonassen and Rohrer-Murphy 1999).
- In the structure, the activity is understood as dynamic and evolutionary, not static nor based on absolute models (Engeström 2015: 32).
- Activity is analyzed as "contextual or ecological phenomenon", and the model focuses on interactions between the individual and the surrounding environment (Jonassen and Rohrer-Murphy 1999; Engeström 2015: 32–33).

Engeström developed the model originally aiming at illustrating the individual–community relationship and its development in work studies (ibid., xvi), originating from the common grounds and theories with administrative sciences. The model was suitable for the examining of the relationship between the citizens and the municipal welfare policymakers and particularly to elucidate a more general view of its development to build the subsequent rounds of the study.

The basis for the following rounds (R2 and R3) was established during the R1 of the study. Panelists were asked to evaluate the probability and desirability of the claims with a seven-level Likert scale (from 1 = improbable/undesirable to 7 = highly probable/desirable) and to give their supportive arguments for each evaluation. Panelists were encouraged to debate on each other's remarks as well as to revise their own responses within the timeframe of 2 weeks. They also received an e-mail notification once there was a comment made on their response in the conversation.

The study was—contrary to the most common types of Delphi studies—dissent oriented with an objective to bring out the profound welfare policy expert perspectives regarding the development of the citizen participation in welfare policymaking. For the controversies to unfold, the future claims were based on the intentionally accentuated presumption of extensive civic engagement in welfare policymaking in 2030. The claims were built in accordance with the human activity system (above), and the discussion was directed to its constituents, briefly described below. Additional information (e.g., further clarification, statistics and previous research results) and supplementary material (e.g., descriptions of innovative methods in citizen participation) were presented to corroborate and validate each claim.

Claim I/Object: "In 2030, citizens are being extensively heard in welfare policy decisions."

> The object is the most significant part of the activity system, extending its problematics over the study and acted on by the subject (Jonassen and Rohrer-Murphy 1999). Here, the object of a system is appointed as problematic issues in welfare services, typically characterized by wickedness and high complexity. Behind the concept of wicked problems lies definition developed by design theorists Rittel and Webber (1974). Opposite to tame problems, the solution of a wicked problem requires generating of innovative methods to engage citizens in decisions made to address even challenging ethical problems in society (e.g., Yankelovich 2015).

Claim II/Subject: "In 2030, the users of welfare services function as policy decision-makers equal to office-bearers and elected officials."

The subject of the activity is a collective subject, acting on the object (Engeström 2015: 122; Jonassen and Rohrer-Murphy 1999). There is an inherent paradox in outlining participants involved in a decision-making process: growing of the number of participants with the diversity of roles and backgrounds simultaneously increases the complexity of the problem, while it is also a prerequisite for collective awareness (i.e., Conklin 2006: 23–30; Stoppelenburg and Vermaak 2009). In order to find sustainable solutions and a collective approach to a complex issue, it is crucial to contemplate it from multiple perspectives.

Claim III/Tools: "In 2030 the current, dual decision-making model is replaced by various and diverse processes of decision making."

In this section different tools of policymaking are reflected upon and conventional (usually board based) structures are questioned. In the background of the claim lies a view of adaptable models of decision-making in approaching varying problems and focus groups. For example, as an answer to an increasing demand for communality among the youth, social media and various sorts of youth councils could be exploited (Möttönen 2012: 28–29).

Claim IV/Rules: "In 2030, the hearing of citizens' juries or service user councils is mandatory and centrally supervised."

This claim argues that the existing practices of representative democracy and bureaucratic administration have created their own pitfalls. With an aim to strengthen the legitimacy of the administration by laws, regulations and different established modi operandi, possibilities to react to societal changes can be time-consuming and limited, whereas the modernization of society requires prompt responses to changing (welfare) needs and open discussion about a fair distribution of limited resources (Möttönen and Kettunen 2011: 384–285).

Claim V/Community: "In 2030, the welfare policies are made across organizational borders.

The two last claims of R1 analyze possibilities to reshape the current model of municipal decision-making and to transcend the organizational and administrative limits. An individual's engagement to a subject under decision can be formed by geographical or functional interests, latter being criticized for being a threat to residence-based representative democracy due to the possibility of uneven distribution of power (Sørensen 1998). Therefore, it is crucial to define the principle of equality when involving participants in decision-making on grounds of functional interests: everyone engaged should have an equal opportunity to be involved in policymaking. At its best, decisions are made in a practical combination of geographical and functional democracy (Ibid.). Increasingly complex societal issues call for a new, holistic and constantly developing approach in organizational governing and cooperation (Clarke and Stewart 2000).

Claim VI/Division of Labor: "In 2030, the welfare policy decisions are serving community's well-being above party politics."

Ambition behind an administrative apparatus is often characterized by its (politicized) protection of achieved position and power, which is rarely perceived as an advance for open and citizen-engaging practices (e.g., Vartola 2005: 98–104). In this claim, the traditional representative system with its political tensions is viewed as a possible inhibitor to the development of the PPM. Behind this claim is an assumption that there should be a transition from politically regulated functioning to a guidance-minded steering based on the mutual respect of different stakeholders in the system, regardless of political activity (Möttönen 2012: 14–17).

Table 6.1 The results of R1 with number of comments

Enabling elements (26)	Inhibiting conditions (86)
Factors affecting the progression of the participative policymaking practices. Reflecting the current system, partly controllable by present-day skills or circumstances	
Technological skills and web coverage (11)	Unfàmiliarity with participative practices (30)
Opportunities in municipal or legislative readjustment (in reference to the reform) (7)	Cultural inertia (24)
Strong (existing) representative system and incipient hearing practices (6)	Challenges in incorporating participative practices with current representative system (15)
Experimental courage (2)	Increasing inequality and consumerism in welfare services (14)
	Challenges in municipal readjustment or governing structures in general (3)

Favorable prospects (45)	Unfavorable consequences (32)
Resultants of the progression of the participative policymaking practices. Associated with the future development, partly nebulous or intangible	
Improvement of legitimacy (18)	Societally poor decisions (12)
More equitable and flexible resource distribution (21)	Tokenistic participation (8)
Regenerating the council work *modi operandi* (2)	Unequal inclusion (7)
Increasing of the health empowerment (2)	Eroding liability for the policies (4)
Improvement in coping with complex welfare policy issues (2)	The decline in political representativeness (1)

6.8 The Results of the First Round

The basic principles of a SWOT analysis were utilized in analyzing and structuring 189 qualitative statements to 61 variables and further to 19 themes (Table 6.1). R1 conversation embraced both current attributes and future prospects of the PPM that were further categorized as positive (enabling elements and favorable prospects) and negative (inhibiting conditions and unfavorable consequences).

Considering the first research question, the factors affecting the development of PPM, concerning current administrative attributes, distinct themes stood out in the results of R1:

- Technological skills and opportunities in the ongoing Finnish welfare reform as enabling elements.
- Cultural stagnation and the unfamiliarity with participative practices, as well as the challenges in PPM integration into current, representative system as inhibiting conditions.
- The increasing inequality and consumerism were brought forward as the inhibitors of PPM development.

The future prospects of the PPM development and novel, inclusive practices were mostly seen as an improvement to the decision-making legitimacy and equity in service distribution, whereas tokenism and inequality as well as the low quality of policies were seen as unfavorable consequences of the participative practices.

Despite the emphasis on the qualitative, discursive part of the study, some interesting features in the statistics of the quantitative data (Table 6.2) of R1 can be perceived:

Table 6.2 The statistics of R1

Claim I:	In 2030, citizens are being extensively heard in welfare policy decisions						
(*N* = 29/34)	Estimates of probability				Estimates of desirability		
	Mean	SD	IQR	M-diff	Mean	SD	IQR
	3.79	1.236	2.00	1.38	5.17	1.197	*1.00*
Claim II:	In 2030, the users of welfare services function as policy decision-makers equal to office-bearers and elected officials						
(*N* = 29/33)	Estimates of probability				Estimates of desirability		
	Mean	SD	IQR	M-diff	Mean	SD	IQR
	3.14	1.302	2.00	0.69	3.83	1.671	*3.00*
Claim III:	In 2030 the current, dual decision-making model is replaced by various and diverse processes of decision-making						
(*N* = 28/30)	Estimates of probability				Estimates of desirability		
	Mean	SD	IQR	M-diff	Mean	SD	IQR
	3.50	1.262	*1.00*	0.54	4.04	1.598	2.00
Claim IV:	In 2030, the hearing of citizens' juries or service user councils is mandatory and centrally supervised						
(*N* = 29/34)	Estimates of probability				Estimates of desirability		
	Mean	SD	IQR	M-diff	Mean	SD	IQR
	3.86	1.246	2.00	0.62	4.48	1.503	1.50
Claim V:	In 2030, the welfare policies are made rising above organizational boundaries						
(*N* = 28/34)	Estimates of probability				Estimates of desirability		
	Mean	SD	IQR	M-diff	Mean	SD	IQR
	4.46	1.621	*3.00*	1.15	5.61	1.571	2.00
Claim VI:	In 2030, the welfare policy decisions are serving more community's well-being than party politics						
(*N* = 28/30)	Estimates of probability				Estimates of desirability		
	Mean	SD	IQR	M-diff	Mean	SD	IQR
	3.39	1.397	1.75	1.43	4.82	1.679	1.5

N numeric estimates given/active panelists by claim, *Mean* the mean of the 7 pt. Likert scale estimates (1 = improbable/undesirable; 7 = highly probable/desirable), *SD* standard deviation, *IQR* interquartile range, (<1.4: *strong consensus;* 1.4–1.75: moderate consensus; 1.75–2.1: moderate dissent; >2.1: *strong dissent*); *M-diff* the difference of probability and desirability estimate means

The *desirability* of "citizens being extensively heard" and the "crossing of organizational boundaries" in welfare policymaking were evaluated the highest of the six claims and, simultaneously, had notable difference with regard to the estimates for probability. The latter had the strongest dissent among *probability* estimates, while the development of novel decision-making models was highly agreed on.

Considering both estimates for probability *and* desirability, the claim of welfare service users to function as equals to current policymakers in welfare policymaking was met with disapproval, but then again, with dissent.

6.9 The Construction of the Rounds Two and Three

The 19 themes from R1 were grouped under three main categories: *service outcomes, structures of involvement* and *administrative configuration*. Following the preliminary analysis of R1, new assertions were constructed and presented to the panelists in the second round (R2). This was repeated for the last, third round (R3) (see Fig. 6.1). A matrix was applied during R2 and R3 to ensure the coverage of all 19 themes in the iterative rounds (Table 6.3).

Before the following rounds, the panelists received a summary of the results from R1. The ten claims of R2 and R3 were built with an objective to clarify the underlying factors affecting the panelists' perspectives. The R2 and R3 claims were constructed by a variety of questions (e.g., multiple-choice questions and evaluation assignments), all including additional information or reference to timely studies or welfare reform updates. Some statements causing lively responses in R1 were added to elaborate the claims.

Table 6.3 The coverage matrix of the iterative rounds

	1st round analysis																		
	189 comments → 61 variables → 19 themes																		
Iteration of the R1 themes in R2 and R3	Enabling elements				Inhibiting conditions					Favorable prospects					Unfavorable consequences				
	1	2	3	4	5	6	7	8	9	10	11	12	13	14	15	16	17	18	19
Service outcomes (claims 7, 9, 10)			X				X				X							X	
				X	X	X	X			X	X			X					X
			X				X		X		X								
Structures of involvement (claims 11, 13, 14)		X	X				X		X	X		X			X	X	X		X
	X		X		X			X	X			X					X		
			X	X		X		X	X	X				X		X			
Administrative configuration (claims 8, 12, 15, 16)		X	X		X	X		X	X	X									
	X	X	X		X				X		X		X		X			X	
			X			X		X	X		X							X	
			X				X		X	X				X					

R2: claims 7–11; R3: claims 12–16

6.9.1 Service Outcomes

The future claims elaborated welfare services by picturing Finland in 2030:

- As a welfare state, offering services and benefits under the Scandinavian tenets of universalism
- With the frames of welfare services provided by public funding established by commonly accepted ethical principles
- Offering welfare services more equal in comparison with the services prior to the reform

6.9.2 Structures of Involvement

The future development of enabling structures for involvement was considered by means of policymaking roles in 2030, in which:

- Citizens/service users are obligated to participate in the evaluation, preparatory work and decision-making of the welfare policies.
- An important role of the municipality is to embrace the communality and support the social capital of the (community as a) "tribe[10]".
- The regional welfare services are outlined by the elected officials, yet the most complex issues being deliberated in regionally coordinated citizens' juries.

6.9.3 Administrative Configuration

The administrative configurations in 2030 were visualized as:

- The municipalities with an altered role (after the reform) emphasizing and promoting well-being and resilient welfare solutions
- The National Institute for Health and Welfare as a strong normative adviser of the independent regions
- The welfare service prioritization coordinated and supervised nationally, in cooperation with various stakeholders (such as the National Advisory Board on Social Welfare and Health Care Ethics, Finnish Medicines Agency) and relative civic statements

The panelists were also asked to arrange the Finnish welfare service stakeholders in the order of importance in affecting the supply of the welfare services in 2030. Additional, missing stakeholders could be added by the panelists.

[10] Expression used and discussed by panelists in R1.

6.10 Study Results

The preliminary analyses were performed after R1 and R2 to construct the claims for the subsequent round(s). The statistical analysis of R1 quantitative data was conducted by SPSS® software, and a more precise final analysis of the qualitative data was conducted by NVivo 11 Pro® software. The statements were classified,[11] numbered[12] and clustered under three main headings originating from the analysis of R1: (1) service outcomes, (2) the structures of involvement and (3) administrative configuration. The following summary, answering the second research question, is categorized accordingly.

6.10.1 *Service Outcomes*[13]

The maintaining of equal and universal public services was perceived to have far-reaching consequences to social order, general trust and productivity. On the other hand, the current welfare service system and its administration was commonly seen as rigid to respond to individual needs with distinct and individual, underlying factors. The inability to design individually flexible, yet prioritized frames for the services was construed to have resulted in "profit seeking cost-effectiveness as primary focus on the evaluation of welfare practices". The myopic economic attitude was also reasoned as the corollary of financial unsustainability as well as the increasing economic asymmetry. The ability to influence welfare policies was increasingly linked with wealth and one's ability to pay for private health services.

The call for a definition of *what and how* in public welfare services by means of prioritization and "the novel methods of measuring economic [service] productivity by taking account of human well-being" were widely expressed and supported by the panelists. There was a wide agreement on the unbearableness of the current implementation of the principles of universalism, which were also contested as merely symbolic, already eroded by increasing service fees and the insufficiency of current livelihood or services equalizing systems.

[11] Comments referring to personal healthcare service decisions (e.g. decisions of medical treatments by the healthcare professionals) were excluded from the analysis.

[12] The numbering of the statements (claim N/statement N) enabled the verification of the statement interpretation during the confirmatory assessment.

[13] 74 clustered statements of the claims 7, 9 and 10 (service outcomes).

6.10.2 The Structures of Involvement[14]

The panelists considered increasing administrative—including feedback—transparency, two-way discourse with a variety of coordinated, undemanding methods as prerequisites for advancing citizens' involvement. The need for promoting the participation was understood resulting from the underlying aspiration for a stronger sense of affinity and "community spirit" which, however, cannot be met by obligating the citizens or service users to participate.

However desirable, the objectives of citizen involvement were treated with reservations and even scepticism. Most doubts were expressed about the practical details and the additional resources required to the implementation of citizens' juries, the excessive representation of the already active citizens and the true policy influence of the public opinion. The representativeness of the underprivileged was considered as a significant issue, not able to be met by merely technological or general solutions.

Doubts were also stated regarding some civic aptitudes, assumed to be required for the engagement, such as subjectivity, willingness to participate, discursive skills and abilities to assimilate the municipal "big picture". The shortages in participative skills were alternatively expressed as developmental targets and to be met by "strengthening the citizens' abilities to influence [the decision-making]" by means of carefully constructed processes.

6.10.3 Administrative Configuration[15]

The changing role of the municipalities (from the provision of healthcare services to the promoting of well-being, due to the ongoing reform) was generally perceived as positive. It was, for example, seen as an opportunity for the municipalities to "take an active role in the cooperation with voluntary associations" and universities. In order to achieve the requirements of the new role, the panelists called for sufficient resources to meet the needs of proactivity, as well as the increasing guidance of the ministries and the National Institute for Health and Welfare (THL) in supporting the municipal, regional and NGO service development and evaluation.

National proposals for the welfare service prioritization were anticipated, rather than leaving the deliberation in the regions, municipalities or single organizations, all in novel roles due to the reform. The national alignment in prioritization was frequently mentioned as a prerequisite to face the future challenges to maintain service equality, menaced by the privatization of the services, and the growth of the regional—and more distant—policymaking power.

[14] 60 clustered statements of the claims 11, 13 and 14 (the structures of involvement).

[15] 85 clustered statements of the claims 8, 12, 15 and 16 (administrative configuration).

6.11 Discussion

Due to the evolving, multilayered and multiagency features of complex systems, to formalize a perfect model for a systematic investigation is not possible. This is naturally a wider challenge for social sciences, unable to achieve the repeatable measures used for natural sciences to illustrate—nor to predict—the creative and imperfect evolutionary processes of human systems. Nevertheless, a multiagent model, even with limitations, creates a most appropriate representation of a complex system (Allen 2018).

The research leaned on the perception of the growing role of public participation in public governance. The shift is scarcely perceptible in documents concerning welfare service planning and reforming in Finland. The Ministry of Social Affairs and Health is framing customer orientation in its strategy as "an offset of developing services as well as a strategic choice aimed to shift emphasis towards preventative and achievable care". The welfare service reform was planned to be implemented through "the active participation of service users", assigning, however, the communities (municipalities, regions) to determine their means of citizen involvement. The Local Government Act, which enables the municipalities to develop a range of participative activities and regulates the inhabitants' right to take part in them, does not ensure the implementation of the law in local welfare policymaking. This has resulted in miscellaneous modus operandi, highly dependent on local administrative actors' motivation to advance participative strategies and structures (Nurmi et al. 2018).

The results of the Delphi study show that regardless of strong trust in technological preparedness and the structural opportunities in the extensive Finnish welfare reform previously well in progress, the cultural stagnation and unfamiliarity generate attitudes inhibitory of PPM development. Even though the resultants in advancing the participative practices were considered influential to decision-making legitimacy in general, as well as the very central idea of welfare services and equal and flexible resource distribution, there were reservations about the true inclusion and the implementation of PPM practices. In some responses, the reservations regarding the issue were implied to rise from its assumed juxtaposition of the traditional, representative policymaking and the participative policymaking practices.

Several undercurrents affecting the development of PPM were discernible in the conversations. Proliferating consumerism in welfare services in tandem with the public funding insufficiency was emphasized, collectively proliferating general inequality and individualism. Put in the systemic frame of the study construction, the results show a notorious, vicious cycle: fiscal limitations and economic restrictions leading to myopic service decisions, increasing service inequality and, further, social inequality and, therefore, the increasing need for services. Wilkinson and Pickett (2010: 190–196), basing on the findings of inequalities causing widespread negative effects beyond income levels, highlight more fundamental causality between the nations' ideological change and well-being of the citizens, inequality functioning as a major denominator of difficulties connecting to social status and having therefore wider and corrosive effects on the society. Esping-Andersen (2005) approaches the mutual causality of the two: "If, as is possible, we are dealing with a chicken-and-egg problem, this may not matter from a *public policy* point of view because, in this case, a reduction of inequality on either of the two dimensions ought to have positive effects on the other".

The complex issue of policymaking participation becomes even more complex considering the disadvantaged falling short of rates of activity (e.g., Verba et al. 2002: 511–513). Various and comprehensive studies underline the importance of structural, social cohesion on civic engagement: the higher the level of income inequality, the higher the range of social issues and lower the rate of participation and development of common interest (Acik-Toprak 2009: 204–205). Arguments for participatory decision-making highlight the socially equalizing outcomes of involvement (Clawson and Oxley 2017: 10). Macpherson (1977: 94) described this ethical requirement: "This is not to say that a more participatory system would of itself remove all the inequities of our society. It is only to say that low participation and social inequity are so bound up with each other that a more equitable and humane society requires a more participatory political system."

It is stated that the past Finnish healthcare reforms have so far failed to meet their objectives due to the disconnection between issues addressed and the challenges of the society (Vartiainen 2010). According to this research, the clear signals of weakening universalism and equality—the very essence of the Nordic welfare system—have harmful effects on the development of participative practices in welfare service policymaking, and yet, diminishing of these values creates a demand for an open dialogue of our welfare policies.

6.12 Implications

- In order to advance the complex welfare systems' abilities to create holistic and more societally responsive and adaptive policies, the views of the service users need to be made explicit.
- The cultural stagnation and unfamiliarity of advantages achieved by citizens' engagement generate attitudes inhibitory of participative policymaking development. It is noteworthy to emphasize the mutual supportive effects of participative and traditional, representative policymaking practices.
- The socially equalizing outcomes of involvement can enhance the communal ability to achieve a more systemic view of a complex entity of the societal well-being. This requires creation and institutionalization of the participative arrangements, as well as ongoing discourse between policymaking establishments, voluntary organizations, community groups and the research institutes.

References

Acik-Toprak, N. (2009). Civic engagement in Europe: A multilevel study of the effect of individual and national determinants on political participation. *Political Consumerism and Associational Involvement*. University of Manchester, Faculty of Humanities. Doctoral thesis. Retrieved from https://www.escholar.manchester.ac.uk/api/datastream?publicationPid=uk-ac-man-scw:94093&datastreamId=FULL-TEXT.PDF.

Adams, D., & Wiseman, J. (2003). Navigating the future: A case study of growing Victoria together. *Australian Journal of Public Administration, 62*(2), 11–23.

Allen, P. (2018). Complex evolving social systems: Unending, imperfect learning. In E. Mitleton-Kelly, A. Paraskevas, & C. Day (Eds.), *Handbook of research methods in complexity science: Theory and applications* (pp. 18–44). Cheltenham: Edward Elgar Publishing.

Appadurai, A. (2013). *The future as cultural fact: Essays on the global condition*. London: Verso.

Atkinson, R. (2002). The white paper on European governance: Implications for urban policy. *European Planning Studies, 10*(6), 781–792.

Blue, G. (2018). Scientism: A problem at the heart of formal public engagement with climate change. *ACME, 17*(2), 544–560.

Boulton, J. G., Allen, P. M., & Bowman, C. (2015). *Embracing complexity: Strategic perspectives for an age of turbulence* (1st ed.). Oxford: Oxford University Press.

Byrne, D. (2001). *Complexity theory and the social sciences: An introduction* (2nd ed.). London: Routledge.

Cairney, P. (2012). Complexity theory in political science and public policy. *Political Studies Review, 10*(3), 346–358.

Capra, F., & Luisi, P. L. (2014). *The systems view of life: A unifying vision*. Cambridge: Cambridge University Press.

Clarke, M., & Stewart, J. (2000). Handling the wicked issues. In C. Davies, L. Finlay, & A. Bullman (Eds.), *Changing practice in health and social care* (pp. 377–386). London: Sage.

Clawson, R. A., & Oxley, Z. M. (2017). *Public opinion: Democratic ideals, democratic practice*. London: SAGE.

Collins, B. (2010). Energy, transport, environment and the policy challenge. *Emergence: Complexity and Organization, 12*(2), 77–80.

Conklin, E. J. (2006). *Dialogue mapping: Building shared understanding of wicked problems*. Hoboken, NJ: Wiley.

Dalkey, N., & Helmer, O. (1963). An experimental application of the Delphi method to the use of experts. *Management Science, 9*(3), 458–467.

Dennard, L. F., Richardson, K. A., & Morçöl, G. (2008). Editorial. In L. F. Dennard, K. A. Richardson, & G. Morçöl (Eds.), *Complexity and policy analysis: Tools and methods for designing robust policies in a complex world* (pp. 1–22). Goodyear, AZ: ISCE.

Engeström, Y. (1987). *Learning by expanding: An activity-theoretical approach to developmental research*. Orienta-Konsultit: Helsinki.

Engeström, Y. (2001). Expansive learning at work: Toward an activity theoretical reconceptualization. *Journal of Education and Work, 14*(1), 133–156.

Engeström, Y. (2015). *Learning by expanding: An activity-theoretical approach to developmental research* (2nd ed.). New York, NY: Cambridge University Press.

Eppel, E. (2012). What does it take to make surprises less surprising? The contribution of complexity theory to anticipation in public management. *Public Management Review, 14*(7), 881–902.

Eppel, E. (2017). Complexity thinking in public administration's theories-in-use. *Public Management Review, 19*(6), 845–861.

Eriksson, M., & Lindström, B. (2014). The salutogenic framework for Well-being: Implications for public policy. In T. J. Hämäläinen & J. Michaelson (Eds.), *Well-being and beyond: Broadening the public and policy discourse* (pp. 68–97). Cheltenham: Edward Elgar.

Esping-Andersen, G. (2005). Inequality of incomes and opportunities. In A. Giddens & P. Diamond (Eds.), *The new egalitarianism* (pp. 8–38). Cambridge: Polity Press.

Eurocientist. (2016). *Bringing RRI forward*. Retrieved from http://www.euroscientist.com/bringing-rri-forward/.

Goergen, M., Mallin, C., Mitleton-Kelly, E., Al-Hawamdeh, A., & Chiu, I. H.-Y. (2010). *Corporate governance and complexity theory*. Cheltenham: Edward Elgar.

Haynes, P. (2015). *Managing complexity in the public services* (2nd ed.). London: Routledge.

Hemerijck, A. (2002). The self-transformation of the European social model(s). In G. Esping-Andersen, D. Gallie, A. Hemerjick, & J. Myles (Eds.), *Why we need a new welfare state* (pp. 173–213). Oxford: Oxford University Press.

Hiltunen, E. (2011). Crowdsourcing the future: The foresight process at Finpro. *Journal of Futures Studies, 16*(1), 189–196.

Inglehart, R. (1999). Postmodernization erodes respect for authority but increases support for democracy. In P. Norris (Ed.), *Critical citizens: Global support for democratic government* (pp. 236–256). Oxford: Oxford University Press.

Jonassen, D. H., & Rohrer-Murphy, L. (1999). Activity theory as a framework for designing constructivist learning environments. *Educational Technology Research and Development, 47*(1), 61–79.

Kernick, D. P. (2008). Facilitating resource decision making in public organizations drawing upon insights from complexity theory. In L. F. Dennard, K. A. Richardson, & G. Morçöl (Eds.), *Complexity and policy analysis: Tools and methods for designing robust policies in a complex world* (pp. 105–115). Goodyear, AZ: ISCE.

Köhler, J., Wendling, C., Addarii, F., Grandjean, M., & Wilkinson, A. (2015). Concurrent design foresight. In *Report to the European Commission of the Expert Group on Foresight Modelling*. Luxembourg: Publications Office of the European Union.

Kuntaliitto. (n.d.). Retrieved from https://www.kuntaliitto.fi/tilastot-ja-julkaisut/kaupunkien-ja-kuntien-lukumaarat.

Kuusi, O. (2002). Delfoi –menetelmä. [The Delfoi-method.]. In M. Kamppinen, O. Kuusi, & S. Söderlund (Eds.), *Tulevaisuudentutkimus: Perusteet ja sovellukset [Futures research: Foundations and directions]* (pp. 204–225). Helsinki: Suomalaisen Kirjallisuuden Seura.

Linstone, H. A., & Turoff, M. (1975). *The delphi method* (pp. 3–12). Reading, MA: Addison-Wesley.

Linturi, H. (2007). Delfoin metamorfooseja. [The metamorphoses of Delfoi.] *Futura 26*(1).

Linturi, H., & Rubin, A. (2014). Metodi, metafora ja tulevaisuuskartta. [The method, metaphor and the future map]. *Futura 33*(3).

Macpherson, C. B. (1977). *The life and times of liberal democracy*. Oxford: Oxford University Press.

Mannermaa, M. (1988). Complexity and systems thinking in futures research: From "neutral" scenarios to value considerations. *Systems Practice, 1*(3), 279–205.

McGlade, J., & Garnsey, E. (2006). The nature of complexity. In E. Garnsey & J. McGlade (Eds.), *Complexity and co-evolution: Continuity and change in socio-economic systems* (pp. 1–21). Cheltenham: Edward Elgar Publishing Ltd.

Ministry of Finance. (2017). *Open Government III Action Plan 2017–2019 Finland*. Retrieved from https://www.opengovpartnership.org/sites/default/files/Finland_NAP_2017-2019_EN.pdf.

Ministry of Finance. (2018). Open government partnership. National Action Plan—Finland 2017–2019: *Mid-term interim evaluation*. Retrieved from https://avoinhallinto.fi/assets/files/2018/09/In-English_OGP_Self-assessment_Finland_Midterm2017_2019-FINAL.pdf.

Mitleton-Kelly, E. (2003). Ten principles of complexity and enabling infrastructures. In E. Mitleton-Kelly (Ed.), *Complex systems and evolutionary perspectives on organisations: The application of complexity theory to organisations* (Vol. 1, pp. 23–50).

Mitleton-Kelly, E. (2011a). Identifying the multi-dimensional problem-space and co-creating an enabling environment. *Emergence: Complexity and Organization, 13*(1/2), 1–25.

Mitleton-Kelly, E. (2011b). A complexity theory approach to sustainability: A longitudinal study in two London NHS hospitals. *The Learning Organization, 18*(1), 45–53.

Monno, V., & Khakee, A. (2012). Tokenism or political activism? Some reflections on participatory planning. *International Planning Studies, 17*(1), 85–101.

Möttönen, S. (2012). Kunnan poliittisen johtamisen uudistaminen—kokemuksia, näkemyksiä ja ehdotuksia. [*Reshaping the political leadership in municipalities—experiences, perceptions and proposals.*] Helsinki: Suomen Kuntaliitto.
Möttönen, S., & Kettunen, P. (2011). Yksilöosallistuminen ja yhteisöosallistuminen kuntien hyvinvointipalveluissa: Pohdintaa taustoista, periaatteista, vahvuuksista ja heikkouksista. [Individual participation and community participation in municipal welfare services: Reflection on backgrounds, principles, strengths and weaknesses.]. *Kunnallistieteellinen aikakauskirja, 39*(3), 281–293.
Nabatchi, T. (2012). Putting the "public" back in public values research: Designing participation to identify and respond to values. *Public Administration Review, 72*(5), 699–708.
Nurmi, H., Syväjärvi, A., & Leinonen, J. (2018). Osallistava toimintaote hyvinvoinnin edistämistyössä. [Participatory manners in the advancement of well-being.]. In J. Lammintakanen & S. Laulainen (Eds.), *Towards sustainable decision-making and management in welfare services* (pp. 113–126). Kuopio: University of Eastern Finland.
Parsons, W. (2004). Not just steering but weaving: Relevant knowledge and the craft of building policy capacity and coherence. *Australian Journal of Public Administration, 63*(1), 43–57.
Pernaa, H.-K. (2017). Deliberative future visioning: Utilizing the deliberative democracy theory and practice in futures research. *European Journal of Futures Research, 5*(1), 1–10.
Perttola, L., & Pernaa, H.-K. (2016). The absent minority in welfare planning: Entitling or overburdening citizens with responsibility? *Social Research, 39*(2), 48–61.
Pierson, P. (2000). Three worlds of welfare state research. *Comparative Political Studies, 33*(6/7), 791–821.
Pyun, H. O., & Gamassou, C. E. (2018). Looking for public administration theories? *Public Organization Review, 18*(2), 245–261.
Raisio, H. (2009). Health care reform planners and wicked problems: Is the wickedness of the problems taken seriously or is it even noticed at all? *Journal of Health Organization and Management, 23*(5), 477–493.
Raisio, H. (2010). The public as policy expert: Deliberative democracy in the context of Finnish health care reforms and policies. *Journal of Public Deliberation, 6*(2), article 6.
Raisio, H., Valkama, K., & Peltola, E. (2014). Disability and deliberative democracy: Towards involving the whole human spectrum in public deliberation. *Scandinavian Journal of Disability Research, 16*(1), 77–97.
Rask, M. T., Mačiukaitė-Žvinienė, S., Tauginienė, L., Dikčius, V., Matschoss, K. Aarrevaara, T., & D'Andrea, L. (2016). *Innovative public engagement: A conceptual model of public engagement in dynamic and responsible governance of research and innovation.* Retrieved from https://pe2020.eu/wp-content/uploads/2016/05/Innovative-Public-Engagement-FINAL.pdf.
Rask, M., Puustinen, A., & Raisio H. (2018). Toward a theory of fourth sector involvement. *Paper presented in ECPR conference*, Hamburg 22–25 August. Retrieved from https://ecpr.eu/Filestore/PaperProposal/5dc86a23-35c9-4cee-8090-5a3c84c9b8a6.pdf.
Rieger, W. G. (1986). Directions in Delphi developments: Dissertations and their quality. *Technological Forecasting and Social Change, 29*(2), 195–204.
Riikonen, E., Makkonen, M., & Smith, G. (2004). Good marginality? In V. Puuronen, A. Häkkinen, A. Pylkkänen, T. Sandlund, & R. Toivanen (Eds.), *New challenges for the welfare society* (pp. 311–325). Joensuu: Publications of Karelia Institute, University of Joensuu.
Rittel, H. W., & Webber, M. M. (1974). Wicked problems. *Man-made Futures, 26*(1), 272–280.
RRI. (2014). *Rome declaration on responsible research and innovation in Europe.* Retrieved from https://ec.europa.eu/research/swafs/pdf/rome_declaration_RRI_final_21_November.pdf
Seaford, C. (2014). What implications does well-being science have for economic policy? In T. J. Hämäläinen & J. Michaelson (Eds.), *Well-being and beyond: Broadening the public and policy discourse* (pp. 221–243). Cheltenham: Edward Elgar.
Sørensen, E. (1998). New forms of democratic empowerment: Introducing user influence in the primary school system in Denmark. *Statsvetenskaplig Tidskrift, 101*(2), 129–143.
Spicker, P. (2008). *Social policy: Themes and approaches* (2nd ed.). Bristol: The Policy Press.

Stoppelenburg, A., & Vermaak, H. (2009). Defixation as an intervention perspective: Understanding wicked problems at the Dutch Ministry of Foreign Affairs. *Journal of Management Inquiry, 18*(1), 40–54.
THL. (2019). *National Institute of Health and Welfare*. Retrieved from https://thl.fi/en/web/social-welfare-and-health-care-reform.
Vartiainen, P. (2005). Wicked health care issues: An analysis of Finnish and Swedish health care reforms. In G. T. Savage, J. A. Chilingerian, M. Powell, & Q. Xiao (Eds.), *International health care management. Advances in health care management* (pp. 159–182). Bingley: Emerald Group.
Vartiainen, P. (2010). Changes and challenges in Finnish health care management. *Society and Economy, 32*(1), 123–136.
Vartola, J. (2005). Näkökulmia byrokratiaan. [*The perspectives of bureaucracy*.] Tampere: University of Tampere.
Verba, S., Lehman Schlozman, K., & Brady, H. E. (2002). *Voice and equality: Civic voluntarism in American politics* (4th ed.). Cambridge: Harvard University Press.
Warren, M. E. (2009). Governance-driven democratization. *Critical Policy Studies, 3*(1), 3–13.
Wilkinson, R., & Pickett, K. (2010). *The spirit level: Why equality is better for everyone*. London: Penguin Books.
Yankelovich, D. (2015). *Wicked problems, workable solutions: Lessons from a public life*. London: Rowman & Littlefield.
Ziglio, E. (1996). The Delphi method and its contribution to decision-making. In M. Adler & E. Ziglio (Eds.), *Gazing into the Oracle: The Delphi method and its application to social policy and public health* (Vol. 5, pp. 3–33). London: Jessica Kingsley Publishers.

Part III
Innovation as an Interaction Space

Chapter 7
How Overlapping Connections Between Groups Interact with Value Differences in Explaining Creativity?

Antti Gronow, Anssi Smedlund, and Aasa Karimo

Abstract We build on recent developments in network theory and the sociology of valuation, and we propose that the overlapping connections that groups have with each other (i.e., structural folds) and differences in within-group values are substitutes for explaining creativity (coming up with new ideas and practices). Thus, only groups that lack overlapping connections with other groups stand to benefit from within-group value differences. In order to test this proposition, we developed a scale to measure differences in values in organizational cliques. We constructed 280 cliques of 104 employees at a professional service firm on the basis of their advice relations and tested whether group overlaps and diverging values were positively associated with a group's creativity and their joint effect. As expected, group overlaps only have a positive effect on creativity when values do not diverge. Furthermore, divergence of values contributes to creativity only when overlapping connections between groups are lacking. These findings are explained by presenting a compensatory theory of the function of overlapping group memberships and differences in values. The findings contribute both to the research on group processes and creativity in network theory as well as the effects of values in social sciences.

7.1 Introduction

Why do groups of people come up with new ways of doing things? There is an increasing awareness that the *connections* between people can be crucial in explaining creativity—coming up with new and meaningful ideas for organizations to use (Amabile 1988; Zhou and George 2001; Woodman et al. 1993). Network analysis

---

A. Gronow (✉) · A. Karimo
University of Helsinki, Helsinki, Finland
e-mail: antti.gronow@helsinki.fi; aasa.karimo@helsinki.fi

A. Smedlund
Research and Development, Finnish Institute of Occupational Health, Helsinki, Finland
e-mail: anssi.smedlund@ttl.fi

H. Lehtimäki et al. (eds.), *Society as an Interaction Space*, Translational Systems Sciences 22, https://doi.org/10.1007/978-981-15-0069-5_7

provides a useful way of mapping connections between people and the ensuing social structures that these connections give rise to. Network research on creativity has traditionally revolved around two arguments. On the one hand, brokering connections between groups is said to be essential because connecting disconnected actors gives access to novel information (Reagans and McEvily 2003). On the other hand, dense social relations promote social cohesion, norms, and trust, all of which help in the cultivation of information which is also essential for creativity (Obstfeld 2005). Both views suggest the structures of social ties act as social capital which brings benefits for individuals and groups in search of new ideas.

During the past decade, theories and studies have emerged that combine both of these views of social capital. This line of research has, for example, shown that brokerage and closure can join hands (de Vaan et al. 2015) or differ in their function in time (Burt and Merluzzi 2016). A recent addition to such combinatory views is the theory of structural folds which argues that the creativity of groups is positively affected when people with different values are connected by belonging to overlapping group structures—so-called structural folds (Stark 2009). Structural folds refer to situations where everyone in a group is connected with each other but there is at least one individual who is connected with another group that consists of similar, dense ties (i.e., everybody is connected). The theory of structural folds argues that, in such cases, a clash of different views on what is valuable is likely to occur while at the same time the intimate connections within and between groups produce social cohesion. While both values at the workplace (Halaby 2003) and group-level social capital (Oh et al. 2004) have been the focus of previous research, the theory of structural folds presents a novel take on the way in which values and connections between groups come together to explain creativity in organizations. It argues that creativity is more likely when densely connected groups have overlapping links with other groups—structural folds—because this brings people with different and even dissonant values together (Stark 2009). If this thesis holds, it could turn into practical advice on what sort of teams are most likely to be creative.

Even though the theory of structural folds presents convincing arguments for both overlapping groups and differences in values explaining creativity (Stark 2009), previous research has not empirically tested for the joint effect of these two factors. Our results indicate that the overlapping of groups and differences in values among group members do not result in creativity in a linear fashion. Instead, our study demonstrates that there is a compensatory relationship between differences in values and structural folds when it comes to explaining creativity. We explain this result in the light of network theory and studies in innovation management: when there are groups with homogenous values, overlapping group structures make a positive contribution to creativity because structural folds bring about the disruption that is essential for new ideas. However, when both value differences and group overlaps occur at the same time, this can be too disruptive for the cultivation of new ideas and practices.

The data for the study was derived from a professional service firm. We conducted a self-administered social network and creativity survey with a response rate of 90% in order to obtain a full social network of the organization in question and collect demographic data. We have answered the call for more research in combining structural social network analysis and cultural theories (Pachucki and Breiger 2010). Our findings also provide a novel take on the debate on the network structures that promote creativity. Organizational management practices are often turned into increasing divergence of employees by, for example, intentionally grouping individuals with different personalities together. As a managerial implication, our results suggest that increasing diversity is not necessarily always a good thing.

7.2 Theoretical Background

Dense subgroups of actors, where everybody is connected with each other, are called cliques by network analysts (Scott 2000). Actors that are members of multiple, overlapping cliques are in positions that Stark (2009) calls structural folds because the multiple group memberships of these actors *fold* the groups into each other. The idea of structural folds can be further elaborated by explaining and contrasting folds with the constructs of brokerage and closure. According to Burt (2002), brokerage is a position which connects two or more groups, and these groups exhibit closure by consisting of densely connected individuals. Brokers thus connect dense groups and span so-called structural holes between groups; if the brokers were not connecting the groups, no connections would exist between them. As Fig. 7.1 demonstrates, brokers are not members of the dense groups that they connect with each other, whereas actors in positions of structural folds are (i.e., they are connected with everyone else in the groups in question).

Brokerage is related with creativity by providing access to novel information and by thus challenging old ways of knowing and doing things (Hansen 1999; Reagans and McEvily 2003). However, the social cohesion brought about by dense connections can also contribute to creativity by making the development of shared norms and trust within groups possible (Zhou and George 2001). Social cohesion has been shown to enable the coordination of actions in implementing ideas to practice and the application of new ideas to specific contexts (Bavelas 1951; Obstfeld 2005; Shaw 1964).

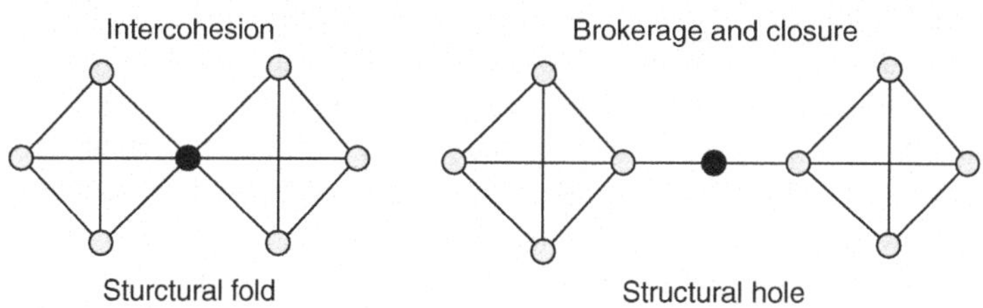

Fig. 7.1 Structural folds and structural holes. Figure based on Vedres and Stark (2010: 1157)

Research has often focused on either the benefits of brokerage or closure (Cross and Cummings 2004; Sparrowe et al. 2001). However, studies have increasingly pointed out that brokerage and closure can complement each other. For example, Tortoriello and Krackhardt (2010) found that brokering ties embedded in dense social structures have positive effects on creativity (measured with patenting activity). Oh et al. (2004) have, in their turn, insisted that closure and the bridging circuits of brokerage should not be examined separately. This is because social capital can follow when actors are central in their local network and brokers in organization-wide networks (Oh et al. 2004; Reagans and Zuckerman 2001). Dense social connections, in combination with brokerage, confer benefits by enabling both the search for nonredundant knowledge (due to brokerage) and efficient within-group knowledge transfer (because of dense connections) (Burt 2002; Hansen 1999; Uzzi and Spiro 2005).

The theory of structural folds differs from previous research in that it insists that the bridging connections between groups must themselves be *embedded* in dense group relations—in group overlaps (as shown in Fig. 7.1). In addition, this theory maintains that group overlaps bring about diverging ways of valuing things and this, in turn, is a property that tends to make groups more creative. In the case of structural folds, nonredundant knowledge is introduced into the cohesive groups, although to a lesser degree than in brokerage, because a broker connects entirely disconnected alters, whereas folds are about overlapping groups. For Vedres and Stark (2010: 1152), the social cohesion produced by overlapping group memberships "is a significant factor in explaining outstanding group performance: groups with more structural folds show higher revenue growth." In the traditional brokerage theory, access to information is the key because the lack of structural holes equals redundancy of information. However, if the problem is "the production of new *knowledge* rather than simply access to information, the bridging ties of brokerage are insufficient" (Stark 2009: 17, emphasis in original). Stark (2009) refers to terminology made famous by March (1991): creativity is about exploration that breaks away from familiar routines by bringing together originally incompatible traditions. According to this view, creativity is about recombining rather than replacing existing practices, because the generation of new knowledge is brought about by combining previously unconnected knowledge bases (e.g., Fleming 2001; Henderson and Clark 1990; Rogers 2003).

For recombination to take place, different groups should not just be in contact with each other but should engage in proper interaction via ties embedded in dense groups. The theory of structural fold argues that because brokers only connect groups but are not members of those groups (as shown in Fig. 7.1), they cannot understand the way things are valued in the groups in question. Actual recombination can therefore take place only when groups are connected by people who are insiders in the groups that they connect (i.e., they are in positions of structural folds). In the structural folding perspective, creativity and social capital are thus group-level processes (cf. Oh et al. 2004).

In addition to pointing out beneficial structural properties of networks, the theory of structural folds also builds on ideas presented by the French school of thought known as the economics of convention (Boltanski and Thévenot 2006). Representatives of the economics of convention school maintain that "economic exchange is only possible to the extent to which there is a pre-existing understanding (a 'convention') on the 'quality' of the exchanged goods and on the cognitive instruments that allow that quality to be measured" (Vatin 2013: 35). This means that arriving at a basic agreement on what counts as being valuable is a prerequisite for economic exchange to take place. However, there are obviously also instances of disagreement on issues of valuation. For example, is nature valuable to the extent that it can be measured in economic terms, or does it contain some inherent values that do not come down to economic growth? Boltanski and Thévenot (2006) argued that, when people disagree on what is valuable, they tend to rely on six or seven kinds of justifications to make their point. These include justifications that rely on inspiration, fame, the market, the environment, or on domestic (as in the family), industrial, or civic issues as criteria for judging what is deemed valuable. We won't go through these value traditions in detail, but Boltanski and Thévenot (2006) traced the roots of each logic of justification to the history of philosophy and their study has spurred empirical analyses which, for example, compare value-based justifications used in different countries (Moody and Thevenot 2000; Ylä-Anttila and Luhtakallio 2016).

The original economics of convention school assumes that agreement about what is deemed valuable facilitates cooperation because then disagreements are absent. This is where the theory of structural folds disagrees, as it postulates that action can also be facilitated by the *divergence* of values (Stark 2009). Divergence, and even the rivalrous collision of principles of valuation (what counts as valuable and how it can be measured), can be fruitful for creativity because uncertainty about the value of things can generate new ideas. When it comes to creativity, it is thus not agreement that matters but the dissonance brought about by the meeting of more than one value system (Hutter and Stark 2015). Stark (2009) also underlines that values determine what is considered to have worth (i.e., what is valuable) in an ongoing process of *valuation* (we use both terms, "values," and "valuation" in what follows).

The theory of structural folds thus directly links differences in values with creativity, because creativity entails the "ability to keep multiple evaluative principles in play and to exploit the resulting friction of their interplay" (Stark 2009: 15, emphasis deleted). It is not just individual entrepreneurs that stand to benefit from multiple evaluative principles but groups and organizations as well. Generative friction produced by the recombination of evaluative principles, which "disrupts received categories of business as usual and makes possible an ongoing recombination of resources" (Stark 2009: 16–17), should thus have an effect on the extent that organizations bring about new ideas. For example, Stark (2009, Chap. 3) studied a new-media start-up in the 1990s and argued that what made the projects of the firm creative was contention over which sort of criteria are used to value the websites they were building. That is, criteria for the value of websites were not set in stone and this caused contention which was productive in terms of allowing for the flowering of creativity.

One might still wonder whether a collision of values is a source of creativity or just a recipe for organizational chaos. In order to avoid chaos, rivalry of values has to be principled, which means that adherents to different values must present reasoned justifications. However, there is still the possibility that "arguments displace action and nothing is accomplished" (Stark 2009: 27). This is where structural folds enter the scene, because the folding of dense, cohesive groups into each other supposedly keeps organizational chaos in check. Members of dense groups are insiders of the values prevalent in these groups, unlike brokers who are outsiders who happen to connect different groups with each other. The "insiderness" of structural folds is thus supposed to ensure that conflicts over values are productive and there is enough social cohesion *between* groups.

Based on ethnographic case studies of a post-Soviet Hungarian firm, a new media start-up, and an arbitrage trading room, Stark (2009) suggests that coexistence and even active rivalry among several diverse evaluative principles within an enterprise can increase its adaptive potential. Furthermore, in an analysis of the personnel ties of firms, Vedres and Stark (2010) showed that structural folds predicted high growth. Their study also documented the potentially disruptive forces of structural folding; it showed that folds decrease the stability of groups. De Vaan et al. (2015), in turn, proposed that teams in the video game industry stand to benefit vis-à-vis creativity and also economic success if the teams are composed of individuals who are cognitively distant in terms of being exposed to different kinds of video games in their previous line of work. This effect is more visible if the teams also exhibit structural folding in that they are composed of game developers who have previously worked in different teams. These studies indicate that both divergence of values within groups and the existence of group overlaps (i.e., structural folds) can be related with creativity. However, previous research has not empirically tested for the associations between all of these factors. Researchers have given rich and detailed ethnographic descriptions of value recombinations (Stark 2009) and analyzed structural folds in relation to other issues than creativity (Vedres and Stark 2010) or value recombinations (de Vaan et al. 2015). However, it is surprising that the association between diverging values and structural folds—an essential ingredient of the theory of structural folds—has not been tested before. Therefore, we first test whether this relationship exists and present the following hypothesis:

***H1**: Structural folds and diverging values are positively associated at the group level.*

The underlying idea of a structural fold type of structure is already evident in research based on the ideas of the classical sociologist Georg Simmel (Krackhardt 1992, 1999). When individuals are embedded in cliques, in which all parties are connected with each other (so-called Simmelian triads when they consist of three people), the mechanism of closure takes placę and shared values, norms, and trust often emerge. However, Krackhardt (1999) argues that when triadic network structures overlap with each other, individuals can become constrained and even "tortured" by conflicting norms. The theory of structural folds would agree that overlapping network structures can be sources of friction but it would add that the folding between cohesive groups is supposed to ensure that some of that cohesion is split into the relationship between groups, thus ensuring that friction is kept in check. However, we suspect that things are more complicated than the theory of structural folds assumes.

Research on brokerages traditionally underlines that tapping into nonredundant information has positive effects on creativity, but some research results indicate that such nonredundancy can also have its share of problems. Ter Wal et al. (2016) argue that, unlike the theory of brokerage assumes, redundancy of information is not necessarily always bad because it enables the cross-checking or triangulation of information (e.g., by hearing it from many sources). When unfamiliar knowledge is circulated in a network with structural holes, the actors may in fact face an information overload due to difficulties in interpretation. We suspect that something similar might be going on in the case of structural folds if they bring together very diverging ways of valuing things. It is possible that the socio-emotional support that is needed for the cultivation of creative ideas (Parker and Hackett 2012) is lacking in groups that have several structural overlaps with other groups. Ter Wal et al. (2016) showed that different aspects of diversity—either diversity of knowledge or diversity brought about by nonredundant network structures—act as substitutes rather than as complements: diversity of knowledge is a substitute for the lack of diversity in social structures and vice versa (when explaining the success of venture capital in their case study). Therefore, a combination of nonredundancy *and* redundancy can be ideal because it pools the advantages of receiving novel information with ease of interpretation.

Furthermore, research by Goldberg et al. (2016) suggests that there may be a trade-off between structural and what they call cultural embeddedness. They found that brokerage has a positive effect on individual attainment at the workplace only if one is culturally embedded in the organization culture (in the sense of using similar concepts as others in the organization). This finding points toward a trade-off and the fact that being a broker without cultural embeddedness can be problematic. Even though the focus of the research by Goldberg and his colleagues' study is on work-related advantages at the individual level, we surmise that a similar kind of trade-off can be seen in the case of diverging values and structural folding at the group level. This means that if our supposition is correct, divergence of values and structural folding should be beneficial for the creativity of groups, but too much of both *at the same time* may be detrimental. Here is where we build on but also contradict the theory of structural folds, because it assumes that diverging values and structural folds jointly produce creativity in a linear fashion.

We suspect that, if people's values are highly divergent, the cognitive dissonance this produces can act as a source of problematic friction within groups. This is because divergence means that there is less social homogeneity in the group and the socio-emotional support that creative ideas need may be lacking (Parker and Corte 2017). Social homogeneity can foster a socio-emotional culture that motivates in the creation of innovative ideas and also shelters these ideas from negative criticism (Parker and Hackett 2012: 22). With structural closure, an atmosphere of trust is more likely and it is helpful in situations of dissonance, which can result from diverging values. While the idea of structural folding is not anathema to closure (folding implies dense groups but they should have overlapping connections with other groups), the interpenetration of groups by structural folding can still result in less trust and less socio-emotional support.

Our argument is that *less* folding can help in overcoming the friction that follows from diverging values. If values clash with each other, but this happens in clearly delineated groups (i.e., they lack folding), this may be conducive to the ease of interpretation of value differences. Social cohesion is likely to make people more willing to put in the extra effort required to be understood in settings with diverging values. If values divergence occurs, but the only thing that is accomplished is friction and conflict, this is not likely to be beneficial for creativity. However, in those cases where groups are fairly homogeneous in terms of their values, having structural folds that lessen redundancy (due to less social closure) can have, we suspect, a positive effect for creativity.

According to this logic, structural folds and divergence of values compensate for the lack of the other in explaining group-level creativity. Therefore, we hypothesize:

***H2**: Structural folds have a positive effect on group creativity when values do not diverge.*

Figure 7.2 presents the logic of our hypotheses. Our first hypothesis considers the relationship between structural folds and divergence of values (what we call divergence of valuation), while the second hypothesis is about their joint effect on creativity.

7.3 Methods

7.3.1 Research Setting and Data Collection

We surveyed the employees in a subunit of a professional service company in Northern Europe, which specializes in energy-related technical consulting. The company had 148 employees, 19 of whom were supervisors and the rest were contributors. Our background interviews revealed that the company was organized around teams and was characterized by open and flat hierarchies. Hence, it was

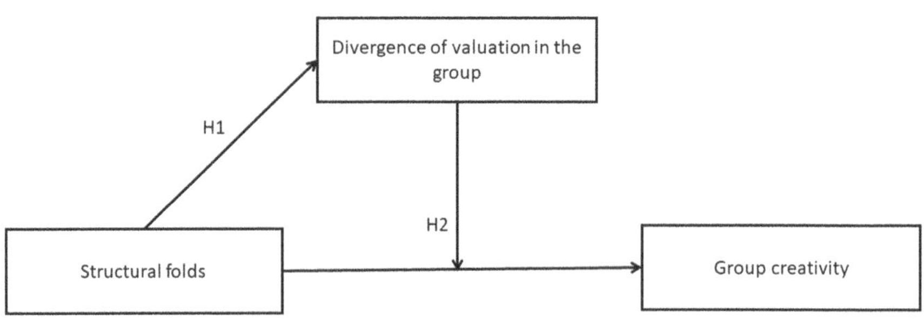

Fig. 7.2 The logic of the paper

ideal for testing our hypotheses because the theory of structural folds assumes that it should be applicable in the case of such "heterarchical" companies (i.e., they lack hierarchies; Stark 2009). In our case study firm, contributors worked in projects based on their in-depth expertise, while supervisors, who are also professionals, contributed to project management, sales, and strategies.

The data was collected during September and October of 2016 with two questionnaires. The first concerned the social networks, valuations, and demographic information of all employees, whereas the second measured creativity. A personal invitation to fill out the online questionnaire was sent to all employees via e-mail in cooperation with the company's research department. Moreover, all supervisors received an additional invitation to evaluate their own subordinates with a separate questionnaire. The data to test the hypotheses consisted of 132 responses for the first questionnaire and 18 responses for the supervisor questionnaire, resulting in response rates of 89% and 90%, respectively. The sample of our study is fairly homogeneous in terms of the background of the population. This means that the research is designed in a way that divergence of background factors should not be driving the results. However, we controlled for the effects of gender, age, and education, as is explained subsequently.

The social network data consisted of information on self-reported advice-seeking relationships where we presented the respondents with a list of all coworkers and asked them to name up to 10 coworkers from whom they seek advice if they faced a situation at work that they could not resolve on their own. This is a common measure in intraorganizational network analysis (Reagans and McEvily 2003). For example, Ibarra and Andrews (1993) argued that social relationships affect people's attitudes, and therefore the information people obtain from others when receiving advice has an effect on their own attitudes. It has also been noted that personal interactions are a primary means of organizational learning especially when tacit knowledge is being codified and transferred (Siciliano 2015). Tapping into people's advice networks is a way of analyzing the transfer of such tacit knowledge (Nebus 2006).

7.3.2 Dependent Variables

A dependent variable for group creativity was constructed based on the supervisors' evaluations of the creativity of their employees. We operationalized creativity as a so-called explorative tendency in individuals' behaviors. Exploration has been used as a synonym for creativity in the theory of structural folds (Stark 2009), although in empirical research it has not been operationalized before in this context. Researchers working in the context of other theoretical traditions have used exploration as a synonym for creativity in survey settings. For example, Rogan and Mors (2014) measured creativity as exploration in a similar type of a professional service firm that we studied. The concepts of exploration and exploitation date back to a conceptualization by March (1991), and they measure whether employees are better at implementing existing business practices (exploitation) or at developing new business ideas (exploration). In our survey questionnaire, exploitation and exploration were measured with a five-point trade-off scale. First, we asked the supervisors to evaluate their subordinates on a scale where exploitation was at one end and exploration at the other (1 = "much better at implementing existing business"; 2 = "better at implementing existing business"; 3 = "equally good at both"; 4 = "better at new business development"; 5 = "much better at new business development"). We then constructed a group-level measurement for creativity by calculating the mean of individual supervisor ratings for each group and generated a continuous dependent variable. The groups are constructed by the clique analysis procedure described below. The members of a clique might have several different supervisors and therefore it was not possible to ask the supervisors to evaluate the creativity of each clique. Aggregating the measures does have its limitations, and caution is needed when interpreting the results (we address these limitations in the concluding section of this chapter).

A 14-item absolute scale to measure explorative or exploitative behavior also exists (Mom et al. 2009), but we chose the trade-off scale used by Rogan and Mors (2014) since it is based on the view that exploitation and exploration are a continuum. Thus, an individual cannot score high on both ends at the same time. Moreover, the absolute scale relies on self-reported measures, which can lead to biases if there is a social expectation that one has to be creative. Previous research related to the theory of structural folds has relied on measures of creativity that are not based on self-report, and we feel that this is an additional justification for measuring creativity with supervisor ratings.

7.3.3 Independent Variables

Structural folding. We constructed a continuous measurement for structural folding from the sociometric survey data by measuring the number of overlaps that cliques had with other cliques. This method is described in more detail in the section on Clique Analysis.

Divergence of values. We measured the difference in how members of cliques value different things. This measure is called divergence of valuation. Stark is the main proponent of the theory of structural folds and his ideas on valuation are based on Boltanski and Thévenot's (2006) conception. Boltanski and Thévenot (2006) suggest that valuing things can be based on seven different kinds of "worlds" with their own logics, namely, the worlds of inspiration, domestic, fame, civic, the market, industrial, and ecology. We operationalized these worlds as 21 questions on values, three for each type of valuation (or "world") that Boltanski and Thévenot (2006) present (see Appendix 1 for the questions of each value type). Respondents were asked to evaluate how important they considered different types of values to be. Each question was measured on a five-point scale (1 = "not at all important"; 2 = "not very important"; 3 = "somewhat important"; 4 = "fairly important"; 5 = "very important") and the wording of the items was checked with the company representative before gathering the data. We also had a separate question for each type of value that had to do with the extent that the respondents think each value is realized at their workplace in practice. Thus, the questionnaire introduced a distinction between what the respondents valued and how they thought these values were realized in practice. This distinction was made in order for the respondents not to answer according to what they think is appropriate but rather based on what they actually value. We tested for the correlations between what people value and how they think each type of valuation is realized, and some of the answers to these questions correlate with each other but others do not. We take this to indicate that the respondents were able to distinguish between the normative (what they value) and the descriptive (how things are in practice). The normative values were the basis of our analysis because the theory of structural folds assumes that divergence in actual values has an effect on creativity.

We checked correlations and reliability for each type of value separately and, in addition, ran an exploratory factor analysis with varimax rotation (see Appendix 2). On the basis of the results, we constructed four composite variables which represent the valuation types that rely on markets (Cronbach's alpha 0.634), fame (Cronbach's alpha 0.688), inspiration (Cronbach's alpha 0.682), and ecology (Cronbach's alpha 0.776). Thus, although we operationalized all seven types of valuation in the survey, only four were included in the final analysis based on the results of the factor analysis. We also conducted the analyses using all seven types of valuations with similar results, but both the R squared of the models and parameter estimates were weaker than with four types of valuations. In the final analyses, we used only those valuation types that made sense based on the factor analysis, since it was not clear what the remaining valuation questions were actually measuring. Stark (2009) maintains that, in studying processes of valuation, one should pay attention to the local context and thus follow a principle of so-called methodological situationalism. Following this principle to the extreme would mean conducting only ethnographic research. We incorporated Stark's (2009) situationalist insight by focusing only on the four (rather than all seven) types of valuations that work in the particular context of our study (based on the factor analysis).

After constructing the composite variables, we coded which types of values the respondents thought of as important by including answers 4 or above (see the aforementioned scale). This cutoff point was chosen for two reasons. First, the middle point (3 in this case) of a Likert scale is usually regarded as a neutral stance rather than as a positive response. Second, if the middle point had been coded as something that a respondent values, cliques would have had so many types of valuations that it would have been difficult to discern any differences between them. The average number of the types of valuations that clique members bring into a clique was divided by the total number of the different types of valuations per clique. This procedure ensured that when there were multiple valuations these were not only based on the multiple valuations of a single individual, but on different types of valuations that members thought of as being important. The direction of this scale was reversed so that the larger the value the greater the divergence of valuation in a clique.

7.3.4 Control Variables

Multiple valuation. Whereas divergence of valuation measures the existence of different kinds of valuations in a clique, we also measured multiple valuation as the total number of values in a clique. Adding this measurement controls for the possibility that the presence of multiple valuations (everybody values similar but several things) rather than the valuations that are different from each other has an effect.

Proportion of project managers in a clique. We included the proportion of project managers in a clique as a control variable. In the preliminary discussions with the company representatives, we came to the conclusion that the engineering projects undertaken by the company included both contributors focusing on their core tasks and managers representing the firm to customers and managing the work of the project members. Based on their job descriptions, the managers were expected to engage in tasks that demonstrated more new business developments, whereas contributors implemented their competencies to existing businesses.

Average duration of employment in a clique. We included the tenure of the clique measured as the average tenure of the clique members. Tenure has been found to be a relevant variable in previous social network studies at the individual level (Reagans and McEvily 2003; Reagans and Zuckerman 2001), and it has also been connected with the phenomenon of exploration (March 1991).

Association of structural folding and diverging valuations with group creativity. A central claim of the theory of structural folds as proposed by Stark (2009) is that both structural folds and diverging valuations are associated with group creativity. Therefore, we test also for this association although our own expectation was that diverging values and the structural folds in fact do not increase creativity in a linear fashion.

As *demographic control variables*, we used the share of men, mean age, and mean education in a clique. All of these variables were aggregated from the individual level. Finally, we also controlled for *the size of the group* using the number of members in a clique.

7.3.5 Statistical Modeling

7.3.5.1 Clique Analysis

Vedres and Stark (2010) maintain that, in order to map structural folds, it is essential to be able to identify the overlapping of groups. This entails that actors (or nodes in network parlance) can be members of more than one group. Group overlap is often treated as a methodological problem that must be overcome in order to assign nodes to just one subgroup. The method used by Vedres and Stark (2010) is the clique percolation method, which relaxes traditional clique membership criteria. This means that all nodes do not need to relate to everyone in a group for it to count as a clique. The beauty of this method is that it enables an analysis of group overlaps. However, clique percolation often identifies relatively few subgroups. For this reason, we find that it is not the best option in the case of small data sets, such as ours.[1] This is to be expected since the method is designed for the analysis of large networks (Palla et al. 2005). Hence, we developed a novel version of group overlap analysis, which is better suited to smaller data sets. First, to identify cliques, we used clique analysis in UCINET. The aim of clique analysis is to examine the cohesive subgroup structures of networks.

Before running our analysis, we dichotomized and symmetrized the network matrix. This means that nonrespondents were also included in the analysis if a respondent had indicated that they were linked to a nonrespondent (i.e., a respondent said that (s)he received advice from a nonrespondent). This procedure excludes analysis of directions and the reciprocity (or lack thereof) of relations, even though the advice relations of our data are directional. However, clique analysis requires that ties are treated as nondirectional. Information on direction of ties is therefore lost but, then again, the theory of structural folds does not base its claims on the directionality of ties.

In order to identify cliques, we used a minimum clique size of three nodes. This means that an actor must be connected with at least two other actors and they also have to be connected with each other for a clique to exist. Three is the lowest number for a clique and therefore it is the essential structural ingredient of groups. The classical definition of a group by Georg Simmel is indeed a triad. As Krackhardt (1999:186) explains, all members of cliques are by definition "Simmelian tied," that is, part of triads. Minimum clique size of three was also chosen in order to keep as many respondents in the analysis as possible. Only 13 respondents were omitted from the analysis (they did not have at least two ties to such actors that are also connected with each other) compared to losing 31 and 63 nodes with minimum clique sizes of four and five, respectively.

Next, we generated a clique-by-clique co-membership matrix in order to identify overlaps between groups, thereby calculating *the number of cliques each clique has overlaps with* but not the cliques that individual employees are members of (which would have been an individual-level measure). We think this procedure captures the essence of structural folds, as the concept refers to dense groups that are interconnected with each other. Other clique-level variables were computed and aggregated on the basis of information on the clique members listed in the clique analysis output.

[1]We also used the CFinder software to analyze our data with the clique percolation method. With k value 3, CFinder identified only two subgroups; with k values of both 4 and 5, there were 10 subgroups. With so few subgroups, no statistically significant differences can be found.

7.3.5.2 Linear Regression and Modeling

To test our hypotheses, we used a linear regression analysis with OLS estimation. Our hypotheses suggested a proportional relationship between structural folds, divergence of valuation, and creativity. In addition, visually examining the scatterplots of the association between the variables leaned toward a linear relationship, which was confirmed with the post-estimation of the models.

Modeling was performed in two steps to study the effects of independent variables on the dependent variables. The first set of models examined the effects of structural folds on divergence of valuation (Table 7.2). The second set of models (Table 7.3) tested whether, and how, structural folding and divergence of valuation were associated with creativity. We z-standardized all independent variables to better facilitate interpretation of the moderation effect, as suggested by Dawson (2014).

7.4 Results

The number of identified cliques with a minimum size of three was 280.[2] These cliques had 9646 overlaps with each other in total, and the mean amount of overlap was 34.45 with a variance of 3 to 81. The mean divergence of valuation in a clique was 0.41 on a scale from 0 to 1, where 0 indicated a lack of divergence and 1 represented that all clique members value different things. The mean score for creativity per clique was 2.5 on the original Likert scale from 1 to 5. We found that creativity correlated significantly with divergence of valuation and the proportion of supervisors in a clique. We also found a significant correlation between structural folds, divergence of valuation, proportion of supervisors, and multiple valuations. Divergence of valuation correlated with the proportion of supervisors and average duration of employment. Bivariate correlations of the main variables are presented in Table 7.1.

Our first hypothesis stated that structural folds and the divergence of valuation are associated at the clique level. We found support for this hypothesis. The more structural folds a clique has (i.e., overlaps with other cliques), the higher the divergence of valuation. However, the proportion of supervisors in a clique explains a larger degree of variation in the divergence of valuation than structural folds. The results of these analyses are presented in Table 7.2.

Our second hypothesis implies two things: first, structural folds should have a positive effect on creativity when the divergence of valuation is low and, second, the effect should be negative when the divergence of valuation is high. We found that the interaction effect between folding and divergence of valuation is significant (Model 4). This means that, when it comes to creativity, the effect of each is dependent on

[2] When the N of the network is only 147, 280 subgroups may sound like a high figure. However, this figure is not that high considering that nodes are members of 1.9 cliques on average.

Table 7.1 Descriptive statistics and Pearson correlation coefficients for the variables

Variable	Min	Max	Mean	SD	1	2	3	4	5	6	7	8	9
1. Creativity	1	4	2.50	0.59									
2. Divergence of values	0	0.75	0.41	0.16	−0.127*								
3. Structural folds	3	81	34.45	14.85	−0.085	0.184**							
4. Share of supervisors in a clique	0	1	0.53	0.35	0.168**	−0.342**	0.387**						
5. Average duration of employment in a clique	2.33	6	4.91	0.95	0.01	0.140*	0.407**	0.128*					
6. Share of men in a clique	0	1	0.63	0.29	0.068	0.113	−0.101	0.205**	0.103				
7. Mean age in a clique	29.33	56	43.65	5.11	−0.05	−0.271**	−0.092	0.361**	0.148*	0.139*			
8. Mean education in a clique	2	5	4.04	0.71	0.145*	-0.049	0.477**	0.625**	0.204**	0.093	-0.007		
9. Number of members in a clique	3	7	3.97	0.9	−0.192**	0.250**	0.531**	0.098	0.369**	0.026	0.015	0.164**	
10. Number of values in a clique	1	4	3.6	0.74	0.021	−0.092	0.156**	0.052	0.015	−0.184**	−0.117	−0.012	0.241**

$^{**}p < 0.01$, $^{*}p < 0.05$

Table 7.2 The relationship between structural folds and divergence of valuation

	Model 1		Model 2	
Divergence of valuation	B	Std. error	B	Std. error
Constant	0.413**	0.009	0.413**	0.008
Structural folds	0.03**	0.01	0.049**	0.012
Share of supervisors in a clique			−0.092**	0.012
Average duration of employment in a clique			0.001	0.009
Share of men in a clique			0.041**	0.009
Mean age in a clique			−0.012	0.01
Mean education in a clique			0.019	0.011
Number of members in a clique			0.019	0.01
R^2	0.034		0.325	
Sig of R^2 change	0.002		0.000	
N	280		280	

$^{**}p < 0.01$, $^{*}p < 0.05$

Table 7.3 The effect of structural folds and divergence of valuation on creativity

	Model 3		Model 4	
Creativity	B	Std. error	B	Std. error
Constant	2.315**	0.182	2.546**	0.175
Structural folds	−0.116*	0.052	−0.032	0.051
Divergence of values	−0.013	0.041	−0.047	0.039
Structural folds*Divergence of values			−0.205**	0.034
Number of values in a clique	0.052	0.05	−0.002	0.048
Share of supervisors in a clique	0.137*	0.058	0.114*	0.054
Average duration of employment in a clique	0.079*	0.039	0.086*	0.037
Share of men in a clique	0.012	0.038	0.026	0.036
Mean age in a clique	−0.1*	0.041	−0.101**	0.039
Mean education in a clique	0.055	0.048	0.051	0.045
Number of members in a clique	−0.108*	0.043	−0.097*	0.041
R^2	0.120		0.224	
Sig of R^2 change	0.000		0.000	
N	280		280	

$^{**}p < 0.01$, $^{*}p < 0.05$

the *lack of the other*. The estimate for the interaction shows that the more structural folds a clique has the less divergence of valuation is associated with creativity. Conversely, higher levels of divergence in valuation make folding less likely to be associated with creativity.

As a control, we checked whether structural folds and divergence of valuation are positively associated with creativity. The results of Model 3 in Table 7.3 show a statistically significant negative association with structural folds and creativity. However, a simple bivariate regression does not result in an association between creativity and structural folds. The standard procedure for regression diagnostics in

Stata did not show heteroskedasticity or multicollinearity between the variables, although the proportion of supervisors correlates with the structural folds. After omitting the proportion of supervisors from the model, the structural folds become nonsignificant. This warrants further examination, but one explanation for these results could be the collider bias (e.g., Greenland 2003) caused by the proportion of supervisors on the association between creativity and structural folds. This would normally show in the post-estimation procedures, but the logic may be different with our clique analysis method. We also observed that the proportion of supervisors in a clique and average duration of employment in a clique were positively associated with creativity, both in line with previous research. The mean age of the people within a clique and group size were instead negatively associated with creativity. This meant that a higher mean age and bigger group size were associated with lower creativity. Other control variables used in the model did not exert significant effects on creativity. Furthermore, according to the model diagnostics, multicollinearity between structural folds and divergence of valuation should not pose a problem. The variance inflation factor (VIF) for the direct effects was 1.035 for both structural folds and divergence of valuation.

To further test hypotheses 2, we investigated the interaction pattern with simple slope analysis, as suggested by Dawson (2014). We did so by computing a categorical variable to represent low, medium, and high levels of divergence of valuation (see Fig. 7.3). The cutoff points for low and high levels were defined as one standard deviation from the mean. The coefficient for the simple slope of structural folds on creativity was significant and positive for low levels of divergence ($b = 0.174$, $p = 0.012$). With high levels of divergence, the simple slope was significant and negative ($b = -0.237$, $p < 0.000$). However, the simple slope for the medium level of divergence was nonsignificant. The relationship between structural folding and innovation for different levels of divergence of valuation is shown in Fig. 7.3. With low levels of divergence, structural folding had a positive effect on creativity, but the effect was negative for both medium and high levels (although the result is nonsignificant for medium levels). Furthermore, for high levels, the negative effect was significantly stronger compared to medium levels. We take these results as further validation of our second hypothesis, which postulated that divergence and folding act as substitutes for each other.

7.5 Discussion and Conclusion

It has become widely accepted that a network analysis of the social determinants of creativity holds potential. However, there is no universal agreement about the kinds of network structures that explain creativity. The theory of structural folds suggests that creativity is positively affected when groups have overlapping connections (i.e., structural folds) with other groups and when the values that people have differ from each other. Our analysis shows that, instead of both diverging valuations and group overlaps increasing creativity in a linear fashion, there is a compensatory

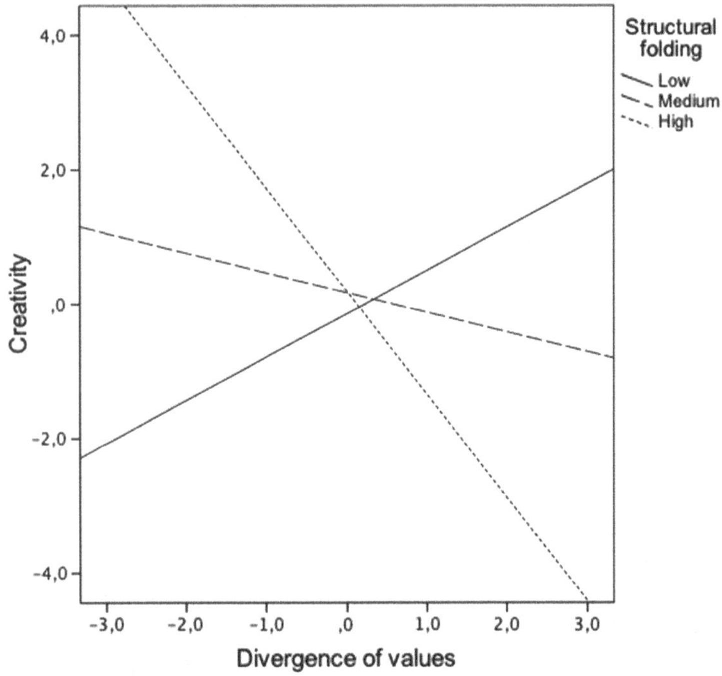

Fig. 7.3 The relationship between divergence of valuation and creativeness for low, medium, and high levels of structural folding

mechanism in which a combination of *many* structural folds with *low* levels of diverging valuations, or *few* structural folds with *high* levels of diverging valuations, are the most beneficial for creativity.

The structural folding theory presents divergence of valuation and structural folding as joining hands in explaining creativity by stating that the key "is not the overlapping structure of the network itself, but the generative tension that overlapping groups experience when their cognitive makeup is different" (de Vaan et al. 2015: 1179). De Vaan et al. (2015: 1154–1155) aimed to convey an image of "a topology in which structural folding is pulling groups closer while cognitive dissimilarity [diverging values] is pulling them apart." While this image is powerful, our results imply that the association between folding, divergence of valuation, and creativity may be more complicated than the theory of structural folds suggests. Why is this, then, the case?

Both folding and divergence are factors that increase heterogeneity and make cliques less cohesive. A plausible explanation, supported by innovation theories of closure (e.g., Obstfeld 2005), is that, with concurrent folding and diverging values, a lack of cohesion prevents the group from concentrating on enhancing creativity. This is in line with the findings of Parker and Corte (2017) who argued that social homogeneity can provide creative interactions because of associated shared cultural capital and personal familiarity. Having both diverging values and overlapping connections with other groups at the same time can call into question the basic agreement needed for cooperation. However, when the group is cohesive and lacks folding, divergence of values brings with it the freshness of ideas that cohesive structures can lack. Differences can thus bring added value, as De Vaan et al. (2015: 1154) argued, but with the caveat that too much of a difference can cause problems. If creativity is the "ability to keep multiple evaluative principles in play and to exploit the resulting friction of their interplay" (Stark 2009: 15, italics removed), then exploiting this interplay may be easier with less overlap of social structures at the group level.

Stark (2009: 27) has admitted that it is possible that diverging values can lead to problems if "arguments displace action and nothing is accomplished." However, he still maintains that those occupying positions of structural folds should be able to suppress such tensions because they are trusted insiders in the groups in question. Based on our results, we suggest that folding does not necessarily suppress the tensions produced by diverging values but rather can make them more acute. Our results resemble arguments presented by Krackhardt (1999) when he argues that overlapping triadic network structures can lead to conflicting norms. It seems that structural folding does not ensure a sufficient level of cohesion in the face of the challenges that divergent valuation presents to a group. Organizational diversity may be a source of adaptive potential "when several diverse evaluative principles coexist in active rivalry within the enterprise" (Stark 2009: 26), but our research highlights that cohesion without excessive folding is needed to encounter the forces of diverse evaluations.

Even though the theory of structural folds assumes that both divergence of valuation and structural folds enhance creativity, previous research has mainly focused on analyzing the effects of these factors on creativity separately. In an empirical analysis of computer games, de Vaan et al. proposed that "the effects of structural folding on inventiveness and game changing creative success are especially strong when overlapping groups are cognitively distant" (2015: 1147). However, the measurement of cognitive distance used in their study is different stylistic codes of the video game industry, not diverging values. Instead of differences in stylistic exposure, our study highlights differences in actual values and, therefore, we believe our research has been more in line with what the theory of structural folds argues.[3]

Our study complements the findings of Goldberg et al. (2016) who showed that brokerage is helpful only for the culturally embedded. Although the context of our research is different,[4] we encountered a somewhat similar dynamic: folding enables creativity when valuations do not vary and people are thus, either or but not both constitutes the lesson. Social network analysts have pointed out that homophily seems to be an almost universal feature of social networks in the sense that likeness

[3] Stark (2009) has explored the connection between divergence of values and structural folding in the methodological context of ethnographic research. A methodological focus on ethnographic research is logical if one wants to underscore (as Stark does) that valuation always takes place in particular situations. However, ethnographic research is better suited to the formulation of new theories rather than to testing them.

[4] Goldberg et al. (2016) studied career advancement with a dual focus on the effects of similarity of vocabulary of senders and receivers of e-mails (cultural fit) and the structural positions of nodes in e-mail networks.

breeds connections (McPherson et al. 2001). Our results imply that forcing different, heterophilous actors into densely connected groups is not always a good idea. Finding the correct balance between divergence and homogeneity of valuation within groups remains a managerial challenge to be reckoned with.

The theory of structural folds is partly based on Boltanski and Thévenot's (2006) influential theorizing toward seven different kinds of value-based justifications. For example, job-related values have been the topic of previous studies (Halaby 2003), but our study is the first in which the types of values that the theory of structural folds assumes to have an effect on creativity are operationalized in the context of an organizational survey. An additional methodological contribution is our novel way of measuring the structural folding of groups by analyzing clique overlaps. This method is suited to the analysis of small N data, unlike the clique percolation method which has previously been used in the literature on structural folds.

Despite its contributions, this study has some limitations, which will hopefully provide motivation for further research. The first concerns the case study character of our research. Our data was collected with a survey from a subunit of a professional service company, which limits the generalizability of the findings. We hope that future research will analyze how structural folds and the divergence of valuation are related with different kinds of organizations. This will entail either aggregating individual-level data on valuations or coming up with variables that can be measured at the organizational level. The latter option may prove to be difficult, because it is not easy to operationalize the types of values presented by Boltanski and Thévenot (2006) at this level. Nevertheless, we encourage experimenting with other possible measures in future research.

With surveys, it is always possible that people answer in a manner they think is socially desirable. It was for this reason that we did not ask the employees to evaluate their own creativity but rather relied on their supervisors' assessments. However, it is still possible that supervisors do not know how good their employees are in coming up with new business ideas in reality or that they base their answers on superficial criteria, such as identifying more extrovert persons. Nevertheless, we were able to gather social network survey data, along with attribute data, from the participants with an exceptionally high response rate. In discussions with the human resource managers of the case organization, it became evident that the company should be ideal for testing the theory of structural folds because it displays the distributed authority of so-called heterarchical organizations, which should be an ideal breeding ground for the network structures of structural folds (Stark 2009).

Future research could also try developing measures that are not reliant on subjective responses. One option would be to analyze the content of communication within an organization with the help of big data. For example, examining the content of e-mails that individuals send to each other (cf. Goldberg et al. 2016), and dividing the content between creative and noncreative content, could shed light on the folding and divergence of values on a larger scale. However, access to such data is often limited and there might also be problems with issues of operationalization (what counts as creative content in an e-mail and how to measure its effect on the creativity of the employee). Field experiments are another interesting direction of future research (Hoogendoorn et al. 2017). For example, employees could first be assigned to different teams based on the types of values they prefer and afterwards teams with different ways of valuing things could be brought together while measuring for existing links between teams and for their creative output.

An additional limitation is the aggregate nature of our dependent and independent variables that may cause concerns of generalizability of our findings. Finding a suitable measure for creativity is always context-specific and depends on the operation and goals of the organization. We used a proven measure (Rogan and Mors 2014) of superior ratings of explorative versus exploitative behavior. The case organization of Rogan and Mors (2014) was similar to ours, and the construct of exploration originally coined by March (1991) is connected to the theory of structural folds (Stark 2009). There are naturally other possibilities for assessing creativity of organizations, such as measuring patenting activity. However, patenting data is usually used for comparing the creative output of different business organizations, whereas we focused on the creativity of small groups within an organization.

While we feel confident that supervisors' assessments of employees' exploration capture something about actual creativity, there are aspects of creativity that we did not cover. Exploration measures the ability to come up with new business ideas and does not differentiate between incremental and radical innovations. There are previous indications that the "unknown unknowns" associated with radical innovations call for managerial strategies where different solutions are examined simultaneously (Lenfle et al. 2016). One thing that the development of radical ideas requires is sheltering them from initial skepticism (Parker and Hackett 2012). Such sheltering is possible in diverse groups that show solidarity with each other and are closed in terms of their connections to outsiders. Even though we cannot demonstrate that the dynamic we diagnose between diverging values and structural folds would be at play in the context of radical innovations, we think that this is likely. This is because groups with low levels of structural folds and with diversity in values are relatively closed at same time as they bring different values together (which, at least in principle, makes it possible to examine different solutions simultaneously). However, it remains for future research to find out whether incremental and radical innovations behave differently in relation to diverging valuations and structural folds.

Social identities have known to have an effect on, for example, work motivation and task performance (Van Knippenberg 2000) and future studies should also test whether it has an effect on creativity if the groups that fold into each other exhibit social identities or not. The groups of our study consist of cliques (everybody is connected with everyone else) that were constructed based on advice links and therefore members might not identify with the groups in question. We feel that measuring the existence of groups the way we did is justified because the original theory of structural folds does not posit that creativity would come down to group identities. The respondents thus did not "choose" the cliques we placed them into. The positive outcome of this is that we should not be measuring self-selection of individuals with different dispositions toward exploration or exploitation into groups with different levels of clique overlap. However, it is possible that group identities would have something to do with the way in which the dynamics of structural folding and diverging values play out. For example, it is conceivable that groups in which the members identify with a single group can maintain high levels of creativity even with high levels of value divergence and structural folding at the same time. Perhaps the normative pressures exerted by overlapping and diverging group memberships can also be more manageable if group identity is stable. Future research could also look into what explains the particular kinds of values that employees bring into the workplace. Halaby (2003) found that family backgrounds can have an effect on the extent that employees value riskier entrepreneurial or safer bureaucratic job properties. The types of valuations that the theory of structural folds builds on (Boltanski and Thévenot 2006) have not been studied with the aim of finding out what explains the types of values employees favor. We hope that future researchers also approach this topic.

Appendix 1

Operationalization of the valuation questions (the titles of the "worlds" were not shown in the questionnaire)

Please indicate how important you consider the following factors to be (1 = "not at all important"; 2 = "not very important"; 3 = "somewhat important"; 4 = "fairly important"; 5 = "very important").

1. **Market World**

   My salary or other monetary compensation is good.
   My company pays a better salary than its competitors.
   My company succeeds better than its competitors.

2. **Industrial World**

   My company operates efficiently.
   The targets of the company are clear.
   The division of responsibilities among employees is functional.

3. **Civic World**

   Employees can participate in the company's decision-making.
   All employees are being treated equally.
   Employee rights are explicit in the company.

4. **World of Fame**

   My job is valued in society.
   My company is well known.
   I am able to network widely in my job.

5. **World of Inspiration**

   I am able to fulfill myself at work.

Company culture promotes my creativity.
I am passionate about my work.

6. **Domestic World**

I trust my closest colleagues.
In my company, the superiors are held in esteem and respected.
In my work, I accumulate competence that is being transferred to future employees.

7. **World of Ecology**

I am able to promote environmental welfare in my work.
The company functions in accordance with sustainable development.
My work promotes the use of renewable energy.

Appendix 2

Reliability statistics for all valuations

	Cronbach's Alpha	Number of items
Market	**0.634**	**3**
Industrial	0.488	3
Civic	0.241	3
Fame	**0.688**	**3**
Inspiration	**0.682**	**3**
Domestic	0.568	3
Ecology	**0.776**	**3**

The valuations used for constructing the composite variable are indicated with bold characters

References

Amabile, T. M. (1988). A model of creativity and innovation in organizations. *Research in Organizational Behavior, 10*(1), 123–167.

Bavelas, A. (1951). Communication patterns in task-oriented groups. In D. Lerner & H. D. Lasswell (Eds.), *The policy sciences*. Stanford, CA: Stanford University Press.

Boltanski, L., & Thévenot, L. (2006). *On justification: Economies of worth*. Princeton, NJ: Princeton University Press.

Burt, R. S. (2002). Bridge decay. *Social Networks, 24*(4), 333–363.

Burt, R. S., & Merluzzi, J. (2016). Network oscillation. *Academy of Management Discoveries, 2*(4).

Cross, R., & Cummings, J. N. (2004). Tie and network correlates of individual performance in knowledge-intensive work. *Academy of Management Journal, 47*(6), 928–937.

Dawson, J. F. (2014). Moderation in management research: What, why, when, and how. *Journal of Business and Psychology, 29*(1), 1–19.
de Vaan, M., Vedres, B., & Stark, D. (2015). Game changer: The topology of creativity. *American Journal of Sociology, 120*(4), 1144–1194.
Fleming, L. (2001). Recombinant uncertainty in technological search. *Management Science, 47*(1), 117–132.
Goldberg, A., Sameer, B., Srivastava, V. G. M., Monroe, W., & Potts, C. (2016). Fitting in or standing out? The tradeoffs of structural and cultural embeddedness. *American Sociological Review, 81*(6), 1190–1222.
Greenland, S. (2003). Quantifying biases in causal models: Classical confounding vs collider-stratification Bias. *Epidemiology, 14*(3), 300–306.
Halaby, C. N. (2003). Where job values come from. *American Sociological Review, 68*, 251–278.
Hansen, M. T. (1999). The search-transfer problem: The role of weak ties in sharing knowledge across organization subunits. *Administrative Science Quarterly, 44*(1), 82–111.
Henderson, R. M., & Clark, K. B. (1990). Architectural innovation: The reconfiguration of existing product technologies and the failure of established firms. *Administrative Science Quarterly, 35*(1), 9–30.
Hoogendoorn, S., Parker, S. C., & Van Praag, M. (2017). Smart or diverse start-up teams? Evidence from a field experiment. *Organization Science, 28*(6), 1010–1028.
Hutter, M., & Stark, D. (2015). Pragmatist perspectives on valuation: An introduction. In A. Antal, M. Hutter, & D. Stark (Eds.), *Moments of valuation: Exploring sites of dissonance*. Oxford: Oxford University Press.
Ibarra, H., & Andrews, S. B. (1993). Power, social influence, and sense making: Effects of network centrality and proximity on employee perceptions. *Administrative Science Quarterly, 38*(2), 277–303.
Krackhardt, D. (1992). The strength of strong ties: The importance of Philos in organizations. In N. Nohria & R. G. Eccles (Eds.), *Networks and organizations* (pp. 216–239). Boston, MA: Harvard Business School Press.
Krackhardt, D. J. (1999). The ties that torture: Simmelian tie analysis in organization. *Research in the Sociology of Organizations, 16*, 183–210.
Lenfle, S., Masson, P. L., & Weil, B. (2016). When project management meets design theory: Revisiting the Manhattan and Polaris projects to characterize 'radical Innovation' and its managerial implications. *Creativity and Innovation Management, 25*(3), 378–395.
March, J. G. (1991). Exploration and exploitation in organizational learning. *Organization Science, 2*(1), 71–87.
McPherson, M., Smith-Lovin, L., & Cook, J. M. (2001). Birds of a feather: Homophily in social networks. *Annual Review of Sociology, 27*(1), 415–444.
Mom, T. J. M., van den Bosch, F. A. J., & Volberda, H. W. (2009). Understanding variation in managers' ambidexterity: Investigating direct and interaction effects of formal structural and personal coordination mechanisms. *Organization Science, 20*(4), 812–828.
Moody, M., & Thevenot, L. (2000). Comparing models of strategy, interests, and the public good in French and American Environmental disputes. In M. Lamont & L. Thevenot (Eds.), *Rethinking comparative cultural sociology: Repertoires of evaluation in France and the United States* (pp. 273–306). Cambridge, MA: Cambridge University Press.
Nebus, J. (2006). Building collegial information networks: A theory of advice network generation. *Academy of Management Review, 31*(3), 615–637.
Obstfeld, D. (2005). Social networks, the Tertius Iungens orientation, and involvement in innovation. *Administrative Science Quarterly, 50*(1), 100–130.
Oh, H., Chung, M.-H., & Labianca, G. (2004). Group social capital and group effectiveness: The role of informal socializing ties. *Academy of Management Journal, 47*(6), 860–875.
Pachucki, M. A., & Breiger, R. L. (2010). Cultural holes: Beyond relationality in social networks and culture. *Annual Review of Sociology, 36*(1), 205–224.

Palla, G., Derényi, I., Farkas, I., & Vicsek, T. (2005). Uncovering the overlapping community structure of complex networks in nature and society. *Nature, 435*(7043), 814–818.

Parker, J. N., & Corte, U. (2017). Placing collaborative circles in strategic action fields: Explaining differences between highly creative groups. *Sociological Theory, 35*(4), 261–287.

Parker, J. N., & Hackett, E. J. (2012). Hot spots and hot moments in scientific collaborations and social movements. *American Sociological Review, 77*(1), 21–44.

Reagans, R., & McEvily, B. (2003). Network structure and knowledge transfer: The effects of cohesion and range. *Administrative Science Quarterly, 48*(2), 240–267.

Reagans, R., & Zuckerman, E. W. (2001). Networks, diversity, and productivity: The social Capital of Corporate R&D teams. *Organization Science, 12*(4), 502–517.

Rogan, M., & Mors, M. L. (2014). A network perspective on individual ambidexterity in organizations. *Organization Science, 25*(6), 1860–1877.

Rogers, E. (2003). *Diffusion of innovations*. New York, NY: Free Press.

Scott, J. (2000). *Social network analysis. A handbook* (2nd ed.). London: SAGE.

Shaw, M. E. (1964). Communication networks. In L. Berkowitz (Ed.), *Advances in experimental social psychology* (pp. 111–147). New York: Academic Press.

Siciliano, M. D. (2015). Advice networks in public organizations: The role of structure, internal competition, and individual attributes. *Public Administration Review, 75*(4), 548–559.

Sparrowe, R. T., Liden, R. C., Wayne, S. J., & Kraimer, M. L. (2001). Social networks and the performance of individuals and groups. *Academy of Management Journal, 44*(2), 316–325.

Stark, D. (2009). *The sense of dissonance*. Accounts of Worth in Economic Life: Princeton University Press.

Tortoriello, M., & Krackhardt, D. (2010). Activating cross-boundary knowledge: The role of Simmelian ties in the generation of innovations. *Academy of Management Journal, 53*(1), 167–181.

Uzzi, B., & Spiro, J. (2005). Collaboration and creativity: The small world problem. *The American Journal of Sociology, 111*(2), 447–504.

Van Knippenberg, D. (2000). Work motivation and performance: A social identity perspective. *Applied Psychology, 49*(3), 357–371.

Vatin, F. (2013). Valuation as evaluating and valorizing. *Valuation Studies, 1*(1), 31–50.

Vedres, B., & Stark, D. (2010). Structural folds : Generative disruption in overlapping groups. *American Journal of Sociology, 115*(4), 1150–1190.

Wal, T., Anne, L. J., Alexy, O., Block, J., & Sandner, P. G. (2016). The best of both worlds. *Administrative Science Quarterly, 61*(3), 393–432.

Woodman, R. W., Sawyer, J. E., & Griffin, R. W. (1993). Toward a theory of organizational creativity. *Academy of Management Review, 18*(2), 293–321.

Ylä-Anttila, T., & Luhtakallio, E. (2016). Justifications analysis: Understanding moral evaluations in public debates. *Sociological Research Online, 21*(4).

Zhou, J., & George, J. M. (2001). When job dissatisfaction leads to creativity: Encouraging the expression of voice. *Academy of Management Journal, 44*(4), 682–696.

Chapter 8
Disaster Management as a Complex System: Building Resilience with New Systemic Tools of Analysis

Petri Uusikylä, Paula Tommila, and Ida Uusikylä

Abstract This chapter introduces an alternative perspective to study disaster preparedness and risk reduction (DP/DRR) systems. Study shows that by applying systems thinking and complexity theory we understand better the dynamics and interconnectedness of the DP/DRR. This applies both to interconnected risks (multirisk landscapes) and interconnected actors (multi-actor networks).

These results are part of the broader study commissioned by the Finnish Red Cross (FRC). The aim of the thematic study was to promote institutional learning on DP/DRR project experiences and practices that can benefit better programming in the future. The overall objective of the study was to identify critical issues in designing, implementing and monitoring and evaluation by the FRC and its partnering National Societies (NS).

This chapter consists of two main parts. The first part presents the results of the meta-analysis of the ten countries and 17 projects. The meta-analysis utilises the IFRC evaluation criteria (relevance, impact, effectiveness, efficiency, sustainability and coherence). From this sample, the final case studies were selected. The last part is the case study section introducing the findings and results of the field missions to the Philippines. Case study analysis uses a set of systems methods and tools to better understand the dynamics and interconnection between the risk factors and stakeholders in the field. These results will be presented in Chap. 8.3. The systems approach utilised in the case study provides insights about the dynamics and interconnectedness of risk landscapes and inter-organisational Disaster Management (DM) networks. The study shows that by applying systems methods such as network analysis, the risk components helped local disaster risk management units to better understand the interconnectedness of risk elements and the joint impact of those risks. Also, identifying the relations and connections between the disaster risk

P. Uusikylä (✉)
Frisky & Anjoy, Helsinki, Finland

P. Tommila
Osma Advisory Ltd, Helsinki, Finland

I. Uusikylä
Hanoi, Vietnam

H. Lehtimäki et al. (eds.), *Society as an Interaction Space*, Translational Systems Sciences 22, https://doi.org/10.1007/978-981-15-0069-5_8

agencies and stakeholders helps to explain why certain risk preparedness actions produce better results and effects. The study concludes that the more actors are connected to the network, the more versatile the understanding of the risk preparedness and thus the higher the resilience of preparedness actions.

8.1 Introduction

The interest and need for developing new systemic tools for analysis in the field of disaster risk reduction (DRR) stems from the ever-increasing complexity of systems and the non-linear interdependence between the socio-technical systems and the natural environment in which they function. This chapter introduces an alternative perspective to study disaster preparedness and risk reduction (DP/DRR) systems. The study shows that by applying systems thinking and complexity theory we can better understand the dynamics and interconnectedness of the DP/DRR. This applies both to interconnected risks (multirisk landscapes) and interconnected actors (multi-actor networks).

This chapter is based on the thematic study commissioned by the Finnish Red Cross (FRC) (Uusikylä et al. 2017). The aim of the project was to promote institutional learning on DP/DRR project experiences and practices that can contribute to better programming in the future. The overall objective of the study was to identify critical factors in the way the FRC and its partnering National Societies (NS) are currently designing, implementing and planning for the sustainability of their DP/DRR projects. Specifically, the evaluation was expected to assess the overall impact, effectiveness and sustainability of selected programmes to identify the most common factors related to planning and implementation approaches and practices that have enabled or hindered the programmes to reach their DP/DRR-related goals and objectives in a sustainable manner.

The main emphasis of the study was on learning and development rather than identifying problems or highlighting flaws and failures. Every single project and country programme has its context-specific weaknesses and caveats and the implementation of such programs in a complex environment is challenging. Therefore, one of the main purpose was to find out what programme designs, implementation practices and methods work best in DP/DRR projects.

First, this chapter discusses the DRR strategy of the Red Cross Crescent, where the thematic programme forms the ground for the strategic analysis. Second, it presents the theoretical underpinnings of systemic thinking, complex systems and resilience. Third, the meta-analysis of 10 countries covered in the thematic study commissioned by the FRC is presented. The main focus of this chapter, however, is on the case study of the Community-Based Disaster Risk Reduction (CBDRR) Project in Aklan Province in the Philippines, which is one of the original 10 countries covered in the study. The Philippines is one of the most high-risk countries in the world experiencing natural disasters, and therefore identifying project experiences and practices was crucial in improving the sustainability and resilience of the project. The analysis utilises multirisk analysis, network analysis and outcome harvesting, which are carried out in the case of the Philippines. Finally, the chapter presents conclusions and recommendations for future research.

8.1.1 Disaster Risk Reduction Operations Under the Red Cross Crescent Strategy

According to the International Federation of Red Cross and Red Crescent Societies (IFRC), disaster management can be defined as "*the organisation and management of resources and responsibilities for dealing with all humanitarian aspects of emergencies, in particular preparedness, response and recovery in order to lessen the impact of disasters*". The Red Cross and Red Crescent National Societies, supported by the International Federation, work with communities to reduce risk, mitigate the effects of, prepare to respond, respond to and recover from disasters.[1] During disasters, the immediate aim is to save lives, to reduce suffering, damage and losses and to protect, comfort and support affected people. These actions combined with preventative risk reduction, preparedness and resilience building constitute the core components of the disaster and crisis management work of the Red Cross Movement.

Besides health, DP and DRR are the key thematic areas in the FRC in the long-term programme support it provides for its partnering sister societies under its development cooperation framework. During 2005–2015, the FRC has supported the implementation of around 40 DP/DRR projects and programmes in Latin America, Africa, Central Asia and Asia co-funded by the Ministry for Foreign Affairs of Finland and the European Commission. In addition, the FRC has regularly supported IFRC DP/DRR policy development by funding global DPDRR tools, approaches and programmes. According to the IFRC's disaster management approach, Red Cross seeks to support and build local, community and NS capacities by strengthening household, community and national resilience, reducing disaster risk, ensuring effective and efficient DP and response and facilitating durable and sustainable recovery that goes hand in hand with development.

However, there is a constant concern that the top-down managed programming does not meet the needs on the ground and the current linear tools and methods are insufficient to measure the reality in the implementation countries. As Fiksel (2006: 1) has described it, "there is an urgent need for a better understanding of the dynamic, adaptive behaviour of complex systems and their resilience in the face of disruptions". Therefore, new analytical frameworks need to be introduced that better describe the realities of DP/DRR field and provide better anticipation of unforeseen risks. Viewing the DP/DRR ecosystem through the lens of systems thinking and complexity provides us with new tools and methods of analysis to utilise to

[1] https://www.ifrc.org/en/what-we-do/disaster-management/about-disaster-management/

describe the existing realities. This chapter proposes tools such as outcome harvesting and participatory dialogue and methods such as network analysis and multirisk assessment tools which help to capture the dynamic relationships and emergent behaviours that characterise complex systems.

8.2 Complex Systems and Resilience

This chapter proposes systems thinking approach as an alternative to the traditional results-based orientation to planning or evaluating development interventions in complex settings. The chapter identifies disaster management systems essentially as complex adaptive systems in which a group of agents (institutions, donors, NGOs, volunteers, subcontracted service providers, etc.) interact in interdependent ways to produce system-wide patterns, such that those patterns then influence behaviour of the agents.

8.2.1 Systems Thinking as the New Paradigm

Complex Adaptive System can be characterised by "apparently complex behaviors that emerge as a result of often nonlinear spatio-temporal interactions among a large number of component systems at different levels of organization" (Chan 2001: 1). Systems thinking can be defined as a cognitive process of studying and understanding complex systems. There are several definitions available. Richmond (1994) defines systems thinking as the art and science of making reliable inferences about behaviour by developing an increasingly deep understanding of underlying structure. Senge (1990), another leader in the field, defines systems thinking as a discipline for seeing wholes and a framework for seeing interrelationships rather than things, for seeing patterns of change rather than static snapshots. Sweeney and Sterman (2000), authors and researchers in the field of systems thinking, found that much of the art of systems thinking involves the ability to represent and assess dynamic complexity (e.g. behaviour that arises from the interaction of a system's agents over time). They list specific systems thinking skills as including the ability to understand how the behaviour of a system arises from the interaction of its agents over time (i.e. dynamic complexity), discover and represent feedback processes (both positive and negative) hypothesised to underlie observed patterns of system behaviour, identify stock and flow relationships, recognise delays and understand their impact, identify nonlinearities and recognise and challenge the boundaries of mental (and formal) models.

There has been an increasing criticism that the results-based management (RBM) model and logic model approach in evaluation are not sufficient tools for studying or evaluating development interventions in complex settings (see, e.g. Patton 2011;

Ramalingam 2013). Rationalistic (in the meaning synoptic) planning frameworks, which embed the causal logic behind actions (from inputs to outcomes and impacts), have been developed and used extensively, especially in the field of international development aid. Too often, the inflexibility of the logical framework approach (LFA) can limit staff capacity to adapt to emergent trends by holding them accountable to predicted cause and effect, rather than accountable for the ability to learn from the use of rigorous evidence analysis in implementation, and to adapt to changing circumstances and understand the conversion mechanisms that translate inputs into outputs, outcomes and impacts (Virtanen & Uusikylä 2004).

Ben Ramalingam uses in his book "*Aid on the Edge of Chaos*" complexity concepts to reveal the deep reasons and underlying patterns for why development aid either works or not (Ramalingam 2013). In addition, the developmental evaluation (Patton 2011) supports innovation development to guide adaptation to emergent and dynamic realities in complex environments.

Compared to linear logical framework, logic model or results chain approaches, the systems models focus more on transformation mechanisms that translate inputs into outputs and outcomes. Logic model thinking considers the end product to be sum of the actions, whereas systems thinking sees that has emerged as a product of interactions. The LFA treats the process planning and implementation as linear process where A leads to B and B leads to C, etc., whereas in systems approach A can lead to B and C simultaneously and B and C can fire back to A (see Fig. 8.1).

Table 8.1 summarises the differences between LFA and systems thinking. Traditional programme theory and LFA rely on linear programme logic and predetermined and fixed results and outcomes that are constructed as sums of the indi-

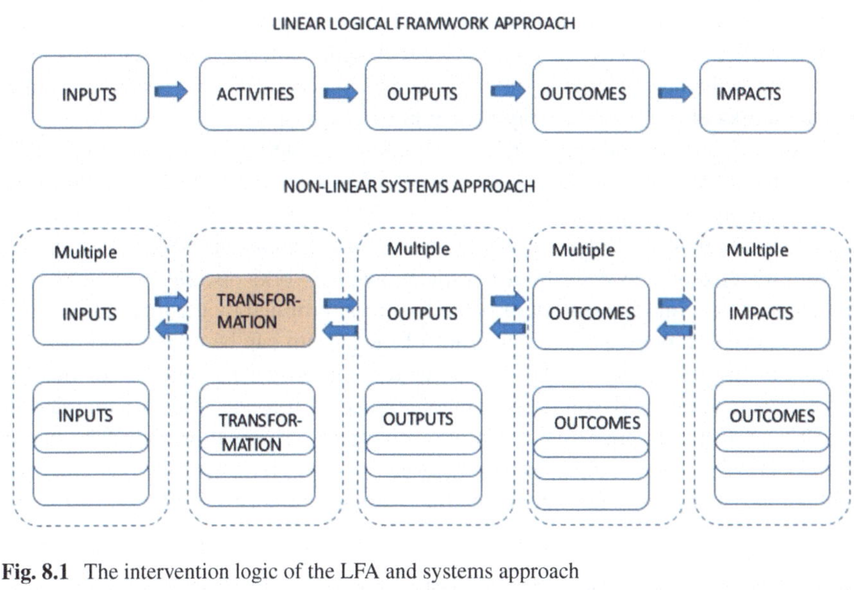

Fig. 8.1 The intervention logic of the LFA and systems approach

Table 8.1 Differences between traditional LFA and systems approach (Uusikylä 2019)

Elements	Logical framework	Systems model
Intervention logic	Linear	Non-linear
Idea on results	Predetermined and fixed	Emerging and changing
End product	Sum of the actions	Product of interactions
Key actors	Defined stakeholders	Nodes of the network
Project manager	Controller and coordinator	Enabler
Outcomes	As defined in the project plan	Real-life changes and outcomes
Coordination mechanism	Compliance, rules	Learning, trust
Success story	Achieving results	Understanding patterns

vidual actions. Actions are to be coordinated according to predefined project or programme plan. According to the systems approach, social reality comprises interacting parts, which consequently cannot be first treated independently and then simply aggregated to describe the whole as in the analytical micro to macro approach. Systemic approach takes the systems approach even further by analysing not only systems and their subsystem but also potential trajectories emerging from collision of interconnected agents in a policy space (i.e. exploration of the space of possibilities). Interconnectedness and trust are main characteristics of a complex socio-economic system.

8.2.2 *Disaster Management as Complex Adaptive System*

DP[2] platform can be seen as a complex adaptive system in which a group of agents (institutions, donors, NGOs, volunteers, subcontracted service providers, etc.) interact in interdependent ways to produce system-wide patterns, such that those patterns then influence behaviour of the agents. We can call this nested structure preparedness culture or commonly agreed policy or strategy.

To specify our systemic approach, we should next elaborate our model in the DP/DRR context. As a starting point, we see DP/DRR work not as technical atomistic projects but as an ecosystem. DP ecosystem is formed by community supported by a foundation of interacting organisations and individuals—the organisms of the disaster management system. Inter-organisational networks operate in an open system environment and the system of behaviour is determined by the interactions, not solid isolated components. The dynamics of the system can be understood only by looking at the interactions. DP/DRR networks comprise large number of institutions, organisations and voluntary groups connected through multiple interaction ties. These agents interact dynamically, exchanging information and ideas based upon heuristics that organise the interactions locally. Network relations are very contagious. Even if only few agents interact with one another, the effect spreads and

[2] We use the term disaster preparedness in its broader meaning covering both DP and DRR.

propagates through the system. As a result, the system has a memory that is not located at the specific place, but is distributed through the system (Innes and Booher 2010: 32). This means that even a loosely coupled system can be very effective in getting and spreading new information and knowledge through its weak links (Granovetter 1973). The DP/DRR community produces goods and services of value to beneficiaries, who are themselves members of the ecosystem. This complex ecosystem provides a platform to design effective, realistic and coordinated planning, reduces duplication of efforts and increases the overall effectiveness of National Societies', households' and community members' disaster preparedness and response efforts.

Preparedness ecosystem has many properties that easily create a gap between "preparedness planning" and "preparedness system". Preparedness ecosystem is characterised by the following:

Emergence Rather than being planned or controlled, the DP agents in the system interact in apparently random ways. From all these interactions, patterns emerge which informs the behaviour of the agents within the system and the behaviour of the system itself.

Co-evolution All systems exist within their own environment and they are also part of that environment. Therefore, as their environment changes, they need to change to ensure best fit. But because they are part of their environment, when they change, they change their environment, and as it has changed they need to change again, and so it goes on as a constant process. That is, communities where DP/DRR work takes place are not static but in a process of constant evolution and change.

Connectivity The ways in which the DP agents in a system connect and relate to one another is critical to the survival of the system, because it is from these connections that the patterns are formed and the feedback disseminated. The relationships between the agents are sometimes more important than the agents themselves. This would mean remarkable change of existing *modus operandi* of NS on how to train and build capacity of the DP project staff and volunteers.

Simple Rules Complex adaptive systems are not complicated. The emerging patterns may have a rich variety, but like a kaleidoscope the rules governing the function of the system are quite simple. From the DP/DRR point of view, this means only some changes of perception on DP/DRR work.

Iteration Small changes in the initial conditions of the system can have significant effects to the system as a whole (often referred to as the butterfly effect). These changes are often spurred by different feedback loops within the organisation. These are likely to have an effect on DRR methods and training.

Self-organising In a pure model, there is no hierarchy of command and control in a complex adaptive system. There is no planning or managing, but constant reorganising takes place to find the best fit with the environment. In the real (organised) world, this naturally is a naïve assumption but it might give some new ideas especially in developing community-based DP/DRR projects.

Figure 8.2 presents our understanding of the DP governance model. The model is based on interlinked and interconnected component both *vertically* (hierarchical levels of governance) and *horizontally* (cooperation or coordination among subsystems). It is important to notice that the IFRC, the NS and their partners play an important role as partners, brokers and supporters both in the field of horizontal and vertical coordination.

In the systems analysis, an intervention and change process makes sensitivity critical in understanding the systems dynamics, that is, actors' values, interests, choices and inter-linkages and interdependencies. DP/DRR environment (context) can be treated as a dynamic field that fluctuates rather than being static. No system is constantly in a simple and static state nor does it operate in a continuous complexity or chaos. Even a minor change in systems dynamics can have dramatic impacts on the system as a whole. In systems language, this is called bifurcation. Bifurcation occurs when a small smooth change made to the parameter values (the bifurcation parameters) of a system causes a sudden qualitative or topological change in its behaviour. For example, a shift in power relations or exit of an important DP/DRR actor could cause major changes in the DM network.

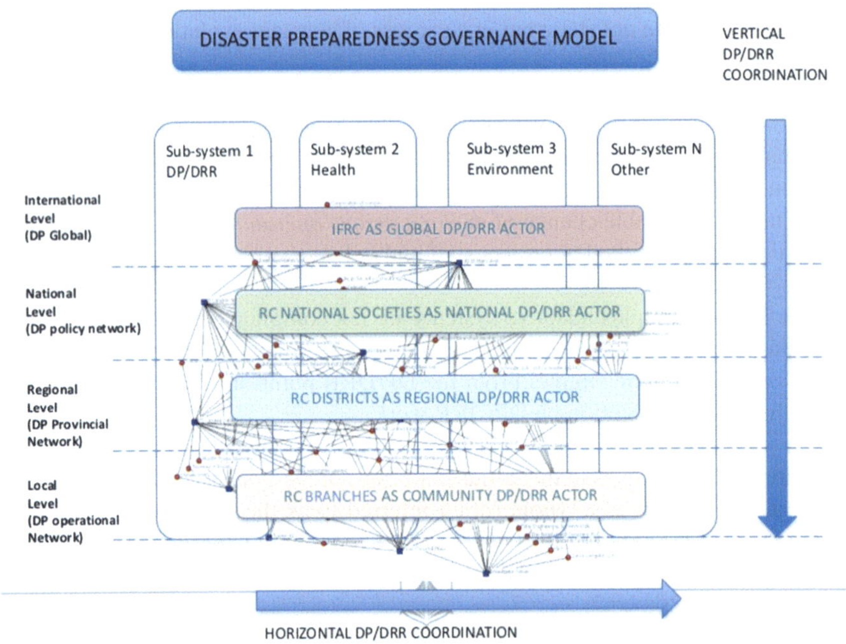

Fig. 8.2 DP governance model

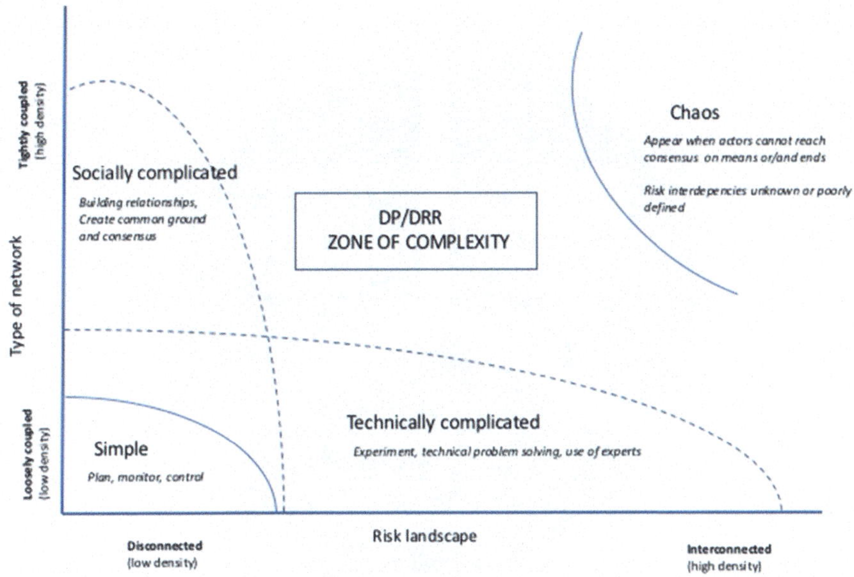

Fig. 8.3 DP/DRR environment as a zone of complexity (adapted and modified from Patton 2011)

Homeostasis on the other hand is the property of a system in which a variable is actively regulated to remain very nearly constant. In DP/DRR system, the highly regulated environment or strong position of powerful institutions normally stabilises the system and thus brings it back to the state of homeostasis. Normally, system displays both capacity to maintain its viability and capacity to evolve. With sufficient diversity, the agents will adapt to each other, and the system can reorganise its internal structure without outside agents involvement. It is important to remember that the system is open, the behaviour of the system is determined by interactions and the behaviour of the system cannot be understood by looking at the components. Instead, it can be only understood by looking at the interactions.

Figure 8.3 presents our analytical framework when analysing the DP/DRR networks from a systems perspective. Horizontal axis describes the risk landscapes where risks can be isolated or highly interconnected and vertical axis illustrates the network types, that is, whether a network is loosely coupled (low density) or tightly coupled (high density). We operationalise these by calculating the risk and stakeholder network density[3] and centralisation[4] scores for each case study networks. This leads to the following expectations (working hypotheses):

[3]Density is the measurement of network cohesion. The density (*D*) of a network is defined as a ratio of the number of edges (*E*) to the number of possible edges. We apply valued data so density is defined as the average strength of ties across all possible (not all actual) ties. Where the data are symmetric or undirected, density is calculated relative to the number of unique pairs $((n*n - 1)/2)$.

[4]The concept of point centrality originates in the sociometric concept of the star. A central point was one which was at the center of a number of connections, a point with a great many direct

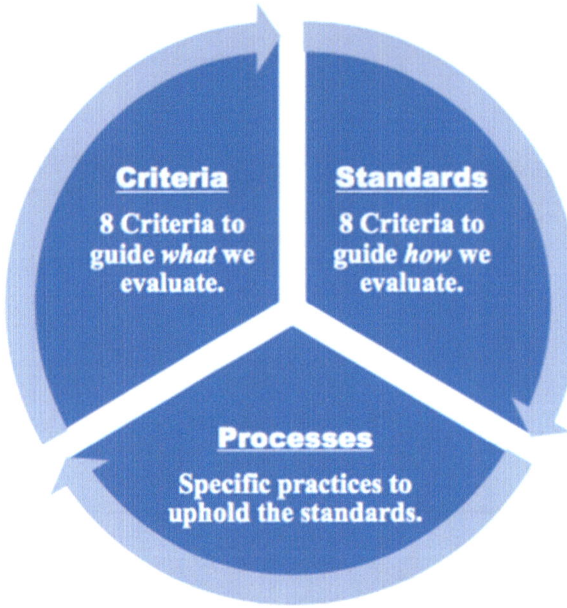

Fig. 8.4 The IFRC Evaluation Framework

1. The higher the risk density, the more complex the risk environment.
2. The higher the risk centralisation, the more dependent are other risk factors on root cause.
3. The higher the stakeholder network density, the more connected and interdependent the actors are (sometimes it can also be an indicator of high trust).
4. The higher the centralisation, the more dependent the actors are on one or few powerful agents.

There are four spheres of complexity in Fig. 8.4. Simple environment is the one where risks are disconnected and actors are operating in loosely coupled network. Socially complicated sphere is the one where actors are highly interconnected but risks are disconnected. In the technically complicated sphere, actors are loosely connected but risks are highly interconnected. Zone of complexity exists in a situation where both actors and risks are highly interconnected. Simple problems (such as implementing training or drill according to a manual) may encompass some basic issues of technique and terminology, but once these are mastered, following the recipe carries with it a very high assurance of success. Complicated problems (like building a water sanitation system) are different. Their complicated nature is often related not only to the scale of the problem but also to their increased requirements

contacts with other points. The simplest and most straightforward way to measure point centrality, therefore, is by the degrees of the various points in the graph. Tie degree, it will be recalled, is simply the number of other points to which a point is adjacent.

around coordination or specialised expertise. In contrast, complex systems are based on relationships, and their properties of self-organisation, interconnections and evolution.

On the far ends of the complexity, we enter the zone of chaos. In that zone, there is intense conflict among key stakeholders and extreme uncertainty about the risk landscape and lack of understanding and knowledge on how to achieve the desired outcomes. There is no clear dividing line between complexity and chaos. According to Patton (Patton 2011: 93), "it is a matter of degree that has to do with how rapidly things are changing and the extent to which reverberations, ripple effects and turbulent interactions are multiplying and cascading". In the state of chaos, things are uncontrollable and unpredictable.

8.2.3 Resilience in Complex Adaptive Systems

Resilience building constitutes as the core component of the DPDRR work of the Red Cross Movement and as a term has been widely used in the DRR literature. Resilience has in fact become a buzzword and has obtained diverse meanings in different academic disciplines (Bahadur et al. 2010). There has been a concern that resilience "may collapse into meaninglessness that results from having too many meanings" (Lundberg and Johansson 2015: 2). The difficulty in conceptualisation of resilience lies in the varying views on whether the "system" is considered as "constant, stable and/or has the capacity to adapt" (Bosher 2014: 4). Bosher (2014) has categorised the different definitions of resilience into four categories: resistance/robustness, recovery/"bouncing back", planning/preparing/protecting and adaptive capacity. This confusion has led to the difficulty in conceptualising resilience and subsequently measuring it. There is also divergence in whether resilience is being used to describe outcomes or processes leading to outcomes. Here, resilience is conceptualised in the framework of systems thinking fitting to the characteristics of complex adaptive systems such as DP platforms.

In this chapter, resilience is defined following Manyena (2006) and Holling (1973) emphasising its processual nature as well as the persistence of relationships within a non-equilibrium system. According to Manyena (2006), resilience is understood as a process, comprising "series of events, actions or changes to augment the capacity of the affected community when confronted with singular, multiple or unique shocks and stresses". "...Resilience does not deal with regularities ...but rather, it is an art that addresses singularities as we experience them" (Weinberg 1985 in Manyena 2006). Understanding resilience as a process is central to systems thinking approach as the inflexibility of the traditional results-based approach can limit capacity to adapt to emergent trends by being accountable to predicted cause and effect rather than accountable for the ability to learn from evidence analysis in implementation and to adapt to changing circumstances. According to Manyena (2006), in the current usage of the term resilience in the field of DRR, there is a risk that it is being used too extensively to describe the quality of end results of disaster

DRR interventions. "The danger of viewing disaster resilience as an outcome is the tendency to reinforce the traditional practice of disaster management, which takes a reactive stance" (McEntire et al. 2002 in Manyena 2006). This has the possibility to skew activities towards following "supply rather than demand", neglecting activities such as emergency preparedness planning and community capacity building (Manyena 2006). Manyena (2006) also emphasises as part of the process-oriented resilience the importance of local knowledge and culture in forming resilient DRR strategies (Bahadur et al. 2010). This is supportive of a bottom-up approach unlike the top-down mechanism embedded in the traditional results-based log-frame thinking. In the case of the Philippines, the bottom-up approach was successfully utilised as the local stakeholders were included in the process from early on.

"The theory of complex dynamic systems describes the periodic, rhythmic dance between order and chaos, between stability and transformation as a fundamental pattern of self-organization in complex (living) systems" (Wahl 2017). Holling (1973: 17) draws his understanding of resilience from the fundamental nature of this thought, characterising ecological systems "by two distinct properties: resilience and stability". DRR programmes can be seen as complex adaptive systems and "systems-of-systems", part of the bigger surrounding ecology subordinate to the characteristics of self-organisation and non-linearity. Holling (1973: 17) defines resilience as "the persistence of relationships within a system and … the ability of these systems to absorb changes of state variables, driving variables and parameters and still persist". Holling (1973: 17) sees resilience as a "property of the system and persistence or probability of extinction is the result and stability the ability of the system to return to an equilibrium state after temporary disturbance". This approach is necessary as the DP platforms are understood as complex adaptive system in which a group of actors interact in interdependent ways. Holling's understanding of resilience stems from the view of "natural systems as dynamic and being away from an 'equilibrium' or stable state at any point, instead being organised in a domain of attraction in which different elements of a system are organised around different, individual equilibriums" (Bahadur et al. 2010: 7). Following the logic of systems thinking, Holling understands ecological systems essentially as non-linear, which human actions inherently make even more unpredictable. Ecological resilience therefore emphasises the adaptive capacity of systems, which may lead to new equilibria (Carpenter et al. 2001 in Fiksel 2006). However, these fluctuations can improve resilience instead of harm it. While some elements in the system might be changed due to the disturbance, "the system will persist if the nature of the relationships between these elements broadly remains the same" (Bahadur et al. 2010: 7).

8.3 Meta-Analysis

This chapter presents data, methods and results of the meta-analysis covering ten countries and 17 projects covered in the thematic study commissioned by the FRC. The country/project selection is introduced first, followed by describing the differences between meta-evaluation and meta-analysis (focus mainly on meta-analysis but some observation on the quality and accuracy of the evaluation reports is also reported). Finally, the results of the meta-analysis are presented by comparing eight IFRC evaluation criteria and the ten country cases.

8.3.1 Data and Methods

Thematic programme level forms the ground for a strategic analysis. It starts with the main goals and objectives of the DP/DRR activities set by IFRC, FRC, NS and other donors or co-founders (e.g. ECHO). The aggregation of empirical results from the various project levels analyses feedback to programme level and is supposed to give answer to the questions such as: Are the goals and objectives valid, realistic and relevant vis-á-vis the problems and needs? Should they be changed or fine-tuned? What revisions need to be made at the programme level?

The basic assessment criteria included geographical regions, focus areas, donors and time spans of the projects. The criteria were complemented with more dynamic evidence from the experience and the tacit knowledge of the FRC experts in mapping workshop participated by seven FRC staff members and facilitated by the consultants (Table 8.2).

Table 8.2 Project assessment criteria

Criteria	Variables
Geographical region	South America/Caribbean/Central Asia and Caucasus/Asia
Funding agencies	ECHO/MFA/FRC or others
Number of implementing agencies	2 (FRC and NS)/consortium
Preparedness emphasis	Community preparedness/institutional preparedness/both in equal shares/other
Multiple phases	Yes/no
National society's institutional position in national preparedness systems in the beginning of the project	Strong position/have a position but could have a stronger one/no official position, aspire to have one
National society's potential (assumed) interest in learning from the DP study	Strong interest assumed/intermediate interest/no interest/no information
Variance in project's multirisk approach	Only natural disaster risks considered/only man-made risks considered/different kinds of risks considered (natural and man-made)

8.3.2 Concept of Meta-Analysis

Meta-analyses are often, but not always, important components of a systematic review procedure. For instance, meta-analysis may be conducted on several DP/DRR reports and evaluations in an effort to obtain a better understanding of how successfully projects have been implemented and what are the main results and impact of these projects. In this study, meta-analysis is used as a practical inquiry to combine evidence and lessons learned to have an overall understanding of the DP/DRR programme planning, implementation and M&E dynamics.

Meta-analysis refers to a synthesis of existing programme evaluation studies in a given area and aims to summarise the current knowledge about a particular type of programme and analytical synthesis of evaluation findings, outcomes and lessons learned. The study followed the logic of IFRC Evaluation Framework (IFRC 2011). The purpose of this IFRC Framework for Evaluation is to guide how evaluations are planned, managed, conducted and utilised by the secretariat of the IFRC. The framework is designed to promote reliable, useful, ethical evaluations that contribute to organisational learning, accountability and the mission to best serve those in need.

Both IFRC and MFA evaluation criteria are applied as an analytical framework for carrying out the meta-analysis (see IFRC 2011: 17). The evaluation criteria applied here (six out of eight) are:

Relevance and appropriateness. The extent that the IFRC's work is suited to the needs and priorities of the target group and complements work from other actors.

Impact. The extent that the IFRC's work affects positive and negative changes on stakeholders, directly or indirectly, intended or unintended.

Effectiveness. The extent that the IFRC's programmes meet their targets set and produce positive results.

Efficiency. The extent that the IFRC's work is cost-effective and timely.

Sustainability and connectedness. The extent the benefits of the IFRC's work are likely to continue once the IFRC's role is completed.

Coherence. The extent that the IFRC's work is consistent with relevant policies (e.g. humanitarian, security, trade, military and development) and takes adequate account of humanitarian and human-rights considerations.

These criteria are used to draft the meta-analysis framework. Also the eight IFRC evaluation standards (utility, feasibility, ethics and legality, impartiality and independence, transparency, accuracy, participation and collaboration) were taken into account although they were used only implicitly. In the meta-analysis framework, the first column presents the criteria described earlier. The second column consists of the list of critical research questions to operationalise the criteria. After that, each project is rated according to each criterion by applying the applied MFA rating scales, where:

1 = criteria mostly not fulfilled or totally absent
2 = criteria partially fulfilled
3 = criteria nearly fulfilled

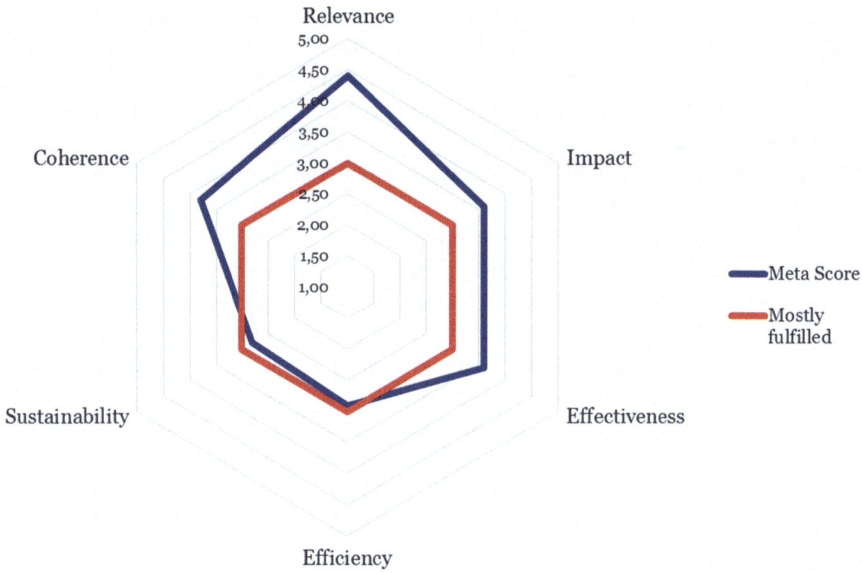

Fig. 8.5 The average scores of the DP/DRR meta-analysis according to the IFRC criteria

4 = criteria entirely fulfilled
5 = criteria entirely fulfilled in a clear and original way
n/a = not addressed

8.3.3 *Results of the Meta-Analysis*

In comparative terms, the overall result of the DP/DRR programme or project meta-analysis is rather positive.[5] Figure 8.5 shows that all criteria reach at the average (score 3) and most are above it. **Relevance** (4.40) and **coherence** (3.80) are rated as highest factors. This clearly proves that the FRC's DP/DRR projects are suited to the needs and priorities of the target group and complement work from other actors. High coherence indicates that FRC's projects are consistent with relevant policies (e.g. humanitarian, security, trade, military and development as well as national strategies and government policies) and take adequately into account humanitarian and human rights considerations. More generally, success in both of these areas also indicates that strategic planning and alignment during the pre-programing phase has been appropriate and well done.

The second layer consists of two criteria that are both above average score, that is, **impact** (avg. = 3.60) and **effectiveness** (avg. = 3.60). Positive impact score

[5] With the comparative aspect, other meta-analyses are referred to carry out during the last 3 years. This is a naturally very subjective statement and should be treated as one.

suggests that FRC's work affects positive changes on stakeholders, directly or indirectly, intended or unintended. Positive effectiveness score tells that FRC's projects have mostly achieved or are likely to achieve their intended, immediate results and long-term impacts. In most of the evaluation reports, the impact of a project is analysed in the phase were project has just ended or is running during the evaluation. Therefore, the impact usually is more of an expected impact or a perception of the stakeholders.

Efficiency (avg. = 2.90) and **sustainability** (avg. = 2.80) requirements are only nearly fulfilled in the FRC's DP/DRR projects. Both criteria score below average value of 3 which are the lowest overall scores. This still indicates that in future projects FRC should pay more attention to efficiency (i.e. cost-efficiency, cost-effectiveness and timeliness of the implementation) and especially to sustainability. As far as efficiency is concerned, several programmes have had a slow start, which made management costs seem proportionally high. In addition, in some cases, inefficiencies were beyond the influence of the programme/project, since it was mostly due to partner government processes. Relatively low sustainability score can be explained by high external support or donor dependency, which means that after the project ends, the activities (e.g. trainings, drills, capacity building) are likely not to continue. In some cases, one programme cycle (in some cases only 1 year) was seen as too short for setting ground for an appropriate level of sustainability. In some of the cases, the next project phase would have been needed to ensure sustainability.

Coherence scores of the projects analysed were also rather high (avg. = 3.80). This indicates that projects have been consistent with relevant policies and have taken adequate account of humanitarian and human-rights considerations.

Considering the results per country, the Philippines achieved the highest scores (Fig. 8.6). In both cases, the projects were strategically well aligned, accurately planned and well implemented. Also, monitoring and evaluation reports in these

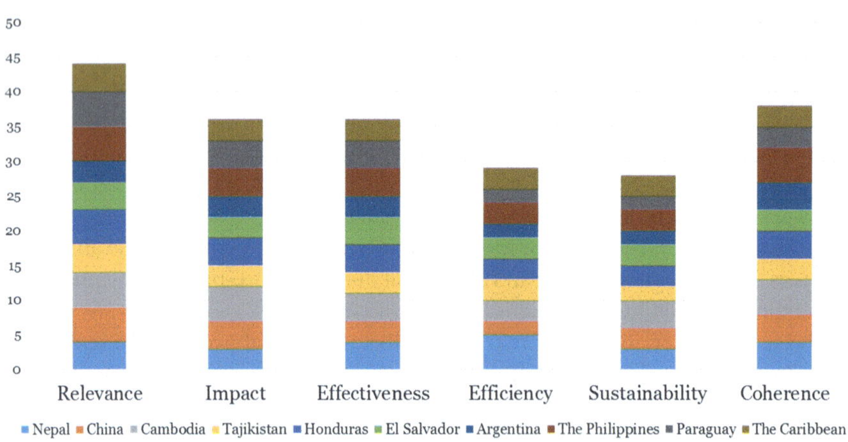

Fig. 8.6 Results of the meta-analysis on selected DP/DRR projects aggregated to country level

two country cases were sound, clear and well written (in meta-analysis, this could cause a minor positive bias).

Still, the overall conclusion drawn from the country comparison is that the differences between the eight case study countries according to the six IFRC criteria are not that remarkable. There is some minor variation (e.g. low efficiency in Argentina and China, high impact in Cambodia or low sustainability in Tajikistan) but differences are not vast. The scoring depended also highly on the quality and accuracy of the evaluation reports. If the evaluation criteria were not applied appropriately, it was extremely difficult to get the relevant information for meta-analysis and scoring.

8.4 Case Study: DP/DRR Programmes in the Philippines

The Philippines is one of the most high-risk countries in the world for experiencing natural disasters. The list of possible natural disasters includes earthquakes, floods, mudslides, typhoons and volcanic eruptions. The Philippines is considered to be one of the most storm-exposed countries on Earth. On average, 18 to 20 tropical storms enter Philippine waters each year, with 8 or 9 of those storms making landfall. It has been estimated that the extensive risk, accounting to 2/3 of all losses in the Philippines, is mainly associated with flash floods and droughts. According to Hatakka and Gogcio (2016), disaster trends for the Philippines show that the impacts of disasters are increasing, not only by total number of people affected, but also by the impacts of disaster trends by estimated damage. Demographic growth and urbanisation have also affected the provision of basic services resulting in deteriorating solid waste management and aggravating flooding in urban areas for the past years. Economic vulnerabilities manifest these, as for instance, when poor households lack the assets or resources to repair, rebuild or replant their livelihoods, or workers in informal employment with no access to social safety nets face immediate or ongoing loss of incomes.

8.4.1 DP/DRR Policy Framework in the Philippines

Policy and legal frameworks have been established and guided by international treaties such as the Hyogo Framework for Action (HFA) and the ASEAN Agreement on Disaster Management and Emergency Response (AADMER) as well as the Sendai Framework for Disaster Risk Reduction. Based on those treaties, the Government of the Philippines has introduced the Philippines Strategic National Action Plan for Disaster Risk Reduction 2009–2019 (SNAP). At the national level, the Disaster Risk Reduction (DRR) Management Act of 2010 (RA 10210), also referred to as "DRR Law", aims at building resilience of local communities to disasters, including climate change impacts. The DRR Law mandated the Department of Interior and Local Government (DILG), which is also the vice-chair of the Preparedness Committee of the National Disaster Risk Reduction and Management Council (NDRRMC), to take the lead on DP and build capacities in the local government units (LGUs) and to integrate DRR and climate change adaptation (CCA) in development planning. The Philippine Red Cross (PRC) is the only non-governmental member of the NDRRMC and is therefore uniquely positioned to support the implementation of RA 10210. The PRC, by virtue of RA 10072, is an independent, autonomous, non-governmental organisation auxiliary to the authorities of the Republic of the Philippines in the humanitarian field. It offers a range of programmes on blood services, disaster management services (DMS), safety services, health services, social services, Red Cross Youth and volunteer services targeted to the most vulnerable population. At present, the PRC Headquarters has around 400 staff including the directors and managers and a total of 102 chapters and subchapters manned by a total of approximately 1500 staff composed of chapter administrators and technical personnel supported by thousands of volunteers located across major cities and provinces in the country (Hatakka & Gogcio 2016).

8.4.2 Community-Based Disaster Risk Reduction Project in Aklan Province

The CBDRR Project in Aklan Province started from April 2011 until December 2012. Project planning for the 2013–2015 took place during January to February 2013 for assessment and preparation. The new cycle of CBDRR Project was extended in Aklan Province while sustaining activities in 5 "existing" project areas (community and schools) until 2014 and adding 5 "new" project areas until 2015. Likewise, the CBDRR Project expanded to an urban environment—Caloocan City wherein 5 project areas were selected in January 2013. The design of the project remained to adhere to the PRC Disaster Risk Reduction and Management (DRRM) framework and at the same time applying new CBDRR approaches such as improved Red Cross 143 (RC143) volunteer programme, inclusive programming of thematic issues and health integration to DRR. As the programme was implemented by DMS, the CBDRR project also seeks to contribute to the PRC DMS strategic plan 2012–2016 most particularly in contributing to the development of a safe and disaster resilient community and schools and capacity building of PRC.

The CBDRR project aimed to improve the capacity of targeted communities and institutions to better prepare for and reduce disaster risks. The direct beneficiaries are the people living in targeted barangays of Aklan and Caloocan. The project activities in the barangays are divided in four categories and closely interlinked components. RC143 established in all barangays trained and mobilised communities in DRR activities and developed barangay disaster actions plan (BDAP) and sustainable small-scale mitigation measures. School-based DRR increased knowledge on hazards, climate change and DRR and response in case of disasters. The project also aimed to strengthen organisational links of chapter-level PRC with municipal and provincial levels and to strengthen coordination and cooperation among the stakeholders in DM. It was also targeted to capacity building of NHQ, Aklan Chapter and Caloocan Chapter of PRC for Project and Financial Management.

The project's principal and specific objectives according to its log frame is "to increase safety and resilience of targeted communities in disasters" and "to improve the capacity of targeted communities and institutions to better prepare for and reduce disaster risks", respectively. The thrust of PRC in achieving these objectives is to organise a network of RC143 volunteers who will assist the community and school to prepare for disasters and respond rapidly in emergencies. Multiple capacity building and mobilisation activities were organised and implemented for the RC143 volunteers such as trainings, equipping, assessment, planning sessions, awareness campaigns and small-scale mitigation measures. The relevance of the RC143 volunteers is recognised by local officials due to its limitation in manpower and resources to organise and capacitate them. Retaining the activeness of trained RC143 volunteers was a major challenge in view of their livelihood activities or academic obligations and few instances of personal differences with local officials; however, it is advocated to the chapter and local officials to exert efforts in mobilising them in its different activities whenever possible. Beyond the capacity building for RC143 volunteers, community residents and school pupils were also engaged in the project through their participation in assessment activities, awareness campaigns, evaluation (midterm and final) and surveys (baseline and end line).

Prior to the project, there has been limited involvement of residents in DRRM implementation. However, they are often perceived as receivers, not co-implementers. There is, however, consultation of communities and pupils in assessing their locality's vulnerabilities and capacities to prioritised hazard and larger number of participants in simulation exercises. Various awareness campaigns facilitated by RC143 volunteers were organised for and participated by residents and pupils; however, the efforts were not sufficient to influence significant change in knowledge and attitude.

The final Annual Report of 2015 (extended to Spring 2016) gives a very positive overall assessment of the results of the Philippines Programme. The report states that the CBDRR project contributed to DMS achievement of its share in the Goal 1, Objective 1 of the PRC Strategic Plan 2012–2016 which is "to develop resilience in communities vulnerable to disasters and public health emergencies through a sustainable community-based preparedness and response plan". It continues that "the CBDRR project to the chapters is its increased capacity to manage DRR projects and improvement of its image as a development partner and not only as an organisation that provides relief aid and safe blood. The project also strengthened the capacity of the chapter in emergency response through volunteer training and minor equipping, and in daily office operations through the purchasing of equipment, office furniture and vehicle used by the chapter during and after project's duration". The Final Evaluation (May 11, 2016) was a bit more critical and lists also several recommendations to further enhance the DP/DRR awareness, capacity and activities in Caloocan City and Aklan Province.

8.4.3 Multirisk Analysis

During the field mission to Aklan and Caloocan City on November 14–19, 2016, PRC staff (HQ, chapters and volunteers) were interviewed together with main stakeholders and beneficiaries (52 total). Assessment of the main risks related to both communities was one of the interview topics. Instead of repeating the risk part of the vulnerability and capacity assessment (VCA), a more comprehensive systems approach to risk identification and analysis was introduced. This approach was warmly welcomed by the participants of the risk assessment workshops in Caloocan City and Kalibo (Aklan). In their opinion, VCA process is helpful in identifying the main risks that are more or less known a priori. Risk definition should be broadened to cover also political, economic, health-related, social, technological and cultural risks. Secondly, risks should not be seen as independent or atomistic phenomena but tightly interlinked web of risk patterns (WEF 2014). In this case, the risk assessment framework of the World Economic Forum (see, e.g. WEF 2014) was applied. In addition to natural disaster, the so-called systemic risks that have sometimes explanatory power when explaining human behaviour in critical disaster environments were also included. Systemic risk is the risk of "breakdowns in an entire system, as opposed to breakdowns in individual parts and components" (Kaufman and Scott 2003). Systemic risks can be characterised as follows (WEF 2014):

- modest tipping points combining indirectly to produce large failures
- risk-sharing or contagion, as one loss triggers a chain of others
- "hysteresis", or systems being unable to recover equilibrium after a shock

According to the CBDRR Project 2015 Annual Report, the planning process in Caloocan City remained to be difficult. Only one community was able to complete their barangay DRRM 2015 plan; however, a copy could still not be secured from the community or city, and only 2 communities (12 and 176) were able to finalise their contingency plan (these were also the barangays that participated in workshops).

Three most critical risks were identified as: (1) floods, (2) earthquakes and (3) fire. Given the urban context, these are also the most dangerous for the inhabitants and livelihoods in the area. However, when mitigation measures are considered, it is not sufficient to tackle these risk factors separately. Most of the risks listed earlier are highly interconnected and therefore also mitigation measures, drills and evacuation plans should be planned from the multirisk perspective.

In Fig. 8.7, the numerous and complex interconnections between risks can create consequences that are disproportionate and difficult to contain or predict. The Risks Interconnections Map (RIM) seeks to connect the dots by identifying and visualising the underlying patterns. This allows for a better understanding of the impact of systemic risks so as to mitigate them by identifying the transmission channels between risks and potential second- and third-order effects. These interconnections do not represent direct causality. They are likely to be indirect, for example, through parallel impacts or mitigation trade-offs.

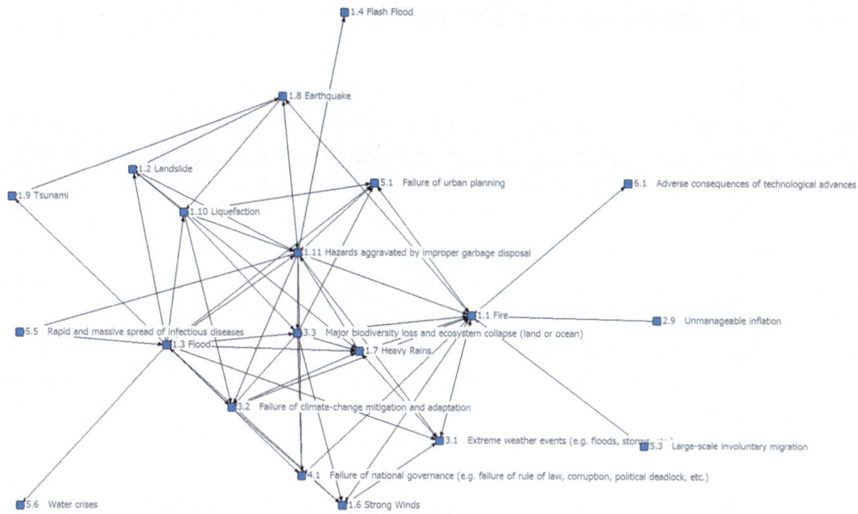

Fig. 8.7 Caloocan multirisk map of interconnectedness

The RIM shows how all global risks are connected to others and underlines the complexity of dealing with global risk in an effective manner. The map visualises the strength of connection between individual risks—the most strongly connected risks could merit additional attention due to the multiple ways they affect or are affected by other risks.

Interestingly, hazards aggravated by improper garbage disposal (listed as No. 4 in prominence) together with fire (No. 2) and major biodiversity loss and ecosystem collapse (No. 10), seem to be the most centrally positioned risk factors that bridge several other risk areas. These risks together with failure of the national governance are not typically listed in VCAs or other risk assessment exercises. During the focus groups discussions, many participants announced that when they carry out risk assessments next time, they are willing to apply a broader, systemic multirisk approach. This also indicates that there should be special risk identification maps and mitigation measures for urban DP/DRR projects.

The systemic multirisk mapping widened the risk landscape both in Aklan (multirisk map presented in Annex) and in Caloocan City. It showed that risks such as failures in urban planning and infrastructure are directly connected phenomena with hazards aggravated by improper garbage disposal and liquefaction. Likewise, failure of national governance directly increases major biodiversity loss and failures of climate change mitigations. When planning a future urban DRR project, these second layer risk factor should be embedded into the overall risk landscape and taken into consideration when planning project activities.

8.4.4 *Inter-organisational DM Networks*

In the complex world, relations (collaborative and competitive) between individuals and organisations need to be given a special attention. The introduction of general systems theory into discussions of management theory by Johnson et al. (1964) served as a stimulus, and a way forward, for those seeking to explore relations between organisations. They described systems theory as a way of integrating diverse internal and external factors that managers faced. In their view, systems theory also helped managers to cope with the complex nature of these factors. There are two dimensions across which organisations can be related. They can have interactive relationships, for instance, in the exchange of information or resources, or noninteractive relationships when they share particular attributes—such as status, identity, cognitive structures, strategic positioning or core technology—that induce the same behavioural stimuli in related members and/or expose the organisations to the same evolutionary forces (see, e.g. Gharajedaghi 2011; Holland 2014). Here, the focus is on direct interactions between the organisations and group of actors in Caloocan and Aklan DP/DRR networks.

During the workshops and interviews, the participants were first asked to list the most important/prominent organisations and groups in their local DP/DRR networks. Participants were given the list of organisations and they could add additional organisations to this list. This produced a traditional stakeholder mapping (refer to the Caloocan and Aklan stakeholder prominence scores).

Stakeholders were asked to list and rate the most influential DP/DRR groups and organisations in their area. According to these ratings, the most prominent actors in the Caloocan list consist of government organisations or service agencies (barangay LGUs, schools, the DRRM Office and the Division Office) with PRC Chapter being ranked 5, followed by Bureau of Fire Protection and DILG. In Aklan, the two most prominent organisations or groups were PRC Chapter and barangay residents and after LGUs again the 143 members of PRC and the volunteers.

After listing all the relevant stakeholders related to DP/DRR activities in Caloocan City and Aklan, the respondents were given a matrix (with additional stakeholders included) and asked to define the relationships between all actors (organisations and groups) in the matrix. Individual Excel matrices were thereafter aggregated (mean) to form a synthesis matrix containing all the responses. This matrix was then copied to UCINET programme for network analysis and mapping. Figure 8.8 show the overall structure of the inter-organisational DP/DRR networks in Caloocan and Aklan.

The two networks (Aklan Province and Caloocan City) were found to be very dense and highly interconnected. In practice, this means that all organisations and groups can reach each other at least through paths (i.e. via brokerage). Strong government-driven culture in Caloocan can be seen by analysing the organisations that occupy central positions in the middle of the networks. This brokerage position increases their power in resource and information sharing. The EuropeAid project states in its 2015 Annual Report that "close and formal links with the DILG and

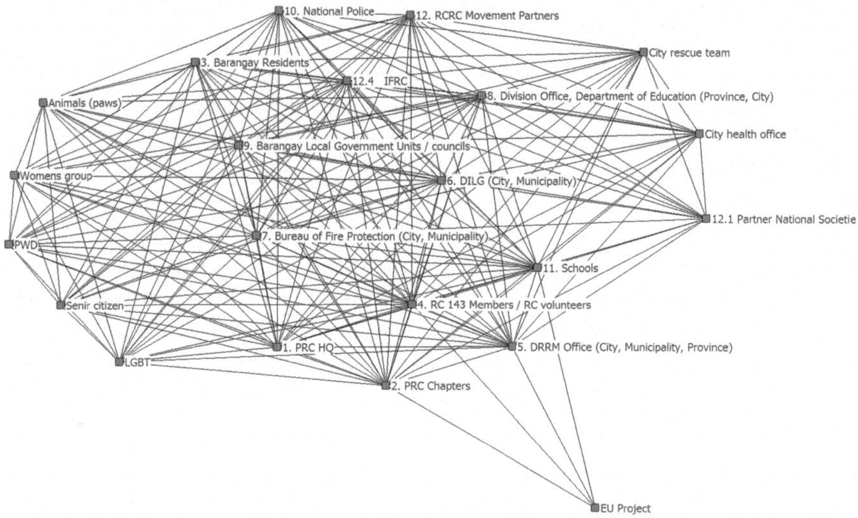

Fig. 8.8 Inter-organisational DP/DRR network in Caloocan City

LGUs have not been established, risking that they are not very much interested in the products of the project". The project sees the LGUs as target for the envisaged advocacy activities, instead of considering them as partners or allies working for the same cause. The opportunities for influencing local planning were found very limited. In addition, during the field mission, it was clearly seen that barangays that received funding from the projects were not willing to disseminate the knowledge gained to other barangays (winner takes it all). This is not a very positive cultural mode from the sustainability perspective.

Network analysis of the Aklan and Caloocan City stakeholders showed that there were many groups or agencies that were rather actively participating in the implementation of the project without having formal status in the CBDRR project framework. In Aklan network, other NGOs (e.g. World Vision), charities and associations (Rotary Club) and especially the Catholic Church and companies were considered to be important actors in DP/DRR work. In Caloocan, the role of the citizen groups (women groups, senior citizens) and healthcare agencies was more important than expected in project plans. These groups provide additional resource that gives the CBDRR project more opportunities and are likely to increase resilience in the area.

The roles of different collective actor groups in the DM networks will be discussed next[6]. Although, we have argued that DM networks are self-organising social systems which manifest certain characteristic that may retain even if all its individual members are replaced (see Laszlo 1972), each actor occupies a certain structural

[6] Network data was aggregated by coding each actor into a collective actor group. The adjacency matrix was partitioned into submatrices by computing the average scores for each subgroup. This data was thereafter used as $N \times N$ network matrix.

position in a network that either constrain or enable actors to pursue their goals and ambitions. Consider the dynamics of the diffusion of new ideas or information in a network. Central individuals, organisations or groups embedded in a system of strong ties not only have a high potential for transmitting ideas but also can send messages to those who share those ideas and practices (Kadushin 2012: 145). To analyse the network positions of various collective DM actors, we use two indicators to measure their influence. First is Freeman's centrality index, which measures the number of direct ties that an actor has to other members of the network. The score we have calculated from the case study DM networks is the betweenness centrality.[7] A practical interpretation for the betweenness centrality is the position of a brokerage. An actor with high betweenness centrality links groups that might otherwise not be connected. The less constrained broker or organisation that bridges structural holes (Burt 2005) can be a very effective opinion leader. This gives four DM roles in a DP/DRR network:

1. **Power brokers** are DM actors that have *high brokerage* position but a *low centrality*. These actors normally build bridges between agents in a network. Their position could also be characterised as an enabler, that is, an agent that provides possibilities, opportunities and contacts to other members of the network but does not actively play a leading role.
2. **Support agents** are DM network members that have both *low centrality* and *low betweenness* scores. These agents typically have certain restricted or limited responsibilities or very specified tasks in a network.
3. **Guardians** are well connected (*high centrality*) but do not occupy strategically central positions connecting other members of the network (*low betweenness*). In DM networks, this means that network members are not dependent on guardians but still frequently interact with them.
4. **Game changers** are the most influential actors in a DM network. Game changers have vast amount contacts with other network member (*high centrality*) and occupy strategically critical positions that give them an opportunity channel information and other resources (*high betweenness*). Game changers are agents that can change an existing situation or activity in a significant way. On the contrary, they can also block a change they are not willing to support (Fig. 8.9).

The Philippines DM network is led by the RC Chapters, network of RC 143 volunteers and schools that play an important role in the implementation of the DP/DRR projects and activities. Quantitative network analysis formalises and supports the qualitative information and observation gathered during the Caloocan and Aklan field mission. The capacity of PRC is extremely high and its projects are well pre-

[7] Degree centrality can be defined as the number of links incident upon a node (i.e. the number of ties that a node has). Betweenness centrality quantifies the number of times a node acts as a bridge along the shortest path between two other nodes. It was introduced as a measure for quantifying the control of a human on the communication between other humans in a social network by Linton Freeman (see more in Freeman 1979 or Johanson et al. 1995).

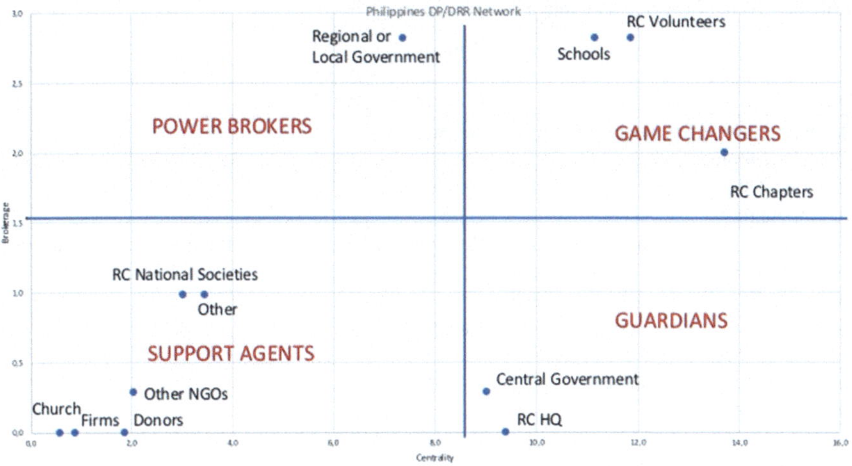

Fig. 8.9 Collective actors' roles in the Philippines DM network

pared and implemented. This is one of the main reasons and explanations for the strong position of the RC actors in the DM network. The role of the Philippines Red Cross Head Quarter (HQ) is more of a guardian (together with the central government). The HQ mobilises the resources needed for DP/DRR activities, is in close contact with the central government (advocacy) and steers the activities from the arm's length. Regional and local government actors are typical power broker. They enable DP/DRR activities and connect various actors in the field. Support agents group in the Philippines consists of organisations such RC NS, NGOs, firms, the Church and other donor organisations. All these agents have a limited scope for their actions and carry out specific tasks in the DM network.

8.4.5 *Outcome Harvesting*

One of the problems with LFA-driven approaches is that they steer focus too narrowly on the programme/project outputs and outcomes and easily neglect other important changes, results and outcomes. Outcome harvesting is a method that enables evaluators, grant makers and managers to identify, formulate, verify and make sense of outcomes. The method was inspired by the definition of outcome as a change in the behaviour, relationships, actions, activities, policies or practices of an individual, group, community, organisation or institution.

Unlike some evaluation methods, outcome harvesting does not measure progress towards predetermined outcomes or objectives, but rather collects evidence of what has been achieved and works backwards to determine whether and how the project or intervention contributed to the change.

Table 8.3 Aklan Province outcome harvesting results

What?	Why?	What was the impact?	Who contributed? Who were the change agents?		
Behavioural change—people are dependent on outside support	Project cycle and exit	Negative			
Community resilience and preparedness	Typhoon Yolanda showed that people were more prepared	Positive	Community volunteer	Barangay officials	Barangay leaders
Low sustainability of the activities in the community	Less monitoring from the project implementer	Negative			
Participation of the community people	Active participation to activities	Positive	MDRRMO	RC143	
Good governance and awareness of the LGU and the community	Active collaboration between the PRC and LGU	Positive	Civil Society Organisations		
Development of DRRM system in Aklan	Active collaboration between the LGU and stakeholders	Positive	Private sector	International NGOs	Volunteers
DRR awareness	When typhoon hits, people know what to do	Positive	PDRRMO	MDRRMO	BDRRMO
Advocate participatory approach in planning	By disseminating information to communities by drills and simulation	Positive	LGU	International NGOs	
Public awareness has risen dramatically	When typhoon frank hit Aklan people started to notice the importance of DRR work	Positive			
Proactive culture	The school children learned to value "preparedness through training"	Positive			
Community has become more proactive, prepared and resilient	After several trainings	Positive	MDRRMO	PDRRMO	

Outcome harvesting method was tested both in Caloocan City and Aklan to measure all possible changes (either positive or negative) observed by the mission informants. Participants of the workshops were given three outcome forms each and were instructed to list the most important changes (from the DP/DRR perspectives) that have taken place in their operating environments. Results of the Aklan outcome harvesting are presented in Table 8.3.

Table 8.3 reports the most relevant changes and outcomes by the respondents. All except two (behavioural change and dependency on outside project support and low sustainability) are positive. Most outcomes relate to behavioural or cultural changes such as: DRR or public awareness has risen, participation has increased, orientation and culture has become more proactive and governance and DRRM system has developed. Respondents were also asked what the main causes for these changes were. External shocks and disasters such as Yolanda and Haiyan in 2013 have been among the most important causes. Also, participation to various drills and trainings has played a major role. Outcome harvesting questionnaire had also one question (scale 1–10) related to the impact of externally funded projects (mainly PRC/FRC project in Aklan) on outcomes listed earlier. Figure 8.10 summarises the main results of the Aklan Study.

The projects seemed to have rather high impact on most of the outcomes (especially on public and DRR awareness), whereas proactive culture and community resilience are more multidimensional phenomena that are not only results of the successful project. Also, two negative outcomes seemed to be caused mainly by other factors beyond the project scope.

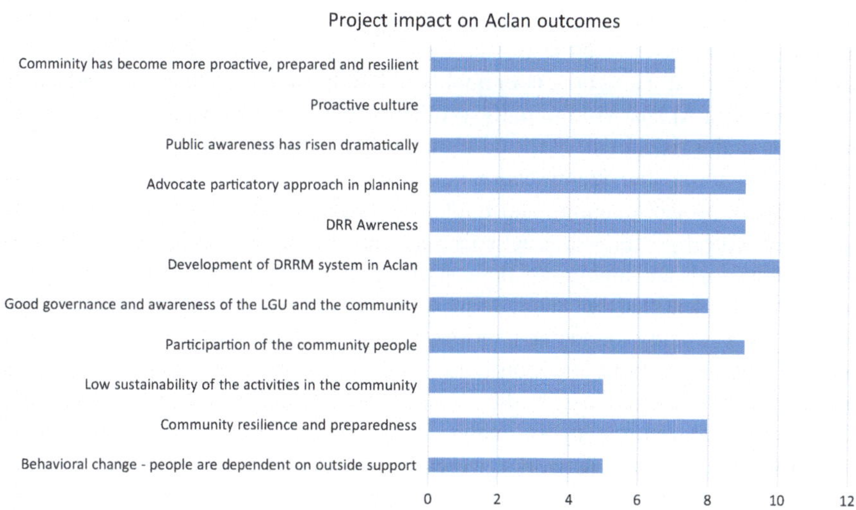

Fig. 8.10 The impact of the project on Aklan outcomes

8.5 Findings and Conclusions

This paper has intended to provide an alternative perspective to study DP/DRR systems. It shows that by applying systems thinking and complexity theory we can understand better the dynamics and interconnectedness of the DP/DRR ecosystems. This applies both to interconnected risks (multirisk landscapes) and interconnected actors (multi-actor networks).

The study has found that systems thinking and complexity theory can provide useful tools for disaster preparedness and reduction. Looking at the DP/DPRR ecosystem as a whole and as a result of interactions and interconnections helps in anticipating risks that otherwise would have gone without noticing and understanding linkages that are useful in increasing resilience in the communities. The study finds that proactive and participatory project design and planning are key factors in successful project implementation and exit as it increases local ownership in projects and thus is likely to improve both the sustainability of a project and the overall resilience. This is also in line with the assumptions of process-oriented resilience which emphasises local knowledge and culture as the basis of resilient DRR strategies. Also, the study states that projects contributing to long-term collaboration practices generate good results. Close collaboration and needs assessment as early as possible was emphasised continuously in the field study interviews and stakeholder workshops.

The study found that vulnerability capacity assessments (VCA) and individual risk maps mostly pointed out the expected major natural risks such as floods, heavy rain, earthquakes and typhoons. However, the analysis of multirisk landscape carried out during the field missions increased participants' understanding on interconnectedness of risks. This helped FRC and local partners to incorporate a broader risk scenario into projects' activities, outputs and outcomes and thus enhanced the future impacts and increased resilience in the communities. In the Philippines, the broadened risk landscape covered also risks related to health issues and urban planning (especially road infrastructure, poor quality of buildings in Caloocan City and waste management in Aklan). Additionally, problems in governance were pointed out as one of the major risks in all of the case studies.

The study found that, identification of major stakeholders is a very important part of successful project planning and implementation because each actor occupies a certain structural position in a network that either constrains or enables actors to pursue their goals and ambitions. In most of the case study projects, the main stakeholders were identified but there were some difficulties in defining the network boundaries. The study found that interlinkages between stakeholders were unknown and there was very little attention paid to cross-sectoral coordination with other critical policy domains (e.g. health, social sector, housing and urban planning). During the field visits, network analysis was introduced as a tool to map inter-organisation stakeholder networks, which illustrates better the complex interlinkages of stakeholders in the ecosystem. Participants in various workshops found this very useful and were willing to get more information and training on network analysis.

The study analysed the stakeholder networks of the case studies and report the main network structures and aggregated the data to see which organisations are acting as power brokers, support agents, guardians and game changers. In all of the case studies, the RC organisations (either headquarters and/or chapters, districts or branches) had a position of a game changer, which was a very positive result. Identifying stakeholder networks and relationships increases the resilience of the ecosystem as it eases collaboration and cooperation among stakeholders in a complex system.

Successful and sustainable DP requires a very good understanding of the overall DM governance in a country. As discussed earlier, community-based DP/DRR cannot provide long-lasting and sustainable results if it is not embedded into a broader institutional DM framework. Likewise, institutional DM does not function if it is not able to mobilise local resources such as volunteer and NGOs.

The results of the study stated that sustainability and long-term resilience are the most critical areas of development in the DP/DRR programmes. Sustainability and resilience can be enhanced by fostering synergy at multiple levels. This includes strong participant and community engagement, strong coordination with several international NGOs and government agencies. The continuation of commitments and resource allocation are also critical measures of sustainability and resilience. Understanding the DP/DRR ecosystem as complex adaptive system and utilising the tools and methods presented in this chapter can help in better anticipating risks to create more resilience and better synergies.

References

Bahadur, A. V., Ibrahim, M., & Tanner, T. (2010). *The resilience renaissance? Unpacking of resilience for tackling climate change and disasters. Strengthening Climate Resilience*. Discussion Paper 1.

Bosher, L. (2014). Built-in resilience through disaster risk reduction: Operational issues. *Building Research and Information, 4*(2), 240–254.

Burt, R. S. (2005). *Brokerage and closure: An introduction to social capital*. Oxford: Oxford University Press.

Carpenter, S., Walker, B., Anderies, J., & Abel, N. (2001). From metaphor to measurement: Resilience of what to what? *Ecosystems, 4*(8), 765–781.

Chan, S. (2001). Complex Adaptive Systems ESD.83 Research Seminar in Engineering Systems October 31, 2001/November 6, 2001.

Fiksel, J. (2006). Sustainability and resilience: Toward a systems approach. *Sustainability: Science, Practice and Policy, 2*(2), 14–21. https://doi.org/10.1080/15487733.2006.11907980.

Freeman, L. C. (1979). Centrality in social networks. Conceptual clarifications. *Social Networks, 1*, 215–239.

Gharajedaghi, J. (2011). *Systems thinking. Managing chaos and complexity*. Amsterdam: Elsevier.

Granovetter, M. S. (1973). The strength of the weak ties. *American Journal of Sociology, 78*(6), 1360–1380.

Hatakka, I., & Gogcio, R. (2016). *Final evaluation report of community based disaster risk reduction Programme 2011–2015 (CBDRR) in Aklan province and Caloocan city*. Manila: The Philippines Red Cross.

Holland, J. H. (2014). *Complexity. A very short introduction*. Oxford: Oxford University Press.
Holling, C. S. (1973). Resilience and stability of ecological systems. *Annual Review of Ecology and Systematics, 4*(1973), 1–23. Retrieved from http://www.jstor.org/stable/2096802.
IFRC. (2011). *IFRC project/programme monitoring and evaluation guide*. Geneva: IFRC.
Innes, J. E., & Booher, D. E. (2010). *Planning with complexity. An introduction to collaborative rationality for public policy*. New York: Routledge.
Johanson, J. E., Mattila, M., & Petri, U. (1995). Johdatus verkostoanalyysiin. *Kuluttajatutkimuskeskuksen menetelmäraportteja ja käsikirjoja 3/1995*. Kuluttajatutkimuskeskus. Helsinki.
Johnson, R. A., Kast, F. E., & Rosenzweig, J. E. (1964). *Systems Theory and Management Science, 10*(2), 367–385.
Kadushin, C. (2012). *Understanding social networks. Theories, concepts and findings*. Oxford: Oxford University Press.
Kaufman, G. G., & Scott, K. E. (2003). What is systemic risk, and do Bank regulators retard or contribute to it? *The Independent Review, 7*(3), 371–391.
Laszlo, E. (1972). *Introduction to systems philosophy: Toward a new paradigm of contemporary thought*. New York: Gordon & Breach Science Publishers.
Lundberg, J., & Johansson, B. (2015). Systemic resilience model, 2015. *Reliability Engineering & System Safety, 141*, 22–32. https://doi.org/10.1016/j.ress.2015.03.013.
Manyena, S. B. (2006). The concept of resilience revisited. *Disasters, 30*(4), 433–450. É The Author(s). Journal compilation É Overseas Development Institute, 2006. Published by Blackwell Publishing.
Patton, M. Q. (2011). *Developmental evaluations. Applying complexity concepts to enhance innovation and use*. New York: Guilford.
Ramalingam, B. (2013). *Aid on the edge of chaos*. Oxford: Oxford University Press.
Richmond, B. (1994). *System dynamics/systems thinking: "Let's just get on with it"*. A paper presented at the 1994 International Systems Dynamics Conference, Sterling, Scotland.
Senge, P. (1990). *The fifth discipline. The art & Practice of the learning organization*. New York: Random House.
Sweeney, L. B., & Sterman, J. D. (2000). Bathtub dynamics: Initial results of a systems thinking inventory. *System Dynamics Review, 16*(4), 249–286.
Uusikylä, P., Tommila, P., Rinne, P., & Valtari, H. (2017). *FRC International Disaster Preparedness and Disaster Risk Reduction (DPDRR) programmes thematic study*. Helsinki: Finnish Red Cross.
Uusikylä, P. (2019). Endeavour to find evidence. *The role evaluation in the complex systems of governance*. Doctoral Dissertation. University of Helsinki, Unigrafia, Helsinki.
Virtanen, P., & Uusikylä, P. (2004). Exploring the missing links between causes and effects. A conceptual framework for understanding micro-macro conversions in programme evaluation. *Evaluation, 10*(1), 77–91.
Wahl, D. C. (2017). The adaptive cycle as a dynamic map for resilience thinking. *Medium*. Retrieved from https://medium.com/@designforsustainability/the-adaptive-cycle-panarchy-as-dynamic-maps-for-resilience-thinking-793fad49de5e.
WEF. (2014). *Global risks 2014* (9th ed.). Geneva: World Economic Forum.

Chapter 9
Translations in Biobanking: Socio-Material Networks in Health Data Business

Ilpo Helén and Hanna Lehtimäki

Abstract This study examines commercialization in the context of biomedical R&D, biobanking and personalized medicine as a manifold and transformative texture of socio-material relations in which an innovation—or even a prospect of innovation—is conjoined with and put to the test by multiple human and non-human actors. The empirical study of a Finnish biobank foregrounds the interplay between social and material elements in innovative business. Our analysis unfolds the commercialization of biobank activities as a series of transformations in relations between social, technical and material biobank actors. The study enriches the theorization of commercialization of innovation by addressing the dynamic and malleable nature of socio-material relations as the groundwork of innovation business and by showing how innovation and business become entangled through translations.

9.1 Introduction

Innovation is considered vitally important for business growth and economic prosperity in society. Research on commercialization of innovation is focused on entrepreneurial activity (Datta et al. 2015), networks for commercialization (Aarikka-Stenroos et al. 2014; Mattila et al. 2019), inter-organizational processes (Markman et al. 2009) and channels of interaction between universities, start-ups and established companies (Kirchberger and Pohl 2016). Much of the literature on commercialization of innovation conceives of innovation as a strategic and entrepreneurial activity and as a linear process from idea to product or service (Kirchberger and Pohl 2016). Datta et al. (2015) show that entrepreneurial activity in commercialization of innovation involves identification of sources of innovations, classification across types of innovation, varying strategies related to market entry competence and feasibility and strategies for protection, development and deployment of innovation. Aarikka-Stenroos et al. (2014) point out a variety of actors joining the network for

I. Helén · H. Lehtimäki (✉)
University of Eastern Finland, Kuopio, Finland
e-mail: hanna.lehtimaki@uef.fi

H. Lehtimäki et al. (eds.), *Society as an Interaction Space*, Translational Systems Sciences 22, https://doi.org/10.1007/978-981-15-0069-5_9

commercialization. These actors—such as customers and users, distributors, complementaries, suppliers, investors, associations, public organizations and policymakers and regulators—contribute to practical commercialization tasks, facilitate innovation adoption or diffusion and create markets.

In this study, we lean on 'actor–network theory' (ANT) (Latour 2005; Law 2007) and demonstrate how innovative R&D is not a linear process but a web of entangled socio-material relations (e.g. Orlikowski and Scott 2008). With the help of ANT, we detach the analysis from a mainstream view in organization and management studies that conceives of innovation as a process in which a new idea, model or practice is implemented or 'pulled through' in an organization (Crossan and Apaydin 2010). From an ANT perspective, innovation and commercialization unfold as multidirectional metamorphoses of actors and their relations, both human and non-human, social and material (Miettinen 1998; see also Stokes 1997). In accordance with this view, we claim that commercialization in innovation business takes place when actors are conjoined through challenging each other.

We study commercialization of innovation in biomedical business focused on 'personalized medicine' (Tutton 2014) and examine how data management is modified into a commercial service in biobanking. The term *biobank* refers to a variety of social and technical arrangements for the collection, storage and exchange of biological specimens and associated medical and other health-related data for biomedical research (e.g. Yuille 2011; Yuille et al. 2008). The biobanks are widely considered as a vital infrastructure for biomedical science and R&D advancing personalized medicine (e.g. Gottweis and Petersen 2008; Lauss et al. 2011; Yuille 2011). The economic and commercial aspects of biobanking have been repeatedly pointed out in several studies (e.g. Fortun 2008; Mcmeeking and Harvey 2002; Parry 2004; Sunder Rajan 2006; Turner et al. 2013). In fact, the prospects of wealth are crucially important in connecting biobanks to personalized medicine, equal to or even more prominent than the ties of scientific and medical expectations (Tarkkala et al. 2018; see also Prainsack 2017).

The term 'personalized medicine' refers broadly to the visions of future medicine in which diagnoses and treatments based on knowledge of 'average' patients will be replaced by individually tailored diagnoses, risk assessment and medical care. The latter are derived from biomedical knowledge capable of precisely capturing 'all' health-related individual differences and singularities (e.g. NAS 2011; Tutton 2014). At the turn of the millennium, medical and commercial imaginaries of personalized medicine were attached to the promises of genomics to 'revolutionize' medical care (Collins 2010; Hedgecoe 2004; Tutton 2014: 113–132). In 2010, the prospect of personalized medicine is associated more closely with data-driven medicine. The promise of future medicine is now predominantly dedicated to the 'mining' of masses of digitalized biological and health data with the help of high-throughput computers and advanced bioinformatics that will result in more precise and individualized prevention, diagnoses and treatments and more efficient health care in general. High hopes attached to the deployment of health-related big data have engendered a new commercial domain of collection, circulation, management and utilization of digital data masses, related to both commercial and scientific domains of biomedical R&D and to consumers of 'digital' health information (Hood and Friend 2011; Prainsack 2017; Swan 2012). Biobanks are situated within this new health data economy.

Our empirical analysis of commercialization of biobanking is focused on Auria Biobank in Finland (see also Lehtimäki et al. 2019). We analyse the transformation of collection and maintenance of a tissue sample and health data repository into a data management service for both public and private biomedical R&D as *a series of modifications in socio-material relations* that essentially constitute biobanking. We deploy ANT (e.g. Latour 2005; Law 2007) and its key concept *translation* as analytical tools. They enable us to see two things: first, how different actors—both 'human' and 'non-human' (Latour 2005: 91)—conjoin and challenge each other when pursuing innovative R&D and business; second, how these alignments and contestations bring about changes in socio-material relations. The concepts of translation (Callon 1986; Latour 2005: 106–109; Law 2007) provide us with the perspective to analyse biobanking and its transformation into a business as actor–networks and, consequently, direct us to ask two sets of questions. We start with the question about what connects diverse things and holds them together in biobanking, in a situation in which 'we do not know in advance what the world is made up (…) who are the main actors, what happens to them, what trials they undergo' (Latour 1988: 9–10). The first set concerns *relations*:

- How are human and non-human actors connected in biobanking? What sort of translations, challenges and resistance constitute relations between the actors? Which actors attempt to translate what and by which powers? What sort of capabilities are required and involved?

The second set, in turn, concerns the dynamics of networks and *modifications*:

- Which additional actors are connected in the network and which are removed when management of the biobank data transforms from maintenance of data depository to service and when data management service is refined as business? What sort of translations, with mutual adaptation and challenge between the actors, are involved in these transformations?

This chapter is structured as follows. First, we present actor–network theory (ANT) as a method to study translations and the analytical concepts deployed in our analysis. After that, we present the data and methods of our study, focusing on the way we modified the ANT approach and its rather broad concepts operational for a concrete empirical analysis. Then we move on to our analysis of biobanking. It consists of four sections, unfolding in sequential order from one translation to another. We start from the basic operations of collection and the 'making up' of biobank data. Then we proceed to the transformation of data repository maintenance to data management service and further to commercialization of that service in collaborative relations with pharmaceutical and other medical companies. The fourth analytical section shows that translation in biobanking does not end with consolidation of commercial collaboration. Instead, commercialization engenders new problems and challenges between the actors and brings new actors into the network. Our study ends with a summary of findings and a conclusion that commercialization should be thought of as capabilities to pursue changes in socio-material networks that form a field of innovative R&D and business. This view of commercialization is new, since it highlights relations of collaboration and contestation instead of products and implementation processes.

9.2 Theoretical Approach: Innovation Business as Actor–Networks

9.2.1 Translation as Modus Operandi of Actor–Networks

The concept of translation implies the idea of the actor–network. The actor–network theory (ANT) (e.g. Latour 2005; Law 2007) takes the analysis further than just mapping a network of biobank business. First, ANT brings in 'non-human' elements and entities as actors. This means that an ANT analysis emphasizes the capabilities of material things and substances, organic entities and organisms, tools, devices and machines, and texts and documents in various forms to act and bear influence upon other actors in a network—to challenge—in a more or less consistent and sustaining manner. For example, the Ebola virus is not just an object of a campaign to prevent an epidemic. Rather, the virus affects human bodies and is contagious. Because of this, it is capable of influencing a number of activities and actors. Physicians treating fever patients in Congo start to wear breath masks and rubber gloves. The government and local authorities in Western African countries start to organize civil servants, police forces and information networks into a system for surveillance and quarantine of certain areas. And health authorities around the world get prepared to receive, handle and distribute risk information on Ebola. As ANT highlights 'non-human' elements in networks as actors equal to human actors, it blurs distinctions between the material and discursive, the social and technical and the subjects and objects.

Furthermore, ANT encourages us to abandon any presumptions about the qualities and capabilities of the actors, except for a sort of minimalistic premise that everything is relational. In other words, an actor exists in the world only due to its relations to other actors, and relations that form an actor–network engender and delineate what actors are and what they can do. When we lean on these ANT premises in our study, we approach all that is involved in biobanking—biobank data, data management service and business activities—as networks consisting of diverse social, technical and material actors.

ANT conceptualizes connections between actors in a network as translations. John Law (2007: 5) uses language as the model for describing the idea of translation:

> To translate is to make two words equivalent. But since no two words are equivalent, translation also implies betrayal: 'traduction, trahison'. So translation is both about making

equivalent and about shifting. It is about moving terms around, about linking and changing them.

ANT studies expand this linguistic idea to every existing thing, activity and power; translation becomes a concept of practical ontology, referring to a modality of both practice and existence. Things, or 'actors', are connected to each other by translations, so that an actor—human or non-human, discursive or material, social or technical—tries to translate other actors to become compatible with its own order. A translation affects the object–actors in two ways: first, it remains equal to what it is (i.e. what it is capable of) in a new order; second, it adapts itself to match the new order. Thus, translation is adaptation and modification—a sort of 'fitting in'—that happens and effects in a two-way manner: the translated actors also force the actor pursuing a translation to adapt and change.

The conceptual trinity of actors, relations and translation can be summarize in five axioms. First, the concept of *actor* means a thing that relates to other things in a network, bears effect and 'act' on them and is capable of influencing the being and capabilities of the other actor(s). Second, *translation* means a formation of a new actor or actors in a network, i.e. attaching a thing as an actor in a network. Third, being in an actor–network is 'actantial', i.e. of *capability*, and a translation makes actors capable and defines (tentatively) what the actors are capable of doing and being. Fourth, actors *challenge* each other, i.e. an actor resists attempts at conjoining and translations that other actors bear upon it. Finally, the actors that have most capabilities for translations also have the most power to exist and be 'objective'.

9.2.2 Analytical Concepts

To adapt the ideas of actor–network and translation in our analysis of biobanking business, we take some actual ANT analyses as a model and select certain analytical concepts deployed in those studies to guide our analysis. From John Law's pioneer study on an actor–network that enabled the Portuguese colonial fleets to sail the high seas from Lisbon to India in the sixteenth century (Law 1986), we take the division of actors into devices, documents and 'drilled' people. Law showed that a cornerstone of colonial 'long-distance' power was an arrangement in which devices of navigation and sailing, manuals that provided knowledge of star positions, sea currents and winds, and a crew trained to carry out specific tasks were related to each other in a manner that allowed each individual ship to sail overseas and back. In a similar way, we approach biobanking as a set of relations between devices, documents and trained personnel that enable and carry out collection, modification and delivery of biological specimen and patient data as biobank data for biomedical R&D.

Furthermore, Michel Callon provides us with conceptual tools for an analysis of translations. In his study on a study and breeding experiment on scallops at St. Brieuc Bay in the late 1970s (Callon 1986), he divided the process of translation into four phases: problematization, interessement, enrolment and mobilization. Our analysis of biobanking business is focused on the first two, which we consider the aspects of translations rather than the phases. *Problematization* refers to pointing out or performing something as a problem, an obstacle or a shortcoming in the functioning of a network and to reasoning out the scope, causes and solutions to the problem. Problematization initiates, motivates and justifies *interessement*. Callon (1986) defines the latter in the following way: 'pursuits of an actor to direct an effect and capability of other actors according to its own interest by preventing or weakening the intentions of other actors directed to alternative directions'. Thus, interessement is at the heart of the translation process, since any act of interessement engenders a situation and encounter in which the actors challenge and contest each other.

9.3 Data and Methods

The background of our empirical study is provided by involvement of the first author in research on biobanks in Finland and Europe for over a decade. In several research projects, he has participated in collecting and analysing interviews, documents and observational material and has become very familiar with the technical, epistemological, ethical, economic and governance aspects of biobanks and personalized medicine (see, e.g., Gaskell et al. 2013; Helén 2004; Lauss et al. 2011; Raivola et al. 2018; Snell et al. 2012). Against this background knowledge, the authors focused the collection of data on Auria Biobank (today Auria), a biobank founded by the University of Turku and three hospital districts in 2012 and closely associated with Turku University Hospital. Auria Biobank was selected because it is the first clinical biobank in Finland. It also managed to start early on the operations of both collection of new tissue samples and delivery of biobank data to both academic research groups and medical companies. Furthermore, Auria's strategy emphasizes commercialization of biobanking and collaboration with private medical enterprises as a means to guarantee financing and sustainability of the biobank as a public organization that serves public academic science as its primary task, whose operative rationale is adopted by biobanks in other countries, too (e.g. Timmons and Vezyridis 2017; Turner et al. 2013). In 2018, approximately 40% of Auria's projects were executed in collaboration with large pharmaceutical companies such as Bayer, Roche and Novartis.

In Auria, the authors interviewed the managing director in 2016 and conducted six additional interviews with a project manager, a lawyer, a quality manager, data scientists and a laboratory specialist in 2017. The interviews were held at the premises of the biobank, which allowed us a sense of the office space and an introduction to the equipment used in processing the samples into data. The interviews were open-ended, which provided us with full-bodied and detailed information about the practices of data management and business development in Auria. Open-ended interviews also enabled us as researchers to engage with the perspective of each interviewee. During the interviews, the respondents were asked about their career in biobanking and their work at Auria. During the discussion, specifications and clarifications of specific terminology and technical details were asked. The interviews lasted approximately 60 min, and they were recorded and transcribed verbatim in Finnish (the language of the interviews). In addition to expert interviews, we used company documents, minutes of meetings, website postings and other industry-related documents, media coverage and other publicly available documents about Auria and Finnish biobanks in general as research material.

It is commonplace for studies applying ANT to take an ethnographic approach to the domain of science or technology under study. In this paper, we do not explicitly back up interviews and textual sources with systematic observations from the 'field'. The examples of the classic ANT studies—Latour (1988) on the conquest of bacteriology in France and Law (1986) on the success of the Portuguese colonial navy in the sixteenth century—taught us that this is not absolutely necessary. Moreover, we noticed that interviews and other material were abundant with descriptions and normative evaluations of biobank actors and their relations. In fact, we found interviews overwhelming for applying ANT as a research method. We were also confident that the first author's experience in biobank studies would help us to contextualize our findings from the interviews and documents properly.

Applying ANT means in this study, first, focusing the analysis on actors, their relations and challenges between them, and, second, using certain ANT concepts as analytical tools. Before we could do that, however, we needed to find an answer to the question of how to approach the actor network *empirically* and analyse translations and its components out of our abundant research material. It is obvious that a description and analysis of the 'whole' network would be counterproductive, if not impossible, because actors, their relation and modalities of action are so numerous that even naming them would exhaust the analysis (Hyysalo 2016). According to Hyysalo (2016), ANT studies tend to face this difficulty by 'flattening' the analysis of actors, relations and challenges, either conceptually or empirically. We would rather talk about 'narrowing', and we chose to narrow the scope of the empirical analysis. This choice led us to a route from an 'extensive' analysis of networks to a 'demonstrative' analysis of translations.

We conducted the analysis in three phases. First, we identified key issues of biobanking and its commercialization with the help of intensive reading and content analysis of the interviews and other texts. After that, we picked up a few key issues for further analysis. At this point, we noticed that the phrase 'real-life data' was repeated very often in the interviews, referring to patient data from EMRs, other hospital databases and public registers. It was an obvious choice for our key analytic theme because Auria's key persons consider 'real-life data' as its main asset in making business in the biomedical R&D market. In addition, utilization of personal health data *en masse* has become the focus of public and professional debates on biobanking and personalized health during the past decade, in Finland and internationally (NAS 2011; Prainsack 2017). In the second phase of our analysis, we collected extensive textual excerpts surrounding the key themes. In the excerpts, actors, their relations and dynamics of action in biobanking were described and discussed.

In the third phase, we conducted a systematic content analysis of the excerpts with the help of ANT concepts. We sorted out three topics: first, documents, devices, expert people and their relations involved in biobanking; second, dynamics of problematizations and interessements that change these relations; and finally, lines of changes on different scales and decisive turning points, which constitute a lineage of translation towards commercialization.

9.4 Findings

9.4.1 Biobank Data as an Actor–Network

Biobank data are collected and combined from many data sources. Such making up of biobank data creates and requires an extensive network of human and non-human actors. When tissue samples are collected at the hospital clinics, patients turn to donors, and they are related to nurses and physicians not only by clinical examinations and laboratory tests but also by consent protocols and forms and by sample-taking devices. Hospital wards and their personnel are connected to the biobank through equipment of both clinical and sample-processing laboratories, sample-preservation equipment and ICT systems. Moreover, tissue samples from the patient donors or from old pathological or other tissue collections reformatted to biobanks samples are associated with electronic personal health data from the patient record databases, databases of clinical laboratories and population registers. Obviously, ICT and ICT experts at the various sites of data handling are indispensable for facilitating and maintaining these relations.

Biobanks have become an essential element of biomedicine in the past two decades. During that time, biobank experts have been (and still are) inclined to see almost every encounter and relation enabling collection, storage and distribution of biobank data either actually or potentially problematic. Issues of consent have been subjects of critical debates since the emerging of the idea of biobanking (e.g. Hoeyer 2008; Lauss et al. 2011; Ursin et al. 2008). In addition, the heterogeneity of 'raw' sample and health data is frequently pointed out as a core problem of biobanking. In interviews, the experts from Auria referred often to such problems. One complaint points out devices of preservation of tissue sample and the documentation practices of sampling that can be problematic and pose a challenge for collecting and making up biobank data. In addition, there are other factors that may compromise the data:

> (…) in a hospital, there is no single information system for the patient data but, I don't know if 20, 30 or 40 is the right amount, but anyway a large number of different systems; and the first task is trying to collect data out of them in a single place and in a form that it is usable at all, and then connect this data to the samples and be in control of this whole 'system'.

> (…) the data need to be collected in the data lake so that the clinician would see what kind of shit there is, that we were able show that data here are awful garbage, to alarm them that hey, look how you inscribe [clinical] information so that the data you provide is entirely

> useless (...) hence, data can be also used to show this aspect [of clinical data] and to point out what requires to be reformed. (IT expert, 2017)

As these quotations express, a large variation of ICT systems used in clinical settings can be problematic for collecting and combining datasets at the biobank. In addition, how clinicians and clinical laboratories inscribe and document patient data (diagnoses, medication, lab test results) is seen as potentially subversive for biobank data formation. While pointing out problems with 'raw' data, these quotations manifest reasoning that brings heterogeneous elements in a unified context and attempts to direct effects and capabilities of actors—patient records, clinicians, laboratory IT systems, for example—in a direction supporting biobanking. Thus, problematization of 'raw' data implies or even includes interessement of devices, documents and 'drilled' people involved in handling biospecimen or health-related data. Pointing out a problem initiates or implies translation. And because translation is a trial and challenge for the actors, problematization indicates a situation in which actors—both human and non-human—challenge and test each other and need to negotiate with each other.

Such relations of trial and negotiation are particularly clear in translations of clinical data into biobank data. Examining the patients, making diagnoses and prescribing treatments at the clinic take place in a wide information network in which data are created and transmitted by various devices at the different sites together with physicians, nurses, laboratory personnel and ICT experts and regulated by numerous technical and epistemic standards. Information created and passed in this network serves and is compatible with treating the patients. Attempts to turn the flow of clinical data and information to serve the collection of biobank data demand a change in existing practices, standards and habits of creating, inscribing, handling and passing clinical data. However, challenging implies two-way traffic, since the clinicians with their habits with patient and other clinical data, documentation and data management devices from laboratory and imaging equipment to patient record software are actors that put harvesting of biobank data from multiple sources to the test.

> There can be a lot of different tissue samples from, for instance, the area of surgery and, also, lymph nodes from all over the mediastinum. And they are just one number [for] all of these samples (...) because they are a part of the pathologists' report evaluating whether the surgery has gone as it should have, and if the cancer has spread [to the area under surgery] or not. Biobank wants all the lymph nodes to be numerated separately. So we have lymph node material and lung tissue, and we have tumour tissue and a bit of bronchus—but we don't have the information. Thus, we have to reorganize the whole database in order to get all the samples numerated; so that we would know for real what there actually is in the archive from this particular patient. (IT expert, 2017)

Against the background of these challenges, the vital role of ICT and experts in data analytics in translation of clinical data to biobank data becomes very clear. The collaborative relation of devices—computers, appropriate software and data mining algorithms—and expert craft makes the different data components match by correcting, cleaning and standardizing clinical and sample data from tens of data management systems. As an IT expert says, 'cleaning and re-ordering the data that comes out of the hospital (...) that takes 90 per cent of our working time, I'd estimate'. He continues:

> The analyses customers want are really easy (...) But to be able to make the required calculations, for that you need first to collect data from a million different places, and [while collecting data] you need to pay attention to that somebody may have inscribed information in centimetres, while others have used millimetres, some have used dots, and other commas or letters (...), and all sorts of issues you can imagine; all this you need to take into consideration. (IT expert, 2017)

Our previous analysis leads to a conclusion that no piece of health data, sample, laboratory result, X-ray image or diagnosis in a patient record is biobank data without documents, devices and trained people that form a network for collecting and making up data deployable in biomedical science and R&D. The existence of biobank data is dependent on such a network of multiple relations between human and non-human actors. In fact, as biobank data is a compilation of health-related data from various sources, it is essentially a fabric, a network that enables combination of heterogeneous personal health data for multiple medical R&D purposes.

9.4.2 Management Service for 'Real-Life Data'

Since biobanks belong to an infrastructure for biomedical R&D, they are supposed to deliver data from its repositories to research labs and groups, both academic and company-based. The task of delivering biobank data puts the biobank as collector and storage-keeper to the test, as an evaluation by Auria's CEO after 2 years of actual biobank operations testifies: 'Biobanking has appeared to be in many ways different from what we expected when founding it'. In Auria's case, encounters with both non-profit and profit R&D institutions have added new actors and rearranged the relations between the actors, thus altering the actor–network which the biobank data are embedded in. They also have redirected the interest of biobank actions and brought additional focus on biobanking. A new *interessement* is epitomized by the idea of data management service, which is highlighted as the core activity of Auria Biobank.

The turn towards data management service remarkably challenged the way to conceive of the biobank data. Experience from collaboration with research labs and groups has made people at Auria realize that their clients are predominantly interested in the clinical data (patient records, lab results, prescription records, etc.) attached to the tissue samples. In particular, collaboration with pharmaceutical companies has made biobank people see that 'it is the patient data that is unique and utterly interesting' (IT expert, 2017). Key persons at Auria reason that especially their commercial clients see such 'real-life data' being of great help in targeting biomedical research in drugs or diagnostic biomarkers, and for that reason Auria's data are 'attractive':

> They are particularly interested in our phenotype data (…) it is precisely the clinical data of our hospital patients that allows deep phenotyping, so that we can find exactly the right patient for the right study. (CEO 2016)

> If [the clients] need more data associated with the sample, then there are not many places where they can get similar data as we have. Elsewhere in the world, there are not clinical data collected from such a long period of time, and then we have PIN [= national personal identity number] through which we can connect all the data [from different sources] with each other. And the law allows the biobank to acquire data from public registers, like the cause of death from Statistics Finland or information on drug reimbursements from the Social Insurance Institution of Finland. (Project Manager 2017)

The latter quotation implies a view presented also in other interviews and documents at Auria that the biobank does not consider its depository of ‘real-life data’ per se as its main asset. Rather, the ‘competitive’ advantage of Auria lies in its expertise and experience combining sample management, bioinformatics and administrative skills. They allow Auria to provide to their commercial and academic partners tailor-made and codesigned datasets that unite data from sample collections, patient records and national health care and population registers. A project manager (2017) says:

> We have invested in our service. We serve our customers so that they can get what they want, and we take care of all that needs to be done on behalf of our customer. And indeed, we have been thanked for being flexible, that it’s easy to discuss with us, and that the projects proceed smoothly and both partners are in dialogue all the time. (Project manager 2017)

The provision of a wide variety of data management services for medical R&D demands both biobank activities and the data to be more malleable. Making the data accessible to potential users requires making a catalogue and descriptive metadata available in the website of the biobank. Such communication to potential users and the public, in turn, brings in a new kind of expertise in ICT and communication in digital networks and social media. Moreover, the scope of biobank activities expands. This can be seen in Auria’s service portfolio, which lists sample delivery, sample collection, real-life data analyses, consultation and project development, feasibility studies and tissue microarrays.

In the first translation of biobanking at Auria, the focus on ‘real-life data’ and widening the scope of data management are aligned. The changes mean expansion of the network as new tasks bring in new actors in the form of technology, experts and institutions. Eventually, these changes result in a reorganization that put more emphasis on the management of clinical data. A shift manifesting this development took place in 2018. Then the biobank and an organization providing services in clinical informatics were conjoined under the brand of Auria. In practice, there is now single access to both the biobank repository with related services and the platform for data mining of patient data repositories. According to the website (2018), clients of the biobank may now have access to ‘careful organization, harmonization and maintenance of clinical data in the commensurated data warehouse and provision of both research as a service and secure data analysis platform service for data-driven real-world analyses'.

Auria seeks to provide both standard and customized data management services to its clients. The customization of data introduces new aspects in data management and requires new capabilities of the actors. Actions within the network for collection and storing of biobank data are primarily focused on making heterogeneous 'raw' data applicable by standardizing of collection and inscription practices and by curating existing data. In turn, provision of datasets customized to the needs of a particular research project or a customer requires flexibility from services and the data. Such 'tailoring' of the data requires 'iteration' to make the needs of the research partner and the services of the biobank match technically, economically and ethically. It also engenders new problems and attempts to redirect interests, which leads to negotiations between the actors. An IT expert (2017) described the problems and situations of negotiation with clients in the following way:

> In principle, we have all the possible data from the patient defined in this hospital, all sorts on numbers, lab results, imaging results, yes, all possible kinds [of data]. (…) If the client does not have a clear idea of what we would like to look at, then it is a bit difficult to get going with the collaboration; (…) many clients are so accustomed to the clinical trials or similar R&D in which the paperwork is painstakingly rigid. But their thinking is stuck to that pattern, even though you repeatedly tell them that, hey, if you list in the first draft of the plan all possible tasks, you will never be to able to accomplish them all. (IT Expert 2017)

Not only relations with clients and potential data users cause problems and require negotiation; the data put technology and 'drilled' people at Auria to the test. An IT expert (2017) describes how experts and data mining technology negotiate with biobank data and rearrange the network when making customized data for biomedical research:

> (…) we have had to develop tools how particular information is caught from the text mass (…) smoking, for example, it is a central predictive factor to all sorts of issues. But there is no database in the hospital that would provide information, in Excel for instance, whether the patient smokes or not. Then we have had to develop some tricks how to read—or how would an algorithm read—from the patient record whether he or she smokes, has stopped smoking, or does not smoke. (…) Even the most enthusiastic researcher cannot possibly read through the files of 10,000 patients, while with our tools this can be done in few seconds. And we can, with the help of a certain algorithm, guess right whether a patient smokes, does not smoke or has stopped, with 90 per cent probability. (IT Expert 2017)

All in all, the translation of biobanking—from collection and compiling of data in a repository to data management services—has several dimensions. First, widening the scope of biobank activities brings in medical research institutions with their own expertise, devices, protocols, documentation and interests. New actors pose challenges to the operations of actors and their mutual relations in a biobank network and thus introduce changes. Auria's experts refer to these changes by talking about the shift of the focus on 'real-life data' and about being engaged with more diverse tasks of handling the data. Second, provision of a data management service requires rearrangement of the relations between expert skills and knowledge—especially those between medical experts as clients and users of biobank data and data analysis experts at Auria—and modification of relations between documents (e.g. patient records) and IT devices (algorithms), as our aforementioned analysis exemplifies. Finally, the shift to data management services requires malleability from the network of 'documents, devices and drilled people' (Callon 1986) that maintains and generates biobank data and from the data itself.

9.4.3 Business Collaboration by Contract

In order to ensure continuity of biobanking in terms of financing and usability of its data repository in biomedical R&D, Auria seeks commercial collaboration with big transnational pharmaceutical corporations and other medical companies. Auria's key persons consider such commercialization to be indispensable for sustaining biobank operations in the future. For a biobank, data management services are central in commercial collaboration; as said earlier, it is not just biobank data but expert services for management of such data—'real-life data', in particular (see previous texts)—that makes a biobank an 'attractive' partner in biomedical R&D. In this, the contract becomes a central actor in enabling the collaboration with commercial actors and transferring the data into a commercial good.

Delivering biobank data for biomedical R&D use follows a certain, international standard procedure, regardless of what kind of potential customer approaches Auria. Both academic research groups and private companies have to first fill in an application form and provide a research plan that specifies the data requested and its use. At this point, a new compound of actors entered the network, namely, Auria's scientific steering group, which consists of 'specialists from different scientific and clinical fields' (Project Manager 2017).

The scientific steering group reviews the application. It investigates whether the purpose of the research is scientifically and ethically sound and the research will not violate research ethics and protects the security, anonymity and privacy of the participants. It also compares the research proposal with other ongoing studies conducted with the biobank data to ensure three issues: first, that there is no overlap between the previous or ongoing studies; second, that there are enough samples and data for conducting the proposed research; and third, that a sufficient repository of samples will remain for future research. Once the steering group has made a decision, the contract can be written and signed, and then the biobank may give access to the data.

Collaboration between Auria and its potential partner, however, usually begins before filling in the application and making the contract:

> Before we take [an application] to the scientific steering group, we discuss with the applicant and work on the application so that it can be considered as biobank research, and pass [the evaluation] (Project Manager 2017).

The issues concerning data are at the heart of the contract, as the most important clauses are related to:

> (…) what data and/or samples can be given out from the biobank, what it can be used for, and that it is protected properly if it is actually given out or not, or operated here [at Auria]. Then there are issues that are derived directly from the law. We have to agree about publishing results of the study after some period of time, so that the research would be of [public] benefit. Usually the default timeframe is 12 months after the end of the study. (Lawyer 2017)

The contract is negotiated between Auria and the customer. These negotiations are different from those between Auria's data management experts and researchers of the customers, as the contract brings in a legal framing and lawyers. The legal dimension is emphasized especially in collaboration with private enterprises. The contract that enables access to biobank data and delivery of data to an outside party and defines the terms of collaboration is negotiated between the lawyer of the biobank and corporate lawyers. In these negotiations, issues of confidentiality, research protocols, assessment of data quality and ethical guidelines are addressed and agreed upon:

> The [contracts] may seem different, but the clauses are largely the same, so that some come directly from biobanking law, for instance that the research results have to be made publicly available, so all these types of clauses they have to be included in all contracts. But when there are large companies that are accustomed to operating with their own types of contracts, we need to put everything that is needed into their contract template. They often think that they are buying a service and often start with their own template that has not been designed for this type of operation; then we have to modify their contract so that we can proceed. So these contracts may involve a bit more work compared to contracts with academic research groups who may not be as enthusiastic to negotiate the detailed words as are the companies, particularly the large ones. (Lawyer 2017)

The translation that brings Auria's data and data management service into the domain of commerce obviously modifies action by relating biobanking and biomedical R&D with profit seeking. However, when we analysed this shift, we ended up highlighting a concrete actor, namely the contract. The contract is pivotal for commercialization because it is the basic requirement of commercial collaboration between the biobank and private companies. More essentially, the contract has the power to relate actors and mediate between them around the biobank data and its management. For example, the legal framework of private business enters the domain of biobanking through contract making, and new documents like the corporate contract templates and corporate lawyers as new experts challenge the biobank network. In contract negotiations, a new situation with new actors sets new and concrete demands on data management at the biobank concerning confidentiality, quality control, ethical evaluation and other protocols of corporate R&D. This may bear a profound influence on the core activities of collecting, formatting and storing the biobank data, as well as to data management services.

Corporate actors also face challenges when collaborating with a public biobank like Auria. The contract allows the Finnish law and public authorities entry to the realm of the practices and protocols of corporate biomedical R&D; and as outside regulating actors, they set demands on commercial actor–networks regarding donor protection, ethical conduct of research and returning results back to the biobank. In order to get access to the biobank data, the private company has to adapt some of its practices and arrangements to these demands. And all modifications are negotiated and inscribed in the contract by the lawyers.

The contract between the biobank and the customer translates biobank data into a network of relations between actors who seek to appropriate the data. It modifies relations into commercial relations, and negotiations between actors become negotiations about the rights, obligations and limitations on the ownership and governance of the data, and the risks and the potential earnings related to the use of the data. With such shifts, biobank data and biobanking become commercialized. Since the contract is capable of facilitating this, it is not just a document but a market device (Muniesa et al. 2007) that can be simultaneously characterized as discursive, social and technical.

Yet translation does not necessarily stop with a finalized contract. When biobank research for which Auria provides data and data management services is conducted by private companies and thus becomes commercial R&D, this change may affect the relations between the biobank and actors that are crucial in biobank data and data management networks. For example, access to personal data in public health registers may become problematic and uncertain:

> (…) it may become troublesome and problematic (…) There was a study, and the National Institute for Health and Welfare gave access to the required data in its repository, but additional data was needed from the databases of the Social Insurance Institution of Finland; but they evaluated that the proposed project did not meet the criteria of scientific research because it was a study sponsored by a private company, and they refused to provide the data (…) We took the case to the court, all the way to the Supreme Administrative Court, but we never got the data. (Lawyer 2017)

9.4.4 Continuous Translation

So far, biobanking at Auria has been modified through a series of problematizations and interessements from collection and maintenance of biobank data repository to data management service focused on 'real-life data' and further to commercial collaboration upon biobank data management for biomedical R&D. However, it seems that this trajectory of commercialization does not have closure. The interviews and documented action plans and evaluations give an impression that Auria is continuously concerned about its future. For Auria's key persons, it is not self-evident that the biobank will be able to provide appropriate and high-quality data for biomedical R&D and to attract pharmaceutical companies and other commercial partners to profitable collaboration in the future.

Auria's problematization is similar to concerns raised in international discussions in which many biobank experts and executives have asked whether or not biobanks will be able to maintain quality and expand their activities to meet scientific, ethical and social standards in the future or not. They identify several sustainability issues in biobanking: continuation of sufficient financing after the foundation and starting periods are over; means and resources to keep the data in biobank depositories usable, of high-quality and attractive for scientific and commercial users in an emerging situation with abundant genomic data available; maintenance of donor recruitment on a high-enough level to keep biobank data extensive; and capability to maintain sufficient data protection and ethical standards (Albert et al. 2014; Caulfield et al. 2014; Chalmers et al. 2016; Kongsholm et al. 2018; Tupasela et al. 2015; Tupasela and Stephens 2013; Vaught et al. 2011).

At Auria, a response to forecasted problems was a call for action that would reinforce biobanking by reorganizing it. In a report preparing the plan for a merger of Auria and two other regional biobanks, this was stated as follows:

> Great expectations are associated with biobanking, especially on the national level; however, keeping biobanks sustainable and cost-effective has been considered to be a challenge internationally, and tentative experiences from Finland support these observations. The Biobank Act has been in force for two and a half years, and hospital biobanks are still at the start line, except for Auria. The biobanks should be seen as the guardian of national resources [that] should be harnessed as productively as possible. To achieve an optimal situation, the biobanks and their owner organizations have to do their share; but also the government and public authorities need to take measures that will be described in this report. (Selvitystyö 2016: 5)

The core of problematization at Auria and among Finnish biobank people was a concern whether repositories of biobank data in the Finnish biobanks are 'extensive enough' to attract scientific and commercial collaborators from abroad. This concern is very acute, as giant global platforms for harvesting and mining genetic and health data, like the Chinese WuXi NextCODE, are emerging on the biobank scene. The merger plan of three regional biobanks was a response to this concern. The government responded by launching a project in 2016 to combine the collections of all Finnish biobanks, so that tissue samples and related health data would be available as if stored in a single national repository. Eventually, the project resulted in the Finnish Biobank Cooperative (FINBB), which began operations in 2018.

A major task of the project was to get the biobanks interested in the national 'merger' and negotiate between a variety of actors and their interests involved in biobanking. Such interessement and negotiation essentially took place in many relations between documents, devices and expert people in the biobank network. Those relations were under modification and challenge when consenting procedures and related documents, quality assessment standards and protocols, practices of data curation and IT systems in charge of management, transfer and protection of data in ten biobank organizations had to be synchronized. Obviously, these are engendered additional problems which the FINBB is still working on.

Translations related to national unification of biobank repositories and to the shift in focus of biobanking on 'real-life data' had repercussions beyond the domains of biobanks and biomedicine. For instance, they lead to demands to reform legislation and regulation of biobanks so that access and a combination of health-related data from different databases would become more flexible (see Tarkkala et al. 2018; Tarkkala 2019). This, in turn, brought new juridical and policymaking documents, experts and stakeholders, with their powers and interests, into the socio-material texture of biobanking. Multiple translations, new relations and challenges between the actors caused uncertainty and confusion about the nature, objectives and benefits of the innovation process. Biobank experts attending seminars and workshops were to some extent puzzled about the new situation. Besides worries about the integration of ICT systems, a major issue was (and still is) the division of labour between the national cooperative and the regional biobanks like Auria. The FINBB was planned to serve potential customers of the biobanks by providing one access route—'a one-stop shop'—to all biobanks' data collections in Finland and the associated administrative and consulting services. This posed a challenge to the business model of Auria. According to the plan, the data management service would be shifted to the national centre, which leaves the role of regional biobanks unclear.

Concern over sufficiency of the data in the biobank repository for international collaborative R&D in the future did not radiate only 'upwards'. It was also reflected in the level of basic operations of collecting tissue samples and patient data. At Auria, the objective of collecting biobank samples was to 'catch all incomers', but shortly after they had started collecting samples, they noticed that the majority of the hospital patients did not provide consent for taking a sample and use of personal patient data, even though their attitude to biobanking was very positive. Auria people thought that most patients take time to consider the consent but then 'forget' to send the signed consent form back to the biobank. Auria was worried that this tendency would make its repository of new data futile in terms of quantity and representativeness of the patient population and thus severely harm the biobank operations. A suggestion for resolving this problem was replacing the informed consent procedure with an 'opt-out' model. In it, every patient in the hospital would give a tissue sample for the biobank, and then they would have the personal option to actively withdraw—to opt out—their sample and patient data from the repository and biobank use.

> The burdensome consent procedure is the most crucial bottleneck at the moment. Citizens surely have a positive attitude to biobanking, but the active percentage of active provision of consent is approximately 20, and 1–2% of the patients actively refuse to donate. The situation becomes unbearable in the long run. It is very congruent with the functioning of public health care that collection of the samples and data will be based on an opt-out system; in other words, all tissue samples taken and data archived in the hospitals will be automatically available to the biobank unless the patient explicitly denies it. (Selvitystyö 2016: 6)

This problematization touched the elementary operation of data collection, the relationship between the donor and the biobank. The suggestion of an opt-out model also challenged the basic practical principle—the one of informed consent—upon which biobanking has been founded all over the world during the past two decades (e.g. Hoeyer 2008). It called for a rearrangement of socio-material relations involved in sample taking and activated an 'old' ethical problem and even controversy at the heart of data collection at the biobanks (see Caulfield and Murdoch 2017), thus making the expertise of ethicists, lawyers and social scientists more prominent in the network. And yet, the Finnish biobank experts and lawyers, ethicists and social scientists involved in the discussion have remained uncertain and divided in their opinion whether or not the shift to an opt-out model should be done:

> The game of consent, it is doubled-edged; I mean do you always have to ask for consent or not? I don't consider it so bad if data is used in research if it is not used against the individual or used for decisions regarding her [and] if data is used for statistical analysis only and the individual is not of interest to anyone. So, if this is the way it goes, then it is ok. But there is a very strong school of thought according to which the consent needs to be asked always, sign here and so forth; there are pros and cons to both views. (Lawyer 2017)

Auria's concerns about the sustainability of biobanking and future usability, or 'attractiveness', of its data repository in the context of international commercialized biomedical R&D exemplify that translation is not a single trajectory that begins from a problem and ends with a rearranged assemblage of actor relations. Instead, translations keep on happening all the time in an actor–network of innovative business like biobanking. As particular sequences of problematization and interessement lead to consolidation of certain relations and capabilities of actors, new problems and tests emerge. They radiate on different scales: both on the level of general juridical and administrative regulation of biobanks, as well as on the level of the basic relations and operations of data collection.

9.5 Discussion

The topic of our study is commercialization in a business field emerging around the utilization of big digital health data reservoirs, related to the innovative biomedical R&D pursuit of 'personalized' or 'precision' medicine (Prainsack 2017; Tarkkala et al. 2018). We approached this topic by studying biobanking, which provides an indispensable data collection and management infrastructure for biomedical R&D (e.g. Yuille 2011) and therefore forms a core element in the new health data economy (on the latter, see, e.g. Tang 2016: 73–98). We emphasize the socio-material character of biobanking and commercialization, and we focused our analysis on a single biobank—a hospital biobank, Auria, operating in southwestern Finland—and its engagement with commercial collaboration with pharmaceutical and other medical companies.

To get a concrete grasp of the socio-materiality of commercialization within the health data economy and biobanking, we based our analysis on the 'actor–network theory' and its key concept of translation (e.g. Callon 1986; Law 2007). In comparison to discussions that emphasize the processual or networked character of innovation and commercialization (e.g. Aarikka-Stenroos et al. 2014) or to a variety of studies that focus on 'translations' (see Waeraas and Nielsen 2016), the ANT approach introduces a new, elementary insight for understanding commercialization in innovation business. ANT extends the sphere of actors in a network to material substances and elements, living entities, tools and devices and documents and other textual items. These 'non-human' elements are equally able to act, i.e. bear influence, in a network as human beings and institutions. Thus, ANT blurs distinctions between the material and the discursive and social and technological aspects of innovation and commercialization. It encourages us to abandon any presumptions about qualities and capabilities of the actors and, instead, to focus on relations of mutual influence that 'determine' what actors are and what they can do. This view allowed us to think of commercialization in the context of biomedical R&D, biobanking and personalized medicine as a manifold and transformative texture of socio-material relations in which an innovation—or even a prospect of innovation—is conjoined with and put to a test by multiple human and non-human actors.

ANT encouraged us to pay attention to details and the 'microlevel' of commercialization process (see Geels 2010). To be able do this, we chose limited examples of the texture of relations and put them under our analytic loupe. We first focused on the core operation of the biobank, namely the collection of biobank data. The results of our analysis show that no piece of tissue sample or health data (laboratory result, X-ray image, diagnosis in a patient record, etc.) is biobank data without 'documents, devices and trained people' (Callon 1986). They align with material items (e.g. a tissue sample or an electronic compound consisting of the result of a blood test) and form a network for collecting and making up data suitable for utilization in biomedical R&D. Biobank data are essentially a compilation of health-related data from various sources and exist as a fabric of relations between human and non-human actors that enables a combination of heterogeneous personal health data for a variety of medical R&D purposes. In fact, biobank data is itself a network.

As our analysis proceeded, we noticed that delivering data from the biobank repository to biomedical R&D clients called for transformations in the texture of relations that forms the biobank and the data. Translations that shifted the focus of biobanking to data management services and to 'real-life data' consisted of both entries of new actors in the networks and changes of the relations between the existing actors. Additional transformations in the texture occurred, and new actors (e.g. 'contract') joined in when the biobank engaged in collaboration with commercial partners.

In sum, our analysis unfolds the commercialization of biobank activities as a series of transformations in relations between social, technical and material biobank actors. In these *translations*, pointing out or performing problems gives impulses for actors to challenge each other, which leads to rearrangement of relations between actors and their capabilities and transforms the socio-material texture of biobanking. Our view resembles in many ways the analysis by Mason et al. (2018), which approaches transformation of a biomedical discovery in the realm of commerce as a series of 'choreographed contestations'.

Our analysis shows that such transformation is not a singular process. As we demonstrated, resettling one problem or contestation leads to other problems and challenges between actors. Thus, translations happen all the time in a biobank network that collects, delivers and commercializes biobank data and its management, and those translations are multilinear and take place on a different scales of action. This understanding of innovation is congruent with the view of many STS studies on cutting-edge science or technology development, whereas it is very different from the emphasis on linearity of mainstream management and organization studies (see Crossan and Apaydin 2010).

Our analysis of biobanking actor–networks leads to a conclusion that opens a new perspective on conceiving collaborative R&D and related pursuits of commercialization. The making of a biomedical novelty, 'an innovation', and its commercial deployment is not essentially about a product, and neither is it a process of implementation. Rather, innovation and its commercialization should be thought of as capabilities and powers to pursue modifications and to challenge—the ability for 'problematization' and interessement' (Callon 1986)—in networked socio-material relations involved in collaborative innovation and business, i.e. relations between documents, material substance, devices and 'drilled' people. Both human and non-human actors may have such powers.

Acknowledgement The authors wish to thank the Academy of Finland for financial support (project number 292492) on this project.

References

Aarikka-Stenroos, L., Sandberg, B., & Lehtimäki, T. (2014). Networks for the commercialization of innovations: A review of how divergent network actors contribute. *Industrial Marketing Management, 43*, 365–381.

Albert, M., Bartlett, J., Randal, N., et al. (2014). Biobank bootstrapping: Is biobank sustainability possible through cost recovery? *Biopreservation and Biobanking, 12*, 374–380.

Callon, M. (1986). Some elements of a sociology of translation: Domestication of the scallops and the fishermen of St Brieuc Bay. In J. Law (Ed.), *Power, action and belief: A new sociology of knowledge?* London: Routledge.

Caulfield, T., & Murdoch, B. (2017). Genes, cells, and biobanks: Yes, there's still a consent problem. *PLoS Biology, 15*(7), e2002654.

Caulfield, T., Burningham, S., Joly, Y., et al. (2014). A review of the key issues associated with the commercialization of biobanks. *Journal of Law and the Biosciences, 1*, 94–110.

Chalmers, D., Nico, D., Kaye, J., et al. (2016). Has the biobank bubble burst? Withstanding the challenges for sustainable biobanking in the digital era. *BMC Medical Ethics, 17*(39). https://doi.org/10.1186/s12910-016-0124-2.

Collins, F. (2010). *The language of life: DNA and the revolution of personalized medicine*. London: HarperCollins.

Crossan, M. M., & Apaydin, M. (2010). A multi-dimensional framework of organizational innovation: A systematic review of literature. *Journal of Management Studies, 47*, 1154–1191.

Datta, A., Mukherjee, D., & Jessup, L. (2015). Understanding commercialization of technological innovation: Taking stock and moving forward. *R&D Management, 45*(3), 215–249.

Fortun, M. (2008). *Promising Genomics: Iceland and deCODE Genetics in a world of speculation. XXXX*. Berkeley, CA: University of California Press.

Gaskell, G., Gottweis, H., Starkbaum, J., et al. (2013). Publics and biobanks: Pan-European diversity and the challenge of responsible innovation. *European Journal of Human Genetics, 21*, 14–20.

Geels, F. W. (2010). Ontologies, socio-technical transitions (to sustainability), and the multi-level perspective. *Research Policy, 39*, 495–510.

Gottweis, H., & Petersen, A. (2008). *Biobanks. Governance in comparative perspective*. London, New York: Routledge.

Hedgecoe, A. (2004). *The politics of personalised medicine*. Cambridge: Cambridge University Press.

Helén, I. (2004). Health in prospect. High-tech medicine, life enhancement and the economy of hope. *Science Studies, 17*(1), 3–19.
Hoeyer, K. (2008). The ethics of research biobanking: A critical review of the literature. *Biotechnology and Genetic Engineering Reviews, 25*, 429–452.
Hood, L., & Friend, S. H. (2011). Predictive, personalized, preventive, participatory (P4) cancer medicine. *Nature Reviews. Clinical Oncology, 8*, 184–187.
Hyysalo, S. (2016). Sosiologinen materia: toimijaverkostoteoreettisen tutkimustarinan ohennus. *Sosiologia, 53*(3), 275–291.
Kirchberger, M. A., & Pohl, L. (2016). Technology commercialization: a literature review of success factors and antecedents across different contexts. *The Journal of Technology Transfer, 41*(5), 1077–1112.
Kongsholm, N. C. H., Christensen, S. T., Herrmann, J. R., Larsen, L. A., Minssen, T., Pedersen, L. B., Rajam, N., Tommerup, N., Tupasela, A. M., & Schovsbo, J. H. (2018). Challenges for the sustainability of university-run biobanks. *Biopreservation and Biobanking, 16*(4), 312–321.
Latour, B. (1988). *The pasteurization of France*. Cambridge, MA: Harvard University Press.
Latour, B. (2005). *Reassembling the social*. Oxford: Oxford University Press.
Lauss, G., Snell, K., Bialobrzeski, A., Weigel, J., & Helén, I. (2011). Embracing complexity and uncertainty: An analysis of three orders of ELSA research on biobanks. *Genomics, Society and Policy, 7*, 47–64.
Law, J. (1986). On the methods of long distance control: Vessels, navigation, and the Portuguese route to India. In J. Law (Ed.), *Power, action and belief: A new sociology of knowledge?* London: Routledge.
Law, J. (2007). Actor network theory and material semiotics. Retrieved August 10, 2016, from http://www.heterogeneities.net/publications/Law2007ANTandMaterialSemiotics.pdf.
Lehtimäki, H., Helén, I., Snell, K., Eriksson, P., & Montonen, T. (2019). Sustainable value creation in the commercialisation of innovation: The case of Auria biobank. *International Journal of Entrepreneurship and Innovation Management, 23*(5), 451–465.
Markman, G. D., Gianiodis, P. T., & Phan, P. H. (2009). Supply side innovation and technology commercialization. *Journal of Management Studies, 46*(4), 625–649.
Mattila, M., Yrjölä, M., & Lehtimäki, H. (2019). Drivers of and barriers to networked commercialization: Business model perspective. *International Journal of Entrepreneurship and Innovation, 23*(5), 479–495.
Mason, K., Friesl, M., & Ford, C. J. (2018). Markets under the microscope: Making scientific discoveries valuable through choreographed contestations. *Journal of Management Studies*. https://doi.org/10.1111/joms.12426.
Mcmeeking, A., & Harvey, M. (2002). The formation of bioinformatic knowledge markets: An 'economies of knowledge' approach. *Revue d'économie industrielle, 101*(4), 47–64.
Miettinen, R. (1998). Materiaalinen ja sosiaalinen. Toiminnan teoria ja toimijaverkkoteoria innovaatioiden tutkimuksen viitekehyksenä. *Sosiologia, 35*(1), 28–42.
Muniesa, F., Millo, Y., & Callon, M. (2007). An introduction to market devices. In M. Callon, Y. Millo, & F. Muniesa (Eds.), *Market devices*. Malden, MA; Oxford: Blackwell.
National Academy of Sciences. (2011). *Toward precision medicine*. Washington, DC: The National Academies Press.
Orlikowski, W. J., & Scott, S. V. (2008). Sociomateriality: Challenging the separation of technology, work, and organization. *Academy of Management Annals, 2*, 433–474.
Parry, B. (2004). *Trading the genome: Investigating the commodification of bio-information*. New York: Columbia University Press.
Prainsack, B. (2017). *Personalized medicine. Empowered patients in the 21st century?* New York: New York University Press.
Raivola, V., Snell, K., Pastila, S., et al. (2018). Blood donors' preferences for blood donation for biomedical research. *Transfusion, 58*(7), 1640–1646.
Selvitystyö Taysin ja Tyksin erityisvastuualueiden biopankkien yhdistämisestä. (2016). Auria.

Snell, K., Starckbaum, J., Lauss, G., et al. (2012). From protection of privacy to control of data streams: A focus group study on biobanks in the information society. *Public Health Genomics, 15*(5), 293–302.

Stokes, D. (1997). *Pasteur's quadrant: Basic science and technological innovation*. Washington, DC: Brookings.

Sunder Rajan, K. (2006). *Biocapital*. Durham, London: Duke University Press.

Swan, M. (2012). Health 2050: The realization of personalized medicine through crowdsourcing, the quantified self, and the participatory biocitizen. *Journal of Personalized Medicine, 2*, 93–118.

Tang, C. (2016). *The data industry*. Hoboken, NJ: Wiley.

Tarkkala, H. (2019). *Reorganizing biomedical research: Biobanks as conditions of possibility for personalized medicine*. Doctoral dissertation in Sociology, University of Helsinki.

Tarkkala, H., Helén, I., & Snell, K. (2018). From health to wealth: The future of personalized medicine in the making. *Futures*. https://doi.org/10.1016/j.futures.2018.06.004.

Timmons, S., & Vezyridis, P. (2017). Market-driven production of biospecimens and the role of NHS hospital-led biobanks. *Sociology of Health Illness, 39*(7), 1242–1257.

Tupasela, A., & Stephens, N. (2013). The boom and bust cycle of biobanking: Thinking through the life cycle of biobanks. *Croatian Medical Journal, 54*(5), 501–503.

Tupasela, A., Snell, K., & Canada, J. (2015). *Patients, business and the state: Translating health information into sustainable benefits (322/2015)*. Helsinki: Tekes.

Turner, A., Dallaire-Fortier, C., & Murtagh, M. (2013). Biobank economics and the 'commercialization problem. *Spontaneous Generations: A Journal for the History and Philosophy of Science, 7*(1), 69–80.

Tutton, R. (2014). *Genomics and the reimaging of personalized medicine*. Farnham: Ashgate.

Ursin, L., Hoeyer, K., & Skolbekken, J. A. (2008). The informed consenters: Governing biobanks in Scandinavia. In H. Gottweis & A. Petersen (Eds.), *Biobanks: Governance in comparative perspective*. London: Routledge.

Vaught, J., Rogers, J., Carolin, T., & Compton, C. (2011). Biobankonomics: Developing a sustainable business model approach for the formation of a human tissue biobank. *Journal of the National Cancer Institute Monographs, 242*, 24–31.

Waeraas, A., & Nielsen, J. (2016). Translation theory 'translated': Three perspectives on translation in organizational research. *International Journal of Management Reviews, 18*, 236–270.

Yuille, M. (2011). Infrastructure Vital to Genome Success. *Nature, 471*, 166.

Yuille, M., van Ommen, G.-J., Brechot, C., et al. (2008). Biobanking for Europe. *Briefings in Bioinformation, 9*, 4–24.

Chapter 10
Digital Platforms and Industry Change

Mikko Hänninen and Lauri Paavola

Abstract Scholars argue that the platform economy spurs both increased efficiency and innovation for participating actors, often opening new ways for radical change and disruption in different industrial settings. However, despite the large academic and practitioner interest towards digital platforms and multisided markets, we are only beginning to understand the scope and impact of the platform economy in our society. In this chapter, we, therefore, explore how digital platforms shape industry dynamics. Based on a non-systematic review of both recent and eminent literature on digital platforms, we construct a literature-based theoretical model of digital platform-led industry change. Our study increases understanding of how a digital platform-led industry transformation evolves and thus serves as a useful basis for future research on the topic.

10.1 Introduction

During recent years, we have seen an increase in initiatives from governments and governmental funding agencies worldwide towards encouraging the development of platform-based businesses in order to promote industry disruption and growth. The increased interest towards platforms comes as digital platforms and multisided markets, along with other digital business models, are creating new mediums for the exchange of products, services, and information in different industrial settings (Parker et al. 2016). Especially digital platforms arguably open novel ways for creating and capturing value (Kenney and Zysman 2016), often creating new economic interactions altogether (Hagiu and Wright 2015). Accordingly, for example, through the digital single market policy, the European Commission has declared that it aims to foster an environment in which online platform ecosystems thrive

M. Hänninen (✉)
Department of Marketing, Aalto University School of Business, Espoo, Finland
e-mail: mikko.o.hanninen@aalto.fi

L. Paavola
Center for Knowledge and Innovation Research, Aalto University School of Business, Espoo, Finland
e-mail: lauri.paavola@aalto.fi

H. Lehtimäki et al. (eds.), *Society as an Interaction Space*, Translational Systems Sciences 22, https://doi.org/10.1007/978-981-15-0069-5_10

and therefore it seeks to create new digital opportunities for both people and business (European Commission 2019). Yet, despite the large recent interest towards the transformative capabilities of digital platforms and multisided markets, scholars are only beginning to understand and examine the impact of digital platforms in our society (e.g., de Reuver et al. 2018).

The transformative capability of digital platforms and multisided markets comes from such platforms providing new exchange and interaction opportunities for economic actors. By definition, digital platforms provide the interface for the interaction between distinct demand and supply-side actors (Adner and Kapoor 2010). Accordingly, digital platforms now bring buyers and sellers of a wide range of products and services together and intermediate transactions between them (Gawer and Cusumano 2002; Parker and Van Alstyne 2005; Gawer 2014; Gawer and Cusumano 2014). In addition, for example, McIntyre and Srinivasan (2017) emphasize that digital platforms intermediate exchange between actors that without a platform as an intermediary would not be able to interact, at least as effectively and efficiently. As such, in the platform economy "much of the provision of labor, products, and services (are) coming from platform-mediated interactions between evermore numerous providers, many of whom work independently and often part-time, and customers" (Laamanen et al. 2018: 214). For example, digital platforms like Airbnb now ensure trust and secure transactions between anonymous individuals which has led to an influx of both new tenants and landlords to the short-term accommodation market as virtually anyone can now become a tenant (e.g., Zervas et al. 2017). Therefore, digital platforms now mediate a large share of economic interactions in the global economy and across diverse industries and sectors (Caldieraro et al. 2018). As such, digital platforms have the potential to transform "how we work, socialize, and create value in the economy" (Kenney and Zysman 2016: 61).

In this chapter, we seek to understand why digital platforms are such a powerful mechanism for driving change in many industrial settings. To inform our analysis, we conducted a non-systematic review of both recent and eminent literature on digital platforms in which we, non-exhaustively, identified, read, and analyzed, both recent and highly cited papers on digital platforms, particularly from leading platform scholars, such as Ron Adner, Michael Cusumano, Thomas Eisenmann, David Evans, Annabelle Gawer, David McIntyre, Geoffrey Parker, Amrit Tiwana, and Marshall Van Alstyne, to understand how existing literature on digital platforms seeks to capture their transformative and evolutionary capabilities. In addition, our analysis seeks to understand to which phase in a platform's lifecycle does the existing literature on digital platforms focus on and in particular to which phase of a platform's lifecycle are the different theoretical concepts regarding digital platforms relevant. This research is important as, despite extensive research on digital platforms and the platform economy from different perspectives (e.g., McIntyre and Srinivasan 2017), most of the extant research on digital platforms focuses on understanding specific digital platform-related questions, such as their effects on employment (Rogers 2016), income volatility (Farrell and Greig 2016), media (Seamans and Zhu 2013), and entrepreneurship (Nambisan 2017), rather than how, in practice, digital platforms transform industry dynamics and particularly how a digital platform-led industry transformation evolves. Therefore, in this chapter, we create a literature-based theoretical model of digital platform-led industry transformation. While previous studies on platforms have been dispersed and focused on identifying different aspects of the platform phenomena (e.g., Gawer 2014), we bridge the recent literature on digital platforms and consider the process in which digital platforms and multisided markets shape industry dynamics, from the initial implementation of a digital platform in a given industry to the creation of competing platforms by incumbent industry players.

We contribute to the literature on digital platforms and industrial change by constructing a model of how digital platforms shape industry dynamics, providing understanding for the phases in which a digital platform-led industry transformation transpires. We argue that due to the characteristics of digital platforms identified in the literature, digital platforms have the potential for creating major disruptions in incumbent industries, for example, by disrupting the existing interaction patterns in the value chain. Particularly, the openness of digital platforms and multisided markets, and the ability for virtually anyone to join a digital platform, often enables digital platforms to reach sustainable competitive advantage in the form of a large user base, which is difficult for rival digital platforms to imitate (e.g., Tiwana 2014). These findings help both scholars and policymakers better grasp the transformative capabilities of digital platforms while also providing a host of research opportunities to further explore such phenomena. In particular, our model of digital platform-led industry transformation can help both scholars and practitioners better understand the societal implications of digital platforms, when digital platforms are implemented in new industrial settings.

10.2 Theoretical Background

Digital platforms and multisided markets are one example of new business and business models that have emerged through advances in information technology and the digital economy (Parker et al. 2016). The platform construct originates in the engineering and economics literature, where platforms are generally used to refer to modules on top of which internal or external third-party collaborators can create complementary products, services, and technologies (Brandenburger and Nalebuff 1997; Jacobides et al. 2006; Gawer and Cusumano 2014). For example, Intel based much of its competitive advantage in the 1990s on a platform-based business model, through which it enabled third-party developers to access its proprietary technology (Gawer and Phillips 2013). From the use of the platform construct in a new product development and innovation context (e.g., Meyer and Lehnerd 1997), lately economics, IS, management, and strategy scholars have increasingly used the platform construct to refer to digital platforms, that is, a specific digital platform-based business model, such as multisided markets and marketplaces (e.g., McIntyre and Srinivasan 2017). As such, digital platforms exist today in a wide range of industrial settings (Han et al. 2016) and have received large multidisciplinary interest from scholars (Gawer 2014).

Accordingly, through digitalization, digital platforms are used to refer to a specific platform-based business model. These digital platforms have several distinct characteristics. First, a digital platform-based business model provides access to the platform to third-party providers. Particularly, industry platforms refer to technological platforms that enable firms to "build further complementary innovations and potentially generate network effects" (Gawer and Cusumano 2014: 420). Accordingly, industries may themselves become platforms, when they tap into the innovation capabilities of external firms that are not directly part of their supply chain (Gawer 2009). Examples of industry platforms include Apple, Google, and Facebook, each having leveraged a platform-based business model as part of their larger business in order to enable third-party complementors to innovate and add their own products or services on top of the, more or less, standardized technology interface (Gawer 2014). For example, in 2018, Google's Android and Apple's App Store each had over two million apps, made by third-party developers (Statista 2018). Second, a digital platform is typically a specific type of network arrangement. Scholars argue that digital platforms can be characterized as a collaborative network where a platform provides the technological interface on top of which third-party collaborators, such as application developers, can create applications to (e.g., Adner and Kapoor 2010). Thirdly, digital platforms generally form a specific technological architecture. Scholars, for example, in IS literature, have defined digital platforms as a "software-based system that provides core functionality shared by the modules that interoperate with it and the interfaces through which they interoperate" (Ghazawneh and Henfridsson 2015: 199). Accordingly, modular design is a central feature of digital platforms (Gawer 2014).

To complement the previously mentioned perspectives to digital platforms, in our study, we define digital platforms as multisided markets and marketplaces, in which a digital platform can be regarded as a "special kind of market that play the role of facilitators of exchange between different types of consumers that could not otherwise transact with each other" (Gawer 2014: 1240). Accordingly, through digitalization, digital platforms have been increasingly implemented across different industries, taking advantage of advances in information technology and the fast-changing customer demands and expectations (Mathmann et al. 2017). By definition, the platform, therefore, "intermediates transactions among firms and/or individuals that may not be able to transact otherwise" (McIntyre and Srinivasan 2017: 472). As such, the digital platform is a structure for the direct and indirect interaction between different user groups (Gawer 2014). Popular examples of such platform-based businesses include Airbnb and Uber, in the accommodation and transportation sectors, respectively, which have both transformed the value creation logic of their industries from, primarily, product to service-based, connecting independent third-party service providers together with potential end users (e.g., Kenney and Zysman 2016). The shift from the exchange of products to facilitating interactions in platform ecosystems (Gawer 2014) enables digital platforms to capture value from businesses that did not exist before and reorganizes how value creation is organized in different industrial settings (e.g., Hänninen et al. 2019).

10.3 Digital Platforms and Industry Transformation

As the review of literature on digital platforms shows, digital platforms have the potential to facilitate change and disruption in several parts of the economy, as digital platforms promote a unique value-exchange logic, which often replaces the incumbent channels in the marketing mix by shifting exchanges from physical to digital channels (e.g., Kenney and Zysman 2016). For example, Eisenmann et al. (2011) argue that digital platforms may create competitive advantage in a given industry when three basic conditions are met: the network effects are strong, multi-homing costs are high, and the demand for differentiated features is limited. As such, a winner-takes-all situation may emerge (Eisenmann et al. 2006), where a few platforms take a dominant position in a given industry, for example, if they are successful in quickly attaining a critical mass of users on different sides of the platform, and at the expense of incumbent industry players (Rysman 2009). This logic explains the success of digital platforms like Airbnb, where a large number of users attained early on in the lifecycle of the platform have prohibited incumbent industry players, such as large multinational hotel chains, developing their own competing digital platforms and multisided marketplaces. Therefore, latecomers wanting to develop and produce a digital platform will often struggle to attain a critical mass of users if a dominant platform has already established itself in the industry.

Bearing these dynamics in mind, based on a non-systematic literature review of 60 journal articles, book chapters, and books on digital platforms and platform economics published between 1982 and 2019, we have converted the characteristics of digital platforms into a model consisting of four phases in which platforms shape industry dynamics, from the initial implementation of a digital platform in a given industry, to the platform becoming the dominant organizing logic in the industry, promoting the creation of further platforms by incumbent industry players and start-ups. Table 10.1 depicts the four identified phases in which platforms shape industry dynamics. Next, we describe these phases in more detail.

10.3.1 Phase 1: Digital Platform Is Implemented

In the first phase, a digital platform is implemented. According to literature, digital platforms emerge as advances in information technology enable the more efficient sharing of products, services, and information (Parker et al. 2016). Through a digital platform, it is generally more efficient to intermediate transactions between individual buyers and sellers, often enabling economic interactions that were not possible before the platform was implemented (McIntyre and Srinivasan 2017).

Table 10.1 Four phases in which platforms shape industry dynamics

Phase	Theoretical construct(s)	Synopsis
Phase 1: A digital platform is implemented	Digital platforms (e.g., Gawer and Cusumano 2002; Rysman 2009; Gawer 2014; Gawer and Cusumano 2014; McIntyre and Srinivasan 2017)	A platform is implemented, enabling more efficient forms of interaction and exchange between buyers and sellers
Phase 2: New users attract further new users	Network effects, Metcalfe's law (e.g., Katz and Shapiro 1986; Shapiro and Varian 1999; Clements and Ohashi 2005; Li et al. 2010)	Each new platform user attracts further users to the platform, driving up the value of the platform exponentially to each platform user
Phase 3: Digital platform creates competitive advantage	Critical mass (e.g., Evans 2009; Evans and Schmalensee 2010; Tiwana 2014) Winner-takes-all, dominant design (e.g., Teece 1998; Eisenmann 2006; Sun and Tse 2007; Tiwana 2014)	The digital platform starts to dominate as a critical mass of users is reached, increasing the likelihood that the platform becomes the dominant design in the given industry
Phase 4: Digital platform creates platforms	Winner-takes-all, dominant design (e.g., Teece 1998; Eisenmann 2006; Sun and Tse 2007; Tiwana 2014) Multihoming (Rochet and Tirole 2003; Adner and Kapoor 2010; (Choi 2010) Envelopment, mutation (Eisenmann et al. 2011; Tiwana 2014)	More digital platforms are created by incumbent industry players that aim to capture similar benefits that the initial platform was able to capture, resulting in diminishing competitive advantage for the initial platform

For example, the sharing economy has emerged through digitalization, and now in many service sectors a digital platform ensures access to market for both buyers and sellers of a wide range of product and services and facilitates trust between users, for example, in the form of transparency through feedback and reviews (e.g., Laamanen et al. 2016).

There are generally two options for creating a digital platform: a closed or open platform (Tiwana 2014). In addition, platforms can follow a so-called 'walled garden' approach, in which the platform is first closed but later is opened to third-party users (Hazlett et al. 2011). An open digital platform is open for external participants (Tiwana 2014), enabling free entry into the supply of the technology (Li et al. 2010) and the ability for external stakeholders to join the platform (Evans 2009). For example, eBay is an open marketplace in which basically anyone can become a seller, with low initial investments required to join the platform (Hasker and Sickles 2010). A closed digital platform is not open for external participants (Tiwana 2014), restricting the development of the platform and enforcing the exclusion of external developers through, for example, patents, copyrights, secrecy, and other restraints (Sun and Tse 2007). For example, many established firms like Walmart have launched a marketplace to support their online business; however, as in the case of Walmart, their platform is often closed, "invitation-only," in order to protect the brand value of the platform owner by, for example, prescreening potential sellers (Tian et al. 2018). However, it is generally argued that all digital platforms have both closed and open elements, in order for a closed platform to also obtain at least some of the innovation and efficiency benefits that open digital platforms deliver. Studies show that, by opening a closed platform to external stakeholders, it is possible to increase the rate of innovation around that platform by up to 500%, measured, for example, by the number of complementors supporting the platform (Boudreau 2010).

10.3.2 Phase 2: New Users Attract Further New Users

In the second phase, through networks effects, more users join the digital platform. According to the concept of networks effects, in open digital platforms, each new user attracts further participants to the platform, thus making the platform more valuable for each existing platform user (Katz and Shapiro 1986; Rochet and Tirole 2003; Clements and Ohashi 2005). For example, the more end-customers use Amazon, the more it makes sense for suppliers to sell on the Amazon Marketplace as well (e.g., Jiang et al. 2011). Accordingly, network effects often drive a platform into a self-reinforcing cycle, as each new user on the platform increases the value of the platform exponentially (Tiwana 2014). This partly explains the popularity of social media platforms like Facebook, which have often seen exponential growth after reaching a critical mass of users (e.g., Hanna et al. 2011).

Generally, in the context of digital platforms, scholars refer to positive cross-side network effects in which a new user on one side of the platform increases the value of the platform for the other side of platform users (Eisenmann et al. 2006). These cross-sided network effects can be either positive or negative. For example, these effects are positive when platforms like Uber are a substitute for existing businesses in specific industry, which means that an increase in the number of Uber drivers in a certain city can actually decrease traffic congestion and other issues (e.g., when alternative modes of transportation diminish from the streets) which increases utility (cross-sided network effects) for all users (e.g., Liu et al. 2016), and negative when free riders on one side of the platform (e.g., an excess number of customers only trying the platform) increase service congestion and thus lower utility (cross-sided network effects) for all users (e.g., Burtch 2011). On the other hand, platforms can also have other types of network effects as well. Same-side network effects, when a new participant on one side of the platform changes the value of the platform to other users on that same side of the platform, can also be either negative or positive (Tiwana 2014). For example, each new seller on a digital platform increases competition between sellers, which leads to negative same-side network effects for all sellers on the platform (e.g., Jiang et al. 2011). Thus, through network effects, digital platforms have the potential to capture exponential growth in value when new users join the platform bearing in mind that they mitigate and manage the potentially negative network effects (Parker and Van Alstyne 2005; Lee and Lee 2014).

10.3.3 Phase 3: Digital Platform Creates Competitive Advantage

In the third phase, the digital platform creates competitive advantage after amassing a critical mass of users as both buyers and sellers. According to theory, network effects enable platforms to achieve a critical mass of users (Tiwana 2014), meaning that it becomes difficult for either side of users to opt out of the platform. For example, Amazon now has an over 40% share of US online retail sales, which makes it difficult for any brand to opt out of selling through Amazon (eMarketer 2018). When a platform is able to reach a critical mass of users rapidly, a winner-takes-all situation may arise (Eisenmann 2006), thus increasing the likelihood that the platform becomes the dominant design that incumbent industry players will eventually be forced to follow and imitate (Tiwana 2014). As such, in many industries like retail (e.g., Amazon), video (e.g., Netflix), music (e.g., Spotify), social media (e.g., Facebook), accommodation (e.g., Airbnb), and transportation (e.g., Uber), often only one global platform now dominates once it has reached a critical mass of users worldwide.

Scholars, however, argue that several factors may limit the degree to which digital platforms capture competitive advantage. For example, uncertainty among the platforms' users may limit the platform from reaching a critical mass of users. The *'penguin problem,'* for example, refers to uncertainty about whether other user groups will eventually join the platform (Farrell and Klemperer 2007). Therefore, to overcome any uncertainty, lock-in is important for keeping users on the platform and restricting their possibility to switch to competing platforms. Lock-in refers to the mechanisms in place for users to stay on a platform, making it costly or even impossible for users to switch to a competing platform due to the incurred switching costs (Monteverde and Teece 1982; Cortade 2006; Farrell and Klemperer 2007). For example, developers in the smartphone industry often invest large amounts of money to develop applications to the Apple iOS or Google Android operating systems, which locks them into the platform, and the contractual terms dictated by the platform owner (e.g., Kenney and Pon 2011). Thus, if a digital platform is able to reach a critical mass of users, the platform often starts to dominate, meaning that the platform becomes the dominant design, which incumbent industry players may eventually be forced to follow, and both customers and suppliers locked into.

10.3.4 Phase 4: Digital Platform Creates Platform

In the fourth phase, the digital platform creates more platforms, as competing digital platforms are introduced in the given industry. According to theory, once a digital platform has amassed a large number of users, the platform often becomes a dominant design for mediating transactions between customers and suppliers (e.g., Tiwana 2014). Accordingly, incumbent industry players often have no option but to also adopt a platform-based business model and also new platform-based start-ups may emerge. For example, in the retail sector, many retailers now follow a marketplace model, after initially launched by Amazon in the early 2000s, as digital platform-mediated marketplaces have become popular among both end-customers and suppliers (e.g., Hänninen et al. 2019). In addition, there is also an increasing number of platform-based start-ups in the retail sector, which seek to grab market share from firms like Amazon by focusing on niche product categories and customer segments like handmade, vintage, and unique products (e.g., Etsy) and sustainability (e.g., Swap.com). Thus, once the platform reaches a critical mass of users, competitors know that there is a viable market for a platform-based business model, which sparks the creation of copycat platforms and differentiated platforms (Cohen et al. 2000). However, if the incumbent platform is not able to identify and control the openings for value creation, it may result in the incumbent platform losing market share as a result (e.g., Eisenmann 2006). For example, in the music industry, Spotify emerged as the dominant platform in 2006, outrivalling existing music streaming services, but recently Spotify has lost market share as rival platforms from incumbent industry players like Apple's Apple Music have sought to capture similar competitive advantage through a subscription-based music streaming platform, the now de facto industry standard (e.g., Datta et al. 2018).

Scholars argue that digital platforms may lose market share particularly if platform users start to multihome (Eisenmann et al. 2011), meaning that platform users use more than one platform for the same service. There is already evidence of this in many sectors of the sharing economy, where both buyers and sellers increasingly use multiple digital platforms simultaneously in order to guarantee service provision and availability (e.g., Sinclair 2016). For example, both drivers and customers may simultaneously use Lyft and Uber platforms to find end-customers and ensure service availability, respectively (Iansiti and Lakhani 2017).

If the core market of the digital platform begins to weaken, for example, due to increased competition or multihoming on behalf of its users, the platform may also mutate and crossover to other markets (Cohen et al. 2000). Mutation refers to the "unanticipated, serendipitous creation of a spinoff platform or app that inherits some properties of the parent subsystem but with a completely different function than its parent" (Tiwana et al. 2010: 682), in which an existing software or interface is applied to another setting. Mutation can also enable the platform to crossover its customers from one service to another. As a result, for example, Google was able to gain over ten million users to its Google+ social media service in just 2 weeks, while it took both Facebook and Twitter over 2 years to achieve the same user base from scratch (Tiwana 2014). At the same time, envelopment, referring to a situation where one platform provider moves to another market in which it combines its own functionality with the target platform in order to form a multi-platform bundle, may also be a competitive tool for displacing dominant platforms if it enables them to develop technically superior alternatives (Eisenmann et al. 2011). For example, Netflix enveloped the rent-on-demand entertainment services provided by cable television companies by combining the existing service with superior functionality and technological supremacy (Tiwana 2014). As such, the potential threat for dominant platforms not only comes from platforms start-ups but also from existing platforms that may mutate or envelop to other markets in order to displace existing dominant platforms.

Therefore, today many digital platforms are crossing over to other markets and also bridging the physical and digital as is the case with Amazon and its increasing brick-and-mortar presence (Hänninen et al. 2019). Thus, once the platform has become the dominant design and attracted a critical mass of users, more platforms are often created by incumbent industry players that seek to capture similar competitive advantage as the initial platform. This can, however, lead to a loss in market share for the initial platform, especially if they lose their technological advantage and other firms mutate or envelop into their market.

10.4 Discussion and Conclusions

In this chapter, we discussed how digital platforms shape industry dynamics. We began with a question of how platforms shape industry dynamics, seeking to understand how digital platforms drive change in different industrial settings. To answer these questions, we created a literature-based theoretical model for how platforms shape industry dynamics, identifying four phases in which platforms shape industry dynamics through an analysis of 60 journal articles, book chapters, and books on digital platforms and platform economics. The four phases identified through our review are: (1) digital platform is implemented, (2) new users attract further new users, (3) digital platform creates competitive advantage, and (4) digital platform creates platforms.

First, platforms emerge as one industry player implements a digital platform or a platform-based business model. During the past couple of decades, advances in information technology have enabled many firms to experiment with new digital business models and accordingly digital platforms have lately been launched in several parts of the economy. Second, network effects enable digital platforms to often grow exponentially. Customers increasingly use a diverse range of digital services, and as such new digital platforms generally attract a large user base from the onset, especially when they seek to make transactions more efficient and secure, or create new markets altogether as is the case both with the sharing and gig economy. Third, digital platforms create a competitive advantage when they reach a critical mass of users. Essentially, a digital platform may reach such a large number of users on both the supply and demand sides of the platform (i.e., buyers and sellers) that it may start to redefine the competitive logic of the industry it operates in and grab market share from incumbent industry players. Fourth, competing digital platforms are created. The competitive advantage of the platform weakens as two dynamics are at play: incumbent industry players launch competing digital platforms and new platform-based start-ups emerge. In addition, through envelopment, dominant platforms in one part of the economy may migrate to other industries in order to displace the dominant platforms and create multi-platform bundles.

Accordingly, through these four phases, a digital platform may become the dominant organizing logic in a given industry. It is important to note however that the four phases presented in this chapter are not mutually exclusive but instead mutually reinforcing, as in order to sustain itself from envelopment the platform should continually develop new services and attract new customers regardless of the lifecycle phase that the platform is in. In the future, technological changes will particularly place pressure on platform-based firms to continue to renew themselves in order to succeed against both current and upcoming competition.

This study suggested four phases of how digital platforms shape industry dynamics, by combining the attributes found in extant literature regarding digital platforms into a literature-based theoretical model. Therefore, we bring forward our model as a useful base for future research on digital platforms and the platform economy. Furthermore, the model helps understand to which phase in a platform's lifecycle does the existing literature on digital platforms focus on and in which phase of a platform's lifecycle are the different theoretical concepts regarding digital platforms, such as network effects, relevant. Accordingly, we invite a multitude of empirical research to examine this model and enhance our understanding of digital platform-led industry transformation in the future. Despite limitations with regard to generalizability as our model emerged from the study of a subset of platform literature from economics, IS, management, and strategy journals, as the topic of digital platforms and the platform economy continues to receive increased interest and is novel as such, the insights generated, along with the literature-based theoretical model, can serve as a useful foundation for future research.

References

Adner, R., & Kapoor, R. (2010). Value creation in innovation ecosystems: How the structure of technological interdependence affects firm performance in new technology generations. *Strategic Management Journal, 31*(3), 306–333.

Boudreau, K. J. (2010). Open platform strategies and innovation: Granting access vs. devolving control. *Management Science, 56*(10), 1849–1872.

Brandenburger, A. M., & Nalebuff, B. J. (1997). *Co-opetition: A revolution mindset that combines competition and cooperation; the game theory strategy that's changing the game of business*. New York: Currency.

Burtch, G. (2011). Herding behavior as a network externality. ICIS 2011 Proceedings.

Caldieraro, F., Zhang, J. Z., Cunha, M., Jr., & Shulman, J. D. (2018). Strategic information transmission in peer-to-peer lending markets. *Journal of Marketing, 82*(1), 42–63.

Choi, J. P. (2010). Tying in two-sided markets with multi-homing. *The Journal of Industrial Economics, 58*(3), 607–626.

Clements, M. T., & Ohashi, H. (2005). Indirect network effects and the product cycle: Video games in the US, 1994–2002. *The Journal of Industrial Economics, 53*(4), 515–542.

Cohen, W., Nelson, R., Walsh, J. (2000). Protecting their intellectual assets: appropriability conditions and why U.S. manufacturing firms patent (or not). NBER Working Paper No. 7552.

Cortade, T. (2006). A strategic guide on two-sided markets applied to the ISP market. *Communications and Strategies, 61*(1), 17–35.

Datta, H., Knox, G., & Bronnenberg, B. J. (2018). Changing their tune: How consumers' adoption of online streaming affects music consumption and discovery. *Marketing Science, 37*(9), 5–21.
de Reuver, M., Sørensen, C., & Basole, R. C. (2018). The digital platform: A research agenda. *Journal of Information Technology, 33*(2), 124–135.
Eisenmann, T. R. (2006). Winner-take-all in networked markets. *Harvard Business School Technical Note*, pp. 806–131.
Eisenmann, T., Parker, G., & Van Alstyne, M. W. (2006). Strategies for two-sided markets. *Harvard Business Review, 84*(10), 92.
Eisenmann, T., Parker, G., & Van Alstyne, M. (2011). Platform envelopment. *Strategic Management Journal, 32*(12), 1270–1285.
Emarketer. (2018). Amazon now has nearly 50% of US ecommerce market. Retrieved April 18, 2019, from https://retail.emarketer.com/article/amazon-now-has-nearly-50-of-us-ecommerce-market/5b48c542ebd4000b24140992
European Commission. (2019). Online platforms digital single market. Retrieved April 18, 2019, from https://ec.europa.eu/digital-single-market/en/online-platforms-digital-single-market
Evans, D. S. (2009). How catalysts ignite: The economics of platform-based start-ups. In A. Gawer (Ed.), *Platforms, markets and innovation*. Northampton, MA: Edward Elgar.
Evans, D. S., & Schmalensee, R. (2010). Failure to launch: Critical mass in platform businesses. *Review of Network Economics, 9*(4), 1–26.
Farrell, D., & Greig, F. (2016). Paychecks, paydays, and the online platform economy: Big data on income volatility. *JP Morgan Chase Institute*.
Farrell, J., & Klemperer, P. (2007). Coordination and lock-in: Competition with switching costs and network effects. *Handbook of Industrial Organization, 3*, 1967–2072.
Gawer, A. (2014). Bridging differing perspectives on technological platforms: Toward an integrative framework. *Research Policy, 43*(7), 1239–1249.
Gawer, A., & Cusumano, M. (2002). *Platform leadership: How intel, palm, cisco and others drive industry innovation*. Brighton, MA: Harvard Business School Press.
Gawer, A. (2009). Platforms dynamics and strategies: From products to services. In A. Gawer (Ed.), *Platforms, markets and innovation* (pp. 45–76). Cheltenham, UK/Northampton, MA: Edward Elgar.
Gawer, A., & Cusumano, M. A. (2014). Industry platforms and ecosystem innovation. *Journal of Product Innovation Management, 31*(3), 417–433.
Gawer, A., & Phillips, N. (2013). Institutional work as logics shift: The case of Intel's transformation to platform leader. *Organization Studies, 34*(8), 1035–1071.
Ghazawneh, A., & Henfridsson, O. (2015). A paradigmatic analysis of digital application marketplaces. *Journal of Information Technology, 30*(3), 198–208.
Hagiu, A., & Wright, J. (2015). Multi-sided platforms. *International Journal of Industrial Organization, 43*, 162–174.
Han, X., Martinez, V., & Neely, A. (2016). Service in the platform context: A review of the state of the art. *Cambridge Service Alliance*.
Hanna, R., Rohm, A., & Crittenden, V. L. (2011). We're all connected: The power of the social media ecosystem. *Business Horizons, 54*(3), 265–273.
Hänninen, M., Mitronen, L., & Kwan, S. K. (2019). Multi-sided marketplaces and the transformation of retail: A service systems perspective. *Journal of Retailing and Consumer Services, 49*, 380–388.
Hasker, K., & Sickles, R. (2010). eBay in the economic literature: Analysis of an auction marketplace. *Review of Industrial Organization, 37*(1), 3–42.
Hazlett, T. W., Teece, D. J., & Waverman, L. (2011). Walled garden rivalry: The creation of mobile network ecosystems. George Mason Law and Economics Research Paper No. 11–50.
Iansiti, M., & Lakhani, K. R. (2017). Managing our hub economy. Strategy, ethics, and network competition in the age of digital superpowers. *Harvard Business Review, 95*(5), 84–92.
Jacobides, M. G., Knudsen, T., & Augier, M. (2006). Benefiting from innovation: Value creation, value appropriation and the role of industry architectures. *Research Policy, 35*(8), 1200–1221.

Jiang, B., Jerath, K., & Srinivasan, K. (2011). Firm strategies in the "mid tail" of platform-based retailing. *Marketing Science, 30*(5), 757–775.

Katz, M. L., & Shapiro, C. (1986). Technology adoption in the presence of network externalities. *Journal of Political Economy, 94*(4), 822–841.

Kenney, M., & Pon, B. (2011). Structuring the smartphone industry: Is the mobile internet OS platform the key? *Journal of Industry, Competition and Trade, 11*(3), 239–261.

Kenney, M., & Zysman, J. (2016). The rise of the platform economy. *Issues in Science and Technology, 32*(3), 61–69.

Laamanen, T., Pfeffer, J., Rong, K., & Van de Ven, A. (2016). Business models, ecosystems, and society in the sharing economy. *Academy of Management Discoveries, 2*(2), 218–221.

Laamanen, T., Pfeffer, J., Rong, K., & Van de Ven, A. (2018). *Editors' introduction: Business models, ecosystems, and society in the sharing economy*. Academy of Management Discoveries. (Forthcoming).

Lee, S., & Lee, S. (2014). Early diffusion of smartphones in OECD and BRICS countries: An examination of the effects of platform competition and indirect network effects. *Telematics and Informatics, 31*(3), 345–355.

Li, S., Liu, Y., & Bandyopadhyay, S. (2010). Network effects in online two-sided market platforms: A research note. *Decision Support Systems, 49*(2), 245–249.

Liu, Z., Hong, Y., & Zhang, Z. (2016). Do ride-sharing services affect traffic congestion? An empirical study of Uber entry. *Social Science Research Network, 2002*, 1–29.

Mathmann, F., Chylinski, M., de Ruyter, K., & Higgins, E. T. (2017). When plentiful platforms pay off: Assessment orientation moderates the effect of assortment size on choice engagement and product valuation. *Journal of Retailing, 93*(2), 212–227.

McIntyre, D. P., & Srinivasan, A. (2017). Networks, platforms, and strategy: Emerging views and next steps. *Strategic Management Journal, 38*(1), 141–160.

Meyer, M. H., & Lehnerd, A. P. (1997). *The power of product platforms: Building value and cost leadership*. New York: Free Press.

Monteverde, K., & Teece, D. J. (1982). Supplier switching costs and vertical integration in the automobile industry. *The Bell Journal of Economics, 13*, 206–213.

Nambisan, S. (2017). Digital entrepreneurship: Toward a digital technology perspective of entrepreneurship. *Entrepreneurship Theory and Practice, 41*(6), 1029–1055.

Parker, G. G., & Van Alstyne, M. W. (2005). Two-sided network effects: A theory of information product design. *Management Science, 51*(10), 1494–1504.

Parker, G., Van Alstyne, M., & Choudary, S. P. (2016). *Platform revolution: How networked markets are transforming the economy—And how to make them work for you*. New York: W. W. Norton Publishing.

Rochet, J., & Tirole, J. (2003). Platform competition in two-sided markets. *Journal of the European Economic Association, 1*, 990–1029.

Rogers, B. (2016). Employment rights in the platform economy: Getting back to basics. *Harvard Law & Policy Review, 10*, 479.

Rysman, M. (2009). The economics of two-sided markets. *The Journal of Economic Perspectives, 23*(3), 125–143.

Seamans, R., & Zhu, F. (2013). Responses to entry in multi-sided markets: The impact of craigslist on local newspapers. *Management Science, 60*(2), 476–493.

Shapiro, C., & Varian, H. R. (1999). The art of standards wars. *California Management Review, 41*(2), 8–32.

Sinclair, M. (2016). Fair and efficient regulation of the sharing economy. *Economic Affairs, 36*(2), 204–211.

Statista. (2018). Number of apps available in leading app stores as of 3rd quarter 2018. Retrieved April 23, 2018, from https://www.statista.com/statistics/276623/number-of-apps-available-in-leading-app-stores/

Sun, M., & Tse, E. (2007). When does the winner take all in two-sided markets? *Review of Network Economics, 6*(1), 16–40.

Teece, D. (1998). Capturing value from knowledge assets: The new economy, markets for know-how and intangible assets. *California Management Review, 40*(3), 55–79.
Tian, L., Vakharia, A. J., Tan, Y., & Xu, Y. (2018). Marketplace, reseller, or hybrid: Strategic analysis of an emerging e-commerce model. *Production and Operations Management, 27*(8), 1595–1610.
Tiwana, A. (2014). *Platform ecosystems: Aligning architecture, governance, and strategy*. Burlington, MA: Morgan Kaufmann.
Tiwana, A., Konsynski, B., & Bush, A. A. (2010). Research commentary—Platform evolution: Coevolution of platform architecture, governance, and environmental dynamics. *Information Systems Research, 21*(4), 675–687.
Zervas, G., Proserpio, D., & Byers, J. W. (2017). The rise of the sharing economy: Estimating the impact of Airbnb on the hotel industry. *Journal of Marketing Research, 54*(5), 687–705.

Part IV
Civic Society as an Interaction Space

Chapter 11
Facilitating Organisational Fluidity with Computational Social Matching

Jukka Huhtamäki, Thomas Olsson, and Salla-Maaria Laaksonen

Abstract Striving to operate in increasingly dynamic environments, organisations can be seen as fluid and communicative entities where traditional boundaries fade away and collaborations emerge ad hoc. To enhance fluidity, we conceptualise computational social matching as a research area investigating how to digitally support the development of mutually suitable compositions of collaborative ties in organisations. In practice, it refers to the use of data analytics and digital methods to identify features of individuals and the structures of existing social networks and to offer automated recommendations for matching actors. In this chapter, we outline an interdisciplinary theoretical space that provides perspectives on how interaction can be practically enhanced by computational social matching, both on the societal and organisational levels. We derive and describe three strategies for professional social matching: social exploration, network theory-based recommendations, and machine learning-based recommendations.

11.1 Introduction

Today, organisations operate in a dynamic environment in which organisational boundaries fade away, actors form new relationships spontaneously, and information flows in a chaotic way (Schreyögg and Sydow 2010; Ståhle and Grönroos 2000; Chatterjee et al. 2017; Stein et al. 2015). Enhancing collaboration within and between organisations is considered a general recipe for improving their productivity and innovation capability (Hsiehchen et al. 2015; Wuchty et al. 2007). Particularly in knowledge work, collaboration is considered an effective means of dynamically solving problems and achieving exceptional results (Frydlinger et al. 2013). Following Schreyögg and Sydow (2010), among others, we conceptualise the more

J. Huhtamäki (✉) · T. Olsson
Tampere University, Tampere, Finland
e-mail: jukka.huhtamaki@tuni.fi; thomas.olsson@tuni.fi

S.-M. Laaksonen
University of Helsinki, Helsinki, Finland
e-mail: salla.laaksonen@helsinki.fi

H. Lehtimäki et al. (eds.), *Society as an Interaction Space*, Translational Systems Sciences 22, https://doi.org/10.1007/978-981-15-0069-5_11

flexible organisational forms that result from these activities as organisational *fluidity*. One manifestation of fluidity is the emergence of more flexible and organic collaboration relationships.

In addition to fluid, we perceive organisations as communicative constitutions. In this vein, we follow recent scholarship in organisation studies arguing that communication is the fundamental constitutive force that brings organisations into being (Ashcraft et al. 2009; Putnam et al. 2009). Organisational fluidity refers to a way of operating in an increasingly complex environment by reducing the role of the boundaries, structures, and processes of the organisational container and, instead, operating through various partnerships, strategic alliances, and outsourcing networks with other organisations, crossing the boundaries of hierarchies, teams, and formal programmes (cf. Schreyögg and Sydow 2010). Fluidity calls for new ways of managing and supporting the process of organising to make the most of increased collaboration while mitigating the problems that accompany increased complexity.

Social matching is an emerging research field that explores the identification and facilitation of new collaboration relationships 'in both physical and online spaces' (Terveen and McDonald 2005). In knowledge work, social matching encompasses functionalities and decision-making related to, for example, networking, recruiting, partner identification, and team formation. Practical examples of social matching in this context include nudging individuals to meet each other (e.g. bringing together an entrepreneur and suitable business partners or advisors) and forming teams on the basis of complementary skills (Olsson et al. 2019). Social matching decisions vary from long-term and high-risk decisions (e.g. recruiting a new employee to an organisation) to short-term and low-risk decisions (e.g. introductions at networking events).

Computational social matching, accordingly, refers to the use of data analytics and digital methods to identify features of individuals or matching actors, to understand the structure of existing social networks, and to offer automated recommendations. We argue that, by developing new computational solutions that utilise and refine data about knowledge workers, we can improve the understanding of individual and organisational features that impact mutual suitability. Related research has been carried out in fields such as person recommender systems (Chen et al. 2009; Guy 2015; Tsai and Brusilovsky 2018) and decision support systems for human resources management (Gal et al. 2017).

In this chapter, we explore the use of computational social matching as a means of facilitating the emergence and evolution of the social connections within fluid organisations. Fluid organisations and their dynamic operating environment provide a fertile context for developing and conducting trials of computational social matching. In a fluid organisation, the organisational boundaries, structures, and processes fade away, and the actors consequently gain the freedom to form new social ties. Such fluidity is also present in cross-organisational settings, where active efforts are taken to facilitate the emergence of new organisations and organisational structures. Examples include cross-organisational collaboration relationships in business and innovation ecosystems (Russell et al. 2015), adaptive spaces (Arena et al. 2017), and other forms of semiformal organisations (Biancani et al. 2014; Dobusch and Schoeneborn 2015). Particularly, flexible social structures are formed through the self-organisation between freelancers and piecework taking place on digital platforms

(Alkhatib et al. 2017). Authors such as Schreyögg and Sydow (2010) and Ståhle and Grönroos (2000) have maintained that such organising is a necessity for organisations working in the modern, dynamic organisational environment.

Computational social matching can be used to drive or support these efforts by facilitating the emergence of social connections within and between organisations, thereby supporting communication and the flow of information. We suggest that computational social matching can enhance the two main phenomena examined in the book, that is, society as an interaction space in general and service ecosystems in particular. First, computational social matching introduces core capabilities to facilitate new interorganisational collaborations that enable the emergence of society as an interaction space in a systemic way. Second, we subscribe to service-dominant logic (Lusch and Nambisan 2015), according to which service ecosystems are emergent actor-to-actor network structures where actors co-create value by developing and recombining services. Both the service ecosystem and its developers form an interconnected structure that can be computationally modelled and presented as networks and that reaches beyond the human capabilities in conventional social matching. Furthermore, the actors in a service ecosystem may include humans, services, and the technology that provides the means of communication.

This chapter takes a conceptual and theoretical approach to examining computational social matching in its role of facilitating the emergence and evolution of fluid organisations that are constituted through communication. Throughout this chapter, we use a fictional but concrete case of organisational partnership to illustrate our theoretical arguments. ACME is a media company that produces digital content both internally and in collaboration with freelancers. Bonk Ltd. is an imaginary digital consultancy that co-creates value with its customer organisations by developing new digital services. Currently, ACME uses an information system to manage the production teams. Over time, ACME has accumulated data and information artefacts about the production teams, the skills, interests, and concrete tasks of team members, and the quality of production outputs. Bonk Ltd. is experienced in developing services that support fluid means of organising.

Below, we first explain our theoretical premise—that is, organisations as fluid, communicative constitutions—connect that premise with the perspective of social networks, and then present the suggested strategies for computational social matching, using the ACME and Bonk Ltd. case as an example.

11.2 Organisations as Fluid, Communicative Constitutions

Recent developments in knowledge work have resulted in the need to rethink how organisations are defined and formed. Of the three types of organisational operating environments—mechanistic, organic, and dynamic—contemporary organisations operate in a dynamic environment, one that is global and forces them to collaborate and co-create value across their boundaries (Ståhle and Grönroos 2000). This introduces changes into the structure and dynamics of interorganisational competition, and it forces organisations to adapt to various global and national political contexts and legislative and cultural environments. Organisations work, for example, in various partnerships, strategic alliances, and outsourcing networks with other organisations (Lee and Hassard 1999). In the dynamic operating environment, the collaboration is so intense that the organisational boundaries fade away and the actors form spontaneous social ties that constitute a complex network in which information flows chaotically (Ståhle and Grönroos 2000). Further, organisations are increasingly embedded in various digital service ecosystems (cf. Lusch and Nambisan 2015), and they must therefore adopt digital practices of work and communication. To thrive, organisations must develop new ways of identifying the needs of their customers and stakeholders in a changing world and must co-create services and products to meet these needs.

Organisational fluidity has emerged as a theoretical and practical response to the 'increasing complexity and environmental turbulence that organisations have to master' (Schreyögg and Sydow 2010: 1251). Whereas the classical view of organisations sees them as bureaucratically organised containers where humans and tasks are managed to produce output and social order (for a review, see, e.g., Reed 2006), recent approaches define organisations as something more fluid and dynamic, such as networks (Borgatti and Foster 2003; Lee and Hassard 1999) or communicative constitutions (Cooren et al. 2011; Putnam et al. 2009). The network paradigm directs attention to the ways in which organisations come into being not as rationally managed entities, but as networks of people, that is, as social structures (Powell 1990). Traditionally, organisations have been seen as sites where people are managed and their actions coordinated in order to achieve a common organisational goal (e.g. Ståhle and Grönroos 2000), but a network perspective makes room for more dynamic views of the constitution of organisations and for an emphasis on interdependence. For example, in our example company ACME, the existing teams might be formed around identified tasks that take care of separate phases of the production process of a new media production. Alternatively, the teams could be formed on a more ad hoc basis, that is, as a changing network that emerges around each production separately, according to the needs of the production.

In line with the service-dominant logic (Lusch and Nambisan 2015), the concept of mutual benefits is embedded in the view of organisations as networks; they are not designed as hierarchies but based on ongoing relationships, mutual reciprocity, and trust (Powell 1990). This means that organisations are not bounded and that their memberships are not predefined; rather, they can form in an ad hoc manner via various collaborations that can also span traditional organisational boundaries. Hence, the ontology of interdependence and relationship is not limited to individuals in organisations but extends to networks, which can also form between organisational teams and even between organisations. However, as we explain in more detail in Sect. 11.3, hierarchical structures and repeated patterns are also found in networks. Such patterns of formal organisation are thought to make organisational structures more durable over time than networks (Porter and Powell 2006).

It can be argued that, in the current service ecosystem, the glue that forms the connections in a network is communication. The communication as constitutive of organisations (CCO) perspective is a theoretical account that advocates the role of communication in fluid organising. This account treats communication as the fundamental constitutive force that brings organisations into being (Ashcraft et al. 2009; Putnam et al. 2009). Instead of seeing organisations as pre-existing entities, the CCO perspective posits that the organisation does not precede communication, but that it exists as communication and is formed in the various flows of communication among its members and other actors (Ashcraft et al. 2009). This makes organisations emergent, processual, and precarious entities that are constantly modified through communication. The CCO approach also acknowledges underlying network structures and the importance of non-human actors, such as technologies and documents, in the process of organising. According to Blaschke et al. (2012), organisations are networks of communication episodes, unfolding over time in spatial and temporal settings. These networks take shape around symbolic or material elements (see also Taylor et al. 1996). In the case of ACME and Bonk Ltd., the launch of a new production project could be considered an element that gives birth to new communication episodes as a given team of people begins to communicate about the project.

This chapter argues that if such communicative networks are allowed to form independently of organisational hierarchies and administrative structures, the organisation can develop more fluidity through the mutual connections between human and non-human actors. Organisational fluidity sets the actors free to form new social ties, which become social structures at the organisational and societal levels. Increasing and enriching human encounters not only adds to the actors' knowledge of the world and other people but enables learning and facilitates inspiration in a very natural way. From this ontological perspective, social matching technologies become a means of supporting the process of organising itself by ensuring that the right people communicate with each other. Instead of managerial team-building decisions, ACME could use a computational matching system to identify potential teams for each new production project and allow the teams to form in a self-organising manner.

It has been argued that the diversification of networks, partnerships, and collaboration brings about advantages at the individual, organisational, and societal levels in terms of exchanging knowledge and therefore improving creative and innovation capabilities (e.g. Mitchell and Nicholas 2006). In certain situations, it would even be advantageous to first bring the actors together and allow the forms of collaboration and specific goals to emerge in interaction, following the principle of 'who before what' (Collins 2001). Human actors, however, are prone to form social ties in a way that reduces diversity and limits the flow of information. Matching facilitates the emergence of communicative connections between actors in an organisation, and when it succeeds, it does so in a way that supports the organisation's goals, its identity, and its existence. In line with the words of Taylor (2009: 156), the product of this intercommunity coordination is the organisation itself.

11.3 Unfolding Organisational Social Networks

Above, we resolved to consider organisations as fluid constellations, born in the network of communicative relationships between actors. In the context of social matching, we start from the premise that these networks form between non-human and human actors. Hence, as our subscription to the CCO perspective implies, we follow the main ideas of actor–network theory and relational sociology, which suggest that objects, such as laboratory tools or technological artefacts, become meaningful only in their interrelations and that various non-human entities play a role in these relational networks (e.g. Latour and Woolgar 1979; Latour 2005; You et al. 2019). In a social matching system, the non-human actors include the matching system and the information artefacts that are used to match people and build the network, commonly things like intangible skills, documents, or points of interest. Hence, this claim is in line with service-dominant logic and its view of service ecosystems as emergent actor-to-actor networks—with the addition, however, that we recognise the agency of non-human entities in such network systems.

The structure of social networks does not form and evolve randomly. Core regularities of networks include their scale-free nature (Barabási and Bonabeau 2003) and small-world structure (Milgram 1967; Watts 1999). In social networks, 'scale-free' refers to the extremely uneven distribution of the number of connections among network actors. At the time of this writing, Katy Perry, Justin Bieber, and Barack Obama each have more than 100 million Twitter followers, whereas most Twitter users have only tens or hundreds of followers. Preferential attachment is the mechanism driving the emergence of scale-free networks. That is, the more connections the actors have, the more likely they will be to form new connections. The preferential attachment mechanism is sometimes referred to as the rich get richer or the Matthew effect. Such phenomena might also occur in smaller contexts; for example, in the case of ACME, it might be that the most senior employees with certain highly valued skills are the employees most frequently asked to join production teams.

The small-world structure is the hypothesis that all the people in the world are within six handshakes of each other (Milgram 1967). The small-world structure is a combination of tightly interconnected communities of actors who are connected to each other through individuals who bridge the communities (Saxenian 2006).

If we assume that fluid organisations are networks that are allowed to form independently, it is likely that they will also demonstrate the small-world phenomenon. A social structure that has evolved organically without constraints is composed of densely interconnected groups that are connected to each other through individuals who bridge structural holes. Following their intuition, a knowledge worker forms new social connections, most likely among their existing social circles, with similar individuals in close geographical or organisational proximity. Two mechanisms drive networking: homophily and triadic closure. The homophily bias posits that individuals seek company based on similarity (Kossinets and Watts 2009; McPherson et al. 2001) and are therefore able to operate efficiently in the short term. At the same time, new connections are likely to be formed between pairs of actors who share a strong connection, that is, friends of friends (Granovetter 1973). These effects have been shown to exist in organisational networks as well (e.g. Brass et al. 2004; Hansen and Løvås 2004).

When the aforementioned mechanisms are allowed to run free, the resulting social network structure likely unfolds as a mycelium of echo chambers or social bubbles. The echo chamber phenomenon involves the formation of densely interconnected groups of actors and the reduction of information within the groups. When a group is established, the group's opinions and information base will likely undergo increasing homogenisation. The phenomenon is amplified when group members who share worldviews continue to enforce each other's opinions. In extreme cases, echo chambers can be detrimental (Van Alstyne and Brynjolfsson 2005). For example, in knowledge work seeking novelty, or when starting a new company or designing a service ecosystem, diversity is imperative (Aggarwal and Woolley 2013), and heterogeneous, complementary knowledge is the driver of organisational success, and especially of innovation capability (Rodan and Galunic 2004). Regarding ACME, would they build better and more innovative productions if the teams were more diverse?

Therefore, computational social matching needs to strike a balance between diversity and bandwidth of information exchange (Aral and Van Alstyne 2011). On the one hand, it is important to support the formation of weak ties that serve as conduits of novel information between existing social groups, such as collaboration partners outside the organisation or the daily social circle. Social ties that bridge the structural holes in social networks enhance creativity and support the career development of the actors who form such connections, because their collaborators perceive them as sources of novel information (Burt 2004). On the other hand, strong ties (Granovetter 1973) enable the high-bandwidth exchange of information, because the actors forming these ties are likely to be similar to each other in terms of domain, knowledge, and shared vocabulary.

11.4 Facilitating Organisational Fluidity with Computational Social Matching

Thus far, we have argued that fluid organisations let their actors operate with a greater degree of freedom than before. Moreover, we have described the mechanisms that come into play when individual actors network and collaborate, guided by limited information and their built-in biases. In this section, we describe how computational social matching can facilitate organisational fluidity.

In our view, a social matching system is a technology artefact that enables and facilitates such constitution by *suggesting and forming relationships of communication between the actors*. A social matching system is an information system artefact composed of technology artefacts, social artefacts, and information artefacts 'that together interact in order to form the IS artifact' (Lee et al. 2015). In this context, a machine learning-based software that runs the social matching service is a technology artefact, the new social ties that the system identifies and facilitates the formation of are social artefacts, and the 'instantiations of information' (Lee et al. 2015: 8), such as messages, articles, and documents of shared interest to the actors, are information artefacts. To facilitate social matching, a system should seek to identify combinations of human actors and information artefacts relevant to them.

When fluid organisations are examined through the CCO ontological lens, the interaction between actors is what forms and reproduces organisational structure. Developing algorithms that can facilitate the identification and formation of these interaction-based social connections is far from trivial. A fundamental challenge in the development of social matching systems is the need to accumulate high-quality data about the characteristics of knowledge workers, including their knowledge, skills, interests, and social networks (Olshannikova et al. 2017). Also necessary is data about and models of the ideal forms, contexts, and objectives of collaboration and networking. The use of mobile devices, digital tools, and collaboration platforms implies that an increasing amount of data about knowledge work interactions has been accumulated (Bunce et al. 2018). In the case of ACME, the prerequisites for a social matching system already exist, because the company has accumulated information about the skills and knowledge of their employees.

Schreyögg and Sydow (2010) pointed to monitoring and timely managerial interventions as means of managing a fluid organisation. Continuous, constantly evolving analysis and enacted sensemaking (Weick et al. 2005) allow individuals to operate independently of structures, support their agency, and transform the role of organisational leadership and management toward continuous development. Organisational monitoring can be considered a first step toward computational social matching when insights into the social structure are used to steer the actors in the organisation toward forming new connections. For example, upon the identification of a structural hole, the ACME organisation can seek to form new social connections, perhaps by refining production team compositions.

To counterbalance the biases in organic network formation and evolution, the default design principle in computational social matching is to increase diversity. There is no formula or even ideal for enabling organisational diversity that could be used to design a service that matches actors. Research has shown that gender, age, culture, and other surface-level differences diminish team performance, whereas attitudes, values, available information, and other deep-level differences enhance it (Mannix and Neale 2005). Although social network structure is a known factor in performance, we do not know enough about the microlevel social interaction mechanisms needed in creative work to effectively utilise these mechanisms in social matching (cf. Holland 2014).

To flesh out the foundation and scaffolding of computational social matching in fluid organisations that are constituted through communication, we now describe three complementary strategies for implementing social matching systems.

The first social matching strategy, *social exploration*, involves providing actors with interactive systems to support their identification of new social connections with suitable knowledge, competencies, and capabilities. A simple ordered list of actors that a user is able to sort by different features has proven to be an efficient approach in social matching (Tsai and Brusilovsky 2018). Examples of measures that support the identification of potential actors include the distance between the actors in terms of social, knowledge, cognitive, and geographic perspectives. In ACME, this is a strategy that could be, to some extent, rather easily accomplished using the employee information already collected by the organisation.

The core design principle of this strategy is to present the data with a minimum amount of refinement. The benefits of such a simple system design include transparency and understandability. Taking a visual analytics approach supports transparency and enables enacted sensemaking (Bendoly 2016), that is, continuous and flexible data exploration with the goal of identifying, creating, and sharing new knowledge about actors and the fluid organisation. Users are able to perform sensemaking and tailor the system to their changing needs and objectives. For example, it is possible to provide support for teasing out truly new ideas from a large social or geographical distance (Tsai and Brusilovsky 2018), with the cost of reduced bandwidth. On the other hand, individuals that are socially and geographically close are able to serve on-demand information needs.

The second social matching strategy, *network theory-based recommendations*, consists of designing systems according to the theories and principles of social interaction and social network formation. When facilitating the communicative constitution of fluid organisations, the system must strike a balance between the diversity and homogeneity of the actors who are nudged to form new social ties. That is, the developers should follow the diversity–bandwidth trade-off (Aral and Van Alstyne 2011) as the guiding design principle. As discussed in Sect. 11.3, introducing new weak ties is important when the social structure becomes static and the actors indicate that they are seeking new sources of information. Strong ties and more static structure is needed in times of convergence. As for the features other than social distance, balancing actor diversity and homogeneity is highly context dependent (Olsson et al. 2019). In this regard, both individual users and organisation management should be able to emphasise matching mechanisms that nudge individuals to form connections that may not seem relevant or intuitive yet could have long-term importance at the organisational or societal level. In ACME, such a strategy could mean that the social matching system would prefer forming connections that connect employees who have not worked together on production projects in order to maximise diversity and the formation of weak ties.

The third strategy for designing computational social matching systems, *machine learning-based recommendations*, rests on a data-driven approach and machine learning. Here, the guiding principle is to derive the social matching rules from data. Following the logic of supervised learning, two types of data are needed: first, data about actors and their interactions and, second, data that represents the actors and their interests, intentions, and subjective experiences during previous interactions. Supervised learning algorithms are trained using features representing actors and their social connections as inputs and the social matching objectives as outputs.

Following this strategy, Bonk Ltd. could offer a computational solution to improve organisational fluidity at ACME by leveraging the existing data about employee skills and interests and by constructing a network of their past interactions and joint production using the historical data collected from the teams. The information about production output quality could be used to infer learning outcomes for the machine learning system, which means it would be defined by existing data about team performance. The performance of the matching rules derived with various combinations of features and algorithms would be compared until a satisfactory performance was achieved. When the algorithm was used in production, data representing the actors, interactions, and organisational social structure would be constantly refreshed.

Table 11.1 summarises and compares the social matching strategies from the viewpoint of the agency of different elements. The impact of a matching system depends on the data, technology choices, service developers' design choices, organisation management's interests, and the individuals' needs.

Computational social matching systems rely on high-quality data about actor interactions and their impacts. The organisations must make sure to accumulate and curate such data to drive the matching logic and to support the knowledge of the teams developing such systems. We are the first to point out that data should not be treated as an objective input of the matching procedure. Both the data that an organisation has accumulated prior to the development of a social matching system and

Table 11.1 Comparison of social matching strategies

Agency	Social exploration	Network theory-based recommendations	Machine learning-based recommendations
Individual	**High.** An individual user can explore options and optimise the use for their own preferences	**Low.** An individual may choose from given options, based on theory-derived reasoning	**Low.** An individual may choose from given options provided by an opaque recommender algorithm
Management	**Medium.** Management defines the general objectives and the rules of access to organisation-specific data	**Medium.** Management defines the objectives and optimisation criteria	**Medium.** Management defines data access rules, the objectives, and optimisation criteria
Developers	**Medium.** Developers can choose which profile and network features are prioritised in the user interface	**High.** Theories and their operationalisations selected by the service developers affect the matching logic	**High.** Developers define the features, select machine learning models, and the training and validation procedures
Technology	**Low.** Software frameworks define the rules and boundaries of visual representation	**Medium.** Technology affects the formal models of actors and their social network	**High.** Machine learning technology is available as modules with built-in rules
Data	**Low.** Actors are able to perceive data categories and values	**Medium.** Actor and social network representations are based on data	**High.** Social matching rules are derived directly from data

the data that is collected specifically for such a system are functions of the data collection systems. That is, the management and system developers have agency in defining how the data comes into being. At the present stage, it is likely that such data does not exist. Solving this issue by collecting subjective data about interactions is bound to change the way individuals act and observe the world. This is because awareness of being the target of observation and measurement changes the way humans behave (Leclercq-Vandelannoitte 2017; Wickström and Bendix 2000).

Moreover, developers and management define the boundaries and objectives for systems in all three strategies. That is, even systems that fall under the category of social exploration may, for example, nudge actors toward forming (or not forming) social ties according to what is perceived as favourable by the organisation. Nevertheless, allowing the actors to explore the data directly, such as with the help of appropriate visual analytics tools, improves the transparency of the system and the actors' awareness of organisational social structure.

11.5 Discussion

Computational social matching seeks to utilise data and algorithms to identify new potential social ties and facilitate their formation in organisations by selecting information and social artefacts of shared interest to the identified actors. In service ecosystems, human actors operate with each other, with services, and with other technological actors. The emerging network structure of such service ecosystems is an important driver of the activity; therefore, facilitating the evolution of the structure with social matching solutions plays an important role in avoiding the often detrimental effects of network mechanisms, including preferential attachment, homophily, and triadic closure. Treating organisations as fluid constitutions of communication further highlights the agency of not only human actors but the technology they use to communicate and to navigate the service ecosystems. Therefore, facilitating communication and interactions with technology has direct consequences for the structure and operation of organisations.

In this chapter, we presented three strategies for designing computational social matching systems: social exploration, network theory-based recommendations, and machine learning-based recommendations. In the first strategy, users are provided with interactive systems that afford a relatively objective means of exploring potential new collaboration partners and shared interests, potentially with a visual analytics approach to supporting actor-driven enacted sensemaking. However, these systems assume that the user is proactive. Moreover, it is likely that the degree of freedom enabled by such transparent systems will result in users following their natural, often suboptimal networking patterns. To overcome these problems, we suggested the use of a network theory-based recommendation system that builds on the mechanisms of social network formation to nudge actors to collaborate in a way that has long-term benefits at the organisational level. Such a system highlights the agency of the developers, who would be responsible for the operationalisation of the matching logic. In the third strategy, a machine learning-based system refines and learns from data collected from the actors and their organisations. This strategy gives developers a leading role in the formation of fluid organisations and therefore insists on transdisciplinary teamwork and close collaboration among the users.

In addition to the strategies for computational social matching presented in this chapter, a computational approach enables additional ways to support the transformation of emergent themes and self-organised groups into more established forms of organised activity, such as work groups, new commercial actors, or voluntary sector institutions. First, clustering the content of communication with, for example, unsupervised machine learning methods enables the identification of emergent themes of interest within broader established communities, such as discussion forums, large enterprises, or innovation ecosystems. Second, with social network analysis and the strategy of interactive sensemaking, one can identify relevant actors who are actively contributing to the substance or building the social capital around an emerging topic of interest. Third, semantic analysis of the communication may help unearth topics that represent relevant needs for new leadership endeavours or product development efforts in the existing organisations or that represent targets for the renewal and restructuring of organisational practices.

All three presented strategies rely on high-quality data about actor interactions and their impacts. While accumulating such data, it must be ensured that the data collection neither violates the rights of the individuals nor introduces unintended mechanisms as users become aware that they are being observed. Therefore, it is important to discuss and reflect on the ethical dimensions of building social matching systems. Do the expected advantages outweigh the potential risks? Are the advantages distributed evenly between individuals, across organisations, and between geographical areas? Building algorithmic systems like computational social matching applications is not a value-free activity, and researchers must be aware of the politics, ethics, and potential future consequences of such development.

First, the data required for computational social matching is personal—potentially sensitive—data and hence must be handled lawfully, fairly, and transparently, as required by the EU General Data Protection Regulation. Access to the data must be carefully controlled and the rights of the data subjects ensured. Who can view the data collected by the automated matching systems? How can individuals, for example, employees at ACME, access their own data? What happens to the data after a person changes their employer or wants to opt out? Even more complex questions will arise if the social matching is done in an interorganisational setting.

Second, data analysis that involves profiling can be seen as suspicious or unethical, and the profiles generated can have profound consequences (Brayne 2017). Several studies have discussed algorithmic bias (Caliskan et al. 2017; Zarsky 2016) and the unintended adverse effects of computational systems (Friedman et al. 1996; O'Neil 2016). For example, many current online recommendation systems in online stores favour popular objects for which data is readily available, leading to the Matthew effect discussed in Sect. 11.3. Essentially, these issues call for transparency of the algorithms (e.g. Kemper and Kolkman 2018; Mittelstadt et al. 2016) behind the matching. Systems based on machine learning, however, are typically unable to explain their recommendations to their users (Wachter et al. 2018).

Therefore, it is of utmost importance to consider the goals and ideals potentially implemented in the social matching system—either explicitly, in designing the matching logic, or implicitly, by carefully selecting the training data (cf. Ruppert et al. 2017). Research in science and technology studies (e.g. Winner 1980) has reminded us that all technology is embedded with implicit values and therefore has consequences beyond its immediate context of use. A social matching system needs some principles or standards that define its goals, and in a machine learning-based system, these principles will change over time as the system learns. Who defines the parameters for optimising the system, and who decides what is measured in the first place? How can the users evaluate the current reasoning behind the system?

11.6 Implications

Computational social matching systems can play an integral role in facilitating the emergence of fluid organisations that are constituted through communication. The success of their design depends on the practices of collecting, refining, and curating high-quality data about actors, their interactions, and the value of the outcomes of these interactions. Computational social matching systems can simply provide the data to the users, draw from the theory of social interaction and social network formation, or learn from past behaviour to recommend new combinations of actors. In all of these approaches, it is important to facilitate the formation of these collaborations by identifying relevant social or information artefacts of shared interest to the actors.

Social matching systems can and, as we argue, also should counterbalance the organic mechanisms driving social network formation and evolution. Densely interconnected social groups are a prerequisite for creating and aggregating knowledge efficiently and in way that facilitates innovation. It is equally important to form ties between social groups in order to establish conduits of novel information and break up echo chambers. Service ecosystems provide an exciting context for theoretical and practical experimentation on the agency of data, technology, and humans that continuously reorganise for ecosystemic value creation. We recommend starting the development from analytics and monitoring services with limited agency and moving gradually toward automatisation. It is imperative that such development ventures are inherently transdisciplinary and conducted in close collaboration with the users of the social matching system and other stakeholders by measuring and making sense of their response to the design.

If the collaboration between ACME and Bonk Ltd. is successful, the envisioned social matching system can be generalised; that is, it can become a digital service that operates in a service ecosystem, drawing and analysing data from different organisations and weaving new social connections to facilitate society as an interaction space.

References

Aggarwal, I., & Woolley, A. (2013). Two perspectives on intellectual capital and innovation in teams: Collective intelligence and cognitive diversity. In *Driving the economy through innovation and entrepreneurship: Emerging agenda for technology management* (pp. 453–460). India: Springer India. https://doi.org/10.1007/978-81-322-0746-7_37.

Alkhatib, A., Bernstein, M., & Levi, M. (2017). Examining crowd work and gig work through the historical lens of piecework. In *Proceedings of the 2017 CHI conference on human factors in computing systems—CHI '17* (pp. 4599–4616). New York, NY: ACM Press. https://doi.org/10.1145/3025453.3025974.

Aral, S., & Van Alstyne, M. (2011). The diversity-bandwidth trade-off. *American Journal of Sociology, 117*(1), 90–171. https://doi.org/10.1086/661238.

Arena, M., Cross, R., Sims, J., & Uhl-Bien, M. (2017). How to catalyze innovation in your organization. MIT Sloan Management Review.

Ashcraft, K. L., Kuhn, T. R., & Cooren, F. (2009). Constitutional amendments: "Materializing" organizational communication. *The Academy of Management Annals, 3*(1), 1–64. https://doi.org/10.1080/19416520903047186.

Barabási, A.-L., & Bonabeau, E. (2003). Scale-free networks. *Scientific American, 288*(5), 50–59.

Bendoly, E. (2016). Fit, bias and enacted sensemaking in data visualization: Frameworks for continuous development in operations and supply chain management analytics. *Journal of Business Logistics, 37*(1), 6–17.

Biancani, S., McFarland, D., & Dahlander, L. (2014). The semiformal organization. *Organization Science, 25*(5), 1306–1324. https://doi.org/10.1287/orsc.2013.0882.

Blaschke, S., Schoeneborn, D., & Seidl, D. (2012). Organizations as networks of communication episodes: Turning the network perspective inside out. *Organization Studies, 33*(7), 879–906. https://doi.org/10.1177/0170840612443459.

Borgatti, S. P., & Foster, P. (2003). The network paradigm in organization research: A review and typology. *Journal of Management, 29*(6), 991–1013. https://doi.org/10.1016/S0149-2063.

Brass, D., Galaskiewicz, J., Greve, H., & Tsai, W. (2004). Taking stock of networks and organizations: A multilevel perspective. *Academy of Management Journal, 47*(6), 795–817. https://doi.org/10.5465/20159624.

Brayne, S. (2017). Big data surveillance: The case of policing. *American Sociological Review, 82*(5), 977–1008. https://doi.org/10.1177/0003122417725865.

Bunce, M., Wright, K., & Scott, M. (2018). 'Our newsroom in the cloud': Slack, virtual newsrooms and journalistic practice. *New Media & Society, 20*(9), 3381–3399. https://doi.org/10.1177/1461444817748955.

Burt, R. (2004). Structural holes and good ideas. *American Journal of Sociology, 110*(2), 349–399. https://doi.org/10.1086/421787.

Caliskan, A., Bryson, J., & Narayanan, A. (2017). Semantics derived automatically from language corpora contain human-like biases. *Science, 356*(6334), 183–186. https://doi.org/10.1126/science.aal4230.

Chatterjee, S., Sarker, S., & Siponen, M. (2017). How do mobile ICTs enable organizational fluidity: Toward a theoretical framework. *Information & Management, 54*(1), 1–13. https://doi.org/10.1016/j.im.2016.03.007.

Chen, J., Geyer, W., Dugan, C., Muller, M., & Guy, I. (2009). Make new friends, but keep the old: Recommending people on social networking sites. In *Proceedings of the SIGCHI conference on human factors in computing systems* (pp. 201–210). New York, NY: ACM. https://doi.org/10.1145/1518701.1518735.

Collins, J. C. (2001). *Good to great: Why some companies make the leap ... and others don't.* New York, NY: Harper Business.

Cooren, F., Kuhn, T., Cornelissen, J. P., & Clark, T. (2011). Communication, organizing and organization: An overview and introduction to the special issue. *Organization Studies, 32*(9), 1149–1170. https://doi.org/10.1177/0170840611410836.

Dobusch, L., & Schoeneborn, D. (2015). Fluidity, identity, and organizationality: The communicative constitution of anonymous. *Journal of Management Studies, 52*(8), 1005–1035. https://doi.org/10.1111/joms.12139.

Friedman, B., Brok, E., Roth, S. K., & Thomas, J. (1996). Minimizing bias in computer systems. *ACM SIGCHI Bulletin, 28*(1), 48–51.

Frydlinger, D., Nyden, J., & Vitasek, K. (2013). Unpacking collaboration theory: What every negotiator should know to establish successful strategic relationships (Tech. Rep.). White paper, The University of Tennessee.

Gal, U., Jensen, T. B., & Stein, M.-K. (2017). People analytics in the age of big data: An agenda for IS research. In Thirty eighth international conference on information systems, South Korea (p. 11).

Granovetter, M. (1973). The strength of weak ties. *American Journal of Sociology, 78*(6), 1360–1380.

Guy, I. (2015). Social recommender systems. In F. Ricci, L. Rokach, & B. Shapira (Eds.), *Recommender systems handbook* (pp. 511–543). New York, NY: Springer US.

Hansen, M. T., & Løvås, B. (2004). How do multinational companies leverage technological competencies? Moving from single to interdependent explanations. *Strategic Management Journal, 25*(89), 801–822. https://doi.org/10.1002/smj.413.

Holland, D. (2014). *Integrating knowledge through interdisciplinary research: Problems of theory and practice*. London: Routledge.

Hsiehchen, D., Espinoza, M., & Hsieh, A. (2015). Multinational teams and diseconomies of scale in collaborative research. *Science Advances, 1*(8), 1–9.

Kemper, J., & Kolkman, D. (2018). Transparent to whom? No algorithmic accountability without a critical audience. *Information, Communication & Society*, 1–16. https://doi.org/10.1080/1369118X.2018.1477967.

Kossinets, G., & Watts, D. J. (2009). Origins of homophily in an evolving social network. *American Journal of Sociology, 115*(2), 405–450. https://doi.org/10.1086/599247.

Latour, B. (2005). *Reassembling the social—An introduction to actor-network-theory*. Oxford: Oxford University Press.

Latour, B., & Woolgar, S. (1979). *Laboratory life: The construction of scientific facts*. Beverly Hills: SAGE Publications. https://doi.org/10.1017/CBO9781107415324.004.

Leclercq-Vandelannoitte, A. (2017). An ethical perspective on emerging forms of ubiquitous IT-based control. *Journal of Business Ethics, 142*(1), 139–154. https://doi.org/10.1007/s10551-015-2708-z.

Lee, N., & Hassard, J. (1999). Organization unbound: Actor-network theory, research strategy and institutional flexibility. *Organization, 6*(3), 391–404. https://doi.org/10.1177/135050849963002.

Lee, A. S., Thomas, M., & Baskerville, R. L. (2015). Going back to basics in design science: From the information technology artifact to the information systems artifact. *Information Systems Journal, 25*(1), 5–21. https://doi.org/10.1111/isj.12054.

Lusch, R., & Nambisan, S. (2015). Service innovation: A service-dominant logic perspective. *MIS Quarterly, 39*(1), 155–176.

Mannix, E., & Neale, M. (2005). What differences make a difference? *Psychological Science in the Public Interest, 6*(2), 31–55. https://doi.org/10.1111/j.1529-1006.2005.00022.x.

McPherson, M., Smith-Lovin, L., & Cook, J. (2001). Birds of a feather: Homophily in social networks. *Annual Review of Sociology, 27*(1), 415–444. https://doi.org/10.1146/annurev.soc.27.1.415.

Milgram, S. (1967). The small-world problem. *Psychology Today, 1*(1), 61–67.

Mitchell, R., & Nicholas, S. (2006). Knowledge creation in groups: The value of cognitive diversity, transactive memory and open-mindedness norms. *The Electronic Journal of Knowledge Management, 4*(1), 67–74.

Mittelstadt, B., Allo, P., Taddeo, M., Wachter, S., & Floridi, L. (2016). The ethics of algorithms: Mapping the debate. *Big Data & Society, 3*(2), 205395171667967. https://doi.org/10.1177/2053951716679679.

O'Neil, C. (2016). *Weapons of math destruction: How big data increases inequality and threatens democracy*. New York, NY: Crown Publishing Group.

Olshannikova, E., Olsson, T., Huhtamäki, J., & Kärkkäinen, H. (2017). Conceptualizing big social data. *Journal of Big Data, 4*(1), 19. https://doi.org/10.1186/s40537-017-0063-x.

Olsson, T., Huhtamäki, J., & Kärkkäinen, H. (2019). Directions for professional social matching systems. Communications of the ACM, Accepted.

Porter, K., & Powell, W. (2006). Networks and organizations. In S. Clegg, C. Hardy, T. B. Lawrence, & W. Nord (Eds.), *The SAGE handbook of organization studies* (2nd ed., pp. 776–799). London: SAGE Publications.

Powell, W. (1990). Neither market nor hierarchy: Network forms of organization. *Research in Organizational Behavior, 12*, 295–336.

Putnam, L., Nicotera, A., & McPhee, R. (2009). Introduction: Communication constitutes organization. In L. Putnam & A. Nicotera (Eds.), *Building theories of organization: The constitutive role of communication* (pp. 1–19). New York: Routledge.

Reed, M. (2006). Organizational theorizing: A historically contested terrain. In S. Clegg, C. Hardy, T. B. Lawrence, & W. R. Nord (Eds.), *The SAGE handbook of organization studies* (2nd ed., pp. 19–54). London: SAGE Publications.

Rodan, S., & Galunic, C. (2004). More than network structure: How knowledge heterogeneity influences managerial performance and innovativeness. *Strategic Management Journal, 25*(6), 541–562. https://doi.org/10.1002/smj.398.

Ruppert, E., Isin, E., & Bigo, D. (2017). Data politics. *Big Data & Society, 4*(2), 205395171771774. https://doi.org/10.1177/2053951717717749.

Russell, M., Huhtamäki, J., Still, K., Rubens, N., & Basole, R. (2015). Relational capital for shared vision in innovation ecosystems. *Triple Helix: A Journal of University-Industry-Government Innovation and Entrepreneurship, 2*(1), 36. https://doi.org/10.1186/s40604-015-0017-2.

Saxenian, A. (2006). *The new argonauts: Regional advantage in a global economy*. Cambridge, MA: Harvard University Press.

Schreyögg, G., & Sydow, J. (2010). Organizing for fluidity? Dilemmas of new organizational forms. *Organization Science, 21*(6), 1251–1262. https://doi.org/10.1287/orsc.1100.0561.

Ståhle, P., & Grönroos, M. (2000). *Dynamic intellectual capital: Knowledge management in theory and practice*. Helsinki: WSOY.

Stein, M.-K., Jensen, T., & Hekkala, R. (2015). Comfortably 'betwixt and between'? Delimiting and blending space, time, tasks and technology at work. In Proceedings of international conference on information systems (p. 19).

Taylor, J. R. (2009). Organizing from the bottom up? Reflections on the constitution of organization in communication. In L. Putnam & A. M. Nicotera (Eds.), *Building theories of organization: The constitutive role of communication* (pp. 153–186). New York: Routledge.

Taylor, J. R., Cooren, F., Giroux, N., & Robichaud, D. (1996). The communicational basis of organization: Between the conversation and the text. *Communication Theory, 6*(1), 1–39. https://doi.org/10.1111/j.1468-2885.1996.tb00118.x.

Terveen, L., & McDonald, D. (2005). Social matching: A framework and research agenda. *ACM Transactions on Computer-Human Interaction, 12*(3), 401–434. https://doi.org/10.1145/1096737.1096740.

Tsai, C.-H., & Brusilovsky, P. (2018). Beyond the ranked list: User-driven exploration and diversification of social recommendation. In Proceedings of the 2018 conference on human information interaction & retrieval—IUI '18 (pp. 239–250). https://doi.org/10.1145/3172944.3172959.

Van Alstyne, M., & Brynjolfsson, E. (2005). Global village or cyber-balkans? Modeling and measuring the integration of electronic communities. *Management Science, 51*(6), 851–868. https://doi.org/10.1287/mnsc.1050.0363.

Wachter, S., Mittelstadt, B., & Russell, C. (2018). Counterfactual explanations without opening the black box: Automated decisions and the GDPR. *Harvard Journal of Law & Technology, 31*(2), 52. https://doi.org/10.2139/ssrn.3063289.

Watts, D. (1999). Networks, dynamics, and the small-world phenomenon. *American Journal of Sociology, 105*(2), 493–527. https://doi.org/10.1086/210318.

Weick, K. E., Sutcliffe, K., & Obstfeld, D. (2005). Organizing and the process of sensemaking. *Organization Science, 16*(4), 409–421. https://doi.org/10.1287/orsc.1050.0133.

Wickström, G., & Bendix, T. (2000). The "Hawthorne effect"—What did the original Hawthorne studies actually show? *Scandinavian Journal of Work, Environment & Health, 26*(4), 363–367.

Winner, L. (1980). Do artifacts have politics? *Daedalus, Modern Technology: Problem or Opportunity, 109*(1), 121–136. https://doi.org/10.2307/20024652.

Wuchty, S., Jones, B. F., & Uzzi, B. (2007). The increasing dominance of teams in production of knowledge. *Science, 316*(5827), 1036–1039. https://doi.org/10.1126/science.1136099.

You, S., Crowston, K., Saltz, J., & Hegde, Y. (2019). Coordination in OSS 2.0: ANT approach. In Proceedings of the Hawaii international conference on system sciences. https://doi.org/10125/59538.

Zarsky, T. (2016). The trouble with algorithmic decisions: An analytic road map to examine efficiency and fairness in automated and opaque decision making. *Science Technology and Human Values, 41*(1), 118–132. https://doi.org/10.1177/0162243915605575.

Chapter 12
Emotions in Customer Experience

Tiina-Kaisa Kuuru, Lauri Litovuo, Leena Aarikka-Stenroos, and Nina Helander

Abstract The aim of this chapter is to display how emotions build experiences in interactive society. To map out the emotions' essential role in experiences, the chapter focuses to look over the literature on emotions in customer experience (CX), which is defined as an umbrella term for diverse experiences. The chapter introduces four key insights to underline the integral relation between emotions in CX in interactive society: (1) we identify eight different types and suggest a framework that captures these key types on how emotions build experiences, (2) emotions in CX are essential both in offline and online environments, (3) the diversity of emotions in interactive society is broad from positive and negative ones, and especially the role of the negative emotions should be acknowledged and further explored, and (4) we propose a set of definitions to clarify different terms used around emotions. The framework serves as a tool that guides practitioners and researchers and other professionals to acknowledge different facets of emotions when aiming to co-create experiences and manage them in the interactive society.

12.1 Introduction

Experiences are a fundamental part of everyday life in all levels of society, being created in various forms of interaction between individuals, organizations, and social system. Thus, we as individuals, professionals, and citizens in interactive society are all continuously creating experiences—building our own and shaping others. This complex foundation makes experiences a fascinating research topic, and furthermore experiences offer organizations a way to gain a competitive advantage by creating memorable experiences for their customers (Pine and Gilmore 1998). To create these memorable experiences, scholars have highlighted the importance of emotions in experience (Bastiaansen et al. 2019). Still, we know only a little about the connection between emotions and customers' experience. Hence, in

T.-K. Kuuru (✉) · L. Litovuo · L. Aarikka-Stenroos · N. Helander
Tampere University, Tampere, Finland
e-mail: tiina-kaisa.kuuru@tuni.fi; lauri.litovuo@tuni.fi; leena.aarikka-stenroos@tuni.fi; nina.helander@tuni.fi

H. Lehtimäki et al. (eds.), *Society as an Interaction Space*, Translational Systems Sciences 22, https://doi.org/10.1007/978-981-15-0069-5_12

this chapter, we are concentrating on building a comprehensive understanding of emotions in customer experience (CX) based on the CX literature.

CX is relevant for multiple industries from retail to wellness and travel to banking. We concentrate on CX as it is often applied as an umbrella term for different experiences including service experiences, user experiences, and patient experiences. CX emerges through the digital and face-to-face interactions customers have during the provision of different services (Bolton et al. 2018). Thus, increasing the understanding how emotions build CX in diverse forms of interaction is a matter of numerous professionals in all levels of society. The interactions occur in different relations both directly and indirectly throughout the society: between customers and an organization, a brand, a product, a technology, other customers, and networks of actors (Meyer and Schwager 2007; Teixeira et al. 2012; Jaakkola et al. 2015). Hence, CX is a constantly ongoing part of interaction in individual, relational, and system levels (Helkkula 2011; Vargo and Lusch 2016).

Despite the notions that emotionally fueled experiences are tightly related to interaction, the understanding how emotions relate to experiences in the interactive society is still missing. Thus far, only a few studies have explicitly linked CX and emotions. Some of these studies focused on the emotional dimension of CX and developed scales for measuring it (e.g., Jüttner et al. 2013; Novak et al. 2000), whereas others examined particular emotions in CX in specific contexts, such as luxury brands (Kim et al. 2016), healthcare (McColl-Kennedy et al. 2017), service failures (Balaji et al. 2017), and service recovery (Mattila et al. 2014). Although these studies among others emphasize the relevance of emotions embedded in various forms of interaction, the studies do not provide a comprehensive understanding on how emotions build CX. Therefore, in brief, more systematic, detailed, and structured analysis is needed to capture and present the diversity of emotions in CX. That is where we contribute.

The purpose of this study is to analyze the role of emotions in CX in individual, relational, and society levels. We systematically reviewed 129 articles (see Torraco 2005), from which we structurally mapped the diversity of research fields where emotions in CX are present so far, identified the theoretical approaches and terms applied to examine emotions in CX, and illustrated how emotions are present in CX research. As a conclusion, we build a structured, clarifying framework, which identifies eight conceptualization types for emotions in CX. By doing so, our study enables researchers and practitioners to use concepts and terms more systematically and to study, develop, and manage emotions in CX in a more advanced way.

We acknowledge that emotions can be studied from many disciplinary and theoretical perspectives, including, business, psychological, and sociological perspectives. In this chapter, we apply business, and particularly marketing and management perspective. The chapter is structured as follows: First, we start by discussing the theoretical background of the two key concepts, CX and emotions. We then explain the methods for data collection and analysis. We introduce key findings regarding emotions in CX from which we develop an integrative framework for emotions in CX. We conclude by suggesting the theoretical and managerial implications and suggest directions for future research.

12.2 Customer Experience and Emotions: Feelers Co-creating Experiences in Interactive Society

12.2.1 Customer Experience

CX research crosscuts many disciplines including economics, psychology, marketing, and management. However, the importance of CX really started to develop in the early 1980s, when consumer research scholars began to consider customers as feelers, thinkers, and doers rather than as rational decision-makers (Holbrook and Hirschman 1982). Shortly after, ignorance of the role of experience in the consumer research was widely noted (Belk 1984; Fennell 1985). Years after, we have seen a dramatic increase in CX research and the shift from a traditional product-based economy to an experience-based economy, where CX is seen as a competitive advantage that is difficult for competitors to duplicate (Pine and Gilmore 1998; Grewal et al. 2009). The shift is noted also in experience research throughout the disciplines, and several types of experiences are distinguished: user experience, service experience (Jaakkola et al. 2015), consumer experience (Howard 1965), product experience (Hoch 2002), and customer experience (Verhoef et al. 2009). In this chapter we focus on customer experience.

The emergence and interest towards experiences are fueled by the pivotal work of Vargo and Lusch (2004, 2008) on service-dominant logic that emphasizes the experiential nature of value. CX and customer's perceived value interrelate with each other. Value is at the same time an individual and contextual function in interaction between subjects which resides in the CX (Echeverri and Skålen 2011). CX incorporates customer's cognitive, emotional, sensory, social, and spiritual responses to all interactions with an organization or other actors (Jain et al. 2017). This definition highlights CX as being strongly individual while also recognizing the importance of social aspects, as experiences are always co-created (Vargo and Lusch 2008). Therefore, CX is strongly connected to interactions as co-creation is defined as a function of interaction. Thus, CX is always co-created in interaction between customer and the organization and/or other actors (Vargo and Lusch 2004; Jain et al. 2017).

The various interactions are taking place in the search, purchase, consumption, and after-sale phases a customer has with an organization through which CX emerges and evolves (Varma 2012; Verhoef et al. 2009). However, CX is more complex to manage compared to interactions, as CX is subjective, has dynamic and unique interpretations of events, and is dependent on many personal and contextual factors (Zomerdijk and Voss 2011). Moreover, in today's networked business environment, multiple actors are participating to CX co-creation within a system of different actors (Vargo and Lusch 2008). Customers are therefore increasingly encountering multiple providers during service delivery forming a social system, which are all affecting the dynamic evaluation of their experience.

Because of the reciprocal nature of the interaction, researchers and practitioners can examine CX from the perspective of either the provider or the individual customer (Helkkula 2011). The provider perspective highlights a firm's ability to understand every facet of the CX throughout all direct and indirect encounters (Frow and Payne 2007), whereas the customer perspective highlights the subjective responses of the individual throughout the customer journey (Lemon and Verhoef 2016).

12.2.2 Theoretical Roots of Emotions

Emotions play a major role in CX. Emotions are produced by an individual's unique appraisal of experience, which is created from an evaluation and interpretation of actions and the prevailing environment. In other words, emotions are always experienced subjectively, and different people can have different emotional reactions to the same action under the same circumstances. Emotions play a significant role in determining behaviors and actions (Carlson et al. 2007) and are therefore critical when investigating, for example, consumer behavior. Emotions are often accompanied by physiological processes and expressed physically (e.g., in gestures, posture, facial features). Just as emotions are perceived individually, they also vary and manifest in different ways. Similar to CX, emotions are also social in nature as emotions are socially contagious, meaning that people are attracted to the emotions displayed by someone with whom they interact (Huang 2001).

Emotion research has roots in psychology (see Mehrabian and Russell 1974). Emotions are usually studied by emphasizing their biological, cognitive, or social aspects, opening up this research area to not only psychologists but also neuroscientists, philosophers, educators, and even economists. This multidisciplinarity of emotions research may have led to nonsystematic use of emotion terminology (e.g., emotions, affects, and feelings) in business-oriented literature, with a few notable exceptions. According to Gentile et al. (2007), affective experience is generated at the system level based on the spectrum of *emotions*, *feelings*, and *moods*. These, in turn, can be further described according to their features, like intensity, duration, cause, awareness, and control (Scherer 2005). Generally, moods are characterized by the enduring predominance of certain types of subjective feelings that affect a person's experience and behavior and may last from hours to days (Scherer 2005) or even months (Jalonen et al. 2016). Although feelings are subjective experiences of individual persons, emotions are projected feelings and are typically manifested in social interaction (Jalonen et al. 2016).

To sum up, experiences are created in various forms of interactions, in which value is resided and emotions embedded. Experiences are subjective in nature while also socially and contextually constructed, mirroring the relevance of experience in the individual, relational, and system level in the society. In other words, the interactive society is full of complex bundles of relations resulting in experiences shaped by emotions. To clarify how emotions actually build experiences in different levels, we next analyze and discuss how emotions are present in current CX literature.

12.3 Methodology

12.3.1 Research Design of Systematic Literature Review: Gathering and Identifying Relevant Articles

To analyze emotions in CX research, we followed an established research procedure for systematic literature reviews. It provides explicit methods for identifying and selecting relevant publications and questioning and analyzing them (see Booth et al. 2012). To gather research on CX examining the emotional aspects, we used a two-phase search: we began by identifying and collecting all relevant research articles on CX and then, in the second phase, focused on those that examined emotions. We selected two databases, Web of Science (WoS) and EBSCO, as they cover a wide range of good-quality journals in marketing and management, and related fields such as technology and innovation management, as well as recent research from all geographic locations. In the first phase, we conducted a systematic search for all articles published before May 2018 in which the title, keywords, or abstract mentioned the words "customer experience." The search yielded a total of 399 articles from EBSCO and 570 articles from WoS. Duplicates were checked and removed. As we focused on scholarly peer-reviewed articles, we excluded book reviews and editorials. This analytical round reduced the number of hits to 336 articles. In the second phase, from these identified CX articles, we zoomed in on those that examined or were related to emotional aspects and included—in their title, keywords, or abstract—at least one of the following search terms or its variation: emotion, feeling, affection, or sentiment. These delimitations and searches resulted in the selection of 129 research articles for final, detailed content analysis. The full citations of these articles are listed in Appendix.

12.3.2 Content Analysis of Selected Articles

In the analysis phase, we conducted a content analysis of the 129 articles. Content analysis employs quantitative and qualitative textual analysis, requires minimal interference by the researcher in the phenomenon studied, and can handle large volumes (Krippendorff 1980; Weber 1985). We emphasized qualitative content and thematic analysis. We first read through all the articles to acquire a general view of the studies and then compared, categorized, and coded the contents. We focused on analyzing the classification of the forum and identifying the key conceptualizations on "emotion" as well as the major theoretical models and approaches. In addition, we classified the major research themes and empirical research contexts.

Researcher triangulation strengthened the analysis throughout the process: four researchers representing different disciplines (marketing, management, service, and engineering) participated in interpreting and categorizing the data. Knowledge of diverse, interlinked research streams was needed in making decisions about categorization, and all the researchers collectively defined the coding procedures and limitations. The researchers assessed and jointly compared the key content of the articles, for example, by employing Excel and Word tabling to ensure consistency of categorization, and the researchers discussed their interpretations of the research findings to improve the quality of the findings, which are presented next.

12.4 Findings: How Emotions in CX Are Co-created in Interactive Society

12.4.1 Overview on Roles of Emotions in CX

Emotions are, indeed, created in complex sets of interaction with other actors in online and offline environments but are always subjectively interpreted and experienced by an individual. In this chapter, we expand the current understanding of how emotions build CX in interactive society and provide an overview of our key findings followed by a more detailed discussion on each of them.

The discussion on emotions and CX is taking place mostly in individual and relational level even though it is acknowledged that emotions in CX are actually becoming real in complex systems. To clarify our findings, we introduce an integrative framework (Fig. 12.1) that illustrates how emotions build CX and highlights the diversity of emotions in CX in interactive society. The framework consists of eight different emotion types. Type 1 concerns emotions emerging in direct person-to-person and online encounters between a customer and an organization or its representative. The type 2 is emotional stimuli or cue (e.g., music or design) the service provider uses to affect customers' emotions. Type 3 addresses customers' emotional responses to providers' different cues. Type 4 focuses on how customers' evaluations of their experience are affected and processed in the emotional dimension (part of the cylinder in Fig. 12.1), which is present in all interactions customer has with the organization or its' elements. The type 5 represents the emotional aspects in different phases of decision-making and buying process, including information seeking, evaluation, purchase, and post-purchase phases (represented as cylinder segments in Fig. 12.1). In type 6, emotions are drivers of experience outcomes (represented as an arrow above cylinder in Fig. 12.1). Type 7 focuses on emotional links and bonds, for example, towards an organization's brand or technology. Type 8 addresses the diversity of emotions in CX and their emergence in all levels in interactive society.

As said, emotions are building CX in both digital, online and offline environments. Driven by the digitalization, the recent literature emphasizes building an understanding on how emotions in CX are created through various forms of interaction, particularly in online environments. That is, organizations also should focus on creating emotional attachment with the customers by, for example, improving the interactive components on their website. Operating only with the static attributes in

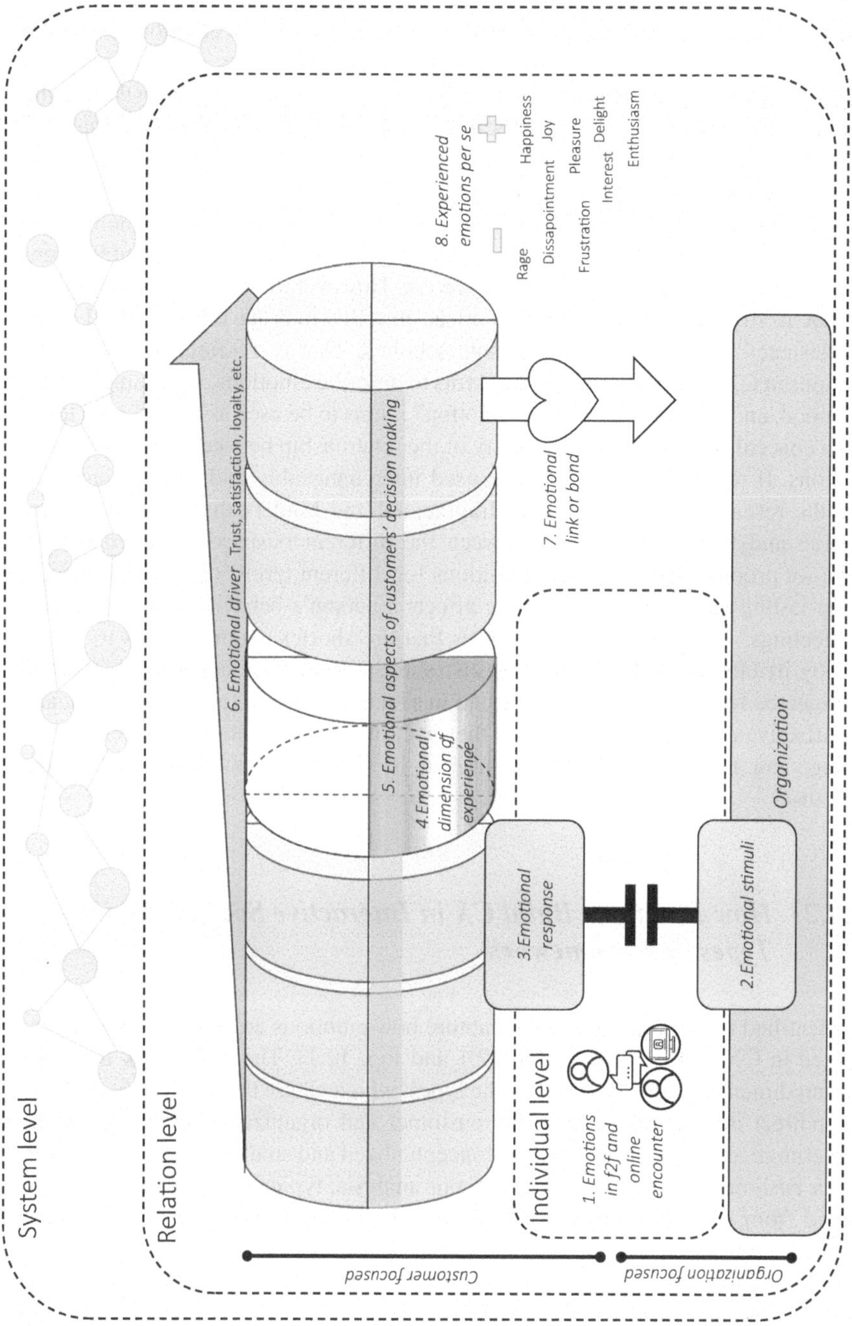

Fig. 12.1 Framework for emotions in CX

online, like visual components, is not enough in the era of experiences, and thus more emphasis should be given to improve the sociality on the online environments. Based on our study, it seems necessary also to highlight that the emotions emerging in interactive society are both positive and negative. Presently, positive emotions have gained a lot more attention in research than negative emotions, even though the diversity of emotions is extensive. Therefore, it is important to understand that also negative emotions define individuals' experiences and they should not be downplayed in research and practice.

In addition, we find it crucial to generate the consensus about the definitions related to emotions as the experience is present in various disciplines, and the centrality of it is underlined in the experience era. However, the research on emotions and CX is still fragmented, and we noticed that this may have also caused some inconsistency in the terminology among scholars. That is, researchers addressing emotions in CX used a lot of different terms to describe emotions, for example, feeling, mood, and affection. The term "emotion" seems to be used as an umbrella term, which conceals the multidimensionality of the relationship between CX and various emotions. If these different terms are used interchangeably and without justification, the research field will remain fragmented and hinders the interdisciplinary research and fruitful discussion between the different businesses. Based on our study, we propose the following definitions for different terms: (1) "mood" depicts a long-lasting subjective emotion that affects a person's behavior and experience, (2) "feelings" are subjective experiences that are shorter (from minutes to hours, e.g., joy, irritation), (3) "emotions" are also short-term feelings but are characterized by projected feelings, usually manifested in social interaction (e.g., love, hate), and (4) "affective experience" is based on the spectrum of all previous terms (emotions, feeling, and mood) and can be described by features like intensity, duration, and cause.

12.4.2 How Emotions Build CX in Interactive Society: Major Types and Framework

We identified eight major types that capture how emotions are applied and conceptualized in CX research (see Table 12.1 and Fig. 12.1). The framework uncovers relevant dimensions that distinguish the types, which all are the result of both direct and indirect interaction between the customer and organization or it's elements. Furthermore, emotions in CX can be conceptualized and studied from *the organization* or *customer* perspective. Based on our analysis, typically emotions in CX are studied from the latter, customer perspective, and thus, our categorization types emphasize this more.

The first type concerned providers' attempts to manage emotions but focused on *competencies*, *personnel*, *procedures*, or *online processes that manage emotions* in customer interactions. For example, the importance of employees' skills in managing

Table 12.1 Types of emotions in CX in interactive society

Category and its focus	How emotion is conceptualized	Example articles
1. Emotions in service encounters and interactions, managed by the firm's personnel *Provider-focused*	As part of frontline interaction, which requires management in online and offline contexts. Firms need to develop the EI of personnel and online practices to successfully manage service encounters characterized by diverse emotions	Rose et al. (2012) and Martin et al. (2015) examined emotions in online services from the management perspective. Johnson et al. (2009) studied emotions in face-to-face service interactions
2. Emotional stimuli or cues triggered by the firm *Provider-focused*	As a product of emotional stimuli and cues (three types: functional, mechanical, and humane) provided by the firm to shape and manage customers' emotions	Wang et al. (2007) examined avatars as emotional stimuli (see also type 3)
3. Emotional response *Customer-focused*	As a response to an element of customer experience, a service process element or event, or other actors, e.g., personnel or other customers	Madzharov et al. (2015) examined how customers respond emotionally to scents in a retail environment. Wang et al. (2007) examined emotional responses to avatars that were considered social cues
4. Emotional dimension of experience *Customer-focused*	As part of the multidimensional customer experience; others are cognitive and behavioral	Cruz et al. (2010) examined multiple dimensions of internet banking experiences
5. Emotional aspects of customers' decision-making *Customer-focused*	As influencing the decision-making, and particularly the purchasing, process	Puccinelli et al. (2009) and Sachdeva and Goel (2015) studied how to manage customer experience and emotions in retailing, focused on the buying process
6. Emotional driver *Customer-focused*	As a driver of long-term customer relationship dynamics because it shapes/affects trust, satisfaction, and commitment	Mascarenhas et al. (2006) examined loyalty and emotions in several contexts (e.g., Disney World, Blyth Industries, and Apple's iMac)
7. Emotional link or bond *Customer-focused*	As a link or bond to a brand, technology, etc.	Morgan-Thomas and Veloutsou (2013) included "emotional aspects" of brand relationships in their model of online brand experiences to supplement the dimension technology acceptance dimension
8. Experienced emotion *Emotion-focused*	As diverse; different emotions are acknowledged as part of the customer experience	Surachartkumtonkun et al. (2015) compared customer rage across countries

customers' feelings during the customer experience was identified (Johnson et al. 2009), while Gabbott et al. (2011) emphasized emotional intelligence (EI) during service failures. The psychological phenomenon of EI was identified by Goleman (1995) and is considered a tool for leaders and employees to manage customer experiences. The articles suggested that positive emotions (Chahal and Dutta 2015) and negative emotions, such as customer rage (Surachartkumtonkun et al. 2015), should be managed by employees. Varma (2012), however, highlights that human emotions are not entirely predictable, and most customers' emotions remain unclear or even totally hidden. The article links CRM to management of customers' emotional states, noting that nothing can deliver a memorable customer experience better than motivated and engaged employees.

The second type focused on *service providers' attempts to manage emotions*. Because providers cannot manage emotions directly, they aim to manage emotions through indirect interaction, which includes stimuli and cues. The main goal for service providers seemed to be creating *positive* emotions among customers as positive emotions favorably affect, for example, customer experience, brand image, purchase intention, satisfaction, and loyalty. Although emotions were positive in principle, the importance of identifying and handling negative emotions should not be underestimated, as removing all cues from service provider performance that could create negative emotions is impossible.

The third type focused on *emotional responses* to different cues or elements of customer experiences. Emotional responses are embedded in customer's interaction with the organization or servicescape, capturing the customer's side in this reciprocal relation. For example, Madzharov et al. (2015) examined how scents elicit emotions and, thus, affect customer experience, while Bagdare and Jain (2013) developed a scale for the experiential responses of retail customers. In this category linking emotions to customer experiences, the aspect is behavioral and customer-focused as these studies examined how customers respond to physical cues and service process elements, such as service failures.

The fourth type analyzed *emotional dimensions* of the whole customer experience, thus conceptualizing emotion as one facet. The other facets were cognitive and behavioral dimensions (Cruz et al. 2010). Again, the customer perspective is emphasized. Customers are involved at different dimensions in all interactions between the organization and its' offerings.

The fifth type linked *emotions and decision-making*, often in the retail context. Positive and negative emotions are usually related to price, information, assortment, process, or interaction, which triggers purchase or repurchase intention. In a study in retail context, Puccinelli et al. (2009) state that, for example, confusing content in a website can induce frustration, which can affect to consumer's decision-making negatively. Authors state that retailers should focus on identifying triggers and focus on interactive attributes, which would pace up consumer's favorable decision making.

The sixth type studied *emotions as a driver of experience outcomes* (e.g., loyalty, trust, and satisfaction). In other words, different forms of interaction create emotions, which influence of experience outcomes. These studies link emotions to long-term relationships and dynamics between the customer and organization. Mascarenhas et al. (2006), for example, examined emotions as a driver of customer loyalty in several contexts.

The seventh type addressed *emotional links* and *emotional bonds* to, for example, a brand (Mollen and Wilson 2010; Morgan-Thomas and Veloutsou 2013) or technology and design (Zomerdijk and Voss 2011). Emotional links and bonds are a result of customer's interaction with these objects (e.g., brand or technology)

(Teixeira et al. 2012). These emotional bonds develop during the customer's interaction with the organization. The role of customer in interaction is active, and thus customer perspective is dominant. Both Johnson et al. (2009) and Zomerdijk and Voss (2011) argue that an emotional connection strengthens the relationship with an organization and can be seen as a competitive advantage (Gabbott et al. 2011) because emotional bonds usually are hard to break.

The eighth type focused on *various specific emotions* per se. Customers are usually interacting with various forms (e.g., with personnel, brand, or technology) during their customer journey, and thus these relations evoke different emotions. Carreira et al. (2013) researched travel experiences and distinguished three categories of emotions: excitement and joy, annoyance and discontentment, and anxiety and fear. Chahal and Dutta (2015) and Arnold et al. (2005) highlighted the importance of identifying the range of emotions customers feel during terrible experiences. Surachartkumtonkun et al. (2015) highlighted the various emotions that customer rage arouses (e.g., disgust, hate, and fury).

12.4.3 CX with Emotions Co-created in Digital Environment

Many organizations in different fields have shifted to multichannel strategies by providing added value both in digital and offline interaction environments (Rajaobelina 2018). The digitalization has also pushed researchers to address this shift and 19 of reviewed articles addressed online or virtual environments. These studies were fragmented under several industries including retail, banking, traveling, virtual, e-learning, and online search engine mirroring the crucial presence of experiences throughout the interactive society in different contexts and levels.

In online environment, experience is formed in interaction between the individual, i.e., customer, and attributes managed by the organization. Interaction in online takes naturally different shapes compared to face-to-face contexts, but still plays a crucial role in CX. Indeed, interaction shapes customer's aroused emotions and emotional attachment in online contexts, which influence customers' decision-making (Bilgihan et al. 2015; Lee 2018), experience outcomes (e.g., loyalty or satisfaction) (Cruz et al. 2010), and future purchase intentions (Bilgihan et al. 2015). At best, the online environment can create a flow experience (Bilgihan et al. 2015) if interactive features generate highly positive emotions like fun, enjoyment, and pleasure.

Emotions are strongly present in online context being embedded in customer's interaction with both static and social cues as well as the e-environment itself. Organizations may interact with their customers by providing a variety of static stimuli including text-based information, visual imagery, video or audio through their website, or other e-environment (see, e.g., Rose et al. 2012). Customer's interaction with the brand (Meyer and Schwager 2007) occurs also in online context. Morgan-Thomas and Veloutsou (2013) concentrated on online brand experiences that include an emotional affective state in the context of search engines. Their findings show that customer's interaction with brand should evoke emotions in order to build trust and loyalty. This is similar with offline retail context. In addition, organizations can influence to their customers and their emotions through social cues and sociality of their websites. This is highlighted by Bilgihan et al. (2015) who stress the importance for organizations operating online to note that to be able to create emotional attachment with the customers, they should shift the focus from static attributes even more to interactive components (Bilgihan et al. 2015). These social components can be provided either as human- or machine-operated as Wang et al. (2007) note that "customers treat computers as social actors even though they are fully aware that they are interaction with machines." For example, Wang et al. (2007) study on sociality of websites showed that customers' interaction between the avatars influence positively on affect and shopping value of the customers. On the other hand, Gefen and Straub (2003) study in online travel agency context showed that social presence of organization has also an influence on consumer trust. However, the social interaction in online goes also beyond the organization interaction with other actors may also influence on customer's emotions (Jaakkola et al. 2015). For example, Tu and Zhang (2013) studied experience in a non-trading virtual community where, according to their findings, experience co-creation has two dimensions: emotional and relationship experience. Interaction with others including emotion sharing is an important building block of co-creation value in non-trading virtual community.

12.4.4 Multidisciplinary Nature of CX with Emotional Aspects

The multidisciplinary nature of emotions in CX highlights that emotions in CX is a real matter of professionals and researchers in diverse disciplines and businesses. Our analysis uncovered the multidisciplinary nature, illustrating the presence of emotions in experiences through disciplines. Table 12.2 presents the main disciplines ranging from marketing to other related disciplines and the focuses regarding emotions in CX. For example, marketing highlights the role of emotions in CX in digitalization and engagement, whereas innovation and technology research emphasizes technological management of CX and its emotional dimension via customer relationship management (CRM) systems, thus also contributing to the emotional aspects of CX. Table 12.2 also presents the main forums in which research on emotional aspects in CX appeared.

Researchers and professionals should be aware of how they talk and name emotions in CX, as we identified a wide range of terms used to describe emotions in CX. Many authors did not clearly justify why they had chosen to use, e.g., "emotion" instead of "feeling" or "affective experience," or used terms interchangeably, although many of the reviewed articles use psychology as a theoretical background. For example, several studies referred to Lazarus's (1991) work in psychology on the relationship between emotion and stress, as well as the role of cognition and motivation in emotions. In addition, scholars often applied Pine and Gilmore's (1998) seminal work on the experience economy. Two other key theoretical models

Table 12.2 Multidisciplinary emotions in CX: disciplines and forums of articles on CX and emotions

Discipline	Emphasis on customer experience and emotions	Main forums, i.e., journal examples	Number of articles linking customer experience and emotions
Marketing	Digitalization, co-creation, engagement, loyalty, branding, strategic marketing, satisfaction	*Journal of Marketing, Marketing Theory, The Marketing Review*	28(22%)
Service	Co-creation, customer relationship, e-services, emotional engagement, quality, emotional labor, intangibility, competitive advantage	*Journal of Service Management, Journal of Service Research, Journal of Services Marketing*	21(17%)
Management	Customer value, emotional bonding, service quality, corporate brand experience, experiential marketing	*Journal of General Management, Strategy and Leadership*	32(25%)
Retail	Online customer experience, experiential consumption, dimensions of retail customer experience, satisfaction, loyalty	*Journal of Retailing and Consumer Services, Journal of Retailing*	16(12%)
Innovation and technology	Customer relationship management (CRM), customer experience management, telecommunication, value creation, social presence, new service development	*International Journal of Innovation and Technology Management, Journal of Product Innovation Management*	14(11%)
Others	E.g., travel experience context, virtual atmosphere	*Entrepreneurial Executive, Tourism and Hospitality Research*	18 (9%)
Total			129(100%)

that were identified was Schmitt's (1999) 15-item general scale of experience and Mehrabian's and Russell's (1974) PAD model (pleasure, arousal, and dominance). Schmitt's model was utilized more on quantitative studies whereas the latter was more utilized in qualitative studies.

12.4.5 A Rollercoaster Between Negative and Positive Emotions

It is valuable to understand that interactive society is full of diverse emotions, which all need to be examined and managed, in all levels of society. Like our study reveals, a wide range of emotions is linked to CX varying from positive to negative (Table 12.3). Many articles we analyzed concentrated on positive emotions like joy, enjoyment, or pleasure (Zomerdijk and Voss 2011) or observed emotions based on their valence without specific identification (Carreira et al. 2013; Gabbott et al. 2011). Strongly *positive emotions* like fun, inspiration, and enjoyment were mostly studied regarding hedonic experiences (Liu et al. 2017), whereas studies linked to utilitarian experiences emphasized other types of emotions, like trust and reliability (Banerjee 2014; Bilgihan et al. 2015). *Negative emotions* were examined in less detail except in a few papers (see Hudson et al. 2017; Surachartkumtonkun et al, 2015). In general, providers were encouraged to focus on avoiding negative emotions (Lucia-Palacios et al. 2016), and the negative effect on experience outcome was outlined (Hudson et al. 2017).

12.5 Conclusions and Implications

At this point we believe it is fair to say that in the very heart of experiences are emotions. Emotions are embedded to experiences in various ways being simultaneously influencing and being influenced by the experiences. In other words, emotions build experiences via interaction in individual, relational, and ecosystem level in society. Thus, we are facing a fascinating research topic, which concerns academicians and practitioners in all disciplines in interactive society. The key contribution for both academicians and practitioners lays in our framework, which opens up our eyes to the embedded complexity of emotions in CX by identifying the types how emotions build CX in diverse relations in society.

We believe our study and framework guides researchers in their quest to investigate emotional aspects in experience. After all, emotions are uncontrollable, difficult to understand, and complex to manage. Emotions in experiences are taking place in several relations between the actors and thus requiring more emphasis on

Table 12.3 Diverse emotions in CX research

Positive emotions	Negative emotions	Example article
Joy, elation, enthusiasm	Disappointment, frustration, irritation, dislike	Johnson et al. (2009)
Delight	Opposite of delight	Chahal and Dutta (2015)
	Rage, disgust, hate, fury, outrage, aggression	Surachartkumtonkun et al. (2015)
Excitement, joy, happiness, pleasure, cheerfulness	Discontentment, annoyance, nervousness, fear	Carreira et al. (2013)
Positive (not specified in more detailed level in the article)	Negative (not specified in more detail in the article)	Gabbott et al. (2011)
Joy, awe, interest, affection, trust		Zomerdijk and Voss (2011)
Good, soft, endearing, friendly	Bad, unpleasantness	Varma (2012)
Peacefulness, excitement	Frustration, stress	Lucia-Palacios et al. (2016)

interaction when studying emotional aspects of experience. As we recognize emotions, central in experiences in individual, relational, and ecosystem level in the interactive society, we are facing a complex set which is hard to manage and control in systems, as well as in the continuously changing society. The framework helps researchers to zoom to this complex phenomenon and illustrate the different forms of interactions, where emotions in experience are taking place and building experiences. The types guide researchers to focus their future studies on emotions in experience by providing guidance to position the studies in different contexts to micro, relational, and system levels. By revealing the close connection between experiences, emotions, and interaction, we highlight that the importance of emotions in interactive society should be taken under serious consideration.

For practitioners, who are aiming to enhance and develop experiences, the managerial usefulness of the framework lays in understanding the contrast between the two main perspectives—organization-focused and customer-focused perspectives—and the different types of emotions in CX. Importantly, the framework clarifies how focus on emotions in experiences actually requires practitioners' concentration on interaction. Framed in a provider-focused way, emotions may be seen as a managerial instrument controlled by an organization. Through this managerial lens, practitioners can identify different types of encounters and emotional stimuli that create experiences for customers. Thus, one important starting point in CX management development is proper recruitment and continuous training and support of employees' emotional intelligence, skills, and behavior to successfully manage encounters that include ranging emotions. However, taking this one-sided perspective organizations may be facing a situation where service design, operations, and CX management monitoring may become blurred by the belief that emotions of customers are largely or solely managed by the organization. Indeed, some emotional types of CX are beyond the view and may be even beyond the control of the organization. The customer-focused perspective in framework helps organizations to open their eyes and to avoid such pitfalls. For example, even though organization designs carefully different kind of cues to arouse specific emotions and feelings in a customer (Type 2), it can never be defined, how the customer will respond to organization's cues (Type 3)—emotions are unpredictable and difficult to control. Therefore, practitioners should concentrate not only on creating and increasing positive emotions in encounters but also on understanding customers' emotions in-depth and systematically identifying different types of emotions, like emotions in decision-making, emotional drivers, and emotional responses. By doing so, companies and other entities in society will be more informed on what they should and can manage in order to better design and implement cues for more appropriate service to fit customers' emotional types and stages.

We hope that our review provides managers and researchers with a deeper understanding of a growing field, yet encourages them. Given the fragmented current state of research and the complex nature of emotions in experience, several future research topics emerged from this study. We want to encourage researchers to carry out multidisciplinary research combining different methodologies as the importance of emotions in CX is widely noted in various disciplines. These further studies could test and validate our suggested types of emotions in CX. In addition, as our study concentrated mainly on emotions in experiences in individual and relational level, more studies in online and offline environments should be conducted concentrating on the ecosystem level. Moreover, we encourage researchers to pay more attention to the role and dynamics of positive and negative emotions in CX as review revealed clearly that researchers have focused on creating positive emotional experiences and considered negative emotions mainly to be avoided or ignored, although it may be an emotional rollercoaster for customers to go through services.

Appendix: Reviewed Articles

Author	Title	Publication
Ali, F., Kim, W.G., Li, J. and Jeon, H.M., 2018	Make it delightful: Customers' experience, satisfaction and loyalty in Malaysian theme parks	*Journal of Destination Marketing and Management*
Bagdare, S., 2015	Emotional Determinants of Retail Customer Experience	*International Journal of Marketing and Business Communication*
Bagdare, S., and Jain, R., 2013	Measuring retail customer experience	*International Journal of Retail and Distribution Management*
Bagdare, S., 2017	Retail customer experience: A research agenda	*International Journal of Research in Commerce and Management*
Balaji, M.S., Roy, S.K. and Quazi, A., 2017	Customers' emotion regulation strategies in service failure encounters	*European Journal of Marketing*
Başaran, A.S., and Nezahat, E., 2014	Experiential Marketing and Vacation Experience: The Sample of Turkish Airlines	*Procedia – Social and Behavioral Sciences*
Banerjee, M., 2014	Misalignment and Its Influence on Integration Quality in Multichannel Services	*Journal of Service Research*
Beltagui, A. and Gandi, M., 2018	Revisiting service quality through the lens of experience-centric services	*International Journal of Operations and Production Management*
Berry, L.L., and Carbone, L.P., 2007	Build Loyalty Through Experience Management	*Quality Progress*
Bhandari, S., 2016	Understanding the models of customer experience	*International Journal of Research in Commerce and Management*
Bolton, R.N., Gustafsson, A., McColl-Kennedy, J., Sirianni, N.J., and Tse, D.K., 2014	Small details that make big differences: A radical approach to consumption experience as a firm's differentiating strategy	*Journal of Service Management*

Author	Title	Publication
Brakus, J.J., Schmitt, B.H., and Zarantonello, L. 2009	Brand Experience: What Is It? How Is It Measured? Does It Affect Loyalty?	*Journal of Marketing*
Bramley, S., Dibben, N. and Rowe, R., 2016	The Utilisation of Music by Casino Managers: An Interview Study	*Journal of Gambling Studies*
Brun, I., Rajaobelina, L., Ricard, L. and Berthiaume, B., 2017	Impact of customer experience on loyalty: a multichannel examination	*Service Industries Journal*
Bustamante, J.C. and Rubio, N., 2017	Measuring customer experience in physical retail environments	*Journal of Service Management*
Butcher, K., 2013	Differential impact of social influence in the hospitality encounter	*International Journal of Contemporary Hospitality Management*
Cachero-Martinez, S. and Vazquez-Casielles, R., 2017	Living positive experiences in store: how it influences shopping experience value and satisfaction?	*Journal of Business Economics and Management*
Calheiros, A.C., Moro, S. and Rita, P., 2017	Sentiment Classification of Consumer-Generated Online Reviews Using Topic Modeling	*Journal of Hospitality Marketing and Management*
Carreira, R., Patricio, L., Jorge, R.N., Magee, C., and Hommes, Q.V.E., 2013	Towards a holistic approach to the travel experience: A qualitative study of bus transportation	*Transport Policy*
Cayaba, Ma, C., Yuting, C., Jurgens, M., Mathews, P.J. and Sefton, A., 2016	Redesigning emergency rooms into experience rooms	*Marketing Health Services*
Cetin, G., Akova, O., and Kaya, F., 2012	Components of experiential value: Case of hospitality industry	10th International strategic management conference 2014
Cetin, G. and Walls, A., 2016	Understanding the Customer Experiences from the Perspective of Guests and Hotel Managers: Empirical Findings from Luxury Hotels in Istanbul, Turkey	*Journal of Hospitality Marketing and Management*
Chahal, H., and Dutta, K., 2014	Conceptualising customer experiences: Significant research propositions	*Marketing Review*
Chahal, H., and Dutta, K., 2015	Measurement and impact of customer experience in banking sector	*Decision*
Chang, T-Y., and Horng, S-C., 2010	Conceptualizing and measuring experience quality: The customer's perspective	*Service Industries Journal*
Chan, S.J., 2015	A Model Linking Store Attributes, Service Quality and Customer Experience: A Study Among Community Pharmacies	*International Journal of Economics and Management*

Author	Title	Publication
Choraria, S., 2015	Managing Emotional Connect between Front-Line Employee and Customers	*Pacific Business Review International*
Choudhury, M., Singh, R. and Saikia, H., 2016	Measuring customer experience in bankassurance: An empirical study	*Market-Trziste*
Cruz, P., Salo, J., Munoz-Gallego, P., and Laukkanen, T., 2010	Heavy Users of e-banking and Customer Experience Management: evidences on intrinsic motivation	*International Journal of Electronic Business*
de Villiers, R. and Po-Ju, C., 2017	Feeling Loyal? The Impacts of Affective Customer Experiences on Business	*International Journal of Business and Economics*
de Villiers, R. and Po-Ju, C., 2017	Achieving Requisite Variety in Customer Experience Research for Improving Marketing Relationship Performances	*International Journal of Business and Economics*
Delcourt, C., Gremler, D.D., De Zanet, F. and van Riel, A.C.R., 2017	An analysis of the interaction effect between employee technical and emotional competencies in emotionally charged service encounters	*Journal of Service Management*
Delcourt, C., Gremler, D.D., van Riel, A.C.R. and van Birgelen, M.J.H., 2016	Employee Emotional Competence: Construct Conceptualization and Validation of a Customer-Based Measure	*Journal of Service Research*
Dennis, C., Brakus, J.J., and Alamanos, E., 2013	The wallpaper matters: Digital signage as customer-experience provider at the Harrods (London, UK) department store	*Journal of Marketing Management*
Deshwal, P. and Phuyan, P., 2018	Cancer patient service experience and satisfaction	*International Journal of Healthcare Management*
Dutta, N.S., 2015	Innovative Product Management Driving Enhanced Customer Experience Management (CEM)	*Telecom Business Review*
Ebrahim, R., Ghoneim, A., Irani, Z. and Fan, Y., 2016	A brand preference and repurchase intention model: the role of consumer experience	*Journal of Marketing Management*
Esmark, C.L., Noble, S.M. and Breazeale, M.J., 2017	I'll Be Watching You: Shoppers' Reactions to Perceptions of Being Watched by Employees	*Journal of Retailing*
Faria, S., Ferreira, P. and Carvalho, V., 2016	Are assortment variety and stock-failures management in Hypermarkets and Supermarkets an important factor for consumers to develop a store-type preference, willing to come back and continue to buy?	*Portuguese Journal of Marketing*

Author	Title	Publication
Gabbott, M., Tsarenko, Y., and Mok, W.H., 2011	Emotional Intelligence as a Moderator of Coping Strategies and Service Outcomes in Circumstances of Service Failure	*Journal of Service Research*
Gefen, D., and Straub, D., 2003	Managing User Trust in B2C e-Services	*e-Service Journal*
Gierlinger, S., 2017	Every Moment Matters: Cultivating a Culture of C.A.R.E.	*Journal of Healthcare Management*
Gilbert, D., and Gao, Y.F., 2005	A failure of UK travel agencies to strengthen zones of tolerance	*Tourism and Hospitality Research*
Gilboa, S., Vilnai-Yavetz, I. and Chebat, J.C., 2016	Capturing the multiple facets of mall experience: Developing and validating a scale	*Journal of Consumer Behaviour*
Gooding, N., 2008	An alternative player's approach against incumbent strategies to make the most of market share	*Journal of Telecommunications Management*
Grewal, D., Roggeveen, A.L., Sisodia, R. and Nordfalt, J., 2016	Enhancing Customer Engagement Through Consciousness	*Journal of Retailing*
Gudem, M., Steinert, M., and Welo, T., 2014	From LEAN product development to LEAN innovation: Searching for a more valid approach for promoting utilitarian and emotional value	*International Journal of Innovation and Technology Management*
Hakanen, T., and Jaakkola, E., 2012	Co-creating customer-focused solutions within business networks: A service perspective	*Journal of Service Management*
Hamzah, Z.L., Alwi, S.F.S., and Othman, M.N., 2014	Designing corporate brand experience in an online context: A qualitative insight	*Journal of Business Research*
Hong-Youl, H., and Perks, H., 2005	Effects of consumer perceptions of brand experience on the web: Brand familiarity, satisfaction and brand trust	*Journal of Consumer Behaviour*
Hsieh, Y.H. and Yuan, S.T., 2016	An application of technology-based design for exhibition services	*International Journal of Quality and Service Sciences*
Huang, R., Lee, S.H., Kim, H;. and Evans, L., 2015	The impact of brand experiences on brand resonance in multi-channel fashion retailing	*Journal of Research in Interactive Marketing*
Hudson, S., González-Gómez, H.V. and Rychalski, A., 2017	Call centers: is there an upside to the dissatisfied customer experience?	*Journal of Business Strategy*
Hung, Y.C., Zheng, X., Carlson, J. and Giurge, L.M., 2017	The weight of the saddened soul: the bidirectionality between physical heaviness and sadness and its implications for sensory marketing	*Journal of Marketing Management*

Author	Title	Publication
Jain, R., and Jain, S., 2008	Towards relational exchange in services marketing: Insights from hospitality industry	*Journal of Services Research*
Jain, R., and Bagdare, S., 2009	Determinants of Customer Experience in New Format Retail Stores	*Journal of Marketing and Communication*
Jain, R., Aagja, J. and Bagdare, S., 2017	Customer experience—a review and research agenda	*Journal of Service Theory and Practice*
Johnson, M.D., Lervik Olsen, L. and Wallin Andreassen, T., 2009	Joy and disappointment in the hotel experience: Managing relationship segments	*Managing Service Quality*
Juettner, U., Schaffner, D., Windler, K., and Maklan, S., 2013	Customer service experiences: Developing and applying a sequential incident laddering technique	*European Journal of Marketing*
Kandampully, J., Zhang, T.T. and Jaakkola, E., 2018	Customer experience management in hospitality A literature synthesis, new understanding and research agenda	*International Journal of Contemporary Hospitality Management*
Keiningham, T., Ball, J., Benoit, Bruce, H.L., Buoye, A., Dzenkovska, J., Nasr, L., Ou, Y.C. and Zaki, M., 2017	The interplay of customer experience and commitment	*Journal of Services Marketing*
Kim, D. and Park, B.J., 2017	The moderating role of context in the effects of choice attributes on hotel choice: A discrete choice experiment	*Tourism Management*
Klaus, P., and Maklan, S., 2011	Bridging the gap for destination extreme sports: A model of sports tourism customer experience	*Journal of Marketing Management*
Klaus, P., and Maklan, S., 2013	Towards a better measure of customer experience	*International Journal of Market Research*
Klaus, P., 2017	Luxury patient experience (LPX): review, conceptualization, and future research directions	*Service Industries Journal*
Kranzbühler, A.M., Kleijnen, M.H.P., Morgan, R.E. and Teerling, M., 2018	The Multilevel Nature of Customer Experience Research: An Integrative Review and Research Agenda	*International Journal of Management Reviews*
Kumar, A. and Anjaly, B., 2017	How to measure post-purchase customer experience in online retailing? A scale development study	*International Journal of Retail and Distribution Management*
Lee, S., 2018	Investigating antecedents and outcome of telepresence on a hotel's website	*International Journal of Contemporary Hospitality Management*

Author	Title	Publication
Lee, C.Y., Chou, C., and Sun, T.L., 2012	An evaluation from presence perspective of customer experiences in virtual environments	*Ergonomics in Asia. Development, opportunities and challenges*
Li, J., Canziani, B.F. and Barbieri, C., 2018	Emotional labor in hospitality: Positive affective displays in service encounters	*Tourism and Hospitality Research*
Liang, C.C., 2016	Queueing management and improving customer experience: empirical evidence regarding enjoyable queues	*Journal of Consumer Marketing*
Lin, Z., and Bennett, D., 2014	Examining retail customer experience and the moderation effect of loyalty programmes	*International Journal of Retail and Distribution Management*
Liu, J.T., 2016	Research on Taiwan theme parks' experience marketing strategy and revisit willingness, purchase willingness and recommendation willingness	*International Journal of Organizational Innovation*
Liu, W., Sparks, B. and Coghlan, A., 2017	Fun, inspiration and discovery: from momentary experiences to overall evaluations	*International Journal of Contemporary Hospitality Management*
Lu, C. and Liu, S.J., 2016	Cultural Tourism O2O Business Model Innovation-A Case Study of CTrip	*Journal of Electronic Commerce in Organizations*
Lucia-Palacios, L., Perez-Lopez, R. and Polo-Redondo, Y., 2016	Cognitive, affective and behavioural responses in mall experience A qualitative approach	*International Journal of Retail and Distribution Management*
Madzharov, A. V., Block, L.G., andMorrin, M., 2015	The Cool Scent of Power: Effects of Ambient Scent on Consumer Preferences and Choice Behavior	*Journal of Marketing*
Malthouse, E.C., Calder, B.J., Kim, S.J. and Vandenbosch, M., 2016	Evidence that user-generated content that produces engagement increases purchase behaviours	*Journal of Marketing Management*
Mann, B., Jit S. and Rawat, J., 2016	The Role of Consumer Personality Trait and Brand Personality Trait in Creating Customer Experience	*The UIP Journal of Brand Management*
Martin, J., Mortimer, G., and Andrews, L., 2015	Re-examining online customer experience to include purchase frequency and perceived risk	*Journal of Retailing and Consumer Services*
Mascarenhas, O.A., Kesavan, R., Bernacchi, M., 2006	Lasting customer loyalty: A total customer experience approach	*Journal of Consumer Marketing*
McColl-Kennedy, J.R., Danaher, T.S., Gallan, A.S., Orsingher, C., Lervik-Olsen, L, Verma, R., 2018	How do you feel today? Managing patient emotions during health care experiences to enhance well-being	*Journal of Business Research*

Author	Title	Publication
Moeller, J., and Herrn, S., 2013	Shaping Retail Brand Personality Perceptions by Bodily Experiences	*Journal of Retailing*
Mollen, A., and Wilson, H., 2010	Engagement, telepresence and interactivity in online consumer experience: Reconciling scholastic and managerial perspectives	*Journal of Business Research*
Morgan-Thomas, A., and Veloutsou, C., 2013	Beyond technology acceptance: Brand relationships and online brand experience	*Journal of Business Research*
Nunes, P.F., Bellin, J. Lee, I., and Schunck, O., 2013	Converting the nonstop customer into a loyal customer	*Strategy and Leadership*
Palmer, A., 2010	Customer experience management: A critical review of an emerging idea	*Journal of Services Marketing*
Palmer, A. and Bejou, D., 2016	Retrospective: service failure and loyalty: an exploratory empirical study of airline customers	*Journal of Services Marketing*
Park, G.W., Kim, Y., Park, K. and Agarwal, A., 2016	Patient-centric quality assessment framework for healthcare services	*Technological Forecasting and Social Change*
Peeroo, S., Samy, M. and Jones, B., 2017	Facebook: a blessing or a curse for grocery stores?	*International Journal of Retail and Distribution Management*
Permutter, K. and Bradshaw, N., 2016	Addressing today's top brand challenges with sonic identity	*Journal of Brand Strategy*
Poncin, I., Garnier, M.B., Mimoun, M.S. and Leclercq, T., 2017	Smart technologies and shopping experience: Are gamification interfaces effective? The case of the Smartstore	*Technological Forecasting and Social Change*
Puccinelli, N.M., Goodstein, R.C., Grewal, D., Price, R., Raghubir, P., and Stewart, D., 2009	Customer Experience Management in Retailing: Understanding the Buying Process	*Journal of Retailing*
Rahman, Z., 2006	Customer experience management: A case study of an Indian bank	*Journal of Database Marketing and Customer Strategy Management*
Rajaobelina, L., 2018	The Impact of Customer Experience on Relationship Quality with Travel Agencies in a Multichannel Environment	*Journal of Travel Research*
Reydet, S. and Carsana, L., 2017	The effect of digital design in retail banking on customers' commitment and loyalty: The mediating role of positive affect	*Journal of Retailing and Consumer Services*
Rose, S., Clark, M., Samouel, P., and Hair, N., 2012	Online Customer Experience in e-Retailing: An empirical model of Antecedents and Outcomes	*Journal of Retailing*

Author	Title	Publication
Sachdeva, I., and Goel, S., 2015	Retail store environment and customer experience: A paradigm	*Journal of Fashion Marketing and Management*
Sato, Y. and Parry, M.E., 2015	The influence of the Japanese tea ceremony on Japanese restaurant hospitality	*Journal of Consumer Marketing*
Schanz, J. and De Lille, C., 2017	Customer Experience Strategy Turned into Hands-On Actions Through a Design Approach	*Design Management Journal*
Sharma, M., and Chaubey, D.S., 2014	An Empirical Study of Customer Experience and its Relationship with Customer Satisfaction towards the Services of Banking Sector	*Journal of Marketing and Communication*
Shim, S.I., Forsythe, S. and Kwon, W.S., 2015	Impact of online flow on brand experience and loyalty	*Journal of Electronic Commerce Research*
Shin, H. and Parker, J.	Exploring the elements of consumer nostalgia in retailing: Evidence from a content analysis of retailer collages	*Journal of Retailing and Consumer Services*
Shobeiri, S., Rajaobelina, L., Durif, F. and Boivin, C., 2016	Experiential motivations of socially responsible consumption	*International Journal of Market Research*
Sit, J.K., Hoang, A. and Inversini, A., 2018	Showrooming and retail opportunities: A qualitative investigation via a consumer-experience lens	*Journal of Retailing and Consumer Services*
Sangyeon, S., 2015	Identifying on-line shopping experiences from the perspective of shopping motives	*Academy of Marketing Studies Journal*
Stachow, G., and Hart, C., 2010	Exploring place image: Formation and measurement	*Place Branding and Public Diplomacy*
Steiner, F., and Harmon, R., 2009	The Impact of Intangible Value on the Design and Marketing of New Products and Services: An Exploratory Approach	Proceedings of PICMET 09: Technology Management in the Age of Fundamental Change, Vol. 1-5
Surachartkumtonkun, J., McColl-Kennedy, J.R., and Patterson, P.G., 2015	Unpacking Customer Rage Elicitation: A Dynamic Model	*Journal of Service Management*
Tehone, A.B., Zo, H.J. and Ciganek, A.P., 2015	Why do people use social computing? An experiential perspective	*Internet Research*
Terblanche, N.S., 2009	Customer experiences, interactions, relationships and corporate reputation: A conceptual approach	*Journal of General Management*
Terblanche, N.S., 2018	Revisiting the supermarket in-store customer shopping experience	*Journal of Retailing and Consumer Services*

Author	Title	Publication
Tosti, D.T., 2009	Customer experience and value: A performance view	*Performance Improvement*
Trudeau, H.S. and Shobeiri, S., 2016	Does social currency matter in creation of enhanced brand experience?	*Journal of Product and Brand Management*
Tu, J., and Zhang, M., 2013	Research on The Effect of Co-creation Customer Experience on Customer Co-created Value in Non-trading Virtual Community	2013 IEEE International conference on service operations and logistics, and informatics (SOLI)
Wall-Mullen, E. and Envick, B.R., 2015	Get a clue: How entrepreneurs can manage the service experience to differentiate themselves and provide value propositions that maximize customer satisfaction	*Entrepreneurial Executive*
van Tonder, C., 2017	More than Just a Stamp in My Passport	*International Journal of Business and Economics*
Varca, Philip E.	Emotional empathy and frontline employees: Does it make sense to care about the customer?	*Journal of Services Marketing*
Varma, R.T.R., 2012	Enhancing and Empowering: Customer Experience	*SCMS Journal of Indian Management*
Vinodhini, G. and Chandrasekaran, R.M., 2017	A sampling based sentiment mining approach for e-commerce applications	*Information Processing and Management*
Wang, L.C., Baker, J., Wagner, J.A., and Wakefield, K., 2007	Can a retail website be social?	*Journal of Marketing*
Wang, S., 2009	Emotional Design Based on Customer Experience Requirement	2009 IEEE 10th International conference on computer-Aided Industrial Design and Conceptual Design. CAID and CD 2009
Wattanacharoensil, W., Schuckert, M., Graham, A. and Dean, A., 2017	An analysis of the airport experience from an air traveler perspective	*Journal of Hospitality and Tourism Management*
Wijaya, A.P., 2017	Role of Experience in Customer Self-Congruity to Maintaining Loyalty: A Study on Fashion Store	*Entrepreneurial Business and Economics Review*
Yang, Z-Y., and He, L-Y., 2011	Goal, customer experience and purchase intention in a retail context in China: An empirical study	*African Journal of Business Management*
Yakhlef, A., 2015	Customer experience within retail environments: An embodied, spatial approach	*Marketing Theory*

Author	Title	Publication
Yoon, S.J. and Lee, H.J., 2017	Does Customer Experience Management Pay Off? Evidence from Local versus Global Hotel Brands in South Korea	*Journal of Hospitality Marketing and Management*
Zaltman, G., Olson, J. and Forr, J., 2015	Toward a New Marketing Science for Hospitality Managers	*Cornell Hospitality Quarterly*
Zomerdijk, L.G., Voss, C.A., 2011	NSD Processes and Practices in Experiential Services	*Journal of Product Innovation Management*
129 in total		

References

Arnold, M. J., Reynolds, K. E., Ponder, N., & Lueg, J. E. (2005). Customer delight in a retail context: Investigating delightful and terrible shopping experiences. *Journal of Business Research, 58*(8), 1132–1145.

Bagdare, S., & Jain, R. (2013). Measuring retail customer experience. *International Journal of Retail and Distribution Management, 41*(10), 790–804.

Balaji, M. S., Roy, S. K., & Quazi, A. (2017). Customers' emotion regulation strategies in service failure encounters. *European Journal of Marketing, 51*(5/6), 960–982.

Banerjee, M. (2014). Misalignment and its influence on integration quality in multichannel services. *Journal of Service Research, 17*(4), 313–327.

Bastiaansen, M., Lub, X. D., Mitas, O., Jung, T. H., Ascenção, M. P., Han, D. I., & Strijbosch, W. (2019). Emotions as core building blocks of an experience. *International Journal of Contemporary Hospitality Management, 31*(2), 651–668.

Belk, R. (1984). A manifesto for a consumer behavior of consumer behavior. In P. F. Anderson & J. Michael (Eds.), *1984 AMA Winter Educators Conference: Scientific Method in Marketing* (pp. 163–167). Ryan Chicago: American Marketing Association.

Bilgihan, A., Khaldoon, N., Okumus, F., & Cabanoglu, C. (2015). Applying flow theory to booking experiences: An integrated model in an online service context. *Information & Management, 15*, 668–678.

Bolton, R. N., McColl-Kennedy, J. R., Cheung, L., Gallan, A., Orsinger, C., Witell, L., & Zaki, M. (2018). Customer experience challenges: Bringing together digital, physical and social realms. *Journal of Service Marketing, 29*(5), 776–808.

Booth, A., Papaioannou, D., & Sutton, A. (2012). *Systematic approaches to a successful literature review*. London: Sage.

Carlson, N. R., Heth, D. C., Miller, H., Donahoe, J. W., Buskist, W., & Martin, N. G. (2007). *Psychology: The science of behavior* (6th ed.). Boston: Pearson.

Carreira, R., Patricio, L., Jorge, R. N., Magee, C., & Hommes, Q. V. E. (2013). Towards a holistic approach to the travel experience: A qualitative study of bus transportation. *Transport Policy, 25*, 233–243.

Chahal, H., & Dutta, K. (2015). Measurement and impact of customer experience in banking sector. *Decision (0304-0941), 42*(1), 57–70.

Cruz, P., Salo, J., Munoz-Gallego, P., & Laukkanen, T. (2010). Heavy users of e-banking and customer experience management: Evidences on intrinsic motivation. *International Journal of Electronic Business, 8*(2), 187–209.

Echeverri, P., & Skålen, P. (2011). Co-creation and co-destruction: A practice theory based study of interactive value formation. *Marketing Theory, 11*(3), 351–373.

Fennell, G. (1985). Things of heaven and earth: Phenomenology, marketing, and consumer research. *ACR North American Advances, 12*, 544–550.

Frow, P., & Payne, A. (2007). Towards the 'perfect' customer experience. *Journal of Brand Management, 15*(2), 89–101.

Gabbott, M., Tsarenko, Y., & Mok, W. H. (2011). Emotional intelligence as a moderator of coping strategies and service outcomes in circumstances of service failure. *Journal of Service Research, 14*(2), 234–248.

Gefen, D., & Straub, D. (2003). Managing user trust in B2C e-services. *e-Service Journal, 2*(2), 7–24.

Gentile, C., Spiller, N., & Noci, G. (2007). How to sustain the customer experience: An overview of experience components that co-create value with the customer. *European Management Journal, 25*(5), 395–410.

Goleman, D. (1995). *Working with emotional intelligence*. New York: Bantam Books.

Grewal, D., Levy, M., & Kumar, V. (2009). Customer experience management in retailing: An organizing framework. *Journal of Retailing, 85*(1), 1–14.

Helkkula, A. (2011). Characterising the concept of service experience. *Journal of Service Management, 22*(3), 367–389.

Hoch, S. J. (2002). Product experience is seductive. *Journal of Consumer Research, 29*(3), 448–454.

Holbrook, M. B., & Hirschman, E. C. (1982). The experiential aspects of consumption: Consumer fantasies, feelings, and fun. *Journal of Consumer Research, 9*(2), 132–140.

Howard, J. A. (1965). *Marketing theory*. Boston: Allyn & Bacon.

Huang, M.-H. (2001). The theory of emotions in marketing. *Journal of Business and Psychology, 26*(2), 239–247.

Hudson, S., González-Gómez, H. V., & Rychalski, A. (2017). Call centers: Is there an upside to the dissatisfied customer experience? *Journal of Business Strategy, 38*(1), 39–46.

Jaakkola, E., Helkkula, A., & Aarikka-Stenroos, L. (2015). Service experience co-creation: Conceptualization, implications and future research directions. *Journal of Service Management, 26*(2), 283–305.

Jain, R., Aagja, J., & Bagdare, S. (2017). Customer experience—A review and research agenda. *Journal of Service Theory and Practice, 27*(3), 642–662.

Jalonen, H., Vuolle, M., & Heinonen, L. (2016). *Negatiiviset Tunteet – Positiivinen Bisnes [Negative emotions—Positive business]*. Talentum: Helsinki.

Johnson, M. D., Olsen, L. L., & Wallin, A. T. (2009). Joy and disappointment in the hotel experience: Managing relationship segments. *Managing Service Quality, 19*(1), 4–33.

Jüttner, U., Schaffner, D., Windler, K., & Maklan, S. (2013). Customer service experiences: Developing and applying a sequential incident laddering technique. *European Journal of Marketing, 47*(5/6), 738–769.

Kim, S., Park, G., Lee, Y., & Choi, S. (2016). Customer emotions and their triggers in luxury retail: Understanding the effects of customer emotions before and after entering a luxury shop. *Journal of Business Research, 69*, 5809–5818.K.

Krippendorff, K. (1980). *Validity in content analysis* (2nd ed.). Thousand Oaks: Sage.

Lazarus, R. S. (1991). Progress on a cognitive-motivational-relational theory of emotion. *American Psychologist, 46*(8), 819–834.

Lee, S. (2018). Investigating antecedents and outcome of telepresence on a hotel's website. *International Journal of Contemporary Hospitality Management, 30*(2), 757–775.

Lemon, K. N., & Verhoef, P. C. (2016). Understanding customer experience throughout the customer journey. *Journal of Marketing, 80*, 69–96.

Liu, W., Sparks, B., & Cighlan, A. (2017). Fun, inspiration and discovery: From momentary experiences to overall evaluations. *International Journal of Contemporary Hospitality Organizations, 29*(7), 1937–1955.

Lucia-Palacios, L., Pérez-López, R., & Polo-Redondo, Y. (2016). Cognitive, affective and behavioural responses in mall experience: A qualitative approach. *International Journal of Retail & Distribution Management, 44*(1), 4–21.

Madzharov, A. V., Block, L. G., & Morrin, M. (2015). The cool scent of power: Effects of ambient scent on consumer preferences and choice behavior. *Journal of Marketing, 79*(1), 83–96.

Martin, J., Mortimer, G., & Andrews, L. (2015). Re-examining online customer experience to include purchase frequency and perceived risk. *Journal of Consumer Marketing, 25*, 81–95.

Mascarenhas, O. A., Kesavan, R., & Bernacchi, M. (2006). Lasting customer loyalty: A total customer experience approach. *Journal of Consumer Marketing, 23*(7), 397–405.

Mattila, A., Hanks, L., & Wang, C. (2014). Others service experiences: Emotions, perceived justice, and behavior. *European Journal of Marketing, 48*(3/4), 552–571.

McColl-Kennedy, J. R., Danaher, T. S., Gallan, A. S., Orsingher, C., Lervik-Olsen, L., & Verma, R. (2017). How do you feel today? Managing patient emotions during health care experience to enhance well-being. *Journal of Business Research, 79*, 247–259.

Mehrabian, A., & Russell, J. A. (1974). *An approach to environmental psychology*. Cambridge, MA: The Massachusetts Institute of Technology.

Meyer, C., & Schwager, A. (2007). Understanding customer experience. *Harvard Business Review, 85*(2), 116–126.

Mollen, A., & Wilson, H. (2010). Engagement, telepresence and interactivity in online consumer experience: Reconciling scholastic and managerial perspectives. *Journal of Business Research, 63*(9), 919–925.

Morgan-Thomas, A., & Veloutsou, C. (2013). Engagement, telepresence and interactivity in online consumer experience: Reconciling scholastic and managerial perspectives. *Journal of Business Research, 63*(9–10), 919–925.

Novak, T. P., Hoffman, D. L., & Yung, Y. (2000). Measuring the customer experience in online environments: A structural modeling approach. *Marketing Science, 19*(1), 22–42.

Pine, B. J., & Gilmore, J. H. (1998). The experience economy. *Harvard Business Review, 76*(6), 18–23.

Puccinelli, N. M., Goodstein, R. C., Grewail, D., Price, R., Raghubir, P., & Stewart, D. (2009). Customer experience management in retailing: Understanding the buying process. *Journal of Retailing, 85*(1), 15–30.

Rajaobelina, L. (2018). The impact of customer experience on relationship quality with travel agencies in a multichannel environment. *Journal of Travel Research, 57*(2), 206–217.

Rose, S., Clark, M., Samouel, P., & Hair, N. (2012). Online customer experience in e-retailing: An empirical model of antecedents and outcomes. *Journal of Retailing, 88*(2), 308–322.

Sachdeva, I., & Goel, S. (2015). Retail store environment and customer experience: A paradigm. *Journal of Fashion Marketing and Management, 19*(3), 290–298.

Scherer, K. R. (2005). What are emotions? And how they can be measured? *Social Science Information, 44*(4), 695–729.

Schmitt, B. H. (1999). *Experiential marketing: How to get customers to sense, feel, think, act, relate to your company and brands*. New York: The Free Press.

Surachartkumtonkun, J., McColl-Kennedy, J. R., & Patterson, P. G. (2015). Unpacking customer rage elicitation: A dynamic model. *Journal of Service Research, 18*(2), 177–192.

Teixeira, J., Patrício, L., Nunes, N. J., Nóbrega, L., Fisk, R. P., & Constantine, L. (2012). Customer experience modeling: From customer experience to service design. *Journal of Service Management, 23*(3), 362–376.

Torraco, R. J. (2005). Writing integrative literature reviews: Guidelines and examples. *Human Resource Development Review, 4*(3), 356–367.

Tu, J., & Zhang, M. (2013), *Research on the effect of co-creation customer experience on customer co-created value in non-trading virtual community*. Paper presented at IEEE International Conference on Service Operations and Logistics and Informatics (SOLI).

Vargo, S. L., & Lusch, R. (2004). Evolving to a new dominant logic. *Journal of Marketing, 68*(1), 1–17.

Vargo, S. L., & Lusch, R. (2008). Service-dominant logic: Continuing the evolution. *Journal of the Academy of Marketing Science, 36*(1), 1–10.

Vargo, S. L., & Lusch, R. F. (2016). Institutions and axioms: An extension and update of service-dominant logic. *Journal of the Academy of Marketing Science, 44*, 5–12.

Varma, R. T. R. (2012). Enhancing and empowering: Customer experience. *SCMS Journal of Indian Management, 9*(3), 71–78.

Verhoef, P. C., Lemon, N., Parasuraman, A., Roggeveen, A., Tsiros, M., & Schlesinger, L. A. (2009). Customer experience creation: Determinants, dynamics, and management strategies. *Journal of Retailing, 85*(1), 31–41.

Wang, L. C., Baker, J., Wagner, J. A., & Wakefield, K. (2007). Can a retail website be social? *Journal of Marketing, 71*(3), 143–157.

Weber, R. P. (1985). *Basic content analysis*. Beverly Hills: Sage Publications.

Zomerdijk, L. G., & Voss, C. A. (2011). NSD processes and practices in experiential services. *Journal of Product Innovation Management, 28*(1), 63–80.

Chapter 13
Sensory Technologies for Improving Employee Experience and Strengthening Customer Relationships

Jari Jussila, Virpi Sillanpää, Mika Boedeker, and Nina Helander

Abstract Emotions are always present when we talk about human interaction and relationships. In this chapter the focus is on studying the role of emotions in employee–customer interaction through theoretical discussion and two practical case examples. Particular focus is on modern sensory technologies, which can be used especially in measuring emotional states in such situations, where emotions are in other ways hard to express and identify. In this chapter, we argue that in the process of turning negative emotions to positive outcomes, the key is to understand the role that different relationships play in value co-creation. Manager–subordinate and employee–employee relationships have the most impact on well-being inside workplace, but especially for those employees that are involved in customer interface, the customer interaction and relationship has a direct impact on job satisfaction. Naturally this applies also vice versa; job satisfaction has direct impact on the customer experience and satisfaction. Without measurement of emotional states of employees and customers, it can be difficult to determine, which relationships and situations cause most stress and negative emotions in the workplace and within the customer interaction. Thus, emotions are in a key role in understanding and developing relationships.

J. Jussila (✉)
Häme University of Applied Sciences, Hämeenlinna, Finland
e-mail: jari.jussila@hamk.fi

V. Sillanpää · N. Helander
Tampere University, Tampere, Finland
e-mail: virpi.sillanpaa@tuni.fi; nina.helander@tuni.fi

M. Boedeker
Tampere University of Applied Sciences, Tampere, Finland
e-mail: mika.boedeker@tuni.fi

H. Lehtimäki et al. (eds.), *Society as an Interaction Space*, Translational Systems Sciences 22, https://doi.org/10.1007/978-981-15-0069-5_13

13.1 Introduction

Employee satisfaction has been shown to be linked to business performance, company profitability, (Harter et al. 2002) and through better customer service (Chi and Gursoy 2009; Yee et al. 2008) to increased customer engagement and more loyal customer relationships (Berry and Carbone 2007). The organization should be aware of the employees' emotions, thoughts, and aspirations so that their dedication and commitment to work and to the organization can be strengthened (Naseem et al. 2011). Furthermore, it's been said that happy employees make happy customers. This phrase might already be a cliché, but it is nevertheless true, as the customer can clearly feel the effects. If a customer service rep, for example, gets off on the wrong foot, and the workplace atmosphere fails to support him in finding positivity, his customer will probably receive service that is inhospitable and strained. The customer will then go on with the day after the service feeling a little sad or confused, or a little irritated, or perhaps even furious. Emotions are therefore reflected and contagious, and the employee in customer service work has a golden opportunity to make the customer's emotional state more positive than it was when the service situation arose.

Emotions are awoken especially in these kinds of social interactions within the service process. Thus, it is not surprising that, e.g., in the latest servicescape studies the focus has shifted from the effect of the physical environment of the service process towards the social interaction between employees and customers, but also between different customers (Kraak and Holmqvist 2016; Carù and Cova 2015). Furthermore, the role of the emotions in building long-lasting customer relationships has already been acknowledged for a long time (DeWitt et al. 2008).

Ultimately, the employee has quite big shoes to fill in the responsibility of what kind of customer experience the organization can create. It is no wonder, then, that particularly in the service sector, employee satisfaction has been shown to have a direct link to customer satisfaction, which in turn affects the results of the organization (Yee et al. 2008). Job satisfaction has been found to have a direct impact on customer satisfaction and an indirect impact on the financial performance of the organization (Chi and Gursoy 2009; Naseem et al. 2011). Especially in services involving close interaction between the customer and the staff, job satisfaction has been found to have a significant impact on service quality and customer satisfaction as well as on the company's profitability (Yee et al. 2008). On the other hand, customer satisfaction also contributes to job satisfaction. Service professions continuously involve interactions with customers and successes or failures in these situations directly affect customer satisfaction and staff satisfaction. In the worst-case scenario, unsuccessful customer encounters can create vicious circles that can spread negative outcomes more widely to the organization's employees and customers (Groth and Grandey 2012; Masuch 1985). Job satisfaction not only affects work productivity but also the quality of work.

Job satisfaction and, in particular, well-being at work are broad concepts that consist of individual, job, organization, and group, as well as factors relating to the managers and employee's superiors (Manka et al. 2007). However, well-being at work is said to be ultimately built on emotions, and the person in the business operations is the only one that "feels" (Juuti and Salmi 2014). As emotions play such a key role in well-being at work and in the employee experience, and through them in the customer's experience, and even in the success of the entire organization, it is appropriate to be closely familiarized with emotions. In this article, special attention is paid to technologies that have strongly developed in recent years for the measuring and reporting of emotional states. The focus of the review is on measurement of emotions using different technologies that (1) measure human physiological functions directly, (2) measure emotions indirectly by analyzing human external behavior (e.g., facial expressions, speech), or (3) measure emotions subjectively by utilizing various applications that allow people to self-report their own emotions. Beyond this article, emotions can be measured also by making use of secondary emotional data that people themselves produce, for example, in the form of text or images in various information systems and networks, such as expressions of emotions in social media.

Following the introduction, this article discusses the concept of emotion and presents many ways of understanding emotions. This is followed by a review of the literature surrounding sensory technologies and emotion measurement. The review of the literature is not meant to be all-encompassing, but rather to create a picture of the commonly used sensory technologies and their measurement principles. After the review, practical examples of the application of sensory technologies in the development of the customer and employee experience in Finland are presented. Finally, the importance of emotions and the potential role of sensory technologies for developing job satisfaction and customer relationships is discussed.

13.2 The Many Forms of Understanding Emotions

Emotion, feeling, mood, etc.; non-emotional affective qualities, emotional state, etc.; primary emotion, secondary emotion, tertiary emotion, etc.; superordinate level, basic level, subordinate level, etc.; valence, arousal, activation, dominance, control, potency, etc.; emotional circumplex, emotional wheel, emotion family, etc.; and basic emotions, categories, dimensions, etc. A beloved child has many names, and a loving phenomenon is described, explained, and attempted to be understood in many ways. Counting the number of definitions of emotion is hopeless, and there is no answer to the question of the number of emotions (Scherer 2005, 707). However, as an umbrella concept, we may consider the effect (Bagozzi et al. 1999, 184; Kokkonen 2010, 14), and in everyday language, we often talk only about "emotions" when we refer to different affective experiences. This article is not so much problematizing or examining what emotions are, per se; therefore as generally the everyday term "emotion" is used to refer to the different affective experiences here.

In the first place, the studying and understanding of emotions is challenging because the concept is really very complex. The second challenge is how emotions can and should be measured; how and where do emotions manifest and appear? Sometimes it is also worth considering are we studying emotions or the terms or expressions that describe them (see, e.g., Tuovila 2005). If one measures a person's behavioral change or physiological reaction (e.g., facial expressions, change in the electrical conductivity of the skin, or heart rate interval), the result is not up to the person to remember or be able to describe. But, on the other hand, if we want to know what a person is subjectively feeling, it should be asked in one way or another (Feldmann Barret 2004, 281; Scherer 2005, 712). And while these descriptions of a person's self-reporting reflect what he or she feels, those emotions mentioned by the person cannot always be considered as separate emotions per se, as individuals use the same terms in different ways to describe their emotions. In addition, some are able to distinguish and describe their experiences very accurately, while others are only capable in more general terms (Feldmann Barret 2004, 267; Scherer 2005, 712). And even though, for example, the so-called basic emotions, such as joy, anger, sadness, and fear, are often perceived as biological and universal (e.g., Kokkonen and Pulkkinen 1996, 406), the culture also affects what these and other emotions bring forth, how they are interpreted and shown, and how they are discussed (e.g., Kokkonen 2010, 13–14; Tuovila 2005).

Roughly speaking, emotions can be conceptualized either as special, discrete emotions, or then usually with the help of two or three dimensions. Discrete emotions are often presented as different lists (like many lists of basic emotions) or hierarchies (Makkonen et al. 2019). For example, Laros and Steenkamp (2005) use 16 different basic emotion lists in their research to form a three-tier hierarchy, in which in the superordinate level emotions are divided into positive and negative experiences, while the basic level has 8 emotions (anger, fear, sadness, shame, contentment, happiness, love, pride) and the subordinate level up to 41 special emotions. A similar type of division can be found, for example, in an article from Shaver et al. (1987) about prototypical emotions and hierarchies.

In dimensional terms, two-dimensional examinations generally give birth to a variety of four- or multi-fields or emotion circles and wheels. Usually, the dimensions are pleasure/valence and arousal (e.g., Seo et al. 2008) or valence and control (e.g., Scherer et al. 2013). Dimensions and their number are not unanimous and, among others, Mehrabian et al. (1997) use three dimensions (pleasure, arousal, dominance) to define "emotional space." In a dimension-based presentation, emotions can be conveniently captured with a limited number of dimensions. On the other hand, the dimensions are rather abstract, and the language used does not always correspond with how people would describe the experiences in their normal way of speaking (Sacharin et al. 2012, 4). A discrete way of presenting provides more accurate information than mere dimensions, as specific terms describing emotions and the categorical or hierarchical relationships between them can also be taken into account. As a hybrid case, we can use the example of Jussila et al. (2018a, b, c), in which specific emotion terms are combined with the three dimensions (pleasure, arousal, dominance) resulting in eight emotion families.

Thus, there are many challenges in understanding emotions and studies, as well as discussion, about the essence and measurement of emotions are continuous. In any case, it is important to know the basics, possibilities, and constraints of each perspective and way of measuring so that one can correctly interpret the results.

13.3 Satisfied and Engaged Employees Can Create Positive Emotions in Customer

Well-being at work can be described as affective/emotional-dimensional, relatively (Fig. 13.1). According to the model of affective well-being at work (Warr 1990), the central dimensions of well-being at work are pleasure and arousal, to which additionally other dimensions of well-being at work are anxiety/contentment as well as depression/enthusiasm. The pattern is elliptical in shape, because pleasure has been found to have greater weighting than arousal. The pleasure dimension is seen to be particularly relevant to job satisfaction.

As can be seen from the picture, work fatigue has a minimal association with arousal and pleasure. Low pleasure but high arousal characterizes stress, the developing of work fatigue and, for example, workaholism, which better describes the work attitude and way of doing things rather than well-being. Relaxation and enjoyment at work include pleasure but little arousal. Work satisfaction can be thought to belong to the right side in the area of the pleasure axis and just above that is the joy of work (Hakanen 2004).

Lately there has been a lot of talk about the engagement of work as a desired state. This work engagement refers to a positive emotional state, characterized by the terms "energy," "dedication," and "immersion." Unlike flow, engagement is not a momentary peak experience, but a more permanent, widespread state that is

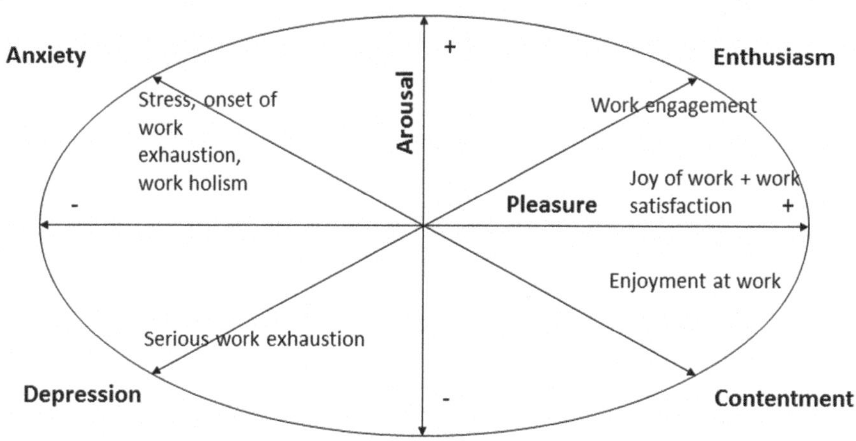

Fig. 13.1 Dimensions of well-being at work. (Hakanen 2004; applied from Warr 1990)

not confined to a particular situation or task. In everyday life, the engagement of work is reflected in the employee's willingness to go to work, to make the work meaningful and enjoy it, to be proud of the work, and to persevere in it when faced with adversity. An engaged worker is a producer and an achiever. The engaged work is located at the top right of the picture and describes positive, pleasure-filled excitement and enthusiasm. It should be noted that the engagement of work does not mean that the work has a "pulling" property, but rather a genuinely positive state of well-being. To experience work that is engaging is important because of the positive satisfaction it produces. Work is also important for workaholics, but they don't enjoy it (Hakanen 2009). Thus, there are differences in the emotional state of the engaged worker and of the workaholic, and it is important to recognize the differences in these emotional states in order to support well-being at work. Measuring emotional states with new technologies and self-assessment methods can help take steps forward on the complicated path of well-being at work. Moreover, measuring emotional states is the first step that can help companies understand both employee and customer experience and develop means to break the vicious circle of negative emotions and steer towards an increasing returns virtuous circle. Based on systems theory approach (Senge 1991; Garud and Kumaraswamy 2005), the role of emotion measurement can be illustrated to impact the process of turning negative emotions and in the one extreme vicious circle of negative emotions towards positive outcomes and ideally an increasing returns virtuous cycle (Fig. 13.2).

In the process of turning negative emotions to positive outcomes, the key is to understand the role that different relationships play in value co-creation. Manager–subordinate and employee–employee relationships have the most impact on well-being inside workplace, but especially for those employees that are involved in customer interface, the customer relationship has a direct impact on job satisfaction. Without measurement of emotional states of employees and customers, it can be difficult to determine which relationships and situations cause most stress and negative emotions at the workplace.

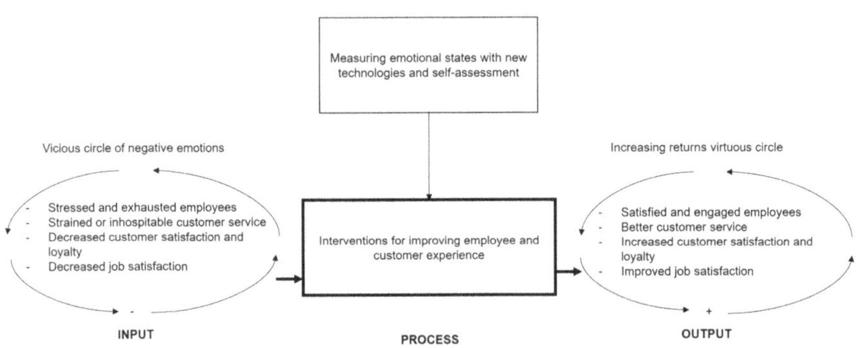

Fig. 13.2 Proposed process of turning negative emotions to positive outcomes

13.4 Sensory Technologies and Measurement of Emotions

There are many types of emotion technologies. Roughly, sensory technologies can be divided into two categories: laboratory-level sensory technologies and field-level sensory technologies. Laboratory-level sensory technologies are scientifically validated measuring instruments that perform measurements in laboratories. The upside of laboratory-level emotion technologies is their accuracy, but the downside is their inadequacy for measurements under authentic conditions in which employees do their work. As an example of this, we can mention electroencephalography (EEG), in which loose electrodes or an electrode cap (Martikainen and Mäkinen 2018) is placed on the head being studied, and with which the movement and the performance of typical work tasks are thereby very limited. Also, appearance reasons may exclude the use of laboratory-level emotion technologies, for example, in customer service. Field-level emotion technologies can be used in the field as their name suggests, allowing measurements under authentic conditions and, as a rule, do not interfere with ability to perform work. Examples of such technologies include various smart bracelets and smart watches (Picard et al. 2017) as well as smart rings (Jussila et al. 2018a, b, c). There are, of course, situations and working conditions that are also unsuitable for field-level sensory technologies. For example, in the manufacture and handling of food, rings, jewelry, and watches can pose a food hygiene risk and must be taken out during the work shift. In general, however, field-level emotion technologies are more convenient to use and typically do not require specific work arrangements or actions from the user side. The disadvantage of the field-level emotion technologies is their lower accuracy. Some of the field-level emotional technologies are so inaccurate that they are not suitable for scientific research at all, but rather produce mainly indicative information about the phenomena being measured.

More subtle emotion technologies can be divided according to the measurement method (e.g., Mauss and Robinson 2009). More generally, emotions are measured based on central nervous system (CNS), autonomic nervous system (ANS), human behavior, or self-reporting (Fig. 13.3).

In the market, there are several emotion technologies based on wearable electronics which can measure the emotions from physiological signals. The most

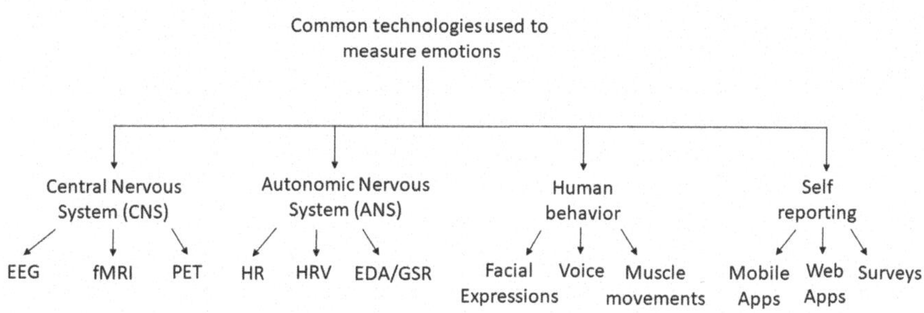

Fig. 13.3 The most common technologies used to measure emotions

common ways to measure the physiological responses of emotions are measured through the skin conductance response (electrodermal activity, EDA, or galvanic skin response, GSR) and the measurement of blood circulation (Mauss and Robinson 2009), which provide information on the functioning of the autonomic nervous system (Martikainen and Mäkinen 2018). Blood circulation is measured by electrocardiography (Martikainen and Mäkinen 2018), which is represented by, among other things, heart rate (HR) and heart rate variability (HRV) measurements (Mauss and Robinson 2009). Based on a meta-analysis (Cacioppo et al. 2000), a single autonomous nervous system activity indicator (EDA, HR, HRV) can mainly be used to obtain information about arousal level instead of a single discrete emotion. On the other hand, there are also studies (Stemmler 2004; Kreibig et al. 2007; Cacioppo et al. 2000), which have found that it is possible to obtain more detailed results by combining several indicators of autonomic nervous system activity and can separate, for example, discrete emotions of sadness and fear with a measurable 85% accuracy (Kreibig et al. 2007).

Laboratory-level emotion technologies that can measure the emotions of autonomic nervous system activity, especially arousal, include the Shimmer GSR (Galvanic skin response) measuring instrument (Burns et al. 2010) and the BIOPAC Systems ECG (Electrocardiogram) electrodes (Wei et al. 2018). Examples of field-level emotion technologies that can be used to measure autonomic nervous system activity are the Moodmetric smart ring (Torniainen et al. 2015), which measures the skin conductance response, Firstbeat (Parak and Korhonen 2013) measuring heart rate variability, and the CardioMood (Okkonen et al. 2017) Android application to measure and analyze heart rate variability with the help of various sensors.

13.4.1 Practical Example 1: Sensory Technology in Developing the Customer and Worker Experience

In May 2018, Rinnekoti and Sailer Research and Development Ltd. launched a pilot study which combined the digital measurement of emotion and stress levels into videographic qualitative research. The goal of the research was to better understand the customer's emotions and, through this, create a better customer understanding. With the help of the study, the desire was to improve both the quality of life of customers and the well-being of the staff.

The study combined a new way of videographic research and technology: The emotion and stress states of Rinnekoti's instructors and clients who participated in the study were followed with the help of a Moodmetric ring. By combining ring information with staff journal entries and video material, one obtained information and understanding of customers who were otherwise unable to express emotions due to illness or disability. By monitoring emotions and stress conditions, customers were able to get their voices heard and thus affect everyday issues. The follow-up also provided assurance on such issues for which the importance or agreeability to customers had previously been based on what it "just feels like." One of Rinnekoti's instructors explains: "I feel that with the help of the ring, I can read a lot more about the customer." "The expressions, gestures, and sounds tell a lot, but with it, you get confirmation of what you feel and what you want to do."

The second part of the study focused on measuring the recovery and stress levels of nursing staff at work and during leisure time. Through the use of sensory technology, employees learn more about themselves, stressful situations, and recovery. For those who work in guidance and nursing, the recovery during sleep was very much based on the individual. A particularly busy working day, for example, could correspond that night with a restless sleep.

Emotion measurement provided meaningful information from the point of view of well-being at work; for example, the stress levels were not necessarily as high as the worker had thought, and the recovery from work was quite fast. For some people, the measurement strengthened the view that work and home affairs remain separate, and therefore the work matters were not stressing at home or vice versa. The results can be used to improve well-being at work and in the work organization. The customer's right to self-determination is emphasized in Rinnekoti's operations. Increasing knowledge of the customers will help employees work according to their customers' wishes and thus work according to the employee's and the organization's goals, which contributes to coping with work. One employee gave this view of the benefits of the research towards their own work: "It feels more demanding in the communication at work. I would like to know what the customer thinks about certain matters. The communication could become smoother. The research makes it easy to get more information about customers, which we may not have otherwise detected or noticed."

The research results are used at Rinnekoti as part of the development of the workplace well-being and in the customer work. The results of the clients participating in the research are valuable because there was an increase in the information about their individual needs. The results also help supervisors to also learn to pay attention to how well the timing of the assistance and guidance situations suits the individual needs of the customers. For example, at meal times it has been possible to make customer-focused concrete changes to make them more appealing for the customer.

The research also highlighted the need for staff to have a sufficient grip on methods for augmentative and alternative communication, and because of this, training has increased for the staff. A large number of different technological aids were provided for the use by the units' staff and customers to support communication and to enhance pleasant multisensory sensory experiences.

The study found that the noise level of some facilities affected both customers and employees. New solutions were sought for the acoustics in the facilities and acquired were, among others, hearing protectors to reduce the noise levels.

The results of the research will also be utilized as part of the development of other facets in personnel well-being. "Good workday!" and "Safe workday!" promotions are taking place at Rinnekoti to further facilitate employee well-being. According to research results, the ability to recover during sleep is a very individual matter. After the research, staff members were offered the opportunity to receive online training for a well-being service in which they were given, among others, instructions and exercises for recovery. A healthy pillow was given by the employer as a Christmas present as a continuation of the well-being theme. At the same time, emotion research took place with a number of other development measures. As a combined effect of all these development activities, the sick leave of Rinnekoti's personnel decreased from 2017 to 2018 by a total of 15%.

– *Hannu Uotila, CEO, Sailer Research & Development Ltd*
– *Anu Kallio, CEO, Rinnekoti*

Sensory technologies, which measure the functioning of the central nervous system, more generally the brain function, are basically laboratory-level devices. Emotional physiological responses can be measured from the brain, for example, by electroencephalography (EEG) and by neuroimaging (Mauss and Robinson 2009). EEG measurements illustrate where brain activation occurs approximately with different emotions (Mauss and Robinson 2009; Martikainen and Mäkinen 2018). For example, the emotion of anger is connected to greater activation on the anterior part of the left side of the brain (Harmon-Jones and Allen 1998) and the sense of anxiety with activation of the frontal lobe of the left side (Heller et al. 2002). Neurographic imaging methods, as well as functional magnetic resonance imaging (fMRI) and positron emission tomography (PET), can be used to identify more precisely which brain areas are active in certain emotions as compared to electroencephalogram measurements (Mauss and Robinson 2009; Martikainen and Mäkinen 2018). For example, it has been found that there is a connection between fear and activation of the amygdala. Recently, consumer-oriented EEG devices have also been developed, such as Emotiv's and Muse's brain helmets (e.g., López-Gil et al. 2016), which can also be used, with certain reservations, in field conditions (e.g., indoors or outside in good weather conditions).

Emotions can also be measured by human behavior. Bodily expressions, such as facial expressions and muscle movements, tell about people's emotional experiences (Martikainen and Mäkinen 2018). Facial expressions can be measured by, for example, electromyograph (EMG). Electromyographs measure the electrical potential of the muscles attached to the face, the most common of which are the measurement of the corrugator supercilii associated with the eyebrows and the zygomatic muscle associated with the raising of the corner of the mouth (Martikainen and Mäkinen 2018). Electromyography is suitable for measuring emotions with respect to the pleasure dimension, whereby the activity of the muscles associated with the elevation of the corners of the mouth increases as the pleasure increases, and the activity of the muscles associated with the eyebrows decreases as the pleasure grows (Cacioppo et al. 2000). To recognize emotions from facial expressions, machine-based vision applications have also been built in which an external device, such as a cell phone camera or camcorder, depicts an object and tries to identify the person's emotion from the image using an algorithm. An example of a machine-based vision application is a mobile application available for Android devices that can recognize six different basic emotional states in real time from video images of people with

86% accuracy (Suk and Prahakaran 2014), Emotient technology capable of simultaneously recognizing multi-person emotion from video (Movellan et al. 2014; Winkler et al. 2016) and a method for identifying micro-expressions (Li et al. 2018) which can be used to identify emotions that a person did not mean to display from a video image.

As part of human use, emotions can also be measured in terms of arousal dimension by measuring the use of voice. Speeches have shown that, for example, during elevated emotions, such as fear and anger, the human pitch is higher than those of lesser-elevated emotions, such as grief (Martikainen and Mäkinen 2018; Feidakis et al. 2011) and also tempo and rhythm, intonation, vibration, key change, and volume have been reported to signal emotional changes (Feidakis et al. 2011). For example, using the Moodies mobile application, it is possible to record sound, and based on a 20-s sample, the application reports a discrete emotion recognized by the algorithm (Marchi et al. 2016).

In addition to the above-mentioned objective emotion sensors, various self-reporting applications have been developed to enable individuals to report their own emotions. These include, for example, various surveys, web applications, and mobile applications. Commonly used surveys to identify employee experience with stress, workload, and well-being at work include Labor Stress Questionnaire (Elo et al. 1990), Better Work Community ParTy Survey (Multanen et al. 2004), and Maslach's general work fatigue evaluation method MBI-GS (Kalimo et al. 2006). Web applications that can be used to self-report emotions include Emotion Tracker, an application for discrete emotional reporting (Kuivanen 2017), the NayDaya web application for storing emotions generated by digital objects, the Vibemetrics emotion meter (Pitkänen 2018), and a VibeVision tool for measuring customer, personnel, and event experience.

13.4.2 *Practical Example 2: Emotions at the Heart of Measuring the Employee Experience*

VibeVision® is a tool for measuring and analyzing emotional experience developed in a university collaboration. The tool is used either as a continuous measure of employee experience or as individual measurement periods, such as, for example, during periods of change. The meter is based on the PAD framework (Mehrabian et al. 1997), according to which emotions can be described by three dimensions—Pleasure, Arousal, and Dominance. The meter therefore takes into account the range of emotions broader than the traditional positive-negative way of thinking. For example, embarrassment and irritability guide us to behave as employees or customers in very different ways, although both emotions are seen as negative.

The most effective way to measure emotional experience and, above all, the reasons behind emotional experience, is to ask about it from the staff or from the customers themselves. The aim of VibeVision® is not to study a person's deepest emotion, but rather the strongest emotions that come from a certain experience and the reasons for those, as well as a few questions related to the business.

In this way, we learn to understand our experience deeper than before and develop our experience in a business-oriented and goal-oriented way. We can also set aims for our emotions. The goal may be, for example, that under a change in strategy, less than 5% of the employees feel fear, or even that the working weeks would start with 80% of the staff in an enthusiastic state of mind.

VibeVision® provides deeper insight into the customer experience, but also more common business metrics such as NPS, Customer Effort Score, or grouping questions. On the staff side, one can monitor employee load and recovery, the meaningfulness of work tasks, attitudes to change, or the impact of training programs on the staff's emotions. At the same time, you will also learn about the influence of emotions on these factors—which emotions predict successful customer meetings or which emotions correlate with a high overtime workload.

Making the results and emotional atmosphere visible is essential. It is important to point out why an organization has a certain emotional atmosphere and what can be done for this or done at its best. The every Monday morning irritation is not always related to work or the organization. Irritation can be caused by very simple things, such as constant traffic or stress can cause very personal issues. However, these things, which are independent of the work, affect our work performance, and therefore the identification of these issues is also important. Is it possible to make it easier for staff in the Monday morning traffic to stagger the work time flexibility or by the work organization giving more support for employees to handle personal life situations? To simplify, by measuring, one also learns what negative emotions stem from—a poor leadership culture or a constantly temperamental copy machine.

Identifying emotions as part of the experience, whether it be employee or customer experience, gives a business not only a competitive advantage, but also helps to identify the risks hidden in the experience. Only through consciousness of emotions can experiences lead to genuine leadership and development of customer relationships.

13.4.3 Julia Flovén, CEO, VibeVision Oy

Mobile applications for reporting emotions include Emotion Gauge (Andersson et al. 2017) for the reporting of emotional states with respect to the dimensions of pleasure, arousal, and dominance, the Moodmetric App (Jussila et al. 2018a, b, c) in which the value of the arousal dimension is based on the measurement of the electrical conductivity of the skin and to which the person can complete his assessment in the pleasure dimension and more accurately record the emotional experience as a journal entry, as well as the Emotion App (Jussila et al. 2018a, b, c) Android application, which allows the user to report the emotion by selecting one of the eight emotional senses according to the emotion family and by giving a free-form explanation.

13.5 Conclusion

Sensory technologies have brought new possibilities for developing both the employee and customer experience, as they provide means to react to affections and, in turn, strengthen emotional linkages and the customer relationship. Sensory technologies, for example, are the only way to identify the emotions of those who cannot express them. In this way, we get better information than the "just feels like" descriptions to find out how people experience different situations, such as what things are felt as comfortable and uncomfortable. Rinnekoti's practical example illustrates how **increasing customer knowledge helps employees work according to their customers' wishes, and so act according to the employee's and the organization's goals,** which contributes to coping well at work. As also shown in the VibeVision practical example, **only by knowing emotions can experience lead genuinely towards leadership and development of customer relationships.**

Objective information on employee experiences through sensory technologies can be used to complement subjective experiences and views on working conditions and well-being at work. For example, studies of well-being at work have shown contradictory results between experienced and objectively measured stress (Oldehinkel et al. 2011). For example, some people underestimate their workload and overestimate their own coping, which in a long-term workload situation may lead to work fatigue and prolonged loss of work capacity. **In addition to making use of well-being surveys and subjective experiences described by the employee, objective sensors could recognize such situations in time and react before negative consequences happen to the person and the organization.**

Emotions have a different meaning depending on the value system of the organization and its management. For example, in the industrial value system which emphasizes efficiency and performance, the importance of emotions may also be neglected, and an effort is made to squeeze out as many resources as possible from the workers. However, the loss of employee and customer emotions can lead to significant problems and business consequences. On the other hand, it is also recognized in the industry's value system that value cannot be obtained or captured if the employees are unproductive, ineffective, or without motivation (Boltanski and Thévenot 2006). In organizations that, in turn, incorporate a value system based on reputation building and maintenance, emotions are seen to play a more central role—and it is understood that reputation and trust can also be easily lost if they do not appreciate the emotions and opinions of their own employees and customers. Furthermore, in the process of turning negative emotions to positive outcomes, the key is to understand the role that different relationships play in value co-creation. Manager–subordinate and employee–employee relationships have the most impact on well-being inside workplace, but especially for those employees that are involved in customer interface, the customer relationship has a direct impact on job satisfaction. Naturally this applies also vice versa; the job satisfaction has direct impact on the customer experience and satisfaction. Without measurement of emotional states of employees and customers, it can be difficult to determine, which relationships and situations cause most stress and negative emotions in the workplace and within the customer interaction. However, in terms of measuring emotions, it is good to realize that, in addition to technologies, it is important for organizations to evaluate and discuss their own value system and their most precious stakeholder relationships that should be nurtured. There is definitely demand for research that links emotions and relationships and applies both the soft side of social science research and modern sensory technologies for the best of both employee and customer experience development.

References

Andersson, T., Boedeker, M., & Vuori, V. (2017) Emotion-gauge: Analyzing affective experiences in B2B customer journeys. In T.A. Kavoura, D.P. Sakas, & P. Tomaras (Eds.), *Strategic Innovative Marketing: 5th IC-SIM*, Athens, Greece, September, 23–26.

Bagozzi, R., Gopinath, M., & Nyer, P. (1999). The role of emotions in marketing. *Journal of the Academy of Marketing Science, 27*(2), 184–206.

Berry, L. L., & Carbone, L. P. (2007). Build loyalty through experience management. *Quality Progress, 40*(9), 26.

Boltanski, L., & Thévenot, L. (2006). *On justification: Economies of worth.* Princeton, NJ: Princeton University Press.

Burns, A., Greene, B. R., McGrath, M. J., O'Shea, T. J., Kuris, B., Ayer, S. M., Stroiescu, F., & Cionca, V. (2010). SHIMMER™—A wireless sensor platform for noninvasive biomedical research. *IEEE Sensors Journal, 10*(9), 1527–1534.

Cacioppo, J. T., Berntson, G. G., Larsen, J. T., Poehlmann, K. M., & Ito, T. A. (2000). The psychophysiology of emotion. In M. Lewis, J. M. Haviland-Jones, & L. Feldman Barret (Eds.), *The handbook of emotion*. New York: Guildford Press.

Carù, A., & Cova, B. (2015). Co-creating the collective service experience. *Journal of Service Management, 26*(2), 276–294.

Chi, C. G., & Gursoy, D. (2009). Employee satisfaction, customer satisfaction, and financial performance: An empirical examination. *International Journal of Hospitality Management, 28*(2008), 245–253.

DeWitt, T., Nguyen, D. T., & Marshall, R. (2008). Exploring customer loyalty following service recovery: The mediating effects of trust and emotions. *Journal of Service Research, 10*(3), 269–281.

Elo, A.-L., Leppänen, A., Lindström, K., & Ropponen, T. (1990). *TSK Miten käytät työstressikyselyä.* Helsinki: Työterveyslaitos.

Feidakis, M., Daradoumis, T., & Caballé, S. (2011) Emotion measurement in intelligent tutoring systems: What, when and how to measure. In *2011 Third International Conference on Intelligent Networking and Collaborative Systems* (pp. 807–812). IEEE.

Feldman Barrett, L. (2004). Feelings or words? Understanding the content in self-report ratings of experienced emotion. *Journal of Personality and Social Psychology, 87*(2), 266–281.

Garud, R., & Kumaraswamy, A. (2005). Vicious and virtuous circles in the management of knowledge: The case of Infosys Technologies. *MIS Quarterly, 29*(1), 9–33.

Groth, M., & Grandey, A. (2012). From bad to worse: Negative exchange spirals in employee–customer service interactions. *Organizational Psychology Review, 2*(3), 208–233.

Hakanen, J. (2004). *Työuupumuksesta työn imuun: työhyvinvointitutkimuksen ytimessä ja reuna-alueilla, Työ ja ihminen tutkimusraportti 27*. Helsinki: Työterveyslaitos.

Hakanen, J. (2009). *Työn imun arviointimenetelmä.* Helsinki: Työterveyslaitos.

Harmon-Jones, E., & Allen, J. J. B. (1998). Anger and frontal brain activity: EEG asymmetry consistent with approach motivation despite negative affective valence. *Journal of Personality and Social Psychology, 74*(5), 13101316.

Harter, J. K., Schmidt, F. L., & Hayes, T. L. (2002). Business-unit-level relationship between employee satisfaction, employee engagement, and business outcomes: A meta-analysis. *Journal of Applied Psychology, 87*(2), 268.

Heller, W., Schmidtke, J. I., Nitschke, J. B., Koven, N. S., & Miller, G. A. (2002). States, traits, and symptoms: Investigating the neural correlates of emotion, personality, and psychopathology. In D. Cervone & W. Mischel (Eds.), *Advances in personality science* (pp. 106–126). New York: Guilford Press.

Jussila, J., Boedeker, M., Helander, N., & Vuori, V. (2018a). Tunnetilojen tunnistaminen Twitteristä. In T. P. Isotalus, J. Jussila, & J. Janne Matikainen (Eds.), *Twitter viestintänä: Ilmiöt ja verkostot* (pp. 256–275). Tampere: Vastapaino.

Jussila, J., Venho, N., Salonius, H., Moilanen, J., Liukkonen, J., & Rinnetmäki, M. (2018b, October). Towards ecosystem for research and development of electrodermal activity applications. In *Proceedings of the 22nd International Academic Mindtrek Conference* (pp. 79–87). ACM.

Jussila, J., Sillanpää, V., Helander, N., Vuori, V., Boedeker, M., Liukkonen, J., Suoja, K., Felicetti, A., & Raso, C. (2018c, January). Design of mobile application for self-reporting affective experiences. In *Proceedings of the 51st Hawaii International Conference on System Sciences.*

Juuti, P., & Salmi, P. (2014). *Tunteet ja työ: Uupumuksesta iloon*. Jyväskylä: PS-Kustannus.

Kalimo, R., Hakanen, J., & Toppinen-Tanner, S. (2006). *Maslachin yleinen työuupumuksen arviointimenetelmä MBI-GS [The Finnish version of Maslach's Burnout Inventory–General Survey]*. Helsinki: Finnish Institute of Occupational Health.

Kokkonen, M. (2010). *Ihastuttavat, vihastuttavat tunteet. Opi tunteiden säätelyn taito*. Jyväskylä: PS-kustannus.

Kokkonen, M., & Pulkkinen, L. (1996). Tunteet ja niiden säätely. *Psykologia, 31*(6), 404–411.

Kraak, J. M., & Holmqvist, J. (2016). The authentic service employee: Service employees' language use for authentic service experiences. *Journal of Service Experience, 72*, 199–209.

Kreibig, S. D., Wilhelm, F. H., Roth, W. T., & Gross, J. J. (2007). Cardiovascular, electrodermal, and respiratory response patterns to fear- and sadness-inducing firms. *Psychophysiology, 44*(5), 787–806.

Kuivanen, T. (2017) "Emotion Tracker" tunneapplikaatio-tunteiden tunnistamisen, tunne-elämän kehittymisen ja arjen hyvinvoinnin tukena.

Laros, F. J. M., & Steenkamp, J.-B. E. M. (2005). Emotions in consumer behavior: A hierarchical approach. *Journal of Business Research, 58*, 1437–1445.

Li, X., Hong, X., Moilanen, A., Huang, X., Pfister, T., Zhao, G., & Pietikäinen, M. (2018). Towards reading hidden emotions: A comparative study of spontaneous micro-expression spotting and recognition methods. *IEEE Transactions on Affective Computing, 9*(4), 563–577.

López-Gil, J.-M., Virgili-Gomá, J., Gil, R., Guilera, T., Batalla, I., Soler-González, J., & García, R. (2016). Method for improving EEG based emotion recognition by combining it with synchronized biometric and eye tracking technologies in a non-invasive and low cost way. *Frontiers in Computational Neuroscience, 10*, 85.

Makkonen, M., Riekkinen, J., Frank, L., & Jussila, J. (2019). The effects of positive and negative emotions during online shopping episodes on consumer satisfaction, repurchase intention, and recommendation intention. In *Proceedings of the 32nd Bled eConference – Humanizing Technology for a Sustainable Society.*

Manka, M.-L., Kaikkonen, M.-L., & Nuutinen, S. (2007) Hyvinvointia työyhteisöön. Eväitä kehittämistyön avuksi. Tutkimus- ja koulutuskeskus Synergos, Tampereen yliopisto & Euroopan Sosiaalirahasto.

Marchi, E., Eyben, F., Hagerer, G., & Schuller, B. (2016) Real-time tracking of speakers' emotions, states, and traits on mobile platforms. In INTERSPEECH (pp. 1182–1183).

Martikainen, H. A., & Mäkinen, E. (2018). Tunnetiloja mittaavat menetelmät epänormaalin pelon hoidossa. *Finnish Journal of eHealth and eWelfare, 10*(1), 167–178.

Masuch, M. (1985). Vicious circles in organizations. *Administrative Science Quarterly, 30*, 14–33.

Mauss, I. B., & Robinson, M. D. (2009). Measures of emotion: A review. *Cognition and Emotion, 23*(2), 209–237.

Mehrabian, A., Wihradja, C., & Ljunggren, E. (1997). Emotional correlates of preferences for situation-activity combinations in everyday life. *Genetic, Social & General Psychology Monographs, 123*(4), 461–477.

Movellan, J., Bartlett, M. S., Fasel, I., Littlewort, G. F., Susskind, J., & Whitehill, J. (2014). U.S. patent application no. 14/180,352.

Multanen, L., Bredenberg, K., Koskensalmi, S., Lauttio, L.-M., & Pahkin, K. (2004). *Parempi työyhteisö*. Helsinki: Työterveyslaitos.

Naseem, A., Ejaz, S. S., & Malik, K. P. (2011). Impact of employee satisfaction on success of organization: Relation between customer experience and employee satisfaction. *International Journal of Multidisciplinary Sciences and Engineering, 2*(5), 41–46.

Okkonen, J., Heimonen, T., Savolainen, R., & Turunen, M. (2017). Assessing information ergonomics in work by logging and heart rate variability. In *International Conference on Applied Human Factors and Ergonomics* (pp. 425–436). Springer, Cham.

Oldehinkel, A. J., Ormel, J., Bosch, N. M., Bouma, E. M., Van Roon, A. M., Rosmalen, J. G. M., & Riese, H. (2011). Stressed out? Associations between perceived and physiological stress responses in adolescents: The TRAILS study. *Psychophysiology, 48*(4), 441–452.

Parak, J. & Korhonen, I. (2013) *Accuracy of Firstbeat Bodyguard 2 beat-to-beat heart rate monitor*. White paper by Firstbeat Technologies Ltd.

Picard, R. W., Migliorini, M., Caborni, C., Onorati, F., Regalia, G., Friedman, D., & Devinsky, O. (2017). Wrist sensor reveals sympathetic hyperactivity and hypoventilation before probable SUDEP. *Neurology, 89*(6), 633–635.

Pitkänen, L. (2018) Fiilismittarin käyttö organisaation henkilöstön tunnetilojen arvioinnissa–kriittinen kehittämisanalyysi.

Sacharin, V., Schlegel, K., & Scherer, K. R. (2012). *Geneva Emotion Wheel rating study (report)*. Geneve: University of Geneva, Swiss Center for Affective Sciences.

Scherer, K. R. (2005). What are emotions? And how can they be measured? *Social Science Information, 44*(4), 695–729.

Scherer, K. R., Shuman, V., Fontaine, J. R. J., & Soriano, C. (2013). The GRID meets the wheel: Assessing emotional feeling via self-report. In T. J. R. J. Fontaine, K. R. Scherer, & C. Soriano (Eds.), *Components of emotional meaning: A sourcebook* (pp. 281–298). Oxford: Oxford University Press.

Senge, P. M. (1991). The fifth discipline, the art and practice of the learning organization. *Performance+ Instruction, 30*(5), 37–37.

Seo, M.-G., Feldman Barret, L., & Jin, S. (2008). The structure of affect: History, theory, and implications for emotion research in organizations. In T. N. M. Ashkanasy & C. L. Cooper (Eds.), *Research companion to emotion in organizations* (pp. 17–44). Bodmin: Edward Elgar.

Shaver, P., Schwartz, J., Kirson, D., & O'Connor, C. (1987). Emotion knowledge: Further exploration of a prototype approach. *Journal of Personality and Social Psychology, 52*(6), 1061.

Stemmler, G. (2004). Physiological processes during emotion. In P. Philippot & R. S. Feldman (Eds.), *The regulation of emotion* (pp. 33–70). Mahwah: Lawrence Erlbaum Associates, Inc.

Suk, M., & Prabhakaran, B. (2014). Real-time mobile facial expression recognition system—A case study. In *Proceedings of the IEEE Conference on Computer Vision and Pattern Recognition Workshops* (pp. 132–137).

Torniainen, J., Cowley, B., Henelius, A., Lukander, K., & Pakarinen, S. (2015). Feasibility of an electrodermal activity ring prototype as a research tool. In *Engineering in Medicine and Biology Society (EMBC), 2015 37th Annual International Conference of the IEEE* (pp. 6433–6436). IEEE.

Tuovila, S. (2005). *Kun on tunteet. Suomen kielen tunnesanojen semantiikkaa*. Oulu: Oulun yliopisto.

Warr, P. (1990). The measurement of well-being and other aspects of mental health. *Journal of Occupational Psychology, 63*, 193–210.

Wei, J., Luo, H., Wu, S. J., Zheng, P. P., Fu, G., & Lee, K. (2018). Transdermal optical imaging reveal basal stress via heart rate variability analysis: A novel methodology comparable to electrocardiography. *Frontiers in Psychology, 9*, 98.

Winkler, R., Wakabayashi, D., & Dwoskin, E. (2016) Apple buys artificial-intelligence startup Emotient. *Wall Street Journal*.

Yee, R. W. Y., Yeung, A. C. L., & Cheng, E. T. C. (2008). The impact of employee satisfaction on quality and profitability in high-contact service industries. *Journal of Operations Management, 26*, 651–668.

Chapter 14
Individual Conditions for Co-production of a Social Innovation in a Living Lab: Case Sunshine PopUp Park

Kaisa Henttonen, Anna-Maija Nisula, Kirsimarja Blomqvist, Anne Horila, and Minna Takala

Abstract Participative processes and the empowerment of citizens are seen as central aspects of social innovation, which involves collaborative activities between the private, public and third sectors. It is important to identify the factors influencing citizen involvement, and we therefore investigate how people can be encouraged to contribute to improving societal well-being and to enhance partnerships between citizens, regions and, also, the profit and non-profit sectors. In particular, we investigate the motivation of citizens involved in the co-production of social innovation. We also provide descriptions of specific citizen- and public authority-related outcomes of the co-production process, which are missing from most previous studies (Voorberg et al., Public Management Review, 17(9), 1333–1357, 2015). We also identify actions that might facilitate the co-production of social innovation. In this study, we report a successful case of co-produced social innovation and derive findings from it.

14.1 Introduction

Participative processes and the empowerment of citizens are seen as central aspects of social innovation that involve collaborative activities among the private, public and third sectors. The involvement of users (here citizens) and collaborative

K. Henttonen (✉)
Business School, University of Eastern Finland, Kuopio, Finland
e-mail: kaisa.henttonen@uef.fi

A.-M. Nisula · K. Blomqvist
LUT University, Lappeenranta, Finland

A. Horila
Growth Corridor Finland, Hämeenlinna, Finland

M. Takala
Regional Council of Häme, Hämeenlinna, Finland

H. Lehtimäki et al. (eds.), *Society as an Interaction Space*, Translational Systems Sciences 22, https://doi.org/10.1007/978-981-15-0069-5_14

partnerships with the private, public and third sectors, also called fourth-sector activity can reduce public expenditure and contribute positively to quality of life and sustainable development via suitable public policy. Empowerment and collaboration can bolster social, economic, environmental and cultural outcomes and models of place-based innovation. Therefore, it is important to identify the factors influencing citizen involvement (e.g. Dutilleul et al. 2010), so as to empower and connect various stakeholders creating a fruitful environment for social innovation. In this paper, social innovation refers to 'the process of collective idea generation, selection and implementation by people who participate collaboratively to meet social challenges' (Dawson and Daniel 2010: 16).

Living labs, on the other hand, are seen as spaces facilitating social innovation. They have been characterised as a methodology that highlights user involvement in innovation. The application of living labs to real-life settings and 'real' experimentation started in Europe around the year 2005 and was based on Nordic countries' experience of involving users. Cunningham et al. (2012) defined the living lab as an environment, a methodology or an approach that facilitates user-driven open innovation within real-life rural and urban settings/communities in which users collaborate with multiple committed stakeholders (non-governmental organisations, small and medium-sized firms, industry, academic/research institutes, governments or donors) in one or more locations to become co-creators or co-designers of innovative ideas, processes or products within multidisciplinary environments. Successful collaboration may result in improved processes or services and new business models alongside social innovations (rules, procedures, programmes and norms) that can be replicated to improve the overall quality of life and the socioeconomic conditions through involvement in communities. In this study, a living lab is seen as a functional place in a real-life context that enables public–private partnerships among individuals (entrepreneurs and citizens), enterprises, public entities and universities. The real-life context in our case is a small, pioneering Finnish town called Hämeenlinna and its surroundings, where citizens took over a public place and turned it into an oasis for all the citizens in town. It became a social space for innovation—a place by citizens for citizens that supported connectivity and social action among citizens. Overall, interest in the potential of citizen involvement is growing among cities and scholars (Wascher et al. 2018), and several attempts to foster involvement of citizens have been made. For instance, the URBACT program—funded by the European Commission Regional Development Fund (ERDF)—targeted the promotion of social innovations (Urbact 2015), highlighting sufficient environment and spaces of experimentation as central for social innovation. However, while most municipally originated social innovation labs are funded experimental projects with a specific theme around which the actors are gathered, in the case of the present study, the idea for social innovation originated from citizens, and it gathered volunteer citizens, firms and public actors to co-produce social innovation without allocated budgets or formal project organisation. Hence, the case of the present study is unique, as it employs citizen potential starting from the initial steps of social innovation. In addition, the present study sheds light on citizen involvement in small cities, which often tend to ignore the potential of citizen initiatives, likely due to a lack of knowledge, skills or sufficient mechanisms to employ the potential of citizens for innovative solutions. Hence, living labs, as seen in our case study example, are mechanisms for stimulating connectivity among citizens (Dutilleul et al. 2010) and enabling 'scaffolding' efforts and intermediation for structuring and managing people involved in co-production in the innovation process (Moulaert and Mehmood 2010).

Co-production is defined in this study as 'the mix of activities that both public service agents and citizens contribute to the provision of public services' (Ostrom 1999). Co-production differs from classic volunteerism in that it concerns services the volunteers also use themselves (Voorberg et al. 2015). Co-production is used here interchangeably with the related concept of co-creation; we assume an interactive and dynamic relationship in which value is created from interaction. (Osborne 2018; see also Brandsen and Honigh on the different types of co-production).

Most previous studies in the field of co-production and social innovation have focused on citizens as co-implementers, while only a few focus on the citizens' degree of involvement as co-designers or co-initiators (Voorberg et al. 2015). First, there is a need to directly address the citizen involvement in the co-production of social innovation. Second, because the stakeholder in co-production is acting in a setting where users and organisations are likely to have contradictory role expectations, it is useful to research the relation between the diversity in roles and the outcomes of co-production processes. Third, it is important to understand under what conditions citizen involvement in the co-production of social innovations can be linked to more positive, concrete and functional outcomes. Only a few prior studies expressly analyse such outcomes (see review by Voorberg et al. 2015). In this chapter, we focus on the problem of how people can be encouraged to contribute to improving societal well-being and enhancing partnerships between citizens, regions and the profit and non-profit sectors. This is an important question, because co-production can help make the best use of resources, deliver better outcomes for people who use services, build stronger communities and develop good citizenship. It also seems to point out a paradigm shift, in which the consideration of citizens as passive consumers of public services has moved towards a view of citizens as co-producers (Voorberg et al. 2017). In this chapter we specifically *investigate which individual conditions foster citizen involvement in co-production of social innovations.* This involves analysing the types of people involved and their motives. The analysis is supported by addressing the questions: What motivates citizens to take part in co-production of social innovation? What value does co-production of social innovation create for the citizens, entrepreneurs and public authorities involved? What are the best practices to foster co-production of social innovation? Do the motivations, perceptions of value and best practices differ according to the degree of involvement (e.g. co-implementer, co-designer or co-initiator) people have in co-production?

Our study results reveal influential factors on the organisational and citizen side of co-production in different degrees of involvement. Furthermore, we also describe specific shareholder-related outcomes of the co-production process absent from most of the previous studies (Voorberg et al. 2015). Finally, we identify actions that can be taken to overcome potential barriers to the co-production of social innovations.

The remainder of the chapter is structured as follows. In the literature review, we discuss which individual conditions foster citizen involvement in co-creating social innovations. This involves themes such as citizen involvement motivation, value gained through involvement, enhancing conditions and best practices for co-production. In the methodology section, we will present the case study design and provide details on qualitative data collection and qualitative content analysis. The results section of the study reviews the motivations, values and co-production best practices in each degree of involvement investigated: co-implementer, co-designer and co-initiator. We also suggest some new degrees of involvement and motivations not present in earlier research. In the final section, we will present conclusions and notes on the limitations of the study.

14.2 Individual Conditions Fostering People's Involvement in Co-production of Social Innovations

In this study we focus, following Voorberg et al. (2015), on three types of citizen involvement, as we are interested in determining whether the motivations, perception of value and best practices differ according to the degree of involvement (co-implementer, co-designer or co-initiator) people have in co-production. The first type of citizen involvement sees the citizen as co-implementer of public services; the citizen performs some implementation tasks. The second type represents the citizen as co-designer. Often, the initiative comes from the public organisation, but citizens decide how the service delivery process is being designed. The third type presents the citizen as an initiator and the government is seen as an actor that follows.

Next, we turn our attention to what we know about the supporting questions of the analysis in this study. These are: what motivates individuals to take part in co-production of social innovation? What value co-production of social innovation creates for the various parties involved? What the best practices are to foster co-production?

14.2.1 Motivation

There is a considerable volume of literature on the factors that motivate citizens and other types of volunteers to offer public service, regardless of the fact that we do not know whether the motives of citizens and other volunteers differ according to their degrees of involvement. In her pioneering work, Sharp (1979) studied citizens' motivations in the context of crime prevention and, as a result, devised a typology of incentives for participant involvement consisting of three parts (based on Wilson 1973). The typology included material incentives (money, goods and services), solidary incentives (socialising, a sense of group membership, being well regarded, fun, etc.) and expressive incentives (e.g. environmental conservation and supporting the needy). Sharp's (1979) study found the effectiveness of motivation depends of the form of co-production. Individualistic forms of co-production emerge from more material and solidary interests, whereas collective action (e.g. block watches or neighbourhood watch initiatives) emerges from solidary interests and not from material interests.

Prior research on volunteer motivations, in contrast, identifies six categories of motivation (e.g. Clary et al. 1996; Clary et al. 1998). These are (1) values (people's willingness to express humanitarian values or to be altruistic), (2) understanding (when people view volunteer work as an opportunity to gain new knowledge of the world and develop their skills), (3) enhancement (when people develop psychologically and improve their self-esteem), (4) career (people volunteering to gain experience to benefit their careers, (5) social (people wanting to be part of or involved with social groups of importance to them) and (6) protective (when people volunteer to aid others' efforts to cope with their own anxieties and conflicts). Of these six functions, values were found to be most important motivation followed by the enhancement, social and understanding forms. The career and protective forms of motivation were found to be the least important (Clary et al. 1996). To summarise, we can identify four possible sources of motivation for co-production: material rewards, solidarity, values and intrinsic rewards.

14.2.2 Value Gained by Citizen Involvement in Co-production

The value of citizen involvement can be a result of involvement in the co-production or of the outcome of co-production or both. Most relevant academic studies have focused on the factors influencing the co-production process, but only a few studies have investigated co-production outcomes (Voorberg et al. 2015). Previous research has found, for example, that in co-production of healthcare for hospital clinic patients, the outcome—treatment quality—improved (Leone et al. 2012). Other research establishes that it is easier to acquire knowledge on how to organise and maintain organic farming when the initiative involves farmers working in organic farming (Baars 2011). There are also previous studies reporting no improvement related to outcomes through co-production. For example, Benari's (1990) study reports how co-production in the context of garbage disposal in Japan failed because people did not separate their garbage as instructed. In addition, Meijer (2011) found that co-production is not necessarily a source of better neighbourhood safety. To summarise, previous research suggests that the concrete outcomes of co-production have mostly been an increase (or reduction) in effectiveness. Additionally, previous studies report contradictory results related to the effectiveness of co-production.

14.2.3 Facilitating Co-production

We examine how to facilitate co-creation, as it seems that there is little specific literature on co-production, and in addition, the two concepts seem to be very closely interlinked (Voorberg et al. 2015). According to the review, both literature streams identify citizens as valuable partners in the delivery of public services. In addition, emergent and multiparty co-production research describes co-production in an open and public living lab space for social innovation.

Prior research suggests that collaborative emergence (co-production) is likely to occur under particular types of conditions that also reflect the circumstances of an open living lab space. Scholars such as Sawyer and DeZutter (2009), Gray (1989) and Prins (2006) present equal characteristics that enable collaborative emergence: (1) interdependence of actors/stakeholders, (2) openness to unfolding interaction, (3) openness towards outcome/solution, (4) equal participation and engagement of actors and (5) collective responsibility and shared leadership of the future direction of the task (or the goal of the event). However, the nature of co-production varies in terms of environment (the people involved, access, the goal of the co-production (task), time and the organisation of the process) and the degree of co-production (ranging from self-organised co-production to a managed form).

The process of co-production is more experimental and iterative than it is preplanned, a fact related to the openness towards emerging interaction and the direction of the solution. As a result, the development evolves and thrives amidst the dynamic interaction between the involved members (e.g. John-Steiner 2006), who feel themselves to be responsible and empowered participants in the co-production event. It follows that equal involvement and empowerment of the people involved are critical for successful co-production. Informal communication and a lighthearted environment encourage participants to express their ideas, to help other involved participants, to contribute ideas and to build on the ideas of the others; these aspects also facilitate theoretical and practical experiments. Non-hierarchical interaction is typical of co-production activity, which is related to shared leadership and decision-making practices. This means that leadership is given and taken according to the situation and that decision-making and direction setting are collectively stated and redefined in the course of the process. In addition, in order to build a shared vision and a future direction of the process, practices capable of recognising and making visible the diverse goals of the people involved are required. The space and facilitation of the co-production process are critical for co-production. The enabling and flexible space (either physical/virtual or mental) support co-production, whereas facilitation is often required in both supporting interaction and relationships between participating members, as well as in directing and structuring the course of the co-production (in terms of the content and process).

To summarise, the previous research on emergent collaboration and co-production describes the conditions under which multiparty co-production is likely to occur. It also indicates that successful co-production is highly dependent on the dynamics and interaction between the members involved, which can be supported by facilitation.

14.3 Methodology

Our theoretical orientation and related methodological approach can be described as theory elaboration (Ketokivi and Choi 2014). We build on past research on co-production of social innovations yet remain open to the idiosyncrasies in the case's context. In the following, we adopt interpretative sensemaking approach to first illustrate and then theorise based on the specific case context (Welch et al. 2011).

14.3.1 Case Sunshine PopUp Park

Nowadays, cities struggle with empty malls and other business spaces, and they appraise novel reuse ideas for such abandoned spaces. The small Finnish city, Hämeenlinna, took the initial steps to involve citizens in the collective building of their city. The Sunshine PopUp Park was an experimental in-house park in a local mall, the concept for which arose via an idea competition. The idea of a group of students at a local upper secondary school, the Hämeenlinna Lyseo, was selected to be implemented on a voluntary basis in collaboration with regional development experts. The original idea behind and aim of the experiment was to create an experimental Sunshine PopUp Park in a local empty mall to bring light and life into the city centre. The park created a green oasis and open meeting place for all ages and was therefore named the Sunshine PopUp Park.

The Sunshine PopUp Park was experimental in nature. It was created according to open innovation principles emphasising open citizen involvement and co-production. The city rented the space from the empty mall for the Sunshine PopUp Park for a test period (3 months). The indoor park was constructed by volunteers and was developed continuously based on original ideas and ideas offered by volunteers and visitors. The volunteers were mainly citizens, representatives of public authorities and local entrepreneurs, but everybody was welcome. In addition to building a space, the volunteers organised social activities and events for citizens in the space. Events organised by a variety of volunteers at the Sunshine PopUp Park included start-up events for companies, information on gardening and fruit tree maintenance, entrepreneurship training sessions, a Valentine's Day event, an Easter event, a flea market, recycling workshops, education and research information events, expert lectures, a bio-economy afternoon, national general election themed events and city meetings targeted at young people and the elderly. Additionally, there was an exhibition of indoor graffiti, watercolour paintings, musical performances and dancing.

What is more, students from educational institutions of all levels, from kindergarten to university, supported the activities. Teachers and a student counsellor also played an important role in guiding the students. Furthermore, the involvement of the members of the regional LUO cooperation network, in the field of natural resources, helped, especially when communicating the opportunity to get involved with the Sunshine PopUp Park project. LUO (Luonnonvara-alan verkosto) is a cooperation network in the field of natural resources in the Kanta-Häme region in southern Finland. The network's main aims are to increase research and development cooperation, use learning spaces together and discover innovations in the field of bio-economy and natural resources.

There was little in the way of monetary resources available, and the Sunshine PopUp Park aimed to operate by borrowing things, using recycled materials and using solicited donations. The use of social media was an important element in communication and coordination. The experiment was successful and results included attracting over 11,000 visits to the park, hosting around 30 workshops and events, assembling a team of around 100 volunteers and trainees, obtaining the support of around 30 firms and gathering around 250 ideas and recommendations. The advent of the Sunshine PopUp Park prompted around ten newspaper articles and five television segments. The park was opened on 16 January 2015 and closed on 18 April 2015, when the experiment ended. Visitors to the park spanned all age groups from infants to the elderly. The majority of visitors came from Hämeenlinna, but there were also visitors from around the world from Africa to Alaska.

14.3.2 Data Collection

The urban living lab case Sunshine PopUp Park was chosen because we were interested in understanding this unique case (Stake 2005). Our case was a successful experiment that attempted to involve citizens in the ideation and implementation of social innovation. Despite the living labs, whose purpose is social innovation, being initiated by the European Union, with funding from the ERDF, there is a scarcity of research and practical understanding of the living labs based on citizens' ideas and volunteer involvement of citizens, firms and public actors. For us, this specific case provided a situationally grounded opportunity to understand contextual idiosyncrasies (Ketokivi and Choi 2014), as our underlying question was to determine what made this active, citizen-volunteer co-production successful. The ten informants of this study were selected from different stakeholder groups to gain a holistic view of the phenomenon. The groups were students, teachers, entrepreneurs, citizens and representatives of public authorities.

The interview questions concerned Sunshine PopUp Park's development since its foundation. We were interested in learning of the actors' subjective experiences and the interviewees were asked to describe their backgrounds and their tasks within the Sunshine PopUp Park project to ensure that they had had direct experience with the studied phenomenon. They were also asked to describe what motivated them to get involved, how they had benefited from getting involved and also what they perceived as the best practices regarding co-production based on their Sunshine PopUp Park experiences.

The interviews were conversational and lasted between half an hour and 1 h. Each interviewee was made aware of the aim of the research. Beyond that, the interviewees were encouraged to talk about their experiences in their own words. The questions were repeated if necessary, and iterative and circular questioning and discussion were allowed. Furthermore, the information received was continually clarified and verified during the interview. All interviews were recorded and transcribed, and, in addition, the researchers took notes. All individual interviewees were guaranteed their responses would remain confidential.

14.3.3 Data Analysis

We conducted a deductive analysis by performing a literature review on motivations, on value gained by the citizens involved and on best practices for co-production. Theory driven template analysis (King 2004) was undertaken to categorise motivations, value and best practices identified in the data. A qualitative content analysis was then used to systematically code the interview data with categories identified in the literature review. During the coding stage, researchers sought theory-driven categories in the interview data, and identified were excerpts that described the motivations, value gained by the citizens and best practices for co-production. The first round of analysis focused on each citizen separately. Thereafter, a cross-citizen group analysis was conducted to gain a more holistic understanding of the phenomenon and to compare and synthesise the findings. Data reduction and classification processes were used to find patterns in the data and to define categories (Gummesson 2005). The results of the analysis are reported in Table 14.1.

14.4 Results

The results from the interviews indicate that citizens/volunteers are motivated to participate by self-interest, as none of the citizens/volunteers (co-implementer, co-designer, co-initiator, and public authority) were motivated by material rewards to co-produce something that could not be clearly defined beforehand (as the Sunshine PopUp Park experiment was); thus, it seems that volunteering citizens are not benefit maximisers, who only co-produce when benefits outweigh costs. However, regardless of the fact that a self-interest motivation has its limitations, some of the citizens/volunteers were motivated by non-material rewards, that is, their desire to boost their own business, aspirations related to their own careers, and carrying out regional developmental plans. This was typical of those as a co-designers and a public authority role. One of them said, 'Yes, I thought I could do my work there and maybe market my work'.

The study results indicate that also social identification with others was one of the motivations of co-production, that is, people were motivated by group affiliation and belonging. They wanted to be associated with and to interact with other people, and to gain their approval. One of the volunteers stated: 'This was a way of getting

Table 14.1 Summary of the empirical results of the study according to the degree of involvement

Role	Motivation	Value	Co-production practices
Citizen as a co-implementer = citizens only perform some implementation tasks (5 persons)	**Extrinsic (material or non-material):** **Solidarity:** wanting to have an impact on society both professionally and as a person; parks are good for human health; meeting people **Values**: the project motivated people because it was congruent with their green values **Intrinsic rewards:** general interest in participating in an experiment	**Increase in effectiveness:** possibility to better diffuse the ideas about gardening to the whole of society **Decrease in effectiveness:** **Other:** increasing citizen involvement; increasing awareness of one's own business; good feeling when doing something that makes other people happy; strengthening social cohesion: making new contacts; increasing awareness of one's own business	**Interdependence of actors/stakeholders:** **Openness to unfolding interaction:** ongoing documentation, coordination in Facebook (secret group for the experiment) **Openness towards outcome/solution:** all ideas were welcomed at any time **Equal participation and engagement of actors:** the role of a public actor as a role model and active participant; just do it-attitude; good spirit/community spirit; the public authority /coordinator encouraged everyone to offer ideas **Collective responsibility:** Volunteering: the experiment is as good as the ideas of the volunteers and the implementation by the volunteers **Shared leadership of the future direction of the event:** the ideas provided by the volunteers created the direction of the experiment; experiment started from 'nothing' **Material rewards:** free coffee (not very significant) **Other:** people who volunteered were open and easy going and easy to get to know; common interest in green/environmental issues
Citizen as a co-designer = citizens decide how the activity is being designed (2 persons)	**Extrinsic (material or non-material):** wanting to boost own business; aspirations related to own career **Solidarity:** possibility to work with other people **Values:** **Intrinsic rewards:** wanting to see how public spaces could be used for this type of purpose	**Increase in effectiveness:** finding new contacts and potential customers, new business **Decrease in effectiveness:** **Other:** increasing awareness of one's own business; using the Sunshine PopUp Park for work purposes (meeting); enjoyment of people's reactions related to organising these types of things voluntarily rather than relying on any authorities	**Interdependence of actors/stakeholders**: **Openness to unfolding interaction:** everybody was welcome to join the experiment **Openness to outcome/solution:** **Equal participation and engagement of actors:** the role of a public actor as a role model and active participant; volunteering (unpaid) **Collective responsibility:-** **Shared leadership of the future direction of the event:**

Citizen initiator = an initiative of citizens themselves(1 person)	**Extrinsic (material or non-material) rewards:** **Solidarity:** **Values:** **Intrinsic rewards:** realising one's own vision of the experiment and seeing it come true	**Increase in effectiveness:** **Decrease in effectiveness:** **Other**: feeling of achievement; gaining a great deal of knowledge on organising an experiment	**Interdependence of actors/stakeholders:** **Openness to unfolding interaction:** **Openness to outcome/solution:** realising that everyone has good ideas (may not be easy for idea owner, who has a clear vision) **Equal participation and engagement of actors:** **Collective responsibility:** no participants could complain about the activities because they were organising them themselves (and no one was paid) **Shared leadership of the future direction of the event:**
Public authority role (2 persons)	**Extrinsic (material or non-material) rewards**: **Solidarity:** **Values:** **Intrinsic rewards**: advancing regional development plan	**Increase in effectiveness:** **Decrease in effectiveness:** **Other:** increasing citizen involvement; realisation that there is need for this type of place, 11,000 visits, over 200 ideas	**Interdependence of actors/stakeholders:** **Openness to unfolding interaction:** ongoing documentation in Facebook; using a notebook for daily notes and challenges; setting house rules **Openness to outcome/solution**: ensuring ideas and actions are feasible; tolerating ambiguity **Equal participation and engagement of actors:** involving people in everything all the time, being a role model and active participant **Collective responsibility:** shared leadership of the future direction of the event **Other:** experiment had a beginning and an end

to know people with similar interests. They also had skills and knowledge that interested me.' Another motivation was the expressive values of citizens/volunteers, which reflected purposive norms and commitment to social issues, that is, environmental issues. *To summarise,* citizens/volunteers are ready to contribute time and effort to experiments like the Sunshine PopUp Park, if they do it for their own reasons. These reasons are far more complex, than just money or other material rewards.

So that co-production would not be considered a value itself—as it is been in many previous studies—we also investigated whether the citizens had found their involvement in co-production beneficial. Increasing effectiveness in terms of information diffusion throughout society and finding new potential clients faster were important benefits to those being co-implementers and co-designers and for those in the public authority role. One co-designer stated: 'Other citizens came to ask for advice and there were also some business cases, for example, someone needed to have their apple trees cut, and such like'. Additionally, one of the public authority representatives said: I think the value I gained was that I realised that there is a need for this type of space, and that this idea can be multiplied, and also there can be many different types of activity. The idea also was that people from some other cities could visit the park and see whether they could do something similar.

Other outcomes reported were; getting a good feeling when doing something and making other people happy, strengthening social cohesion; getting new contacts; and increasing public awareness of one's own business. *To summarise*, the outcomes of co-production did not only relate to gaining more effectiveness or efficiency. Finally, we investigated the conditions under which co-production and, more specifically, successful co-production as in the Sunshine PopUp Park case took place. More specifically, we investigated the best practices for successfully managing co-production. Technology is able to enhance co-production in that it can provide opportunities for dispersed action and it can make co-production more social. In the study case, social media (in the form of a closed Facebook group) was used to provide ongoing documentation and enable coordination. This created the (social) infrastructure for open interaction between all the citizens. There was also a notebook provided at the Sunshine PopUp Park itself to enable citizens in co-production to write down events that happened during the day (with visitors etc.) and potential problems. The citizens had also jointly set what could be called house rules and all new citizens in co-production were informed of those rules, which were visible on the wall at the project. The house rules concerned various issues including opening and closing hours and the rules were designed around the principle of DIT, that is, do it together. All citizens were encouraged to be open to all outcomes or solutions and all ideas were welcomed at any time during the experiment. However, as one of the public authority representatives stated: I had to make sure that all ideas that were to be carried out, were within the scope of the experiment; for example, there were suggestions to bring in a knitting machine or ideas that required a lot of resources like painting the whole place or installing a new floor…these types of ideas were not implemented. However, you cannot have too strong a vision, because it will restrict the experiment…And you have to tolerate things not necessarily being perfect right away and also encourage others to cope with it. If some materials et cetera were needed, then you just had to figure out where to get them. The idea was that we did not have funding for this experiment.

Equal involvement and engagement of actors was further influenced by the willingness of public authorities to support co-production. This was done, for example, by acting as a role model, through active involvement, and by encouraging everyone to provide ideas: You had to also make people realise that it is not just their role to create ideas and then we (the public organisation representatives) would carry them out. The idea is that you do things yourself too.

The citizens/volunteers had a collective responsibility for the experiment and thus shared the leadership of it. One of the co-initiators explained: I think it worked so well because everyone was a volunteer, and no one could complain because no one was paid…In volunteer work everyone can put in the effort they want to.

Hence, the experiment was just as good as the citizens as volunteers co-produced intended it to be. Material rewards, on the other hand were not significant, although coffee was offered to the volunteers. Finally, our study findings show that citizen/volunteer's characteristics also seem to determine whether they are willing to get involved. Personal traits such as openness and being easy going were mentioned. To summarise, it is important to understand that citizen involvement is not just about facilitating citizen involvement and developing managerial practices to motivate them. It is a complex combination of individual motivation, the benefits produced for individuals (value) and enabling circumstances and involvement. Citizens/volunteers need to be motivated to engage in co-production, but also effort is required to overcome the hurdles of citizen involvement.

14.5 Discussion

Below we discuss the results relating to our research questions and the previous studies, and thereby shed light on co-production of social innovations in the context of public experiments and spaces to increase citizen active involvement. *First*, we asked under which individual conditions do people co-produce social innovations. The question required that we understood the degree of citizen involvement and their motives for getting involved. We also investigated whether individual motivational conditions differ according to the degree of citizen involvement (co-implementer, co-designer, or citizen initiator).

Past research has recorded the presence of enhancement motivation (e.g. Clary et al. 1996), and that was also visible in our results, as some citizens learned about themselves and were able to improve their esteem through the self-actualisation process. Career motivation was also part of the motivation through learning, new contacts, and even potential customer relationships. Likewise, social motivation was important for a variety of citizens, from those new to the town to those accustomed to working alone. However, the respondents did not openly express the protective form of motivation, but it could have been seen as a preventive idea for the

Living Lab as a mechanism to combat the dark winter months and the associated low moods and seasonal affective disorder.

Regarding the motivations of citizens of various degrees of involvement, the current research aligns with that of Voorberg et al. (2015) in indicating that citizens as co-designers had both intrinsic and extrinsic motivations. Their extrinsic motivations were related to boosting their own business or career, whereas their intrinsic motivations were related to seeing how public spaces could be used for similar purposes. The distinction between the extrinsic and intrinsic motivations was not very clear, and as were others, they were also motivated by solidarity. Motivational synergy (e.g. Grant 2008) may explain this. The motivation of the citizen initiator was purely intrinsic, the person being driven by a vision and seeing the experiment realised. In addition to the degrees of involvement identified by earlier research, we also identified the critical roles of public authorities, whose involvement was based on intrinsic rewards and who then used the experiment as a means to advance a regional development plan. There were some differences between the degrees of involvement by the citizens in terms of individual intrinsic rewards. Some citizens, especially those being co-designers, were motivated by non-material rewards, such as their boosting own business, their own career, or progressing regional plans. However, the degrees of involvement and motivations are not clear-cut; the co-initiator also actively got involved in every phase of the design and implementation of the experiment. Likewise, the citizens as a co-designers got involved in the implementation. It is therefore not possible to distinguish pure degrees of involvement in this type of emergent and open-ended experiment, the degrees of involvement identified are more like dominant degrees of involvement that differentiate citizens at a certain time, and complementary degrees of involvement supporting the collective effort, yet citizens degree of involvement is less significant and the related effort invested into them less. There were also some signs of role competition, when two people identified themselves as co-initiators. To answer the question of what motivates citizens to get involved in the co-production of social innovation, we found that material rewards are not the main motivators but instead the key drivers of involvement are solidary and expressive incentives and individual intrinsic motivation. Hence, the people who find social relationships (connectivity) valuable both for collective and individual development are motivated to get involved in social innovation events.

Secondly, we also asked what value co-production of social innovation creates for the various parties involved. The findings of our study support previous studies that identified material, solidary and expressive incentives, of which the solidary incentives were found to drive the involvement in the collective forms of co-production (Sharp 1979). Another identified value was the expressive incentives of citizens. These took the form of purposive norms and commitments relating to social issues, which in this case meant environmental issues. Material incentives did not drive citizen involvement in the co-production of social innovation in our case, and were secondary to the impact of solidary and expressive incentives (Sharp 1979; Voorberg et al. 2018). Interestingly, almost all of the interviewed citizens had some experience in volunteer work, which speaks of their value-based involvement.

Citizens value-based involvement manifested, for example, in a willingness to co-create a place for elderly retired people to experience the shrubbery and trees, or a meeting place for young mothers. Many of the citizens stated that they get involved to learn about an interesting experiment, and had found they learned about themselves and others. The citizens also reported that the positive social interaction made the learning experience empowering. They also learned social and entrepreneurial skills, such as those required to organise events.

Thirdly, we investigated what are the best practices to foster co-production of a social innovation? The process of co-production and co-implementation of the Sunshine PopUp Park was more iterative than pre-planned as it developed by planning and experimenting via contributions from the volunteers. Hence, it equates to the literature on emergent collaborative (Prins 2006), living labs (Moulaert and Mehmood 2010; Cunningham et al. 2012; Dutilleul et al. 2010). With regard to factors influencing successful co-production in an open public Living Lab, our results show that the characteristics of emergent co-production identified in previous studies (Sawyer and DeZutter 2009; Gray 1989; Prins 2006; John-Steiner 2006) were also identifiable in the Sunshine PopUp Park case. In the case of a Living Lab, the open access aspect is catered for by voluntary and egalitarian involvement; openness to outcomes; collective responsibility and shared leadership were also identified as enablers of successful co-production. The volunteer and open access involvement allowed people to enter and leave the event at will. This is critical in social innovation events aiming to increase and accelerate citizen involvement. The openness to an outcome element concerns flexibility, acceptance of emerging ideas, and constant co-production. In this case the original idea about the social and co-created public park with minor funding was kept in mind and respected by the organisers, which in principle guided the co-production and the implementation of the park. Within this frame, the openness to the outcome (in the form of the appearance and content of the Sunshine PopUp Park) remained in place throughout the social innovation. The implementation of ideas included some selection in terms of the scope and of the ideas and the feasibility of implementing them. In addition, collective responsibility and shared leadership were related to volunteer involvement. Moreover, the interdependence of actors was also evident in our case, but played a minor role because the Sunshine PopUp Park was run by various small groups and inspired by others' contributions. Accordingly, our findings diverge from the past research that found examples of interdependence facilitating collaboration and impacting shared performance (Hackman 2002; Wageman 1995; Wageman and Gordon 2005). It seems likely that the level of interdependence varies depending on the types of co-production. Specifically, in encouraging active citizenship and self-organising among citizens in social participation, the level of interdependence may be low at the beginning of the co-production and grow during the process of co-production and self-organising as citizens start to build shared goals and co-produce them.

Although the interdependence between open access and social innovation is complex and may have a different role in performance, interdependence (Wageman and Gordon 2005) may occur. In the Sunshine PopUp Park case, we identified two channels that nurtured interdependence: social media and knowledge sharing via the on-site notebook. With regard to the conditions and enablers of successful co-production, our findings show that in an open public Living Lab where the citizens are not necessarily together all the time (new volunteers enter and other volunteers may leave the event at any time during the process) the communication, coordination, and co-production is not only a face-to-face interaction, but is also mediated by social media (the Facebook group). The citizens could follow the course of the development/co-production process, contribute to ideation, and ask for and provide assistance. In this sense, the Facebook group offers a supporting and enabling social space, that is, a (social) infrastructure for successful co-production.

Another way to build interdependence is the use of various visualisations, such as the on-site notebook, which proved a suitable means through which to inform others of the house rules, about emerging problems, and to communicate other important issues. However, it is likely that in the short period of the Living Lab experiment an interdependence was established in smaller groups working on particular contributions on social innovation. Finally, the availability of facilitation and support often has a critical role in the emergence of co-production among volunteers. In this case, the encouragement to take action and implement ideas was provided by the organisers. As the nature of co-production is dependent on the dynamics and interaction of the people involved, the Living Lab kind of open access social innovation is composed of multiple, varied, smaller co-production performances.

Our interpretive sensemaking of the specific case study (Welch et al. 2011) did not intend for generalisation but for elaborating theory on citizens as active co-producers in social innovation by detailing their voluntary and active citizen involvement in innovation, co-production and co-implementation. To conclude, this study contributes theoretically to the research on the co-production of social innovation between citizens and public-sector organisations. The concept of social innovation is becoming increasingly central to scientific and public discussions. Practitioners, policy makers, scholars and others increasingly agree on the merits of social innovations in addressing the significant challenges currently facing society and those that will face society in the future. Active citizenship, such as that described in this paper, has the potential to contribute to environmental, social, and institutional resilience in cities (Buijs et al. 2016).

This study has shown how to promote innovations that provide novel ways to capture opportunities or tackle problems that create collateral outcomes that ultimately benefit societal well-being. Social innovation is about social benefits and public good that supports people in organisations, communities and society in general. We also documented a success case, the Sunshine PopUp Park, and we hope that similar experiments based on the lessons learned could emerge more broadly in society, so enabling self-organising and active citizenship in various contexts.

References

Baars, T. (2011). Experiential science; towards an integration of implicit and reflected practitioner-expert knowledge in the scientific development of organic farming. *Journal of Agricultural & Environmental Ethics, 24*(6), 601–628.

Benari, E. (1990). A bureaucrat in every Japanese kitchen?: On cultural assumptions and coproduction. *Administration & Society, 21*(4), 472–492.

Buijs, A. E., Mattijssen, T. J. M., Van der Jagt, A. P. N., Ambrose-Oji, B., Andersson, E., Elands, B. H. M., & Steen Møller, M. (2016). Active citizenship for urban green infrastructure: Fostering the diversity and dynamics of citizen contributions through mosaic governance. *Current opinion in environmental sustainability, 22*, 1–6.

Clary, E. G., Snyder, M., & Stukas, A. (1996). Volunteers' motivations: Findings from a national survey. *Nonprofit and Voluntary Sector Quarterly, 25*, 485–505.

Clary, E. G., Snyder, M., Ridge, R., Copeland, J., Stukas, A., Haugen, J., & Miene, P. (1998). Understanding and assessing the motivations of volunteers: A functional approach. *Journal of Personality and Social Psychology, 74*, 1516–1530.

Cunningham, P., Herselman, M. E., & Cunningham, M. (2012). Socio-economic impact of growing Living Labs and Living Lab networks into Africa. *IST-Africa 2012 Conference Proceedings*, Dar es Salaam, Tanzania.

Dawson, P., & Daniel, L. (2010). Understanding social innovation: A provisional framework. *International Journal of Technology Management, 51*(1), 9–21.

Dutilleul, B., Birrer, F. A., & Mensink, W. (2010). Unpacking European living labs: Analysing innovation's social dimensions. *Central European Journal of Public Policy, 4*(1), 60–84.

Grant, A. M. (2008). Does intrinsic motivation fuel the prosocial fire? Motivational synergy in predicting persistence, performance, and productivity. *Journal of Applied Psychology, 93*(1), 48–58.

Gray, B. (1989). *Collaborating: Finding common ground for multiparty problems*. San Francisco: Jossey-Bass Inc..

Gummesson, E. (2005). Qualitative research in marketing: Road-map for a wilderness of complexity and unpredictability. *European Journal of Marketing, 39*(3/4), 309–327.

Hackman, J. R. (2002). *Leading teams: Setting the stage for great performances*. Boston: HBS Press.

John-Steiner, V. (2006). *Creative collaboration*. Oxford: Oxford University Press.

Ketokivi, M., & Choi, T. (2014). Renaissance of case research as a scientific method. *Journal of Operations Management, 32*(5), 232–240.

King, N. (2004). Using templates in the thematic analysis of the text. In S. Cassel & G. Symon (Eds.), *Guide to qualitative methods in organizational research* (pp. 256–234). London: Essential Sage Publications.

Leone, R., Walker, C., Curry, L., & Agee, E. (2012). Application of a marketing concept to patient-centered care: Co-producing health with heart failure patients. *OJIN: The Online Journal of Issues in Nursing, 17*, 2.

Meijer, A. (2011). Networked co-production of public services in virtual communities: From a government-centric to a community approach to public service support. *Public Administration Review, 71*(4), 598–607.

Moulaert, F., & Mehmood, A. (2010). Spaces of social innovation. In A. Pike, A. Rodriguez-Pose, & J. Tomaney (Eds.), *A handbook of local and regional development* (pp. 212–225). London: Routledge.

Osborne, S. P. (2018). From public service-dominant logic to public service logic: Are public service organizations capable of co-production and value co-creation? *Public Management Review, 20*(2), 225–231.

Ostrom, E. (1999). Crossing the great divide. Co-production, synergy & development polycentric governance and development. In M. D. McGinnes (Ed.), *Reading from the workshop in political theory and policy analysis*. Ann Arbor: University of Michigan Press.

Prins, S. (2006). The psychodynamic perspective in organizational research: Making sense of the dynamics of direction setting in emergent collaborative processes. *Journal of Occupational and Organizational Psychology, 79*(3), 335–355.

Sawyer, R. K., & DeZutter, S. (2009). Distributed creativity: How collective creations emerge from collaboration. *Psychology of Aesthetics, Creativity, and the Arts, 3*(2), 81–92.

Sharp, E. (1979). *Citizen organizations and participation in law enforcement advocacy and Coproduction: The Role of Incentives.* Ph.D. Dissertation. Chapel Hill, NC: University of North Carolina at Chapel Hill, Department of Political Science.

Stake, R. E. (2005). Qualitative case studies. In N. K. Denzin & Y. S. Lincoln (Eds.), *Handbook of qualitative research* (3rd ed., pp. 443–466). Thousand Oaks: Sage.

URBACT. (2015). *Social innovation in cities.* URBACT II capitalization, URBACT. Retrieved June 17, 2019, from https://urbact.eu/sites/default/files/03_socialinn-web.pdf

Voorberg, W. H., Bekkers, V., & Tummers, L. (2015). A systematic review of co-creation and co-production: Embarking on the social innovation journey. *Public Management Review, 17*(9), 1333–1357.

Voorberg, W., Bekkers, V., Timeus, K., Tonurist, P., & Tummers, L. (2017). Changing public service delivery: Learning in co-creation. *Policy and Society., 36*(2), 178–194.

Voorberg, W., Jilke, S., Tummers, L., & Bekkers, V. (2018). Financial rewards do not stimulate coproduction: Evidence from two experiments. *Public Administration Review, 78*(6), 864–873.

Wageman, R. (1995). Interdependence and group effectiveness. *Administrative Science Quarterly, 40*(1), 145–180.

Wageman, R., & Gordon, F. M. (2005). As the twig is bent: How group values shape emergent task interdependence in groups. *Organization Science, 16*(6), 687–700.

Wascher, E., Hebel, F., Schrot, K., & Schultze, J. (2018). *Social Innovation Labs – A starting point for social innovation.* Dortmund: sfs/TU Dortmund University.

Welch, C., Piekkari, R., Plakoyiannaki, E., & Paavilainen-Mäntymäki, E. (2011). Theorising from case studies: Towards a pluralist future for international business research. *Journal of International Business Studies, 42*(5), 740–762.

Wilson, J. (1973). *Political organizations.* New York: Basic Books.

Chapter 15
Security Cafés: A Deliberative Democratic Method to Engage Citizens in Meaningful Two-Way Conversations with Security Authorities and to Gather Data

Alisa Puustinen, Harri Raisio, and Vesa Valtonen

Abstract The Security Café is a deliberation and data collection method developed for security authorities and researchers to access the opinion of the general public on issues of importance to their safety and security. It is based on the ideals of deliberative democracy, and the method derives from Citizens' Juries and World Cafés. A Security Café typically lasts for 3–5 h and involves receiving information, facilitated small group discussions and the use of idea rating sheets, or pre- and post-deliberation attitudinal surveys. This study examines three projects conducted in Finland and concludes that the method has both intrinsic and extrinsic value: it empowers ordinary citizens and gives them an opportunity to engage in the construction of safer and more secure societies. At the same time, it offers authorities the opportunity to inform the public and most importantly to harvest the opinion of the public. For researchers, the method offers a feasible way to gather extensive reliable qualitative data quickly and effectively.

15.1 Introduction

The Security Café is an adjusted deliberative democratic method deriving from the ideals of deliberative democracy and deliberative mini-publics. Elstub (2010) and Ercan and Dryzek (2015), among others, consider that deliberative democracy

A. Puustinen (✉)
Emergency Services Academy Finland, Kuopio, Finland
e-mail: alisa.puustinen@pelastusopisto.fi

H. Raisio
University of Vaasa, Vaasa, Finland
e-mail: harri.raisio@uwasa.fi

V. Valtonen
The Security Committee, Helsinki, Finland
e-mail: vesa.valtonen@turvallisuuskomitea.fi

H. Lehtimäki et al. (eds.), *Society as an Interaction Space*, Translational Systems Sciences 22, https://doi.org/10.1007/978-981-15-0069-5_15

currently dominates the theory of democracy. Although this theory development is not yet so visible in practice, in a recent article in *Science*, a large number of deliberative scholars optimistically point out that "[t]he real world of democratic politics is currently far from the deliberative ideal, but empirical evidence shows that the gap can be closed" (Dryzek et al. 2019: 1144). One promising example of the spread of deliberative ideals is the proliferation of deliberative mini-publics. In this article it is, however, pointed out that the use of deliberative mini-publics is not yet common within the domains of safety and security. It might be, for example, that questions of safety and especially (national) security call for secrecy and swift and determinate authoritative action, thus becoming barriers for wider citizen participation and deliberation (see Torfing et al. 2016). The Security Café model is one example of how deliberation could potentially be implemented also in the domains of safety and security.

As a parliamentary republic the Finnish society sturdily rests on the traditional ideals on representative democracy. Representative democracy is strong both on national and on local levels of government. Thus, traditionally citizen participation has been channelled through the formal structures of government, such as local committees and city councils. An alternative route to citizen participation has always been the third sector, mostly in the form of voluntary associations.

In addition, *comprehensive Security* is a Finnish preparedness model (a whole-systems approach) in which the vital functions of society are secured through cooperation between the public authorities, the business community, non-governmental organizations and individual citizens (see Aaltola and Juntunen 2018). These various societal actors form a network of comprehensive security in which the sharing of information, setting of joint objectives and cooperation can take place in a flexible manner. The latest *Security Strategy for Society*, a government resolution which harmonises national preparedness principles and guides preparedness in the various administrative branches, emphasizes the role of individual citizens in enhancing the resilience of Finnish society. In order to build a sense of community, citizens are encouraged to contribute to the construction of a resilient society by actively fostering safety and security both at home and in their neighbourhood. The approach is also supported by educational and cultural services that help to improve citizens' knowledge and their ability to act in a changing society. At the same time, the strategy instructs security authorities to include citizens in the local preparedness planning (Security Committee 2017).

In addition to actions such as developing personal preparedness, the strategy calls for agile and flexible models to engage large numbers of citizens in deliberations on safety and security issues, so as to encourage citizens to become "policy-making partners"; that is, preparedness planning becomes something that is done along *with*, not *for* the citizens (Schoch-Spana 2012: 82). The Security Café was developed as one such model of collaboration.

The Security Café model was originally developed as part of a Finnish project called the Role of Civil Society in National Defence (funded by the Scientific Advisory Board for Defence, operating in the administrative branch of the Ministry of Defence), which sought ways to engage ordinary citizens in discussions about their own role as part of the Finnish Model of Comprehensive Security (Raisio et al.

2017a). Subsequently, the Security Café model was tested in two projects. First, it was used as a deliberation and data collection method in a study funded by the Ministry of the Interior seeking to analyse the views of citizens on asylum seekers and asylum seeker policy in Finland (Puustinen et al. 2017). In addition, it was applied as a data collection method in a project funded as part of the Finnish government's analysis, assessment and research activities, which examined the role of the third sector in supporting public authorities' security functions (Jalava et al. 2017). A total of 16 Security Cafés were run during those projects.

This methodological article briefly describes the roots of the Security Café. It also introduces the underpinnings of Security Cafés and the preconditions for their successful operation and particularly demonstrates how the Security Café can be organized and applied in different contexts. Finally, we reflect upon experiences of the use of the method in the different projects mentioned above and how it might be developed further and applied also in different contexts as part of the methodology of security studies.

Two authors of this article (HR & AP) were involved in the implementation of all 3 projects and 16 Security Cafés. The third author (VV) observed the projects as a member of the Finnish Security Committee's Secretariat, and in the third project was part of its advisory board. The intention in this article is to combine these different research-based and practice-based views in order to foster a deeper understanding of the prospects of and challenges facing Security Cafés in the domains of safety and security.

15.2 Roots in the Ideals of Deliberative Democracy and Deliberative Mini-Publics

Deliberative democracy is a form of democracy that values discussion, reflection and consideration over simply voting (Chambers 2003). Among others, the absence of power and the presence of mutual respect, reason giving, sincerity, orientation to the common good and equal opportunities for influence are seen as defining features of deliberation (Mansbridge 2015). In addition, prior research emphasizes the epistemic goals of deliberation ("truth-tracking") as a new standard of deliberation (e.g. Min and Wong 2018). It should be noted that deliberation does not refer to ordinary everyday discussions. According to Mansbridge (2015: 29) and Dryzek (2002) deliberation is instead, at a minimum, "mutual communication that involves weighing and reflecting on preferences, values, and interests regarding matters of common concern". Fundamentally, deliberative democracy is a normative theory and a transformative project. As such, it is not so much a theory explaining and describing political reality (i.e. *what is*), as a theory determining desirable political activity (i.e. *what ought to be*) (Ercan and Dryzek 2015; Elstub and Böker 2015).

Deliberative democracy is often seen as an umbrella term for a wide variety of innovative deliberative democratic processes (e.g. Nabatchi 2010). These are commonly called *deliberative mini-publics* (Grönlund et al. 2014). Ideally, such mini-publics should be inclusive of stakeholder populations, meaning that those participating in the deliberations should as far as possible represent different societal views. Mini-publics should be deliberative, to allow participants to thoroughly consider the topics and weigh different options and the values underlying decisions; they should have influence, to be a genuine collaboration with decision-makers; in other words, they should influence policy (Carson and Hartz-Karp 2005). Examples of such deliberative democratic processes include *Citizens' Juries* (e.g. Scuffham et al. 2016), *Deliberative Polls* (e.g. Fishkin 2009) and *Citizens' Assemblies* (e.g. Carson et al. 2013).

Ryan and Smith (2014), however, consider mini-publics a contested field and distinguish three different categories of mini-publics in an attempt to clarify the concept. The first category encompasses mini-publics of *restrictive definition*. Such mini-publics (Deliberative Polls) emphasize statistical representation and the strict conduct and analysis of pre- and post-deliberation attitudinal surveys. Mini-publics in the category of *intermediate definition* (e.g. Citizens' Juries and Citizens' Assemblies) often use quasi-random sampling techniques and end with the production of collective recommendations. Finally, mini-publics in the *expansive definition* category are deliberative processes that have clear elements of self-selection, that is, they are open to all citizens; *World Cafés* (e.g. Carson 2011) and *Participatory Budgeting* (e.g. Stolzenberg and Wampler 2018) seem to fit in this last category.

The use of deliberative mini-publics is not yet widespread within the domains of safety and security although there are some examples of such activity. One such example is a Citizens' Jury that took place in Finland in October 2014 and was part the Pirkka14 emergency preparedness exercise (Raisio and Virta 2016; Raisio and Ehrström 2017). The fictional scenario for the exercise was an increasingly tense international situation and subsequent cyber-attacks with broad ramifications. The parameters of the Citizens' Jury were delimited by the abovementioned scenario. The issues deliberated upon included citizens' preparedness for an emergency, community resilience, major disruption to the electricity supply and the improvement of emergency and disaster communications. This Citizens' Jury involved 16 jurors and the jury process consisted of 5 h of deliberation per day for 3 days and a subsequent press event. Jurors watched a video where the scenario was described, asked questions of the expert panel, observed a specific accident simulation in the field, participated in facilitated deliberations and, finally, composed a declaration representing the opinion of the jury, which included 20 suggestions for improvement ranging from wider visions to more concrete action plans. Detailed responses of various quality were received in due course from nine relevant stakeholders, including the Finnish Defence Forces, the National Police Board and the Regional State Administrative Agency of Western and Inland Finland.

The value of deliberative democracy and deliberative mini-publics has been discussed in several publications (e.g. Grönlund et al. 2014; Curato et al. 2017). In the context of emergencies and disasters, the following positive aspects have been raised (Schoch-Spana et al. 2007; Shane 2012): through public deliberation of preparedness policy, leaders can tap into the collective wisdom of the citizenry; citizens can then help set policy priorities and, especially importantly, inform value-laden policy decisions. Moreover, inclusive citizen participation initiatives contribute to making contingency plans more robust, feasible and accepted than they might be without any citizen input, as they would include lessons distilled from local experiential knowledge. Trust between public authorities and communities may also be improved and citizens become more interested in and knowledgeable about safety and security matters. In addition, public deliberation may have a positive impact on the development of community resilience and also work as a "protective mechanism against conflict and division in recovery" (Millen 2011: 16). Wilson (2009: 22) scrutinized the deliberative planning for disaster recovery in New Orleans and concluded that: "Not just feel-good by-products of public deliberation, social trust and social healing are important dividends of deliberative democracy, especially in communities on the road to recovery from natural disaster".

Similarly, various obstacles have been identified that hinder the delivery of high-quality deliberative processes in the safety and security domains. Virta and Branders (2016) highlight the risk that deliberation over security strategies and governance processes loses its political meaning, that is, "Citizens' Juries and other participation and deliberation events and forums are recast as capacity-building and preparedness training forums rather than places for true deliberation". If that happens, then the critical transformative project of deliberative democracy becomes questionable, as radical and revolutionary thoughts, as well as alternative options for action, become mere contingencies to be tamed. On the other hand, state-level-oriented security strategies, such as the Security Strategy for Society, aims merely to enhance deliberative democratic collaboration at local and regional levels, where a continuous dialogue is possible.

Lee Jenni et al. (2015) raise the issues of transparency and information sharing. The tradition of providing information only on a "need-to-know basis" and the need to protect operational security affects the way citizens understand the many perspectives on issues deliberated upon (including operational needs and objectives). In addition, the representativeness of deliberative mini-publics can cause issues in that their composition has been rather homogenous in that they tend to attract relatively affluent and security-oriented members of the public (Raisio and Virta 2016). One must also bear in mind that the use of security information and open forums creates a potential risk for the authorities. Citizen efforts need to be legitimized, and authorities must understand the logic underpinning the civil society in order for it to yield benefits rather than creating confusion or establishing pseudo-participation (Valtonen 2010).

15.3 The Security Café: Form and Modus Operandi

The Security Café is a combination of the abovementioned Citizens' Jury and World Café methods (see Table 15.1) and, as such, can be positioned between the intermediate and expansive definition categories of deliberative mini-publics (Ryan and Smith 2014). In comparison to World Cafés, which are generally open events, Security Cafés aim to assemble a large number of enrolled people and to choose a diverse group of around 25–30 participants. In addition, participants at Security Cafés receive extensive information and participate in facilitated discussions on pre-selected topics. The main difference to the more developed deliberative mini-publics, such as Citizens' Juries, is the duration of the event. Instead of several days, the whole event generally lasts only between 3 and 5 h. Similar to Citizens' Juries, the Security Café method emphasizes a direct linkage to decision-making. Relevant security authorities are involved in the implementation of the Security Café from planning to conclusion. The authorities also take a visible position in using the outputs of Security Cafés. The aim is to achieve genuine two-way interaction between citizens and authorities and to produce input into the decision-making processes.

Next, the different phases—the planning, recruitment, execution and impact—of the Security Café method are discussed. The phases are described by reference to the three projects and the 16 Security Cafés implemented in Finland. Table 15.2 presents a summary of the projects and the Security Cafés implemented at the end of the following section, which as a whole is based on the research reports of the three projects (Raisio et al. 2017a; Puustinen et al. 2017; Jalava et al. 2017).

Table 15.1 Features of citizens' Juries, Security Cafés and World Cafés

	Citizens' Jury	Security Café	World Café
Steering	Extensive advisory committee	Compact advisory committee	Conveners decide on the issues to be addressed
Participant selection	Stratified random sampling; scientific polling techniques	Diverse group chosen to participate from larger enrolled number	Usually open to all
Number of participants	16–24	25–30	From 12 to 100 s
Compensation	Often offered, e.g. 50€ per day	Can be used, e.g. 20€/café	Usually none
Duration	3–5 days	3–5 h	Generally, 2 h
Information	Expert witnesses and/or written material	Expert witnesses, present for the whole duration	Usually none; participants are familiar with the topic
Facilitation	Highly skilled and neutral facilitators; various facilitation techniques	Each small group has a neutral facilitator; participants stay in the same groups for the whole duration	Self-facilitated; small groups select "hosts" among themselves; participants move between groups
End result	Written declaration of the jury, presented in news conference	Collective view emerging through idea rating sheets	Insights are shared in a whole group conversation; visual aids may be used
Impact	Relevant decision-makers respond to the recommendations made by the jury	Relevant decision-makers respond to the recommendations made by the café	Conversations have an intrinsic value; however, opportunities for action may emerge

15.3.1 Planning Phase

The Security Café method was originally developed in Project 1. The starting point for the project was to develop a more agile version of the previously described Pirkka14 Citizens' Jury. The requirement necessitated work on the planning phase, as there was no model to pilot at the time. The basic principles for the Security Café

Table 15.2 Summary of the three projects and Security Cafés implemented

	Project 1	Project 2	Project 3
Purpose	To analyse the suitability of deliberative mini-publics in increasing the two-way interaction between the Defence Forces and the citizens	To obtain a comprehensive a picture of the experiences and opinions of the Finnish people relating to the asylum seeker situation and ideas for developing activities in the future	To analyse the extensive role played by the third sector in supporting public authorities' security functions
Timeline	1/2016 to 12/2016	12/2016 to 3/2017	3/2017 to 12/2017
Funder	The Scientific Advisory Board for Defence	The Ministry of the Interior	The Finnish government's analysis, assessment and research activities
Participant recruitment	Cafés were promoted in local newspapers, on street billboards and in social media.	A private company offering assistance services for research recruited the participants.	Direct contact with public authorities and associations. Social media was also used.
Participant profile	Ordinary citizens	Ordinary citizens	Public authorities and third-sector representatives
Number of participants	Three cafés, 78 participants	Five cafés, 123 participants	Eight cafés, 188 participants
Theme(s) of the cafés	Café 1: operation of the registration centre for asylum seekers. Café 2: the roles and tasks of public authorities and citizens in different emergencies and disaster. Café 3: Hybrid threats	Asylum seeker policy; same theme in each café	The role of the third sector in supporting public authorities' security functions; same theme in each café, though slight variations related to the region, e.g. a sparsely populated area
Duration of the cafés	4 h 30 min	3 h 30 min	3 h
Format of output	Idea rating sheets	Pre- and post-deliberation surveys; in addition, small group deliberations were recorded	Idea rating sheets; in addition, small group deliberations were recorded
Impact	Thirteen written responses received from public authorities; various news stories	A major media event; wide discussions in society	Important data to the research project; idea rating sheets were transcribed for the use of the café participants

were drawn up in cooperation with researchers from three universities (the University of Vaasa, the University of Tampere and the National Defence University). More specific planning took place in each of three pilot Security Cafés. Although the project had a strong research focus, each café was structured to address a real-world issue. Each café then recruited a compact advisory committee to advise on setting the questions to be deliberated upon and on choosing the expert witnesses. In addition, the members of the advisory committees committed to participating in the whole process and establishing the impact of the Security Café.

The advisory committee of the first pilot Security Café consisted of representatives from the Finnish Immigration Service (the main collaborator), the Lapland Police Department, the Jaeger Brigade from the Finnish Defence Forces and the Finnish Red Cross. With the guidance of the advisory committee members, the theme of the Security Café was set as the establishment and operation of the registration centre for asylum seekers that was opened in the centre of the city of Tornio during the 2015 European refugee crisis. The centre processed 32,000 asylum seekers during its period of operation. The aim was to collate the experiences of local residents and suggestions for development for the future. The second and third Security Cafés were initiated in a similar fashion. The main collaborator in the second café was the Regional State Administrative Agency of Western and Inland Finland, and in the third café, it was the Guard Jaeger Regiment from the Finnish Defence Forces. The second pilot café dealt with the roles and tasks of public authorities and citizens in the face of various emergencies and disaster situations. In addition, crisis communication was deliberated upon. The focus of the third café was on the topical theme of hybrid threats.

The Finnish Ministry of the Interior became interested in the Security Café method, which led to Project 2. The objective of the project was to obtain as comprehensive picture as possible of the experiences and opinions of the Finnish people relating to the asylum seeker situation. The project also sought ideas for developing activities in the future. The project was then policy-oriented and linked to ongoing work on internal security strategy. Five café events (called Citizen Forums in this project to convey neutrality) were planned with representatives from the ministry, the Finnish Immigration Service and the Emergency Services College. In this case, no specific questions were set for deliberation in any of the café events, the premise being that participants could choose to debate those issues, they themselves considered important in relation to the asylum seeker policy (as such it was a bottom-up approach). Project 2 also included an electronic citizen survey (n = 1047), conducted before the café events. The survey and the outcomes from the cafés were utilized as two separate datasets.

Project 3 was part of the Finnish government plan for analysis, assessment and research, and as such was both policy and research oriented. The objective of the aforementioned government plan is to ensure a strong and horizontal knowledge base to support decision-making in Finnish society. The government invited ministries to suggest topics for projects, and Project 3 under the auspices of the Ministry of the Interior was one of the projects that attracted funding. The project analysed the role played by the third sector in supporting public authorities' security functions. Eight Security Cafés then played a part in extensive data gathering. The advisory group for the project included representatives from the Ministry of the Interior and the Ministry of the Defence. The theme was similar in each café (the role of the third sector), but there were some local specifics such as operating in remote and scarcely populated areas or in the archipelago region. The project also included many traditional interviews with representatives of the public authorities and third-sector organizations.

The research team's experience indicates that the presence of the relevant public authorities, from local, regional and national level (depending on the theme and focus of the Security Café), is of utmost importance to the success of the cafés (see also Setälä 2017). The more engaged the public authorities are in the planning phase, the better they engage both in the actual operational phase and afterwards in the use of the input from the cafés. Participants in the Security Cafés also value the presence of public authorities very highly.

15.3.2 Recruitment Phase

Open door settings or mini-publics is one of the dilemmas in public participation design raised by Bobbio (2018). Instead of being open door arenas, each Security Café was designed to gather together as diverse a group of people as possible, but the selection criteria and methods varied. In Project 1, the cafés were promoted in local newspapers, on street billboards and in social media. The aim was to recruit 30 participants for each café. The participants were chosen from those who enrolled via email, phone or a website, and the selection was guided by the desire that each Security Café would be as heterogeneous as possible. The third café was the most successful in this regard; it had 72 people enrolled. The selection criteria included various demographic (e.g. age and gender) and attitudinal factors (e.g. attitude towards national defence).

In Project 2, a private company offering services to assist research was used to recruit the participants. This was mainly due to a tight project schedule. The company was tasked with recruiting a heterogeneous group of 25 participants for each café based on age, gender, education, societal activity and two predefined measures of attitude to the then current asylum seeker policy. In an effort to increase the diversity of the participants, 20-euro gift vouchers were offered to incentivize participation. The recruitment drive was successful for each of the five cafés. The number of people enrolled ranged between 51 and 83 people.

Project 3 had a distinct recruitment profile because its purpose was to harvest the viewpoints of local and regional public authorities and third-sector representatives. Public authorities were asked to nominate representatives for the Security Cafés, and third-sector representatives were approached through key persons such as the heads of preparedness of the Finnish Red Cross and via associations' websites and social media channels. The aim was to form a heterogeneous group (e.g. by age and gender) of 25 participants for each café. If, in the course of the recruitment process, it appeared that, for example, women did not sign up, contact persons were asked to convey the invitation especially to women. The target of 25 (or nearly 25) participants was achieved in 7 cafés. The exception was the smallest municipality in terms of population (in Northern Lapland), that ultimately assembled only 15 participants. The composition of the cafés was engineered so that approximately two-thirds of the participants represented the third sector.

The most successful project with regard to recruitment was Project 2 where an external operator was hired to manage the recruitment of participants and the associated cafés had the most diverse participant groups. In addition, the recruitment of the third-sector representatives in Project 3 was achieved with ease, because the candidates were already societally active and welcomed the chance to have their voices heard. The most challenging was Project 1, where direct local advertising was used. It was difficult to communicate to potential participants what the Security Cafés were about. Deliberative methods in Finland are still relatively unknown and it can be challenging to overcome strong prejudices (see also Raisio et al. 2012).

15.3.3 Execution Phase

The execution phase of the Security Café can be summarized as taking place over four different steps. The *first step* is to create a welcoming and safe environment for the deliberations to take place (see Carson 2011). In each Security Café, conveners welcomed each participant personally before using a welcoming presentation directed at the whole group to explain the background to each project and the Security Café method, the schedules of the evenings and the deliberation guidelines (such as respecting the opinions of others and contributors justifying their own views). Finally, the conveners addressed any questions that arose. Next, the events continued to *step two*, receiving information. Participants in Security Cafés should have access to the essential facts and figures (see Fishkin 2009), which as a general rule is provided by way of expert briefings. However, written material may be used as a supplement. For example, in Project 1, three to four experts in the relevant topic—referred to as expert witnesses—delivered a 10-min-long presentation after which the participants were invited to ask questions. As an example, in the Security Café focused on the issue of a registration centre, the expert witnesses were from the police, the Red Cross, the Defence Forces and the Immigration Service. A special feature of the Security Café method is that experts are present throughout the event. This means that during the small group deliberations, participants can invite an expert witness to advise the group on issues relevant to that expert's specialism. In Project 3, the participants were themselves experts on the deliberated topic, so it was the project researchers who gave a brief presentation (summarizing relevant research) at the beginning of the event.

Most of the café event is occupied with small group deliberations. In this *third step*, participants were allocated in advance to heterogeneous groups of six to eight people. Each group had a trained facilitator to ensure there was a safe environment for deliberations and well-functioning group dynamics. The facilitator is a neutral actor who does not express his/her own views or opinions on the subject (see Dillard 2013). However, facilitators can often call upon pre-prepared questions to guide the deliberations and to ensure they remain focused. In the 16 Security Cafés, each small group deliberation lasted for 120 min. An important part of the Security Cafés is the use of *idea rating sheets* (see Zhang et al. 2016). However, in Project 2, pre- and post-questionnaires were used instead of idea rating sheets (to be able to analyse whether the participants' views changed during the deliberations). During the small group deliberations, in Projects 1 and 3, participants usually had 10 blank idea rating sheets available in each small group. Each time an idea emerged that they wanted the whole café to evaluate, they wrote it on the sheet (see Fig. 15.1). At this point, nothing else was written on the sheet. As described by Diceman (2014: 4):

> Idea rating sheets are a simple method for recognizing points of agreement among a large number of people. Participants write down ideas on specially designed paper forms called idea rating sheets […] and use pens to fill in one dot per sheet, recording their levels of agreement. The result is a graph-like visual representation of the group's collective opinion.

During the *fourth step*, idea rating sheets are collected and spread on tables or affixed to walls so the participants can evaluate them. Idea rating sheets follow the basic logic of a SWOT analysis, in that each participant should be able to comment

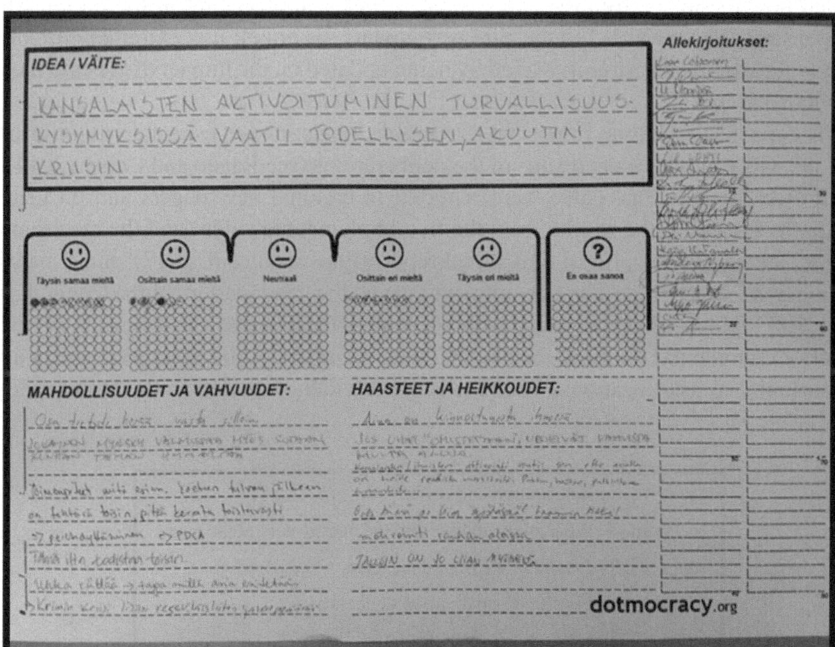

Fig. 15.1 An example of an idea rating sheet: *To activate citizens in security related issues we need an acute and ongoing crisis.* (in Finnish)

on each sheet, write about the opportunities and strengths plus the weaknesses and threats related to the presented idea and sign the sheet. Generally, 20–30 idea rating sheets are generated during the café event. The event usually ends with a speech by one of the experts reviewing the ideas presented in the idea rating sheets. To illustrate the schedule of Security Cafés, the schedule of cafés implemented in Project 1 is given in Fig. 15.2.

15.3.4 Impact Phase

The impact of deliberative mini-publics is a contested issue. Usually a distinction is drawn between binding and consultative deliberations (e.g. Mansbridge 2015; Bobbio 2018). Security Cafés are more consultative in nature; for example, in Project 1, the conveners of the cafés (researchers) prepared a report on each café summarizing the background to the café being implemented, the implementation process and the results (including transcribed idea rating sheets). Those reports were sent to relevant stakeholders (especially those on the advisory committee) who promised to give the outcomes of the cafés serious consideration and also to draw up detailed responses. In Project 1, 13 written responses were received and published. The public authorities commented on the outputs of the Security Cafés and stated how the ideas from the cafés could be taken into account in the future. All responses were forwarded to the café participants via email: it is extremely important that participants are empowered by being updated on the impact of the café they participated in.

The media also has an important role in this impact phase, especially in informing the wider public of the results of the deliberations (see Raisio and Carson 2014). In Project 1, individual cafés were reported in regional newspapers and on local radio. In Project 2, the results from the five implemented cafés (and the electronic citizen survey) were collated into a final report (Puustinen et al. 2017), and a major media event was held in The Government Palace, the headquarters of the Council of State of Finland. Project researchers presented the results; the Minister of the Interior commented on those results; and then members of the press were given an opportunity to ask questions. The results were widely reported in the mainstream

16.00–16.15	Registration and coffee / tea (incl. snack)
16.15–16.45	Welcoming address and the background of the event
16.45–17.45	Presentations from the experts + Q & A session
17.45–19.45	Facilitated small group deliberations
19.45–20.20	Evaluation of the idea rating sheets
20.20–20.30	Final words

Fig. 15.2 An example schedule of a Security Café event

media. In Project 3, the results of the project were presented at a seminar to which relevant stakeholders were invited. The results were also set out in the project's final report (Jalava et al. 2017) and in publications intended for professional communities (e.g. Norri-Sederholm et al. 2018). A summary of all the three projects and Security Cafés implemented is included below in Table 15.2.

15.4 Experiences and Reflection on the Security Café Method

In project 1, pre-filled idea rating sheets were used to collect data, and in Project 2 similar questions were included in a post-deliberation survey. The questions included: "I was able to bring my own opinions into the discussion" and "I would participate again in a similar kind of citizen forum". In Project 1, additional interviews were conducted with the café participants ($n = 16$) and with public authority staff who participated in the cafés ($n = 17$). In addition, in Project 2, ideas generated in the group discussions were coded from the recorded discussions and sent back to the participants for evaluation in electronic form. The questionnaire included an opportunity to give qualitative post-event feedback on the deliberative method applied. In Project 3, no café-specific data was gathered, hence the analysis of that project is based on the reflections of the researchers.

Data from Projects 1 and 2 illustrate a generally positive attitude to the cafés, as is often the case with deliberative mini-publics (e.g. Fishkin 2009). For example, in the Security Cafés on asylum seeker policy, an emotive topic, 86% of the participants reported that discussing in the group was a pleasant experience (figures include those who fully and partially agreed); 88% of the participants felt they were able to express their opinions in the discussions; 96% of the participants would participate again in a similar kind of a citizen forum. Similarly, 96% of the participants felt that similar kinds of citizens' forums should be used to support societal decision-making. A large majority of the participants (83%) reported that participating in the café had boosted their knowledge of asylum seeker policy and 34% stated that their perspective on the issue had changed. For the cafés implemented in Project 1, the views were very similar (See Raisio et al. 2017a, b; Puustinen et al. 2017).

Participants in all of the Security Cafés emphasized how the café brought security authorities closer to the public. The informal deliberation and safe, respectful environment in a way freed the authorities from their uniforms. As one of the café participants in Project 1 commented, "*it gave an impression that [security authorities] are normal people, just like one of us*". Similarly, a café participant in Project 2 stated that "*the people from the Finnish Immigration Office looked like ordinary human beings, and not mere 'machines' talking nonsense on behalf of their organizations*". Participants also pointed out that the cafés offered an opportunity to meet representatives of public authorities who were rarely involved in the café participants' everyday life and who they would be unlikely to meet at other public events.

The staff from the public authorities interviewed in Project 1 also appreciated the encounter with ordinary people. This informal coming together seemed to narrow the perceived differences between authorities and civil society. A representative of the Defence Forces commented that the cafés offered them an opportunity to improve their image, to tell the people "*that we are here for society, not the other way around*". The opportunity to engage in lengthy, in-depth discussions with citizens was seen as a rare one. This is well illustrated by the following comment from a representative of a public authority: "*After all, it is really extraordinary that we can actually hear the opinions of the citizens, and we were essentially calmly discussing [in the café] and not getting opinions through 'shouting' in social media or via emotional e-mails*". The Security Café participants became aware that it was a general challenge that the public debate often showcases extreme opinions and welcomed the fact that voices were heard other than those who shout loudest at the opposite extremes.

The café participants assessed deliberating in small groups to be safer than deliberating in large groups, as might be the case in traditional public meetings. It was also easier to pose questions to the authorities or experts because they could be invited to speak to individual small groups. The conversation was said to be sincere, with almost no political colour to it. The participants felt the atmosphere was safe enough for them to be able to express their opinions freely—even when those opinions differed from those of the authorities or from the anticipated norms. Some participants felt the informal set up of the Security Cafés contributed to the construction of a safe environment, as noted by one of the participants in Project 1: "*When I got there, the atmosphere was relaxed, and everyone was in good spirits. It was not too formal. And I got the feeling that everyone would dare to participate and have their say*". In Project 2, even though the theme of the deliberation—the asylum seeker policy—was more delicate, the reported experiences were largely similar. As one of the café participants commented: "*This was a very good and interesting way to get involved in the discussions [on asylum seeker policy]. In the event I had the courage to speak out, without fear of stigma*". It should be noted, however, not every person in every small group felt they had been fully heard, as was seen in the statistics above. For example, one participant in a more polarized small group stated the following: "*It was interesting to attend [the café]. Somehow it just felt like I did not get my own voice heard in my group. Perhaps it was the other extreme [i.e. anti-immigration] that quieted me*". Nevertheless, participants in Project 1 and 2 often reported that they felt empowered after the cafés. They commented that their personal views really mattered during the cafés:

> I felt myself important. That my opinion really matters. (Project 1)

> It was very enjoyable, and I felt that finally the Finnish people are listened to! (Project 2)

> Great event and great ideas. Thankfully people's opinions are now heard. (Project 2)

Participation in the Security Cafés also influenced the participants' feelings of safety and security, that is, how safe they view society as being and how their own actions matter as part of the whole. One participant from Project 1 commented, "*it made me realize that a lot of things are done [by the security authorities] all the time, that [security authorities] don't just sit and wait for something to happen*".

This increase in trust and understanding of the security authorities' functions and resources seemed to enhance the feelings of safety. The participants also reported that they began to better understand the various threats and that they heard about issues that they would normally never hear about. The influence of the participation in the cafés was also reflected in the level of participants' own activity and awareness. This was depicted, for example, in the following comments, made by participants from Project 1:

> This [café] activated me and made me think that I am able to participate more.

> Participation may have increased my level of awareness on these issues. […] I now keep my eyes open and I am more interested in news, for example, looking for things that are related to the issues we discussed.

In Project 3, a data-gathering project, one of the key values for the participants themselves seemed to be the networking between the actors. In the cafés implemented as part of this project, public authorities and third-sector representatives sat at the same tables deliberating on issues that mattered to all of them. During the evenings spent in the cafés these different actors got to know each other. They started to plan cooperation, and, most importantly, the staff from public authorities became aware of what kind of third-sector actors were active in their own area and obtained information on how to contact them. The Security Café thus acted in a sense as a platform for developing common language and common reality for security authority and third-sector representatives. This can be understood as a spin-off effect of the data-gathering project.

Using Security Cafés also offers value for researchers, in that doing so gives access to data otherwise unobtainable in many research projects. Conducting an extensive number of interviews is very time consuming, and it is often difficult to attract a feasible number of interviewees. The Security Café offers an economic way to quickly gather the opinions and ideas of a large number of people. A researcher participating in a Security Café could easily obtain the opinions of around 30 people in a couple of hours, and hence, five cafés could give a researcher access to 150 interviewees. In addition to the number of participants, the quality of data often differs from that delivered via individual interviews. In our experience, people in facilitated group discussions express their views and ideas very openly and also encourage each other to, for example, justify their opinions. This was most obvious in Project 2 on the asylum seeker policy, where both an electronic survey of citizen's opinions and the Security Cafés were utilized in the same project. Group discussions that were recorded in the cafés afforded access to data normally unavailable when applying only a survey method. Using a survey can deliver the raw opinions of a large number of citizens, which provides a skeleton, or an estimate of the opinion of the larger society, that is, surveys merely gather, "static snapshots of public opinion" (Atlee 2004: 98). Data from the Security Cafés adds meat to the bones, giving access to the reasons, thoughts, fears and feelings of people behind the quantitative data often reported only as facts and figures.

The most prominent problem in the cafés was that of ensuring they were representative. The insufficiently varied representation in some Security Cafés led, among other things, to an insufficient number of dissenting opinions. This was particularly evident in Project 1 when participants were recruited mainly by using social and traditional media to attract the public's attention to the events. In Project 1, the café participants were rather homogenous and safety-oriented. One interviewee from a public authority described the participants as, "*devout believers in security [authorities and policies]*". For this reason, in Project 2 an external recruiter was used to populate the Security Café on asylum seeker policy. This resulted in more heterogeneous groups, and also in more vibrant discussions in the cafés. One café participant for example considered that the Security Café was "*[an] excellent way to obtain ordinary people's view regardless of their background. It is a comprehensive and good way of getting information and for different sexes and different ages to be heard*".

The impact achieved is the second major challenge for Security Cafés. Although the participants in the cafés viewed the act of participating very positively, they questioned the actual impact of their participation. The participants wondered whether their thoughts would be taken into account and whether the authorities would really translate their ideas into action. Café participants hoped that the authorities would screen the most feasible ideas and implement them in the future, because otherwise it would be like "filling a bucket with a hole in it". As a minimum, the participants considered that if the authorities did not act on the ideas generated in the Security Café, they should justify why not, which would make it possible to continue the deliberation. Representatives of the public authorities also worried about the impact of the cafés, and one of them commented in an interview, "*it will dilute the whole idea of the cafés if the ideas and opinions of the participants are not acted upon, if they just come to chat and have coffee, without any real influence*". Weaknesses in their impact were seen as having the potential to compromise the entire concept and core idea of the Security Cafés.

15.5 Discussion

In an environment where complexity is on the rise and psychological and hybrid influencing is becoming an increasingly normal way to affect the minds of people (see, e.g. Treverton et al. 2018; Aaltola and Juntunen 2018), the role of individual citizens in the safety and security domains is becoming ever more important. Ordinary citizens are not only objects of security actions and policies, but active subjects securing their own environment and the resilience of the larger society. Based on our experiences from the three projects, Security Cafés could offer a way to increase both the knowledge base of citizens and their involvement in the matter at hand. Knowledge and active involvement could help counteract the offensive uses of hybrid influence, such as disinformation, and hence increase the resilience of the whole society. These aforementioned features, especially the citizens' shift from object to actor (or the subject) and information sharing, are recognized in the current national Security Strategy for Society. Therefore, Security Cafés could offer a means of identifying ways to implement the national comprehensive security model. The method does seem effective, despite some curable weaknesses.

The advent of social media has meant people can express their ideas anonymously, which seems to increase the polarization of opinions. Our experience of Security Cafés in Finland indicates that they can provide a forum for people with differing views to come together, to deliberate over emotive issues and, most importantly, to listen to the views of others respectfully. This could be one way to enhance empathy in people, merely by ensuring they encounter people from different demographics and encouraging them to understand and respect different opinions (see also Morrell 2010). Having said that, one needs to be careful when addressing the most delicate so-called wicked issues in society. After the project on asylum seeker policy, the results of the project were actively questioned, even purposefully twisted, by various groups and communities, even within academia (see Raisio et al. 2017b). When not handled properly this can worsen the situation. In the case of highly sensitive topics, taking advantage of the different types of deliberative mini-publics might offer an opportunity to progress. For example, Security Cafés could be used to assemble a larger group of people to participate in deliberations around the country after which the results of the cafés could be further processed in a well-executed Citizens' Jury or Citizens' Assembly, increasing the legitimacy of the process (see Carson et al. 2013).

There is also the risk of Security Cafés becoming just one more educational event among others, where security authorities express their own views, without listening to those of the people present (see Virta and Branders 2016). By definition, deliberative methods should always include the opportunity to express even the most critical views and those running counter to the norm, and also those questioning the status quo. This is ultimately a question of balance between the critical transformative project of deliberative democracy and the secrecy and opacity of the safety and security domains.

We have been tracking the potential uses of the Security Café method after the three projects described in this article. Currently it is planned to be used in at least two research projects to facilitate data gathering (the projects will involve the fire and rescue services and military sociology) and as a deliberation method in one development project (The National Defence Training Association of Finland). Two Finnish towns have also taken up the challenge of organizing Security Cafés in their region to enable their citizens to participate in the planning and development of the safety and security of their own neighbourhoods. The Security Café is also recognized as a valid method in the research methods training at the Emergency Services College, where all Finnish fire and rescue personnel are trained. Additionally, the Security Café is piloted at the National Defence University as a pedagogical tool.

It would seem that the method is applicable in different contexts and also feasible both as a method for deliberation and as a data gathering method. Flexibility is a key element of the method in the sense that every municipality, county, region or country has its own security ecosystem. This must be taken into account in the execution of the different phases of the method. As long as the minimum requirements for deliberation are met, the method is sufficiently flexible to meet the varying needs evident in the safety and security domains and contexts. What is still missing in the cases presented in this article is the involvement of private sector businesses. The national Security Strategy for Society acknowledges the private sector as an essential part of the building of a resilient society, yet the sector has no discernible presence in the deliberative processes.

The experiences gathered from three different projects indicate that in Finland, where the comprehensive security model is applied throughout society, Security Cafés function rather well. The model highlights the vital role of citizens as actors in the production and safeguarding of a secure society. Security authorities themselves are both willing and able to participate in such forums, because there is strong support in the government for interaction between citizens and authorities. In the future, the model should be tested in societies where the divide between security authorities and ordinary citizens is greater and where support for cross-sector collaboration on the part of the policy-makers and governments is not so evident.

References

Aaltola, M., & Juntunen, T. (2018). Nordic model meets resilience - Finnish strategy for societal security. In M. Aaltola, B. Kuznetsov, A. Spruds, & E. Vizgunova (Eds.), *Societal security in the Baltic Sea region: Expertise mapping and raising policy relevance* (pp. 26–42). Riga: Latvian Institute of International Affairs.

Atlee, T. (2004). Critiquing America speaks' process and alternative approaches as paths to "collective intelligence". *Group Facilitation: A Research & Applications Journal, 6*(spring), 93–101.

Bobbio, L. (2018). Designing effective public participation. *Policy and Society, 38*, 41. https://doi.org/10.1080/14494035.2018.1511193.

Carson, L. (2011). Designing a public conversation using the world Café method. *Social Alternatives, 30*(1), 10–14.

Carson, L., & Hartz-Karp, J. (2005). Adapting and combining deliberative designs. In J. Gastil & P. Levine (Eds.), *The deliberative democracy handbook* (pp. 120–138). San Francisco: Jossey-Bass.

Carson, L., Gastil, J., Hartz-Karp, J., & Lubensky, R. (Eds.). (2013). *The Australian citizens' parliament and the future of deliberative democracy*. University Park: Pennsylvania State University Press.

Chambers, S. (2003). Deliberative democratic theory. *Annual Review of Political Science, 6*(1), 307–326.

Curato, N., Dryzek, J., Ercan, S. A., Hendriks, C. M., & Niemeyer, S. (2017). Twelve key findings in deliberative democracy research. *Daedalus, Symposium on Deliberative Democracy, 146*(3), 28–38.

Diceman, J. (2014). *Idea rating sheets: Facilitator's handbook*. Retrieved December 21, 2018, from http://idearatingsheets.org/wp-content/uploads/2017/09/idea_rating_sheets_handbook_2-5f.pdf.

Dillard, K. N. (2013). Envisioning the role of facilitation in public deliberation. *Journal of Applied Communication Research, 41*(3), 217–235.

Dryzek, J. S. (2002). *Deliberative democracy and beyond: Liberals, critics, contestations*. New York: Oxford University Press.

Dryzek, J. S., Bächtiger, A., Chambers, S., et al. (2019). The crisis of democracy and the science of deliberation: Citizens can avoid polarization and make sound decisions. *Science, 363*(6432), 1144–1146.

Elstub, S. (2010). The third generation of deliberative democracy. *Political Studies Review, 8*(3), 291–307.
Elstub, S., & Böker, M. (2015). The possibility of critical mini-publics: Realpolitik and normative cycles in democratic theory. *Representations, 51*(1), 125–144.
Ercan, S. A., & Dryzek, J. S. (2015). The reach of deliberative democracy. *Policy Studies, 36*(3), 241–248.
Fishkin, J. S. (2009). *When the people speak: Deliberative democracy & public consultation*. New York: Oxford University Press.
Grönlund, K., Bächtiger, A., & Setälä, M. (Eds.). (2014). *Deliberative mini-publics: Involving citizens in the democratic process*. Colchester: ECPR Press.
Jalava, J., Raisio, H., Norri-Sederholm, T., Lahtinen, H., & Puustinen, A. (2017). *Kolmas sektori vi-ranomaisten turvallisuustoiminnan tukena. [The role of the third sector in supporting public authori-ties' security functions.] Publications of the Government's analysis, assessment and research activi-ties 76*. Helsinki: Finnish Government.
Lee Jenni, G. D. L., Peterson, M. N., & Katz, J. (2015). Military perspectives on public relations related to environmental issues. *Journal of Public Relations, 27*(4), 353–369.
Mansbridge, J. (2015). A minimalist definition of deliberation. In P. Heller & V. Rao (Eds.), *Deliberation and development: Rethinking the role of voice and collective action in unequal societies* (pp. 27–50). Washington, DC: World Bank.
Millen, D. (2011). Deliberative democracy in disaster recovery: Reframing community engagement for sustainable outcomes. In *Centre for citizenship and public policy*. Sydney: University of Western Sydney & newDemocracy Foundation.
Min, J. B., & Wong, J. K. (2018). Epistemic approaches to deliberative democracy. *Philosophy Compass, 13*(6), 1–13.
Morrell, M. E. (2010). *Empathy and democracy: Feeling, thinking, and deliberation*. University Park: Penn State Press.
Nabatchi, T. (2010). Addressing the citizenship and democratic deficits: The potential of deliberative democracy for public administration. *The American Review of Public Administration, 40*(4), 376–399.
Norri-Sederholm, T., Puustinen, A., & Raisio, H. (2018). Järjestöt osana kokonaisturvallisuutta [third sector organizations as part of comprehensive security]. *Kylkirauta [Journal of the Finnish Cadet and Officer Corps Association], 3*, 8–11.
Puustinen, A., Raisio, H., Kokki, E., & Luhta, J. (2017). *Kansalaismielipide: turvapaikkapolitiikka ja turvapaikanhakijat. [Citizens' view: Asylum seekers and asylum seeker policy.] Ministry of the Interior publications 9*. Ministry of the Interior: Helsinki.
Raisio, H., & Carson, L. (2014). Deliberation within sectors: Making the case for sector mini-publics. *International Review of Social Research, 4*(1), 75–92.
Raisio, H., & Ehrström, P. (2017). Taking deliberation to the streets: Reflections on deliberative walks. *Scandinavian Journal of Public Administration, 21*(4), 27–51.
Raisio, H., & Virta, S. (2016). Kansalaisraati turvallisuudesta – Turvallisuuden kontingenssit ja deliberaation mahdollisuudet [Citizens' Jury on security issues – Contingencies of security and possibilities of deliberation]. *Hallinnon tutkimus [Finnish Journal of Public Administration], 35*(3), 223–236.
Raisio, H., Ollila, S., & Vartiainen, P. (2012). Do youth juries enhance youth political and societal participation? Lessons from the Vaasa experiment. *Scandinavian Journal of Public Administration, 15*(3), 41–59.
Raisio, H., Puustinen, A., Hyytiäinen, M., & Wiikinkoski, T. (2017a). *Kansan pulssilla: tarkastelussa deliberatiiviset turvallisuuskahvilat. [People's pulse: Examining the deliberative security cafés.] Re-ports of the University of Vaasa 1*. Vaasa: University of Vaasa.
Raisio, H., Puustinen, A., Huhtinen, A.-M., Lehtonen, T., Vartiainen, P., & Virta, S. (2017b). Pitääkö yhteiskuntatieteiden ideaa jälleen kirkastaa? [should the idea of social science be clarified again?]. *Tiedepolitiikka [Science Policy], 42*(2), 62–65.
Ryan, M., & Smith, G. (2014). Defining mini-publics. In K. Grönlund, A. Bächtiger, & M. Setälä (Eds.), *Deliberative mini-publics* (pp. 9–26). Colchester: ECPR Press.

Schoch-Spana, M. (2012). The People's role in U.S. National Health Security: Past, present, and future. *Biosecurity and Bioterrorism: Biodefense Strategy, Practice, and Science, 10*(1), 77–88.

Schoch-Spana, M., Franco, C., Nuzzo, J. B., & Usenza, C. (2007). Community engagement: Leadership tool for catastrophic health events. *Biosecurity and Bioterrorism: Biodefense Strategy, Practice, and Science, 5*(1), 8–25.

Scuffham, P. A., Moretto, N., Krinks, R., Burton, P., Whitty, J. A., Wilson, A., Fitzgerald, G., Littlejohns, P., & Kendall, E. (2016). Engaging the public in healthcare decision-making: Results from a citizens' jury on emergency care services. *Emergency Medicine Journal, 33*, 782–788.

Security Committee. (2017). *The security strategy for society. Government resolution/2.11.2017.* Security Committee: Helsinki.

Setälä, M. (2017). Connecting deliberative mini-publics to representative decision making. *European Journal of Political Research, 56*(4), 846–863.

Shane, P. M. (2012). Cybersecurity policy as if "ordinary citizens" mattered: The case for public participation in cyber policy making. *I/S: A Journal of Law and Policy for the Information Society, 8*(2), 433–462.

Stolzenberg, P., & Wampler, P. (2018). Partipatory budgeting. In H. Hainelt (Ed.), *Handbook on participatory governance* (pp. 291–311). Cheltenham: Edward Elgar Publishing.

Torfing, J., Sørensen, E., & Røiseland, A. (2016). Transforming the public sector into an arena for co-creation: Barriers, drivers, benefits, and ways forward. *Administration & Society, 51*(5), 795–825.

Treverton, G. F., Thvedt, A., Chen, A. R., Lee, K., & McCue, M. (2018). *Addressing hybrid threats*. Stockholm: Swedish Defence University.

Valtonen, V. (2010). Collaboration of security actors – An operational-tactical view. In *Conference paper at the 2010 ISMS conference*, Stockholm, Sweden, 10–11 November 2010.

Virta, S., & Branders, M. (2016). Legitimate security? Understanding the contingencies of security and deliberation. *British Criminology Journal, 56*(6), 1146–1164.

Wilson, P. A. (2009). Deliberative planning for disaster recovery: Re-membering New Orleans. *Journal of Public Deliberation, 5*(1), 1.

Zhang, L., Wang, W., & Hanks, L. (2016). A comparison of plurality voting sheets and idea rating sheets in judgement-making: A participatory architectural design in the Nottingham Natural History Museum, Wollaton Hall. *Museum Management and Curatorship, 31*(2), 103–140.

The manufacturer's authorised representative in the EU is Springer Nature Customer Service Centre GmbH, Europaplatz 3, 69115 Heidelberg, Germany. If you have any concerns regarding our products, please contact ProductSafety@springernature.com

Printed and bound by CPI Group (UK) Ltd, Croydon, CR0 4YY
25/09/2026
02222901-0011